Carnival and National Identity
in the Poetry of Afrocubanismo

UNIVERSITY PRESS OF FLORIDA

Florida A&M University, Tallahassee
Florida Atlantic University, Boca Raton
Florida Gulf Coast University, Ft. Myers
Florida International University, Miami
Florida State University, Tallahassee
New College of Florida, Sarasota
University of Central Florida, Orlando
University of Florida, Gainesville
University of North Florida, Jacksonville
University of South Florida, Tampa
University of West Florida, Pensacola

Carnival and National Identity in the Poetry of Afrocubanismo

Thomas F. Anderson

University Press of Florida
Gainesville · Tallahassee · Tampa · Boca Raton
Pensacola · Orlando · Miami · Jacksonville · Ft. Myers · Sarasota

The publication of this book is made possible in part by a grant from the University of Notre Dame's Institute for Scholarship in the Liberal Arts.

Copyright 2011 by Thomas F. Anderson
Printed in the United States of America. This book is printed on Glatfelter Natures Book, a paper certified under the standards of the Forestry Stewardship Council (FSC). It is a recycled stock that contains 30 percent post-consumer waste and is acid-free.
All rights reserved

16 15 14 13 12 11   6 5 4 3 2 1

Library of Congress Cataloging-in-Publication Data
Anderson, Thomas F., 1970–
Carnival and national identity in the poetry of Afrocubanismo / Thomas F. Anderson.
p. cm.
Includes bibliographical references and index.
ISBN 978-0-8130-3558-1 (alk. paper)
1. Cuban poetry—Black authors—History and criticism. 2. Cuban poetry—20th century—History and criticism. 3. Carnival in literature. 4. Blacks in literature. 5. National characteristics, Cuban, in literature. 6. Cuba—In literature. I. Title.
PQ7380.A687 2011
861.'609334—dc22
2010032258

The University Press of Florida is the scholarly publishing agency for the State University System of Florida, comprising Florida A&M University, Florida Atlantic University, Florida Gulf Coast University, Florida International University, Florida State University, New College of Florida, University of Central Florida, University of Florida, University of North Florida, University of South Florida, and University of West Florida.

University Press of Florida
15 Northwest 15th Street
Gainesville, FL 32611-2079
http://www.upf.com

Para Marisel, Gabriel, y Mariana
In Memory of Scott Van Jacob

La vida es un carnaval
Celia Cruz

Contents

List of Illustrations xi
Acknowledgments xiii

Introduction. *Comparsas, Congas,* and *Chambelonas*: Carnival and National Identity in Cuba 1

1. Felipe Pichardo Moya's "La comparsa": Afro-Cuban Carnival as Sinister Spectacle 25

2. Carnival and Ñáñiguismo: Poetic Syncretism in Alejo Carpentier's "Juego santo" 49

3. Carnival and Afro-Cuban Ritual in Nicolás Guillén's "Sensemayá: canto para matar una culebra" 79

4. "Comparsa habanera," Emilio Ballagas's Emblematic Contribution to Afrocubanismo 108

5. Drumming Up the Black Vote: *Chambelonas* and Cuban Electoral Politics in José Zacarías Tallet's "Quintín Barahona" 140

6. "La conga prohibida": Felix B. Caignet's Response to Carnival Controversy in Santiago de Cuba 160

7. Representations of Afro-Cuban Carnival in Three Poems by Marcelino Arozarena 181

8. An Outsider on the Inside: Alfonso Camín's "Carnaval en la Habana" 213

Epilogue. Carnival and Cultural Essence 253

Appendix. A Brief Anthology of Poems Inspired by Afro-Cuban Carnival 277

Notes 299
Works Cited 313
Index 327

Illustrations

0.1. Pierre Toussaint Frédéric Miahle, *Día de Reyes*, ca. 1855 — 2
0.2. Alberto Arredondo, "Las comparsas" — 16
0.3. Fernando Tarazona, *La conga*, 1936 — 18
1.1. Cornado Massaguer, illustration for "La comparsa," 1916 — 32
1.2. Members of "El Alacrán" with *farolas*, ca. 1915 — 36
1.3. *Farolero*, ca. 1960 — 37
2.1. Alejo Carpentier, *Dos poemas afro-cubanos*, 1930 — 51
2.2. Musical score for "Juego santo" — 52
2.3. M. Puente, *Fiesta ñáñiga*, 1878 — 55
2.4. Procession from mixed-race Abakuá lodge — 55
2.5. Colonial-era street brawl between Abakuá lodges — 63
2.6. Heriberto Portell Vilá, *Comparsa*, 1948 — 69
2.7. Víctor Patricio de Landaluze, *El ñáñigo*, 1881 — 72
2.8. Manuscript of "Juego santo," ca. 1927 — 73
2.9. Sese Eribó, sacred Abakuá drum — 75
3.1. "The Birth of Ñáñiguismo" — 97
3.2. Sign of Nasakó — 99
3.3. Sign of Nasakó — 99
3.4. Sign of Nasakó — 99
4.1. Decorated carriage with children, ca. 1920 — 119
4.2. Decorated automobile with men in drag, ca. 1915 — 119
4.3. *La brujería y los brujos en Cuba*, 1900 — 123
4.4. Emilio Ballagas, *Cuaderno de poesía negra*, 1934 — 126
4.5. Fernando Tarazona, *La ahijada del santo*, 1936 — 129

6.1. Eusebia Cosme, program for poetry recital, 1936 — 161
6.2. Felix B. Caignet, *A golpe de maracas*, 1950 — 162
6.3. Felix B. Caignet, illustration for "Qué muera er son" — 166
7.1. Marcelino Arozarena, "La liturgia etiópica," 1936 — 183
8.1. Enrique Caravia, carnival poster, 1946 — 231
8.2. Carnival queen, ca. 1915 — 235
8.3. Carnival *carroza* and decorated automobiles, ca. 1920 — 235
8.4. Mario Carreño, carnival poster, 1937 — 236
8.5. Enrique Caravia, carnival poster, 1937 — 238
8.6. Carnival poster by unknown artist, 1941 — 239
8.7. Carnival *carroza*, Chocolates la Estrella, 1920 — 242
8.8. Carnival *carroza*, Pedro Domecq Brandy Fundador — 243
8.9. Carnival *carroza*, Cervecería Polar — 243
8.10. Advertisement for carnival regalia at El Encanto — 245
8.11. Advertisement for carnival regalia at Los Precios Fijos — 246

Acknowledgments

Since beginning my research for this book over five years ago, I have enjoyed the constant support, encouragement, and patience of my wife, friend, and colleague, Marisel Moreno. I am surprised how often I am met with quizzical looks from fellow academics when they learn that I work in a similar field, teach in the same department, attend the same meetings, and spend untold hours in a small home office with my spouse. Many seem to assume that such an arrangement would be hard to bear, but I feel quite the opposite. There is something very special about sharing so many common interests and being able to appreciate, understand, and critique each other's work. Far from being a source of tension, our intellectual collaborations have been stimulating and productive. Marisel's contributions to this book would be difficult to quantify, but suffice it to say that her input has been significant and invaluable in so many ways. I would also like to thank our two children, Gabriel and Mariana, who have always been sources of great joy and inspiration. They have been exceptional travel companions on numerous trips to conduct research or to attend conferences, but the greatest pleasure has come from the many hours that I have spent at home with both of them patiently working at my side—at their own makeshift "offices"—drawing, coloring, reading, and yes, interrupting, but usually in that very special way that only curious and imaginative children can. Already at their tender ages they have both left their indelible mark on how I think and how I approach my work.

Though this book has been a largely solitary undertaking, as these projects often are, I would like to thank a number of individuals who have assisted me in various ways over the last several years. One of the most challenging aspects of putting together a scholarly study of this nature is locating, compiling, and organizing research materials. To this end, I owe my deepest gratitude to Kenneth Kinslow and the Interlibrary Loan staff at the University of Notre Dame's Hesburgh Library. Though much of the material that was invaluable to this study came from the Hesburgh Library's impressive Latin American holdings, or was consulted on site at various libraries and institutions in this country and in the Caribbean, scores of books, articles, and images were delivered either by hand to my campus mailbox, or at breakneck speed to my computer desktop by way of a super-efficient interlibrary loan system that has revolutionized the world of academic research.

I also owe special thanks to my late friend, colleague, and fellow bibliophile Scott Van Jacob, who, in his capacity as Latin American bibliographer at the Hesburgh Library, was instrumental in building what is fast becoming one of the nation's premier collections of Cuban books, journals, and literary manuscripts. It has been such a delight to be able to make use of so much of the material that the two of us worked so hard together to acquire. I also thank Scott for the countless hours that he spent discussing my project with me and for providing so much insight—most of it related to more important things than my work—along the way. Scott was an inspiration, and I will always remember how much he loved life even when he knew he had so little of it left to enjoy.

In Cuba, Elliot Klein provided a great deal of assistance, even when faced with less than desirable personal and professional circumstances: he searched out rare books and journals, dug up answers to difficult questions, and carefully read over various versions of most of this book's chapters. His copious comments and suggestions were very useful and insightful. I am also grateful to Graziella Pogolotti at the Fundación Alejo Carpentier for granting access to so many materials housed at that institution, and for answering several important questions about Carpentier's early career. I owe my gratitude to Olga López Núñez from the Museo Nacional de Bellas Artes and Grisel Martínez from the Museo de Guanabacoa for their attentiveness and rapid responses to my questions and inquiries. Luis Duno-Gottberg deserves thanks for his careful reading of an early version of the manuscript, for his thoughtful suggestions, and for his kind words of encouragement. In the later stages of this project I benefited greatly from the generous assistance of Carrie Caignet and Dr. Robert Caignet, whose rapid responses to my inquiries about Felix B. Caignet were very much appreciated. Marta Salvat, at Ediciones Universal in Miami, graciously pointed me in the right direction when I came looking for information on some of the Cuban exile poets that I discuss in the epilogue. Thanks also to Ivor Miller who, despite being in Calabar and having limited access to e-mail, answered my questions in a very timely manner. Through the assistance of Ivor and Clint Kimberling, from the University Press of Mississippi, I was able to acquire at the very last minute a high-quality image of M. Puente's 1879 painting *Fiesta ñáñiga*, which is reproduced in the second chapter of this study. Albino Suárez Cortina and members of the staff at the Registro de la Propiedad Intelectual del Principado de Asturias were very helpful in their responses to my queries about the Spanish poet Alfonso Camín, and in helping me in my fruitless attempts to contact his heirs.

Much of the research and travel associated with this project was funded by generous grants from the Office of the Dean of the College of Arts and Letters and the Institute of Scholarship in the Liberal Arts (ISLA) at the University of Notre Dame. ISLA also helped to defray the expenses of this project by providing a generous publication subvention. I am very appreciative of this financial support from the University of Notre Dame.

I am grateful to the following individuals and institutions for permission to reprint and/or reproduce materials in this book: Robert Caignet for excerpts of several poems from *A golpe de maracas*, the complete text of "La conga prohibida," and "Letter to Eusebia Cosme," by Felix B. Caignet; The Manuscripts, Archives and Rare Books Division, Schomburg Center for Research in Black Culture, New York Public Library for excerpts from "Letter to Eusebia Cosme," by Felix B. Caignet and a photographic reproduction of a program for a poetry recital by Eusebia Cosme; Fundación Alejo Carpentier, for excerpts from *Écue-Yamba-O*, and "Liturgia," the complete text of "Juego santo," as well as photographic reproductions of *Dos poemas afro-cubanos* and a manuscript version of "Juego santo," by Alejo Carpentier. Most of the remaining poem excerpts, song lyrics, and images that are reproduced in the pages that follow are either in the public domain or fall under the terms of "fair use" according to U.S. and/or Cuban copyright laws. In all other cases every effort has been made to locate possible copyright holders or to acquire necessary permissions.

Finally I would like to express my appreciation for the permission granted to reprint sections from two of my published articles: "Carnival,

Cultural Debate, and Cuban Identity in 'La comparsa' and 'Comparsa habanera'" *Revista de Estudios Hispánicos* 40 (2006): 50–78; "Inconsistent Depictions of Afro-Cubans and Their Cultural Manifestations in the Early Poetry of Marcelino Arozarena." *Afro-Hispanic Review* 27.2 (Fall 2008): 9–44.

Introduction

Comparsas, Congas, and *Chambelonas*

Carnival and National Identity in Cuba

> When we relate any other expression of culture ... to the carnival, we are in a position to learn more about the intricacies and complexities of the Caribbean as a sociocultural system.
>
> Antonio Benítez-Rojo, *The Repeating Island*

As early as the sixteenth century, African slaves in Cuba formed small ensembles on various occasions throughout the year, whose members would dance, sing, and perform sacred rites in the streets of the nation's towns and cities (Feliú Herrera, *Fiestas* 137–38). However, it was not until the 1840s that larger groups that were more akin to the Afro-Cuban carnival street processions of the early twentieth century began to emerge. This was largely due to the establishment of the *cabildos de nación*, social and cultural organizations that at once served to disseminate and preserve African-derived cultural manifestations on the island and to provide guidance, support, and protection for newly arrived slaves. The members of the *cabildos* were granted special permission to parade through the city on January 6, the Feast of the Epiphany—known throughout the Spanish-speaking world as Día de Reyes. "On that day," as Ned Sublette so aptly puts it, "there would emerge into the sunlight a world that was normally hidden: the inner world of Afro-Cuban society" (114).

Large groups of African slaves donned traditional costumes and danced, sang, and played music as they filed through the streets in organized parades and processions petitioning for *aguinaldos* [tips, gratuities] from onlookers who watched the festivities from the streets, or from the doors, windows, and balconies of their homes. The culmination of these celebrations took place in the courtyard of the Palace of the Capitán General of the Island, which was located on the Plaza de Armas in Old Havana. There the participants would congregate and pay homage to

FIGURE 0.1. Pierre Toussaint Frédéric Miahle, *Día de Reyes*. From *Albúm pintoresco de la isla de Cuba* (c. 1855). Plate 16. (Image courtesy of George Glazer Gallery.)

colonial authorities with a festive extravaganza of music, dancing, ritual gestures, and song. Such spectacles, which Ortiz has referred to as "the most picturesque scenes of colonial life" ("Afro-Cuban Festival" 1), were immortalized in nineteenth-century paintings such as *Día de Reyes* (c. 1855) by Pierre Toussaint Frédéric Mialhe (1810–1868) (fig. 0.1), a French painter who taught at the Academy of Painting in Havana, and *El día de los Reyes* (c. 1878) by Víctor Patricio de Landaluze (1828–1889), a Spaniard who arrived in Havana in 1862, and painted many well-known images of Cuban customs and personalities from the mid and late nineteenth century.

The carnivalesque processions of Día de Reyes were banned or put under strict regulations numerous times in the nineteenth century, sometimes as punishment for slave revolts or as a preventative measure during the Ten Years' War (1868–1878) and the so-called Little War (1879–1880) "when combatants took advantage of the masquerades to obtain arms and spread news," (Roy 35). Jory Farr has pointed out that Afro-Cuban carnival processions in Santiago de Cuba were prohibited in 1869 due to their supposed potential to "foment revolution," and that in 1871 several members of "various black carnival *comparsas* were caught and jailed."

Farr also notes that "during the 1895 Cuban War of Independence, Santiago's black *congas* and *comparsas* served as covers for life-and-death political struggles. For it was the chaos and boisterous distractions the groups created during carnival that allowed *mambises*, or freedom fighters, to engage in their clandestine operations" (214).[1] As Robin Moore has noted, there is some disagreement over the precise date that Día de Reyes festivities were banned, but according to most accounts they were definitively prohibited by an official decree in December 1884 (*Nationalizing Blackness* 66). Moore goes on to note that from 1884 until after the Spanish-American War of 1898, "few carnivalesque celebrations of any sort took place in Cuba" (66). However, by the early years of the Republic, traditional Afro-Cuban street processions began to reemerge in the form of *comparsas* and *congas*, which, unlike the ensembles of the colonial period that were typically organized according to ethnic groups, came to be associated with various working-class Havana neighborhoods with high Afro-Cuban populations such as Jesús María, Belén, Regla, and San Lázaro.

During the formative years of the Cuban Republic there was a generalized sentiment among the white, middle-class majority that the repression of African-derived customs and traditions such as *comparsas* and *congas* served the best interests of an emerging nation-state that strove to shed its colonial legacy and forge an image of a people with strong ties to Western traditions. Many middle-class blacks and mulattos supported such measures since they felt that the promotion of certain types of Afro-Cuban music, dance, and religious rituals greatly jeopardized their own hopes of becoming fully integrated members of Cuban society. In March 1916, Ramón Vasconcelos (1890–1965), a prominent mulatto intellectual, wrote several scathing editorials in his widely read column in the Cuban daily *La Prensa* about the traditional Afro-Cuban *comparsas* that he had observed during that year's carnival celebrations in Havana. In an article published on March 7, Vasconcelos made the following observations, which typified mainstream attitudes toward such spectacles:

> [Fue] el espectáculo más bochornoso, más colonial que pudiera imaginarse . . . Y porque la farola, y el tambor y los cencerros y el relajamiento autorizado son coloniales, y por ende anacrónicos, deben desaparecer en esta época de renovación y exaltación de las virtudes cívicas. ("Al primer tapón" 4)

[It was the most humiliating colonial spectacle imaginable... And because the *farola*, the drum, cowbells, and authorized amusement are colonial, and therefore anachronistic, they should disappear in this age of renovation and exaltation of civic virtues.]

Like Vasconcelos, many middle-class Cuban blacks and mulattoes felt that these Afro-Cuban carnival bands, whose masqueraded participants danced through the streets of Havana playing various African-derived instruments during pre-Lenten festivities and at other times throughout the year were damaging to a nation striving for racial equality. To their detractors, such spectacles embodied African atavism and colonial backwardness, and reinforced demeaning stereotypes that served to justify prejudices against all Afro-Cubans. In one of several published responses to Vasconcelos's editorials, Francisco Mendoza Marrero similarly denounced *comparsas* as shameful relics of colonial times and referred to them in the most demeaning terms. In his mind they were little more than "barbarous and obscene mobs" of "incorrigible Negroes"[2] whose drunkenness provoked public scandal, tumultuous brawls, and licentious behavior (4).

As Robin Moore has demonstrated, *comparsas* had been targets of public condemnation and official criticism since the earliest years of the Republic. In the early 1900s, for instance, carnival celebrations in Havana were strictly regulated, and traditional Afro-Cuban troupes were rarely permitted to take part in them since government officials felt that they detracted from the "civility" of the new Republic. Moore notes that in March 1912, *comparsas* became the subject of widespread national condemnation and virulent press coverage after a brawl between two troupes left several individuals dead or wounded (69). Though he is careful to point out that the *comparsas* in question took place just two months before the onset of the Racist Massacre of 1912, he does not stress the impact of the brewing conflict on both official and mainstream attitudes toward the *comparsas* of 1912 and those of subsequent years.[3] Indeed, it is clear that the latent fears of an imminent black rebellion in Cuba had a greater role in the nearly universal condemnation of Afro-Cuban carnival celebrations of 1912 than did the violent confrontations that mainly involved the members of El Alacrán and El Gavilán, two of the best known carnival ensembles.[4] Moreover, it follows that the profound racism and fear of another Afro-Cuban rebellion that were stirred up by the events of 1912 played a decisive role in the decision of Havana's mayor, Fernando Freyre de Andrade (1863–1929), to ban traditional Afro-Cuban *comparsas* in the opening days of 1913.

Afro-Cuban Culture and the Racist Massacre of 1912

Though it is beyond the scope of this study to give a complete history of the Racist Massacre of 1912, a discussion of this conflict is essential to my readings of several of the poems considered here—especially Felipe Pichardo Moya's "La comparsa," which is the subject of Chapter 1. Moreover, an understanding of the events of 1912 is also imperative to any examination of mainstream attitudes toward Afro-Cubans and their cultural manifestations during the early years of the Republic.

Immediately after the defeat of Spain in 1898, Cuban blacks and mulattoes, who made up nearly 30 percent of the population, hoped that their decisive contributions to the liberation of Cuba would be rewarded with the opportunity for full participation in the construction of the new nation. For Cuban blacks, the establishment of a new country "implied a new society, and a new status in that society" (Pérez, "Race War" 510). However, in the opening years of the twentieth century, their dreams of equality and social justice were dashed by a number of factors. Indeed, as Pérez has pointed out, the conditions of many Afro-Cubans actually deteriorated with the advent of the Republic (526). The racist policies of the occupying U.S. military combined with corrupt Cuban administrations—which largely overlooked blacks and did little to reward them for their contributions to Cuba libre—perhaps played the greatest role in the marginalization of Afro-Cubans at the dawn of the Republic, although other factors also served to worsen their status. Massive Spanish immigration (to the tune of 250,000 between 1902–1912), for example, "served . . . to expel blacks from the labor market," and the indisposition of white Cubans to accommodate blacks "within the expanding state bureaucracy" led to their under representation "in elected office, in appointed positions, in the armed forces, and in civil service"(Pérez 527).

In 1908 Evaristo Estenoz, a former slave and a participant in both the War of Independence and the Liberal Party uprising of August 1906, founded the Partido Independiente de Color (PIC). The party's primary intention was to defend the interests of Cuban blacks and mulattoes, not to advocate separatism, as many alleged. Its leaders and members demanded proportional participation in the government, comparable economic and social opportunities, and equal rights as Cuban citizens. Largely because the PIC was seen as a threat to both the Liberal and Conservative political parties, the Cuban Senate passed a bill in 1910, which had been penned by Senator Martín Morúa Delgado, the most prominent Afro-Cuban supporter of President José Miguel Gómez. Morúa's Law, as the bill was commonly known, established "that any group composed of individuals of a single race or color would not be considered a political party" (De la Fuente 72), and it effectively outlawed the PIC. Soon thereafter thousands of Afro-Cubans galvanized in support of the PIC and threatened armed resistance if the bill remained in effect.

In February 1912, just weeks before that year's infamous carnival celebrations in Havana, Estenoz warned President Gómez that he and the members of his banned party would rebel if the president did not revoke Morúa's Law by April 22. Estenoz's demands were not met, and on May 20, 1912, he, along with Afro-Cuban activist Pedro Ivonnet and several hundred supporters of the PIC, led an uprising that was met with fierce repression by the Cuban army. Alejandro de la Fuente points out that "Racist repression became politically possible due to a combination of factors" (73), among which he cites the fact that the revolt of the PIC "was easily construed as an attempt to break the fragile boundaries of Cuban racial democracy and therefore as a threat to the very existence of the republic" (73). De la Fuente adds, moreover, that the members of the PIC were labeled as racists because it was believed that the group placed race above Cuban national identity (73).

According to Louis A. Pérez:

> The political spark ignited the social conflagration, and the countryside was set ablaze. Disorders quickly assumed the proportions of a peasant jacquerie: an outburst of rage and the release of a powerful destructive fury directed generally at the sources and symbols of oppression. As is often the case with peasant movements, the uprising possessed a formless and desultory character. It was a popular outburst, born of social distress and directed not at government but at local social groups and specific conditions of abuse. It was without a program of reform, without commitment to a unifying program, without organization, without defined policy, and without formal leadership. ("Politics, Peasants" 533)

Aline Helg, however, takes issue with Pérez's interpretation of the events of 1912 as a destructive peasant "jacquerie, in which the role of the Partido Independiente de Color was marginal" (*Our Rightful Share* 10). Helg points out a number of methodological problems in Pérez's article, most notable of which is what she refers to as the Cuban historian's uncritical acceptance of "the description of the havoc attributed to the Independientes by the Cuban press and the U.S. officials." According to Helg, Pérez fails "to take into account the long Cuban and U.S. tradition of describing blacks as irresponsible and violent, or the need by the Cuban authorities to mobilize whites against blacks by magnifying the armed protest." Helg adds, furthermore, that Pérez presents the rebels as if they were the only actors in the turmoil, and consequently offers little insight into the impact of "the thousands of troops and volunteers roaming the province to hunt them down" (*Rightful Share* 254 n. 34).

In her convincing interpretation of what she refers to as the "Racist Massacre of 1912"—instead of the more frequently used monikers such as "Guerrita del Doce" or "Race War of 1912"—Helg challenges the common assumptions of many modern Cuban interpretations of the events, which tend to present them as a rebellion or "Race War" launched by Afro-Cubans in Oriente Province against the white establishment. As she sees it, the willingness of the PIC's members to resort to armed protest in order to achieve their goals simply served as a catalyst for an "outburst of racism that swept the entire country" (*Rightful Share* 194). "Although the independientes actually demonstrated only in Oriente," Helg continues, "white repression was nationwide, indiscriminate, and almost unopposed" (194). The protestors' threats to foreign property in Oriente were immediately met with widespread support for "a policy of merciless repression." Moreover, their acts of sabotage, which were largely responses to the increasing antiblack violence, served to justify the suspension of constitutional guarantees in Oriente and "provoked a new escalation of repression of Afro-Cubans in the provinces of Havana, Santa Clara, and elsewhere" (194).

However one chooses to interpret this bloody conflict, its consequences were devastating. In less then two months Cuban troops massacred an estimated three thousand to six thousand blacks and mulattoes, many of whom were innocent citizens with no apparent connections to the PIC or to the peasant rebellion.[5]

It is important to point out that in the years leading up to the crisis and during the armed conflict itself, the Cuban press virulently attacked Estenoz and the PIC, and spread malicious rumors that aimed to create an exaggerated sense of alarm and stir up racial hatred throughout the nation. Numerous newspapers, for example, gave false reports of rapes and kidnappings of white women and children by black men, provided exaggerated accounts of looting and destruction by black insurgents of Cuban towns and U.S.-owned industries, and propagated unfounded accounts of extensive Haitian involvement in the rebellion (Helg, *Rightful Share* 169, 197). Such observations are corroborated by the daily coverage of the conflict in the *New York Times*, which quoted Cuban president José Miguel Gómez's report that "the [Cuban] press in general has exaggerated the importance of the uprising by publishing false rumors and news" ("Gómez Sees End" 1). The newspaper also reported in several articles that official Cuban accounts of black violence and of alleged destruction and pillaging of U.S. property by the rebels were highly exaggerated.[6]

For many years after the massacre—which Cuban authorities made concerted efforts to represent as a "Race War" launched by Afro-Cubans—racial tensions in Cuba ran high, and fear of Afro-Cubans and their potential to mount more rebellions led to increasing efforts to control and suppress African-derived cultural manifestations throughout the island. De la Fuente explains that "since the PIC was a racially defined political party, the widespread perception was that 'blacks' had revolted and that it was only a matter of time before they did it again" (77). One product of the government's campaign of repression was what Helg refers to as a "brujo scare," which was fanned by widespread rumors of white children being murdered for witchcraft-related rituals. Such images haunted the imaginations of white Cubans, and led to the arrests of hundreds of alleged *brujos* [witches, sorcerers], a name used indiscriminately to refer to practitioners of African-derived religions and to members of the Abakuá secret society. In his book, *The Light Inside: Abakuá Society, Arts, and Cuban Cultural History*, David H. Brown similarly writes of the "near-hysterical prohibition[s]" of elite white Cubans, who during the early decades of the Republic forbade their children from "going anywhere near the window, let alone going outside, on the feast days celebrated by Afro-Cubans. Parents feared their children being shot, knifed, kidnapped, or *embrujado* [sic]—that is, ensorcelled. In short, the *brujo* and the *ñáñigo* remained the bogeyman of Cuban cultural fantasy through the 1950s, if not later, lurking just behind the scrim of aestheticized folkloric representation"

(172). The hysteria and paranoia that gripped the Cuban nation were well known even outside the island, as the following parodic verses from "Canción festiva para ser llorada" (1929), by the Puerto Rican poet Luis Palés Matos demonstrate:

> Mira que te coge el ñáñigo
> Niña, no salgas de casa.
> Mira que te coge el ñáñigo
> Del jueguito de La Habana.
> Con tu carne hará compota.
> Con tu seso mermelada.
> Ñáñigo carabalí
> De la manigua cubana. (67)

In the months and years following the 1912 Racist Massacre, traditional Afro-Cuban *comparsas*, which had long been considered degenerate manifestations of Afro-Cuban religion and culture—and were intimately associated with the alleged barbaric practices of *brujería* and *ñáñiguismo* in the public imagination—were turned into targets of a campaign to rid the country of "atavistic" African-derived traditions. For example, shortly before the 1913 carnival season—the first to follow the events of 1912—Havana mayor Freyre de Andrade issued a decree, which was published on January 13 in *Diario de la Marina*. In it, the mayor subjected all carnival celebrations to strict regulations and specifically banned all traditional Afro-Cuban *comparsas* in one of its twenty-three articles, which read as follows: "Artículo 8: quedan prohibidos en lo absoluto, los bailes y comparsas que traigan música, tangos o entonen cantos de los peculiares al ñáñiguismo y otras asociaciones ilícitas" [Article 8: Dances and *comparsas* that involve music, *tangos* or chants related to *ñáñiguismo* and other illicit associations are strictly prohibited][7] (5). Traditional Afro-Cuban *comparsas* did emerge from time to time during future carnival seasons, and the official 1913 ban was lifted briefly in 1916 and again in 1927 (Orovio, *El carnaval habanero* 13). However, it would not be repealed in a truly meaningful way for more than two decades.

The Reemergence of Traditional *Comparsas* in 1937

After some twenty years of carnival seasons with neither authentic nor officially sanctioned Afro-Cuban *comparsas*, certain Cuban government officials and intellectuals began to wonder if depriving the people of such traditions was in the best interests of a nation that on the one hand stood to benefit greatly from the tourist dollars that such spectacles helped to attract, and on the other hand strove to forge a new and unique national identity after decades of political turmoil and U.S. control of the island under the Platt Amendment. As Robin Moore puts it, "in the wake of the successful revolution against Gerardo Machado in August and September 1933, and the abrogation of the hated Platt Amendment soon thereafter, nationalist sentiment in Cuba achieved a degree of intensity that had not existed since the Wars of Independence against Spain" (81). Moore goes on to observe that during the reformist administration of Ramón Grau San Martín (1933–1934) "and the early years of Fulgencio Batista (1934–1944), a new sense of populism and pride" led many Cubans to turn to autochthonous cultural manifestations such as traditional Afro-Cuban carnival celebrations as vehicles through which to express such sentiments (81).

Responding to this palpable change in national sentiment, Havana mayor Antonio Beruff Mendieta composed a letter on January 30, 1937, which he sent to the members of the newly founded Sociedad de Estudios Afrocubanos. In it, Beruff Mendieta asked for their input on his plan to reauthorize traditional Afro-Cuban *comparsas* after nearly two decades of official government bans against them. In his well-known letter of response Fernando Ortiz (1881–1969)—the society's founder and Cuba's leading expert on Afro-Cuban culture—wrote in the name of all of the members of the society. He argued in favor of the reauthorization of *comparsas*, and insisted that these Afro-Cuban cultural manifestations—which he presented as valuable cultural survivals of the colonial era—could be turned into symbols of Cuba's distinctive, mixed-race national identity. Ortiz, who had strongly opposed *comparsas* in the opening decades of the twentieth century, was careful to argue that these traditional cultural manifestations should not be seen as purely African-derived phenomena, since they embodied the cultural heterogeneity that made Cuba unique: "Las comparsas ... [son] mulatas, no porque sean compuestas precisamente por gente de color, sino por la profusa heterogeneidad de los aportes étnicos que en ellas se funden" (138). [*Comparsas* . . . are *mulatas*, not so much because they are made up of people of color, but because of the profuse heterogeneity of the ethnic contributions that meld together in them.] But as Luis Duno-Gottberg has convincingly argued, support from Ortiz and other "administrators of Cuban culture" (85) may have been motivated at least in part by a desire to form an image of a united nation during a time when the Cuban Republic seemed to be on the verge of dissolution and fragmentation (85, 136).

Indeed, in his letter to Beruff Mendieta, Ortiz emphasized the need to develop a stronger sense of national pride, and to reject the cultural imperialism of the United States, which he felt continued to weaken the nation's resolve and sully its self-image. According to Ortiz, he and other members of the Sociedad de Estudios Afrocubanos had determined that such goals could be achieved at least in part by a national embrace, so to speak, of unique and authentic Cuban cultural traditions such as *comparsas*. As Alejandra Bronfman correctly points out, Ortiz and other members of the Society believed that these "relics from the past . . . might still retain the power to harmonize a dissonant society" (169).

Ramón Vasconcelos, who like Ortiz had been an outspoken critic of *comparsas* for many years, advocated the resuscitation of Afro-Cuban carnival ensembles like the ones that had filed down the streets of the capital during the celebrations of the early years of the Republic (precisely those that he had so fiercely attacked from his column in *La Prensa*). He observed in an editorial published in *El País* on February 10, 1937 that there was nothing wrong with "the beauty queens," the "dazzling carnival floats," and the profusion of confetti and streamers that typified Havana's popular white carnival, but he argued that such spectacles hardly demonstrated a budding sense of national pride for the American tourists who came to Cuba to see something more "typical" and "authentic." Like Ortiz, he promoted the idea that *comparsas* would attract both foreign and Cuban tourists—and their money—to Havana, at the same time that they would serve to promote harmony in a nation still reeling from the social, economic, and cultural impacts of U.S. imperialism.

> Nos parece, si se va a presentar al turismo una Cuba cubana, una Habana criolla, carnavalesca de verdad, que no se puede prescindir de las comparsas . . . Nosotros resucitaríamos las comparsas tal y como fueron de pintorescos y originales . . . De ese modo podrían desfilar, con sus farolas, sus canciones, sus tambores, sus güiros, sus guitarras, su colorismo maravilloso: El Alacrán, Los Congos Libres,

Los Moros, Los Negros Buenos, Los Chinos, El Gavilán, Los Guajiros del Jiquí, veinte, treinta, en un espectáculo feérico, lleno de luces y de cantos bajo la noche habanera. ("Complejos" 143–45)

[It seems to us that if we are going to present to the tourists a Cuban Cuba, a truly *criolla*, carnivalesque Havana, that we cannot do without *comparsas* . . . We would revive the *comparsas* to their original, quaint form . . . In that way they could parade through the streets with their *farolas*, their songs, their drums, their guiros, their guitars, their marvelous local color: El Alacrán, Los Congos Libres, Los Moros, Los Negros Buenos, Los Chinos, El Gavilán, Los Guajiros del Jiquí, twenty, thirty, in a fairy spectacle full of lights and songs in the Havana night.]

Vasconcelos, in what amounted to a stunning about-face when read in light of his scathing condemnation of *comparsas* and *congas* in *La Prensa* in 1916, went on to put forth the idea—reminiscent, to be sure, of Nicolás Guillén's famous prologue to *Sóngoro cosongo* (1931)—that reauthorizing these "typical" and "local" traditions was the best way to help all Cubans to discover the African blood that ran through their veins.

Despite such enthusiastic support for the reauthorization of traditional Afro-Cuban *comparsas*, however, Ortiz and Vasconcelos both stressed in their own ways the need for certain changes that would serve to elevate these spectacles in the eyes of the discerning American tourist or the many members of Cuba's middle and upper classes who opposed them. Ortiz stressed, for example, the need for "a stable system of regulation" that would serve to transform *comparsas* into "valuable institutions of Havana life" ("Las comparsas populares" 141). For his part, Vasconcelos revealed some lingering uneasiness about the carnival ensembles that he had once qualified as "the most humiliating spectacles imaginable" ("Al primer tapón" 4) by underscoring the importance of keeping the dancing "decent" and free of "lubricious undertones." Vasconcelos also expressed his hope that the traditional rivalries among *comparsa* troupes remain "inoffensive" ("Al margen" 36). Such comments reflect well Luis Duno-Gottberg's contention that Ortiz, Vasconcelos, and many of the proponents of the literary and cultural movement known as Afrocubanismo aimed not so much to celebrate and embrace African-derived traditions in Cuba, but rather to contain and assimilate the African elements of the Cuban condition (85–87).

Strict government regulation of the carnival celebrations of 1937, and of those of following years, was largely successful and had its desired effect. To be sure, many observers marveled at the transformation of these cultural spectacles, which were suddenly embraced even by certain members of Cuba's cultural and social elite. In a March 1937 article published in the Havana daily *Diario de la Marina*, for example, Armando Maribona had the following to say about the transformation of *comparsas* from an abolished tradition to a widely accepted Cuban cultural manifestation:

> Falso que estas manifestaciones sean pornográficas ... Las comparsas eran cosa abolida. Pero así como el 'son rumbeado' ya no es tabú en las esferas aristocráticas, la comparsa, de repente, ascendió a los clubs más exclusivos. (n.p.)

> [It is false that these are pornographic spectacles ... *Comparsas* used to be abolished. But just as the *son rumbeado* is no longer considered taboo among the aristocratic spheres, the *comparsa* has suddenly ascended into the most exclusive clubs.]

It is important to point out, however, that despite the supposed best efforts of government officials and leading intellectuals and administrators of Cuban culture, Afro-Cuban carnival traditions inevitably lost much of their local color and character following their 1937 reauthorization. Helio Orovio notes, for example, how municipal programs and intense tourism campaigns turned the carnival season and the *comparsas* themselves into a spectacle of extraordinary proportions (*El carnaval habanero* 14). Cuba's ever-growing consumer culture began to be reflected in the increasing commercialization of the *comparsas*, which often included tacky carnival floats that were more like moving advertisements for everything from beer, to chocolate, to perfumes. In terms of their musical components, the local color provided by neighborhood musicians was often trumped by the stronger tourist draw of nationally known orchestras and bands (Feliú Herrera, "Carnavales" 57, Orovio, *El carnaval habanero* 15).

It must be added, moreover, that in 1937 there were still many who opposed the reauthorization and reemergence of Afro-Cuban carnival ensembles. Some of the most vehement voices of opposition to the stance of Fernando Ortiz and the Sociedad de Estudios Afrocubanos came from middle-class blacks and mulattos associated with the progressive journal *Adelante* (1935–1939), a monthly publication that served in part to disseminate literary and artistic creations of Afro-Cubans. The journal's subtitle—"Cultura y Justicia Social / Igualdad y Confraternidad" [Cultural and Social Justice / Equality and Confraternity]—reflects the strong social bearings of its editors and collaborators who included Nicolás Guillén, José Luciano Franco, Ángel C. Pinto, Lino Dou, Salvador García Agüero, Alberto Arredondo, and Marcelino Arozarena, among others. As Bronfman has correctly observed, "the directors of *Adelante* strove not only to galvanize a broadly based black political identity but also to encourage higher degrees of contention and dissent... They also tried to influence the everyday practices and beliefs of blacks throughout Cuba" (166). The heated debate over *comparsas* and *congas* that played out in the pages of *Adelante* in the months following their February 1937 reauthorization in Havana aimed in large part to convince Afro-Cubans to forego their newly granted "right" to participate in these controversial carnival processions. It was the opinion of the directors of *Adelante*—and especially the outspoken journalist, economist, and social critic Alberto Arredondo (1912–1968)—that the white intellectuals and politicians who had "revived" *comparsas* in Havana did not have the best interests of Cuba's black citizens in mind. Arredondo contended that granting Afro-Cubans the right to dance through the streets in carnival processions was in no way beneficial to them, and he therefore saw the reauthorization as a highly politicized move that could hardly be viewed as a step toward racial integration or economic equality in Cuba. In the first official response to the 1937 reauthorization of *comparsas* in Havana, the members of the Asociación Adelante, in a front-page editorial penned by Arredondo (fig. 0.2), expressed their strong disagreement with Fernando Ortiz and other members of the Sociedad de Estudios Afrocubanos (mostly white intellectuals) over their enthusiastic promotion of such "denigrating" and "unedifying spectacles." But their harshest criticism was directed at Havana's mayor, whom they accused of putting politics before the best interests of the nation:

> el señor Alcalde no ha de variar su línea de conducta, porque él, antes que otra cosa, es político que siguió la vieja escuela ... todo lo que hace tiene oculto—más o menos visible—una razón

electoral... estimulará, por todos los medios, los vicios, y las pasiones de las masas, considerando esto, como el más positivo, cómodo y barato sistema para seguirla (sic) explotando, aunque ello venga en detrimento de nuestra condición de pueblo civilizado. (Arredondo "Las comparsas" 1)

[Mr. Mayor will not vary his line of conduct, because he, above all else, is a politician who followed the old school... everything he does hides—though it's more or less obvious—an electoral motive... he will encourage, by all means possible, the vices and the passions of the masses, considering this to be the most positive, comfortable and low-cost system of exploiting them, even if it is detrimental to our condition as a civilized nation.]

Several months later the controversy still brewed, and in July 1937 Arredondo wrote another article in which he expressed his fear that these humiliating public performances simply served to reinforce damaging stereotypes and to justify the systematic exclusion of Cubans of color from meaningful participation in the formation of the new Republic. The following observation about his own experience during the 1937 carnival celebrations in Havana underscores several of Arredondo's concerns:

Fuimos al Malecón y al Prado a contemplar [las comparsas y congas]. Y... por donde quiera que creíamos prudente meter la cabeza y necesario avivar el oído, escuchamos sólo frases por el estilo de éstas: ¡Y luego hablan de que el negro ha evolucionado! ¡A esta gente conga, ron y leña! ¡Son unos degenerados! ¡Están en la selva! ¡En plena barbarie, están los negros por civilizar! ¡Qué se diviertan, que bailen conga¡ ¿qué otra cosa pueden hacer los negros? ("El arte negro" 6)

[We went to the Malecón and to the Prado to contemplate the *comparsas* and *congas*. And... wherever we found it prudent to stick out our heads and necessary to perk up our ears, we only heard expressions like these: And then they'll say that the Negro has evolved! All these people want is *conga*, rum and anything to fuel the fire! They're a bunch of degenerates! They're in the jungle! In the midst of complete barbarity, the Negroes are about to become civilized! Let them have fun, let them dance *conga*! What else can the Negroes do?]

FIGURE 0.2. Alberto Arredondo, "Las comparsas." This editorial from the first page of the March 1937 issue of *Adelante* was the first of more than a dozen articles on the 1937 *comparsa* controversy that were published in this progressive journal. (Evergreen State College Library.)

As the references to traditional *congas* in this passage suggest, Arredondo and the other members of the Asociación Adelante were especially opposed to these traditional carnival processions, which they viewed as unruly spectacles that were completely devoid of artistic merit. What Arredondo and his cohorts found most offensive about *congas* was their unstructured collective dance—commonly known as *arrollao* (from *arrollar*—"to overwhelm," "to crush")—, which tended to be disorderly in nature and often pulled hundreds of rowdy spectators into the frenzy of the procession. As Arredondo saw it, by allowing *congas* to take part in Havana's carnival celebrations, city authorities had essentially halted "the progress of the suffering Cuban Negro," who, thanks to the rowdy *arrollaos*, would continue to be subjected to "damaging theories racial inferiority and Negro backwardness" (*El negro en Cuba* 143).

In another official statement of the Assocación Adelante published at the beginning of the 1938 carnival season, the institution's secretary general, Tomás Acuña L'azcano, reiterated this sentiment—which was shared by many middle-class Cuban blacks and mulattos—with the following declaration: "Jamás podrá estar identificado el movimiento reivindicador del negro con el 'arrollao' retardatorio de las congas" (8). [The movement to vindicate the Negro will never be identified with the retarding 'arrollao' of the *conga*.]

It is worth adding here that Arredondo and those who shared his negative opinions about Afro-Cuban *comparsas* and *congas* could not have been pleased by artistic renditions of them, such as Spanish-born painter Fernando Tarazona's *La conga* (fig. 0.3). In his massive 1936 painting, which measures 6x7 feet, Tarazona highlights the supposedly lubricious elements of the *conga* by placing in the foreground an undulating, hip-swaying Afro-Cuban woman with exposed breasts and thighs. Immediately behind her is an Afro-Cuban man, whose closed eyes, open lips, and widely spread legs exude the stereotypical image of the lustful and uncontrollable black male.

Carnival and the Poets of Afrocubanismo

The history of the debate that surrounded Afro-Cuban carnival traditions during the opening decades of the Cuban Republic has been studied at length by various historians and musicologists, most notably Robin Moore, Helio Orovio, Judith Bettelheim, Alejandra Bronfman, Nancy

FIGURE 0.3. Fernando Tarazona, *La conga*, 1936. This depiction of an Afro-Cuban *conga* is emblematic of the commonly held notion that these Afro-Cuban carnival processions were lewd and offensive spectacles. From *Escenas afro-cubanas*, 1939. (Author's collection.)

Pérez-Rodríguez, and Virtudes Feliú Herrera.[8] However, the present study focuses on a topic that has only been taken up incidentally by two of the figures mentioned above (Moore and Orovio), and has been largely ignored by literary critics—that is, how this controversy played out in Cuban poetry written during the same period. Throughout this book, the multiple social and political controversies surrounding Afro-Cuban carnival celebrations and other similar cultural manifestations—dances, musical genres, religious rituals—will be discussed in light of ten carnival-inspired poems that were written during a period that spans from 1916, the date of Felipe Pichardo Moya's "La comparsa," to 1953, the year in which Marcelino Arozarena penned his "Carnaval de Santiago." All of the poems considered here either belong to or are related in some obvious way to the cultural and intellectual phenomenon known as Afrocubanismo, which flourished in Havana for about a decade starting in the late 1920s.

It is important to point out from the outset that this book does not claim to be a comprehensive study of Afrocubanismo or, for that matter, a complete history of Afro-Cuban carnival traditions. Instead, this study's main focus is a specific and somewhat limited group of poems that are related to this important artistic and intellectual movement, but whose principal significance is their relationship to and evocation of the long-running national controversy that surrounded Afro-Cuban *comparsas, congas, chambelonas,* and other related carnival spectacles throughout the early years of the Cuban Republic. Furthermore, it should be added that many of the close readings of carnival poems in this book focus largely on content and historical context, sometimes at the expense of the type of detailed examination of the poems' formal qualities—rhythm, meter, rhyme scheme—that some readers might expect, and indeed want, to find in a study such as this. However, as the reader will see in the chapters that follow, the issue of poetic form is addressed to varying degrees throughout this study. In some cases—Guillén's "Sensemayá," for example—a detailed discussion of the poem's formal qualities is essential to communicating its deeper meaning, while in others—such as José Zacarías Tallet's "Quintín Barahona"—such a discussion is not as important.

This book is divided into eight chapters, the first seven of which consider carnival poems by well-known Cuban authors: Felipe Pichardo Moya, Alejo Carpentier, Nicolás Guillén, Emilio Ballagas, José Zacarías Tallet, Felix B. Caignet, and Marcelino Arozarena. The final chapter strays from this pattern only in that its subject is a poem by Alfonso Camín, a Spanish-born author who fits squarely into the present study because he is widely held to be one of the founding voices of Afrocubanismo and an initiator of negrismo in the Hispanic Caribbean. Before continuing with a brief discussion of each chapter, it is important to point out that the poetry associated with these related cultural and intellectual movements is often referred to with a confusing assortment of names. In his introduction to *Órbita de la poesía afrocubana 1928–1937*, for example, Ramón Guirao employs all of the following terms interchangeably: "poesía negra," "poesía afrocubana," "lírica oscura," "poética afro-negrista," "poesía afrocriolla," and "lírica afroantillana." In this study I understand "poesía negra" and "poesía negrista" as general terms that refer to poems from anywhere in the Spanish-speaking world (including Cuba) that focus on African-inspired themes. When specifically addressing similar poetry written in

Cuba in the early decades of the twentieth century, I refer either to "the poetry of Afrocubanismo" or to "*afrocubanista* poetry."

In the opening chapter, "Felipe Pichardo Moya's 'La comparsa': Afro-Cuban Carnival as Sinister Spectacle," I examine a poem that is widely held to be one of the most significant precursors to the poetry of Afrocubanismo. Pichardo Moya's "La comparsa" was originally published in 1916—just four years after the Racist Massacre of 1912—and I argue that its reputation as an important precursor has largely overshadowed its obvious conjuration of the deep-seated prejudices against Afro-Cuban carnival celebrations and related cultural manifestations that had led to official bans against them during the early decades of the twentieth century. In this chapter I also demonstrate how "La comparsa," the original version of which was dedicated to Fernando Ortiz, echoes many aspects of the early writings of the man who was, at the time, one of Cuba's preeminent criminologists. Indeed, in two major studies on the Havana underworld that Ortiz had penned by the time Pichardo published "La comparsa"—*Hampa afrocubana: Los negros brujos (apuntes para un estudio de etnología criminal)* (1906) [Afro-Cuban Underworld: The Black Sorcerers (Notes for a Study of Criminal Ethnology)] and *Hampa afrocubana: Los negros esclavos* (1916) [Afro-Cuban Underworld: The Black Slaves]—he revealed his strong prejudices toward Afro-Cubans in general and, more specifically, his disparagement of African-derived traditions and cultural manifestations.

The focus of Chapter 2—"Carnival and Ñáñiguismo: Poetic Syncretism in Alejo Carpentier's 'Juego santo'"—is a little-studied poem by one of the earliest literary proponents of Afrocubanismo. This chapter begins with a brief exploration of Carpentier's decisive role as a founder of this artistic and cultural movement, but the focus is on the poem itself and, more specifically, its relationship to and evocation of Afro-Cuban carnival traditions. I demonstrate how—in an act of poetic syncretism—Alejo Carpentier melds two public spectacles that had long been associated with Ñáñiguismo, or the Abakuá secret society: semi-public, sacred processions that were performed as part of *ñáñigo* initiation ceremonies, and carnivalesque "comparsas ñáñigas," which first emerged during nineteenth-century Día de Reyes celebrations, and then eventually became integrated into traditional carnival festivities. I contend in this chapter that "Juego santo" [Holy Abakuá Lodge] is especially significant because it attests to the fact that Carpentier was the first of the proponents of

Afrocubanismo to focus on the liturgical and ritual elements of Afro-Cuban life and to attempt to interpret the esoteric rites of the Abakuá secret society.

The principal aims of the third chapter, "Carnival and Afro-Cuban Ritual in Nicolás Guillén's 'Sensemayá: canto para matar una culebra,'" are to elucidate past discussions of this poem's relationship to nineteenth-century Día de Reyes celebrations, and to demonstrate that Guillén's widely anthologized but little understood poem can be read as an evocation of the controversies that surround traditional Afro-Cuban *comparsas* during the early decades of the Cuban Republic. I contend that while some critics have already pointed out some of the poem's most obvious connections to nineteenth-century Afro-Cuban Día de Reyes traditions, none have suggested, as I do, that "Sensemayá" can be interpreted as Guillén's reaction or response to the bans placed on Afro-Cuban *comparsas* and the prohibitions of other African-derived cultural manifestations in the twentieth century. In my new reading of the poem, I argue that the act of killing the snake—which has been variously interpreted as a symbol of Cuba's liberation from U.S. domination (Ellis 85) or as an "exorcising [of] ritual violence to prevent social violence" (Benítez-Rojo, *Repeating* 299)—can be read not just as a symbolic eradication of traditional carnival *comparsas*, but also as a metaphor for the attempts to eliminate other Afro-Cuban cultural manifestations, such as the religious rites associated with Santería and Palo Mayombe, and the sacred practices of the Abakuá secret society. Finally, I posit that by "killing" the snake in their carnival celebrations, Afro-Cubans were not acting out a ritual of elimination of evil, but rather were taking part in an act that for them symbolized the creature's rebirth and guaranteed its survival.

Chapter 4 focuses on Emilio Ballagas's widely anthologized poem "Comparsa habanera." I argue here that this lively carnival poem is emblematic in many ways of the ambivalence that middle-class Cubans felt toward Afro-Cubans and their culture during the early years of the Republic. On the one hand "Comparsa habanera" stands out for its vibrant rhythm and colorful imagery, which suggest at least in a superficial manner the festive nature of traditional *comparsas*. These qualities of the poem have led many critics to read it as an authentic recreation and sincere celebration of Afro-Cubans and their cultural legacy in the young Republic. On the other hand, Ballagas's stereotypical depiction of the black *comparseros*—who are marked by their exaggerated *bozal* speech, ignorance, primitive superstitions, drunkenness, and unrestrained sexuality—belies his claims that his *poesía negra* embodied the desire among the poets of Afrocubanismo to replace negative portrayals of black Cubans by authors of previous generations with sincere and authentic images. I also point out that despite the fact that a truncated version of "Comparsa habanera"—which appeared in many important anthologies after the official reinstatement of *comparsas* in 1937—has fewer images that evoke *brujería* and the shameful legacy of slavery, it still echoes the prevailing sentiment in Havana in the mid-1930s that African-influenced cultural manifestations would only be fully accepted as "vital" and "beneficial" components of Cuba's evolving national identity if they were tailored to fit the tastes and standards of the white, middle-class majority.

In the following chapter I delve into the contentious history of the political *comparsas* associated with Cuba's Liberal Party politicians, which were known as *chambelonas*. These carnivalesque ensembles constitute a blatant example of how white politicians exploited Afro-Cubans during the formative years of the Republic by hiring such *comparsas* with the aim of "drumming up support" for their campaigns. The point of departure for my discussion of *chambelonas* is "Quintín Barahona," an underappreciated poem by José Zacarías Tallet. This poem, like much of Tallet's work, has been largely eclipsed by his "La rumba" (1928), one of the first and most significant poems that found its inspiration in Afro-Cuban popular culture. In terms of its open criticism of the sociopolitical plight of Afro-Cubans, "Quintín Barahona" is a relatively rare example of an *afrocubanista* poem whose substantive issues outweigh the seemingly requisite stereotypical images of blacks and their cultural traditions.

Among the many poems of Afrocubanismo that deal with Afro-Cuban carnival celebrations, Felix B. Caignet's "La conga prohibida" [The Forbidden Conga], which is the subject of Chapter 6, is the only one that explicitly refers to and openly denounces governmental prohibitions of traditional *congas* during the early decades of the Cuban Republic. In this chapter I contend that by focusing specifically on the official bans placed on *congas* in Santiago de Cuba during the 1920s and 1930s, Caignet also distinguishes himself as the only poet of Afrocubanismo who poeticized the unique carnival celebrations from Cuba's eastern region during the height of the movement. "La conga prohibida" differs considerably from other poems that deal with Afro-Cuban carnival, largely because it aims to satirize the rampant social and political hypocrisies in Santiago, rather than present an exaggerated sketch of a *conga* and its Afro-Cuban participants. The reader of Caignet's poem will immediately notice that it offers no descriptions of the black musicians and dancers, and contains very few references to the actual carnival celebration. Rather, it focuses on the significant social and political implications of the many prohibitions that were enacted against Afro-Cuban culture in eastern Cuba.

In Chapter 7 I consider three poems by Afro-Cuban poet Marcelino Arozarena: "La comparsa del majá" [The Comparsa of the Majá],[9] "La conga," and "Carnaval de Santiago" [Santiago Carnival]. In my discussion of these poems, I argue that through their widely varying depictions of traditional Afro-Cuban carnival celebrations, each serves as an emblematic example of what we might refer to as the three dimensions of Arozarena's poetic production. "La comparsa del majá," for example, fits neatly into the first dimension, which is characterized by poems that lack political themes and portray blacks as embodiments of a hedonistic world of music, dance, and, sex. In a second, transitional dimension we could place "La conga," which straddles a world in which blacks are portrayed through superficial and retrograde images and one in which they become embodiments of a collective will to denounce centuries of oppression and social injustice. Finally, "Carnaval de Santiago," like some of Arozarena's best sociopolitical poems—"Canción negra sin color" [Black Song Without Color] and "¡Evohé!" immediately come to mind—belongs in a third dimension in which superficial depictions of Afro-Cubans and African-derived cultural manifestations are largely overshadowed by the poet's condemnation of social injustice and his calls for militant action against its every manifestation.

The final chapter focuses on a fascinating poetic rendition of traditional Havana carnival celebrations by the Spanish poet, Alfonso Camín. After a brief discussion of Camín's much-debated role as an initiator of *poesía negra* in the Hispanic Caribbean, I delve into his "Carnaval en la Habana" [Carnival in Havana]. This long poem was first published in *Ma racas y otros poemas* [Maracas and Other Poems] in 1952, but was probably penned in the 1940s when Afrocubanismo was on the wane, but still of considerable interest to the reading public. What intrigues me most about "Carnaval en la Habana" is not so much its relationship to Afrocubanismo or other poems of the movement, but rather the panoramic view that it offers of Havana carnival traditions during the first half of the twentieth century. While the other poems that we consider here focus almost exclusively on Cuban carnival as an African-derived tradition, Camín illustrates the two-faced reality of Havana's carnival season by illustrating the varying ways that it was celebrated by white Cubans and Cubans of color. Echoing the class divisions that dominated Cuban society during the first half of the twentieth century, Camín's poem is clearly divisible into two distinct parts. In the first four stanzas he focuses on traditional Afro-Cuban carnival celebrations and the requisite *comparsas* and *congas* from Havana's lower-class neighborhoods, while in the next four he turns his attention to "white carnival" with its parades of decorated automobiles, elaborate floats, beautiful carnival queens, and dances and balls in exclusive clubs and organizations.

In the epilogue I briefly discuss several additional poems associated with Afrocubanismo that touch on the theme of carnival to varying degrees, but I also suggest other significant sources for the study of representations of Cuban carnival traditions and their intimate relationship to the nation's identity. I explore, for example, several carnival poems that were published during the early decades of the twentieth century in the newspapers of Santiago de Cuba, as well as a selection of poems about Afro-Cuban carnival traditions written by exiles who see these spectacles as embodiments of the nation that they have left behind. In the final sections of the epilogue I stray from the world of poetry first to examine traditional twentieth-century *cantos de comparsa* [comparsa chants] from some of Havana's best-known carnival ensembles, and then to discuss the lyrics to a handful of the scores of Cuban popular songs—from *sones* to salon congas—that found their inspiration in the traditional music of the *comparsas* and *congas* that, as Helio Orovio has observed, are so intricately interwoven into Cuba's "cultural marrow" (*El carnaval habanero* 21).

1

Felipe Pichardo Moya's "La comparsa"

Afro-Cuban Carnival as Sinister Spectacle

> El lector que viva o haya vivido en Cuba habrá visto en las noches de carnaval, o en ocasión de festejos públicos, pasear por las calles abigarradas comparsas formadas por las capas inferiores de la sociedad. A la cabeza de la comitiva poliétnica marcha un sujeto, negro generalmente, sosteniendo una pintarrajeada linterna de papeles multicolores, no siempre desprovista de efecto artístico. Tras él, otros individuos con disfraces chillones y con otras muchas linternas, y rodeándolos a todos una muchedumbre en la predominan los negros, gritando con voces destempladas, y con frecuencia aguardentosas, una cantinela repetida hasta la saciedad con monotonía desesperante.
>
> [The reader who lives or has lived in Cuba will have seen passing through the streets on carnival nights or during public festivities, multi-colored *comparsas* made up of the inferior strata of society. At the head of the poly-ethnic procession marches a subject, usually a Negro, holding up a lantern daubed with multi-colored paper, not always lacking artistic merit. After him, other individuals with gaudy costumes and with many more lanterns, and surrounding all of them a crowd in which Negroes predominate, screaming, with untuned and frequently drunken voices, a chant repeated endlessly and with exasperating monotony.]
>
> Fernando Ortiz, Los negros brujos

> Madera de esclavos, carne de barracón, tribu refractaria a la hygiene social y corporal, canalla inmunda: eso es el cuerpo de una comparsa.
>
> [The temperament of slaves, flesh of the slave barracks, a tribe refractory to social and corporal hygiene, filthy riffraff: that is the body of a *comparsa*.]
>
> Ramón Vasconcelos, "La fuga hacia la selva"

The publication of Felipe Pichardo Moya's "La comparsa" in the Cuban magazine *Gráfico* in March 1916 corresponded to a period during which racial tensions in Cuba were especially acute. Memories of the Racist Massacre of 1912 were still fresh, and many whites lived in fear of Afro-Cubans, their customs, and especially their alleged potential for future rebellions. According to De la Fuente, in the years following the massacre, rumors often surfaced that "blacks were preparing to avenge the killings of 1912" (81). "The first of these rumors circulated in 1913, after the Liberals' electoral defeat," and allegations of an imminent and supposedly well-prepared black uprising emerged again in the final months of 1915, prior to the general elections of 1916 (81).

During the same period, haunting images of murderous and lascivious black *brujos* and *ñáñigos* were irresponsibly disseminated by the sensationalistic press, and served to stir up an ever-increasing sense among the middle-class majority that concerted efforts needed to be made to suppress Afro-Cuban religions and other cultural manifestations. Spectacles that involved large gatherings—such as carnival *comparsas*—were specifically targeted since they were seen to pose the greatest threat to public safety, to the nation's civility, and to its image in the eyes of foreign tourists. That traditional Afro-Cuban *comparsas* were subjected to intense official criticism and negative press during the years following the Racist Massacre is hardly surprising since it was widely held that these collective festivities were atavistic throwbacks to the slave era and hotbeds of moral depravity and criminal violence. In this chapter, I will argue that even if it is an important precursor to the poetry of Afrocubanismo, Felipe Pichardo Moya's widely celebrated poem about an Afro-Cuban carnival ensemble is essentially a faithful reflection of the time in which it was written, and that his depiction of a *comparsa* is very much in keeping with contemporary attitudes toward these and many other expressions of African-derived culture.

In her brief remarks on "La comparsa" in her book *Sugar's Secrets*, Vera Kutzinski notes that it is ironic that the poem was "written and published at a time when actual *comparsas* were banned in Cuba" (181). Though her observation is not completely off the mark, it does not adequately address the nature of the bans that were put in place, nor does it reflect the particular circumstances surrounding *comparsas* in 1916. First of all, when considering the long-running controversy that surrounded Afro-Cuban carnival ensembles in the early decades of the Cuban Republic, it is important to keep in mind that despite the numerous official bans against them, it was not at all uncommon for Afro-Cubans to defy the authorities by parading through their own neighborhoods such as Regla, Jesús María, and Los Sitios (Guzmán Moré, n.p.). Secondly, many bans were not strictly enforced, and *comparsas* and *congas* often managed to slip into the highly regulated carnival processions that paraded through Havana's thoroughfares during the pre-Lenten festivities.

Most importantly, however, Kutzinski overlooks the fact that in February 1916 Havana Mayor General Fernando Freyre de Andrade rescinded his 1913 prohibition of *comparsas*, and allowed several groups to participate in that year's carnival celebrations. His decision, which ended up being reversed after just a few weeks, was vehemently attacked by Havana's elite and middle-class majority—whites and blacks alike—and provoked a flurry of testy editorials in Havana's newspapers. Ramón Vasconcelos, for example, voiced his fervent opposition to *comparsas* and other similar African-derived cultural manifestations in several editorials that were published in *La Prensa* in his column, "Palpitaciones de la Raza de Color: Crónica escrita para negros sin taparabos, mestizos no arrepentidos y blancos de sentido común" [Palpitations of the Colored Race: chronicle written for negroes without loincloths, non-repentant *mestizos*, and whites with common sense]. This provocative title, which appeared above the majority of his editorials from the period, served several purposes: it called attention to the racial tensions in Cuba, underscored the hierarchical divisions that existed among Cubans of color, and reflected the polemical nature of the subjects that Vasconcelos tended to address.[1]

In an editorial titled "Comparsas," which appeared on March 2, 1916, Vasconcelos denounced the mayor for permitting spectacles that so many "civilized" Cubans considered to be humiliating examples of Afro-Cuban atavism and barbarity:

> Dentro de dos o tres semanas tendremos otra vez las comparsas por las calles, pregonando la barbarie negra. Barbarie he dicho y no me arrepiento, aunque debí decir degeneración . . . al son del tambor selvático, ululando, con movimientos lúbricos, recorren la ciudad para exhibir su vergüenza como si fuera un trofeo glorioso.
>
> La bandera del retroceso, la confesión de la incapacidad de adaptación al progreso, tales son las comparsas, o las congas, como las llaman en su jerga esas buenas gentes que no tienen la culpa de su retraso. (4)

> [In two or three weeks we will again have the *comparsas* in the streets preaching black barbarity. I have said barbarity, and I do

not repent, even though I should have said degeneration . . . to the sound of the jungle drum, shrieking, with lubricious movements, they go through the city in order to exhibit their shame as if it were a glorious trophy.

The banner of regression, confession of their incapacity to adapt and progress, such are the *comparsas*, or the *congas*, as those good people that are not to blame for their backwardness call them in their own slang.]

In more than one editorial Vasconcelos warned of the violence that he—and many other middle- and upper-class Cubans, for that matter—believed to be part and parcel of traditional Afro-Cuban *comparsas*. On March 5, 1916, the last Sunday of that year's carnival season, his fears were confirmed when a fight erupted among members of two rival groups, supposedly over a stolen *farola*, or giant, multicolored paper lantern. In "Al primer tapón, zurrapas" [Well, the First Shot Was a Failure], a scathing editorial published the following Tuesday, Vasconcelos condemned the incident, which he believed necessitated the immediate and total suppression of *comparsas*:

> El primer domingo de exhibición antropomórfica . . . la culta y progresiva capital de la República, residencia de los altos dignatarios y centro de turismo, vio a dos hombres acuchillarse, en plena vía pública y en pleno Siglo Veinte: por la posesión de una ridícula farola. (4)

> [The first Sunday of the anthropomorphic exhibit . . . the cultured and progressive capital of the Republic, residence of high dignitaries and the center of tourism, saw two men stab each other in the middle of a public thoroughfares and in the heart of the Twentieth Century: over the possession of a ridiculous *farola*.]

Echoing Fernando Ortiz's *Los negros brujos* and *Los negros esclavos* as well as investigations into forensic pathology by Israel Castellanos ("El tipo brujo" [The Brujo Type](1914), *La brujería y el ñáñiguismo en Cuba desde el punto de vista medico legal* [Brujería and Ñáñiguismo in Cuba from a Medical and Legal Point of View](1916)), in which both authors compared Afro-Cuban religions and cultural practices to pathogens, Vasconcelos made use of pathological metaphors in his editorials in order to illustrate his opinion that *comparsas* were like a highly contagious social illness that could only be "cured" through total eradication. In "Comparsas," for example, he referred to *comparsas* and *congas* as "social ulcers," and posed the following question: "¿Cómo se combate el mal? . . . Yo creo que el enfermo [la comparsa] no tiene cura. La extinción es lo más seguro" (4) [How does one combat the illness? . . . I think that the patient does not have a cure. Extinction is the surest remedy.] Several days later in "Suma y sigue" [And It's Still Going On], Vasconcelos warned that the "plague" of Afro-Cuban *comparsas* was infecting the nation from Havana to Matanzas, to Cienfuegos, to Sagua, to Guantánamo, and finally Santiago, where, he claimed, illicit *congas* were multiplying at an alarming rate. He contended that *comparsas* and related social "ills," such as Afro-Cuban religions, must be isolated and aggressively eradicated to prevent them from being passed down like diseases from one generation to the next:

> Y no piense que el ñáñiguismo, la brujería y los rezagos africanos se pierden con la generación del bocabajo. No. Pasan como un legado precioso a los hijos, y los nietos, que apenas echan el primer diente ya son "hijos" de "Yemayá" o de "Changó" y bailan el "bembé"[2] en los brazos de su madre o de su abuela. (4)

> [And don't go thinking that *ñáñiguismo*, *brujería*, and other African remnants are lost with the generation of the lackey. No. They pass like a precious legacy to the children, the grandchildren, who hardly have sprouted their first tooth when they become "children" of "Yemayá" or of "Changó" and they dance the "bembé" in the arms of the mother or grandmother.]

Comments like these are especially important in the context of the present study since they underscore the widespread opinion that *comparsas* were intimately related to the practices of Afro-Cuban religions and secret societies, which a majority of non practitioners in Cuba essentially equated with witchcraft and all of the nefarious activities that it implied. It should be pointed out here that in the early decades of the twentieth century, *ñáñiguismo*—which was technically a derogative term for the Abakuá secret society—was used interchangeably with *brujería* to evoke the alleged degradation and criminality that characterized all Afro-Cuban rites and rituals. As David H. Brown has noted, "Ñáñiguismo was associated by the white cultural mainstream and nationalist theoreticians with despotic irrationality, teeming Afro-Cuban *barrios*, malicious gangs, murder, savage black men with shaved teeth, and dissipated white men fallen into primitive atavism and the lure of black women" ("Glossary" 84). The truth is that associations between *ñáñiguismo* and brutal violence were not altogether unfounded, as feuds between rival *juegos*, or lodges, were often decided by acts of "mortal revenge" as Lydia Cabrera has observed. Cabrera adds that such rivalries unfortunately bloodied many pages of the history of *ñáñiguismo* in Cuba, and led detractors of the secret society to equate its members with blood, petulance, and terror (*Anaforuana* 13).

On March 10, an anonymous response to Vasconcelos's editorial, signed Lohengrin—evoking the legendary knight of the Holy Grail and the Richard Wagner (1813–1883) opera of the same name—condemned *comparsas* for damaging Cuban society, and called for the immediate formation of a "Comité de Ciudadanos Cívicos" [Committee of Patriotic Citizens], the aim of which would be to "elevate the morality" of black Cubans. In another letter, published in *La Prensa* on March 12, Francisco Mendoza Marrero reiterated Vasconcelos's central argument that *comparsas* were breeding grounds of violence and other social ills. Echoing the typical sensationalism that characterized negative media coverage of Afro-Cubans and their culture at the time, Mendoza Marrero denounced the "wars" and "tumultuous brawls" among the *comparsas*, and called for an end to "these anti-hygienic immoral and criminal spectacles" (4).

Just over a week after the notorious March 5 incident, officials from the Secretaría de Gobernación, moved by Mayor Freyre de Andrade's apparent unwillingness to reinstate laws against illicit Afro-Cuban carnival ensembles, stepped in by enforcing an absolute ban on all *comparsas* from the streets of the capital. This decision was applauded by many critics, such as Vasconcelos, who responded to the government's decision with the following observation: "Hay que aplaudir esa resolución de buen gobierno por los males que . . . evitará: 'Muerto el perro se acabó la rabia'" ("Dos letras" 4) [One must applaud this resolution of good government for the problems that . . . it will prevent: "Dead dog, no more rabies"].

In order to understand and fully appreciate Felipe Pichardo Moya's "La comparsa," contemporary readers must bear in mind these controversies that embroiled traditional Afro-Cuban carnival ensembles in the weeks immediately preceding the poem's first appearance in the March 25, 1916 issue of *Gráfico*. It is also very important to keep in mind that the original version of the poem is followed by a brief footnote, which was cut from most subsequent publications, that reads: "Habana, Carnaval de 1916." This automatically conjures up the violence associated with the carnival processions of that year, as well as the harsh condemnation that it received in the local press, and among prominent intellectuals and government officials. The footnote to the poem also suggests that Pichardo Moya himself might have witnessed some of the traditional *comparsas* that marched through Havana's streets during the infamous 1916 carnival season, and that his experiences inspired him to write "La comparsa."

While "La comparsa" is a significant forerunner to the literary movement associated with Afrocubanismo and "one of the first poems to explore the literary possibilities of Afro-Cuban music" (Kutzinski 181), it is most noteworthy for its reflection of the deeply ingrained prejudices against Afro-Cubans and their carnival traditions that reigned during the early years of the Republic. In the remaining pages of this chapter I will demonstrate that Pichardo Moya's poem focuses on and calls attention to precisely the characteristics of traditional *comparsas* that contemporary audiences found repugnant, and that had provoked so much controversy: the mysterious and monotonous singing, the evocations of Afro-Cuban *brujería*, the unrestrained dancing, the alleged lascivious behavior of the Afro-Cuban participants, and the disagreeable sounds of the music.

It is worth pointing out briefly here that the illustration that accompanies the original publication of "La comparsa" in *Gráfico* does not necessarily reflect the sinister undertones of Pichardo Moya's poem, but instead offers a highly exaggerated caricature of a *comparsa* that recalls the parodic and racist representations of Afro-Cubans in everything from political cartoons to the *teatro bufo* [comic theater] (fig. 1.1). This particular carnival procession is made up of a motley crew of bulbous-nosed, black participants: an ape-like man ringing a *cencerro* [cowbell], an elderly *brujo* carrying a snake, a young child, and two clownish *diablitos* [male Afro-Cuban dancers in masks and raffia costumes], among others. Though this striking image is not signed, it would seem that it is by Cornado Massaguer (1889–1956), the editor and founder of *Gráfico* who provided many of the illustrations for the publication.

In her book, *La poesía negrista*, Mónica Mansour argues that "La comparsa" contains objective descriptions of a traditional Afro-Cuban carnival procession, and she adds that the poem reveals that Pichardo Moya intended to reassess the value of Afro-Cuban customs that had long been

FIGURE 1.1. Illustration by Cornado Massaguer that accompanied the original publication of Felipe Pichardo Moya's "La comparsa" in *Gráfico* (March 1916). (Image courtesy of Fundación Alejo Carpentier, Havana.)

considered inferior or primitive in Cuba (117–18). For her part, Vera Kutzinski contends that Pichardo Moya's perspective in the poem is "that of an unmoved observer of a cultural event that seems to have neither emotional nor political resonances for him" (*Sugar's Secrets* 182). I feel, however, that the poem itself belies such contentions. Pichardo Moya's highly negative poetic recreation of an Afro-Cuban *comparsa* clearly reveals his own negative opinion—fueled, to be sure, by prevailing prejudices—of such spectacles, and it would seem to indicate that the author was very much moved—at least emotionally, and probably politically—by them.

In short, Pichardo Moya's depiction of the Afro-Cuban carnival procession reflects the underlying racism toward and fear and suspicion of blacks and their various cultural manifestations that lingered for years after the Racist Massacre of 1912. And it seems clear that the author was less concerned with conveying the "color, rhythm . . . and the fundamental meaning" (Mansour 117) of traditional *comparsas* than he was with presenting them as strange, sinister, and threatening spectacles that had been transplanted from the "equatorial jungle" of Africa into the civilized streets of the Cuban capital. The opening stanzas of this harsh-sounding and uneven poem serve to illustrate these points:

Por la calleja solitaria
se arrastra la comparsa como una culebra colosal.

En el silencio de la noche
hombres, mujeres, niños, cantan con un monótono compás;
los unos detrás de los otros en una fila inacabable,
van agarrados por los hombros con un temblor epilepsial.
Los ojos brillan en las órbitas
chispeando como un puñal en la siniestra oscuridad,
y los cuerpos se descoyuntan en una furia demoníaca
al impulso irresistible de los palitos y el timbal.

¡Por la calleja solitaria
se arrastra la comparsa como una culebra colosal!

Vienen primero los muchachos
llevando hachones cuyas luces el viento hace temblequear;
y un gran tumulto de mujeres, con los brazos extendidos,
haciendo estremecer sus hombros y sus caderas, van detrás.
Suben las voces por encanto,
y luego vuelven a bajar;
la música, ronca y monótona, va evocando mil raras cosas
como el simún cuando remeda el estertor de algún titán,
y de los pechos que jadean
sale un soplo sibilante: ¡tal el del viento sobre el mar! (8)[3]

One of the most prominent images of Pichardo Moya's poem is that of the snake, which is repeatedly evoked not just in a simile that links this creature to the *comparsa* itself, but also by the frequent repetition of the letter "s," which suggests both hissing and slithering. The association between the figure of the *culebra* and the *comparsa*, which is repeated in most of the carnival poems that are considered in the present study, is especially important for two reasons. On the one hand, many contemporary readers would have recognized in the image of the snake a common symbol of the Devil and the deception and moral depravity associated with this figure. On the other hand, and perhaps more importantly, this image also implicitly evokes the Afro-Cuban cults and religions that were so widely feared and distrusted at the time Pichardo wrote his poem. Indeed, as Lydia Cabrera has noted, the snake represents for many Afro-Cubans a sacred manifestation of a divine force, and it is intimately associated with many deities of the Yoruba pantheon, including Yamayá, Ochún, Ogún, and Changó. The snake is also the inseparable companion of the Santero and the Mayombero brujo, the bodyguards of Lucumí and Congo priests and priestesses (*Animales* 12–13, 16). It should be noted that the references to the snake also conjure one of many traditional forms of collective carnival dancing in which participants in the *comparsas* grab each other by the waist, and twist and coil along the parade route, evoking the undulations of a gigantic snake (Valdés-Cruz, *La poesía* 80–81).

Despite the fact that this particular *comparsa* is described as it passes through an isolated alley, the reader can imagine its eventual arrival at the busy Havana thoroughfares where crowds of spectators line the streets. When carnival ensembles arrived at the crowded streets they often swept hundreds of spectators along with them, resulting in another form of collective dancing known as *arrollao*. Brea and Millet describe the *arrollao* as the "rhythmic movement of a carnival dance group with people joining in behind, winding their way through the streets. It becomes a form of collective dance, marking time with the instruments of the *congas* and parades with a variety of agile steps and body movements, in circle formation, jumping, crouching and whirling, and improvising biting and erotic chants, while constantly on the move. The group of persons is so tightly packed that . . . everything within its radius is swept up and carried along with the crowd" ("Glossary" 177).

This particular tradition, the name of which comes from the Spanish verb *arrollar* (to sweep away, crush, overwhelm), was viewed by its detractors as an especially offensive form of collective dancing because it involved close physical contact that allegedly provoked the inebriated dancers—as well as onlookers who often got swept up in the procession—to lose all notions of moral scruples and to behave lasciviously. As one critic put it in an unsigned 1912 editorial in the Havana daily *Cuba y América*:

> El espectáculo resulta a veces repugnante: hombres y mujeres, perdida la noción del pudor, al son de música africana y cantando monótono estribillo, recorren en tropel las calles reproduciendo en sus movimientos gestos que pueden ser lógicos en África

salvaje, pero que son un contrasentido en Cuba civilizada. ("Las comparsas" 8)

[The spectacle sometimes turns out to be repugnant: men and women, having lost all sense of modesty, file through the streets in a mob to the sound of African music and singing a monotonous refrain, reproducing in their movements gestures that might be logical in savage Africa, but are an absurdity in civilized Cuba.]

Moreover, many critics of traditional *comparsas* and *congas* saw these collective dances as destructive, menacing, and illicit, as Ramón Vasconcelos clearly indicated in two of his editorials from March 1916. In "Al primer tapón, zurrapas," for example, he writes that "las comparsas se desbordaron por las calles de la Habana, 'arrollando' arrollando todo; a los viandantes, la higiene, [la] decencia, las buenas costumbres y hasta la misma ley" [the *comparsas* flood the streets of Havana, 'arrollando' sweeping away everything; pedestrians, hygiene, decency, good customs, and even the law itself]. (4)

Even more telling in terms of its relationship to Pichardo Moya's poem is the following observation that Vasconcelos made while referring to the *arrollao* in a March 13 editorial: "no es justo convertir a una ciudad civilizada en aldea centroafricana y mucho menos sofocarla con el vaho de una turba frenética y sudorosa" [It's not fair to turn a civilized city into a Central African village, and much less to suffocate it with the steam of a frenetic and sweaty mob] ("Dos letras" 4). Vasconcelos's portrayal of the *arrollao* as a hot, suffocating force is clearly echoed in Pichardo Moya's poem when the poetic voice compares the *comparsa* ensemble on two occasions to a *simún* [simoom or simoon], a legendary African desert wind known for its deadly combination of suffocating heat and blowing sand. These winds, whose name originates from the Arabic *samma* [to poison], are greatly feared for their destructive force, and were commonly referred to by mariners, who could see their red-tinged dust clouds from the coast, as "seas of blood." Given that Afro-Cuban *comparsas* were widely considered to be hotbeds of destructive behavior and wanton violence, Pichardo Moya's evocation of the simoom serves as one of many indicators of how "La comparsa" reflected prevailing attitudes toward these and other African-derived cultural manifestations.

The refrain and the opening stanzas of "La comparsa" are significant because they focus our attention on the controversial *arrollao* at the same time that they stress the fact that this particular *comparsa* ensemble slithers through a dark and desolate alley, and not a busy Havana thoroughfare packed with rowdy revelers. These details suggest that what Pichardo Moya describes in his poem is a traditional *comparsa* that he might have observed passing through one of the capital's predominantly Afro-Cuban neighborhoods, were the streets would have been poorly lit and the crowds relatively sparse. Afro-Cuban *comparsas*—and especially those of the late nineteenth and early twentieth centuries—often paraded through the dark streets of Havana's working-class neighborhoods, as Cristóbal Díaz-Ayala has observed ("De congas" 31). To conquer the darkness, *comparsa* troupes began the tradition of fabricating *farolas*—giant, handmade paper lanterns that were carried on poles that were often over ten feet high (figs. 1.2, 1.3). These emblematic Cuban carnival icons make their appearance in this and most of the other poems that we will discuss in the chapters that follow.

Even if Pichardo Moya does accurately reflect the darkness of some of the Havana streets through which traditional *comparsas* passed (often while on their way to the main thoroughfares), however, it is clear that he accentuates—and even exaggerates—the image of the solitary, silent, and

FIGURE 1.2. Postcard depicting the *comparsa* "El Alacrán" with various members carrying elaborate handmade paper lanterns or *farolas*, ca. 1915. (Author's collection.)

FIGURE 1.3. *Farolero* from unknown Havana *comparsa*, ca. 1960. Photographer unknown. (Author's collection.)

dark street in order to infuse his poem with ominous undertones that contradict notions of carnival celebrations as lively, joyful, and colorful spectacles. The reference in the first stanza to the participants' bloodshot eyes that "shine like daggers in the sinister darkness," and the description of their movements as indications of the dancers' "demonic fury" implicitly associate them—and by extension all Afro-Cuban *comparsas*—with Havana's so-called black underworld of violence and criminality, which had been immortalized by early twentieth-century criminological studies such as Fernando Ortiz's *Los negros brujos*, Rafael Roche y Monteagudo's *La policía y sus misterios en Cuba* (1908), and Israel Castellanos's *La brujería y el ñáñiguismo bajo el punto de vista medico-legal*.

Echoes of *Los negros brujos* and the Afro-Cuban Underworld

This last observation brings us to a very important detail about "La comparsa" that is indispensable to any in-depth reading of the poem: that is, that the original version bore a dedication to Fernando Ortiz.[4] Emilio Ballagas, who is one of the few anthologists who include this crucial component of "La comparsa," reads the dedication of the poem to Cuba's preeminent "afrólogo"—a title that was sometimes bestowed upon Ortiz—as an indication of Pichardo Moya's deliberate promotion of a new mode of poetry based on the celebration of Afro-Cuban themes (*Mapa* 106). However, even though "La comparsa" is an important precursor to Afrocubanismo, Vera Kutzinski is more on the mark when she states that the dedication to Ortiz is not surprising, since "the poem can be read as a miniature ethnographic study of *la mala vida habanera* (the seedy side of Havana), inspired . . . by Ortiz's not-so-scientific accounts of Afro-Cuban religious practices in *Los negros brujos*" (*Sugar's Secrets* 182). To be sure, even though Fernando Ortiz was widely known as a champion of Afro-Cuban culture by the time that Emilio Ballagas wrote the brief biographical sketch of Felipe Pichardo Moya for his 1946 anthology, anyone familiar with Ortiz's early writings knows that as a criminal anthropologist he did not always promote or celebrate Cuba's African-derived cultural manifestations, but rather focused on possible ways to eradicate many of them.

While it is certainly true that Ortiz's early work served as a very significant stimulus for the precursors to and poets of Afrocubanismo, as Salvador Bueno has noted (62), Ortiz's influence on this group of poets has often been sugarcoated, such as in the following observation by Bueno, which seems to mollify the patently racist undertones of Ortiz's early writings and the impact they had on everything from "La comparsa" to "Comparsa habanera":

> No debe pasarse por alto en cualquier análisis que realicemos sobre [el Afrocubanismo] que sus cultivadores tuvieron como adelanto mayor a Fernando Ortiz (1881–1969) cuyas obras, desde *Los negros brujos* (1906) y *Los negros esclavos* (1916) abrían el camino hacia la investigación científica de las culturas africanas transplantadas a Cuba y también impulsaban, cada vez con mayor energía, una empresa dirigida contra el racismo y la discriminación. . . . (62–63)

[We should not overlook in any analysis that we undertake concerning Afrocubanismo that its cultivators had as a precursor Fernando Ortiz (1881–1969), whose works from *Los negros brujos* (1906) to *Los negros esclavos* (1916) cleared the way to the scientific investigation of the African cultures transplanted in Cuba and also promoted, with ever-increasing energy, an enterprise against racism and discrimination . . .]

Indeed, in both of these studies Ortiz expressed his strong opposition to the "backward" religious practices associated with *brujería*, which he believed were hindering the progress of the young Republic. He also pushed for the elimination of certain "atavistic" Afro-Cuban cultural manifestations, such as *comparsas*, which he saw as embodiments of the "inferior social strata" of Cuban society (57). In keeping with such an opinion, he denied the artistic value in such spectacles, preferring instead to characterize their dancing as strange and "ritualistic," and the music and singing as "desperately monotonous," "annoying," and "incomprehensible" (*Los negros brujos* 57–58).[5]

The introductory chapters of *Los negros brujos* and *Los negros esclavos* are typical of Ortiz's problematic views on Afro-Cubans and their culture during the initial years of his career. Indeed, they exemplify what Duno-Gottberg correctly sees as Ortiz's preoccupation with the idea that, largely because of the alleged inferiority and the menace that Afro-Cubans posed, the Cuban nation was still a foreigner to modern civilization (126–28). The following passage, which was printed verbatim in the first editions of both books, is typical of the racist undertones that pervade Ortiz's works from the 1900s through the 1920s:

> En Cuba toda una raza entró en la mala vida. . . . En sus amores eran los negros sumamente lascivos, sus matrimonios llegaban hasta la poligamia, la prostitución no merecía su repugnancia, sus familias carecían de cohesión, su religión los llevaba a los sacrificios humanos, a la violación de sepulturas, a la antropofagia y a las más brutales supersticiones; la vida del ser humano les inspiraba escaso respeto . . . Pero la inferioridad del negro, la que le sujetaba al mal vivir, era debida a falta de civilización integral, pues tan primitiva era su moralidad, como su intelectualidad, como sus voliciones, etcétera. (*Los negros brujos* 16–17, *Los negros esclavos* 13)

[In Cuba an entire race became involved in a seedy lifestyle . . . In their amorous relationships the Negroes were extremely lascivious, their marriages ended up in polygamy, prostitution did not deserve their repugnance, their families lacked cohesion, their religion brought them to human sacrifice, to the violation of tombs, to cannibalism and to the most brutal superstitions; the life of a human being inspired little respect . . . But the inferiority of the Negro, which tied him to his seedy lifestyle, was due to his lack of integral civilization, so primitive were his morality, his intellectuality, and his volition, etc.]

In *Los negros brujos,* Ortiz was particularly frank in his condemnation of *brujería,* a term that he used liberally to refer to a wide variety of Afro-Cuban rites, rituals, and cultural manifestations. In the chapter entitled "Porvenir de la brujería" [The Future of *Brujería*] Ortiz argued for the criminalization of *brujería,* and recommended the removal of its practitioners from Cuban society:

Lo primero, pues, en la lucha defensiva contra la brujería, ha de ser acabar con los brujos, aislarlos de sus fieles, como los enfermos de fiebre amarilla, porque la brujería es esencialmente contagiosa . . . Desaparecidos aquellos embaucadores, terminadas sus fiestas, danzas y salvajes ritos, desbaratados sus templos, decomisados sus importantes dioses, cortados todos estos tentáculos de la brujería, que encadenan a sus creyentes al fondo bárbaro de nuestra sociedad, podrán éstos—libres de ataduras—ir aligerando sus aún no desafricanizadas mentes del peso de sus farraginosas supersticiones y subir a sucesivas zonas de cultura. (193)

[The first thing, then, in the fight against *brujería* has to be to do away with *brujos,* to isolate them from their faithful, just like those sick with yellow fever, because *brujería* is essentially contagious . . . Once those frauds are extinct, their fiestas, dances and savage rites are terminated, their temples are destroyed, their important gods decommissioned, once all of these tentacles of *brujería,* which enchain its believers to the barbarous bottom of our society, are cut, they will be able to—freed of their bonds—go about lightening their as-of-yet deafricanized minds from the weight of their muddled superstitions and ascend the successive zones of culture.]

By dedicating "La comparsa" to the author of these two widely read studies of the Afro-Cuban underworld, both of which are filled with observations like those cited above, Pichardo Moya left us with an invaluable clue as to how to read and interpret his poem. Ortiz's writings on Afro-Cuban traditions, and especially his condemnation of witchcraft and related ritual dancing and singing in *Los negros brujos*, left an unmistakable mark on "La comparsa," which is filled with words and expressions—"la siniestra oscuridad" [the sinister darkness], "una furia demoníaca" [a demonic fury], "suben las voces por encanto" [the voices rise by enchantment], "un rapto de locura" [a sudden impulse of madness], "un temor del *más allá*" [a fear of the *otherworld*](emphasis in the original)—that evoke sorcery and the "dark" arts. Moreover, Ortiz's contention that *brujería* was like a contagious disease and that the "parasites" of Cuba's underworld were contaminating the nation with "their pathogenic detritus" (*Los negros brujos* 15) is echoed in what Kutzinski has correctly identified as the "pathological undertones" (*Sugar's Secrets* 182) of "La comparsa." For instance, the epileptic shaking, nervous contortions, glassy eyes, and fits of madness that the poetic voice of Pichardo Moya's poem describes evoke a variety of mental and physical ailments. At the same time they suggest "demonic" possession, which Ortiz described as emblematic of the inane superstitions and antisocial psychology of practitioners of all Afro-Cuban religions. Ortiz claimed that such possessions were brought on by excessive dancing and music, and his many descriptions of them, such as the one below, are clearly echoed in "La comparsa":

> El extenuante ejercicio del baile, la monótona e incesante música de los tambores . . . son los que provocan principalmente la posesión demoníaca . . . 'Es una especie de furia creciente, de rabia, de desesperación, cuyas contorciones acompañan las variaciones cadenciosas . . . hasta la manifestación final del santo.' (93–94)[6]

> [The exhausting exercise of the dance, the monotonous and incessant music of the drums . . . are the things that principally provoke demonic possession . . . "It is a sort of growing fury, of rage, of desperation, whose contortions accompany the rhythmic variations . . . until the final manifestation of the saint."]

In many instances the specific terms and phrases that Pichardo Moya employs in his poem suggest his debt to *Los negros brujos*. For instance,

Ortiz's references to the exasperating monotony, and the incoherence of the songs and music of *comparsas* (57–58), are mirrored in Pichardo Moya's use of expressions such as "monótono compás" [monotonous beat] and "la música, ronca y monótona" [the hoarse and monotonous music]. Likewise, Ortiz's claim that incessant drumming led to demonic possession is echoed in the "furia demoníaca" that the Afro-Cuban subjects of Pichardo Moya's poem display as they dance to strident beats of the sticks and drums. This same notion is reinforced later in the poem when the poetic voice notes that the Afro-Cuban women, who dance about nervously, seem to have been "mordidas por Satán" [bitten by Satan]. Finally, while Ortiz compares Afro-Cuban ritual dancing and the ensuing possessions to an "acceso epiléptico" [epileptic seizure], Pichardo twice refers to the movements of the dancers as a "temblor epilepsial" [an epileptic tremor].

It should be repeated that the pathological undertones of "La comparsa," and especially the references to epileptic shaking, also suggest Pichardo Moya's familiarity with the writings of the prominent forensic pathologist Israel Castellanos, and especially "El tipo brujo." In that essay Castellanos argues that the wild shaking that many Afro-Cubans claim to be a result of possessions by spirits or demons are actually epileptic seizures. Drawing on the writings of Italian criminologist Cesare Lombroso (1836–1909), who theorized that "born criminals" possessed a so-called *substratum epileptoides*, Castellanos posited that the same was true of Afro-Cuban *brujos*, among whom he claimed to have discovered widespread cases of epilepsy (339–43).

The fifth stanza of "La comparsa," which portrays a group of crazed black women dancing in the presence of an elderly man—apparently a *negro de nación*, or a black man born in Africa—who performs acts of sortilege, also suggests the influence of *Los negros brujos*. At the same time, it reflects the kind of stereotypes that served to "justify" the inferior status of blacks in Cuba.

Es "Él" que viene: todos callan:
¡Hay un silencio, se siente el fuerte respirar:
en la cabeza de una joven, sobre el escudo legendario
lleva un simbólico animal!

Entre dos filas de mujeres
que se contorsionan nerviosas como mordidas por Satán,
va un alto anciano tembloroso en cuyos ojos luce el fuego

de una mirada casi irreal.
Lleva un cetro entre las manos y murmura con voz opaca
un misterioso sortilegio que sólo él puede rezar,
un misterioso sortilegio
como un rezo de ritual
que evoca la gloria del trono donde él reinaba cuando niño
allá en su selva ecuatorial,
entre las tribus de guerreros y de sagrados sacerdotes
que lo adoraban al pasar . . . (8)

The frequent allusions to superstitions and witchcraft—which are directly linked to Africa through the references to the shield with an emblem of a totemic animal, the equatorial jungle, and the tribes of warriors—leave the contemporary reader with the distinct impression that Pichardo Moya's opinion of Afro-Cuban religions and cultural manifestations was very much in keeping with contemporary prejudices against them. The modern reader of "La comparsa" must bear in mind, as Aline Helg has demonstrated, that in the early decades of the Republic, and especially during the years that followed the Racist Massacre of 1912, Cuban whites propagated "myths and icons of fear in order to justify the subaltern position of Afro-Cubans in society and to promote repression when necessary" (*Our Rightful Share* 16). Helg further points out that "the threat that Afro-Cubans allegedly represented to whites and the Cuban nation was embodied in three stereotypical images of Afro-Cubans, corresponding to three levels of fear" (16–17). The common myths and related icons that Helg describes all make their appearance in "La comparsa" in some way or another. The dread of an Afro-Cuban uprising, which Helg cites as the first example, often carried over into a more generalized fear of large gatherings of Cubans of color, such as those that inevitably formed during the carnival season. In his poem, Pichardo Moya promotes such anxieties by comparing the *comparsa*, as we have already noted, to a destructive and suffocating desert wind. The poet underscores the intimidating physical strength of the black men by comparing them to Titans and to Hercules, and he also calls attention to the black *brujo*'s magical powers, which give him tremendous control over the crowd.

The second fear that Helg describes is that of African religions and other cultural manifestations, which was embodied in caricatures of black *brujos* and *ñáñigos*. Indeed, stereotypical images of *brujos*—like the fire-eyed, scepter-waving African sorcerer in Pichardo Moya's poem—largely served to bolster the commonly held notion "that Afro-Cuban culture was limited to magic, witchcraft, criminality, and even anthropophagy" (Helg, *Rightful Share* 16–18). Finally, Helg speaks of common fears related to Afro-Cuban sexuality, and especially the widespread belief that black men and women were innately lecherous. This last notion was often presented as a direct consequence of their "dark arts" and "fetishistic" practices, and observations like the following one made by Ramón Vasconcelos in *La Prensa* in 1916 were commonly printed in Cuba's major newspapers:

> Pues la misión cardinal del brujo es esa: saciar la lujuria, proporcionar platos fuertes a los apetitos sexuales . . . ¡Y todavía dicen algunos que la brujería es una religión como otra cualquiera, como si hubiera alguna religión sin fundamento moral. ("La fuga" 4)

> [Well, the cardinal mission of the *brujo* is this: satiate lust, provide heavy dishes to sexual appetites . . . And to think that some still say the witchcraft is a religion like any other, as if there were a religion without a moral foundation.]

Though images of Afro-Cuban sexuality are not as prominent in "La comparsa" as they are in many poems of Afrocubanismo, Pichardo Moya does manage to convey the stereotype by referring to the dancers' lewd gestures, panting chests, and heavy breathing. Moreover, the poet indirectly conjures up the fear of Afro-Cuban eroticism first through the image of the crazed mob of dancers in close physical contact, and later by way of references to the Herculean men whose bare, black chests shine with sweat, and whose imposing figures inspire "un temor del *más allá*." The image of the half-naked, sweaty men is especially provocative as it recalls many observations, such as the following, that Ortiz makes in *Los negros brujos*:

> No transcurre mucho tiempo, una vez empezado el baile, sin que la excitación erótica se manifieste en toda su crudeza africana. Los movimientos lascivos del baile están sometidos al son de los tambores . . . No es raro que los negros sudorosos se despojan de la camisa, mostrando sus bustos lustrosos y sus bronceados brazos que ciñen con febril abrazo el cuerpo de la bailadora. Llegados a este

momento, los bailadores se alocan por la irritación sexual, el *chequeteque*, la música, la danza, etc., y la orgía corona frecuentemente la festividad religiosa. (93)

[Not much time goes by, once the dance has started, before the erotic excitation manifests itself in all of its African crudeness. The lascivious movements of the dance obey the beat of the drums . . . It is not uncommon for the sweaty Negroes to strip off their shirts, showing their lustrous busts and their tanned arms that gird with a feverish embrace the body of the female dancer. Having arrived at this moment, the dancers act crazy because of their sexual exasperation, the nasty potion, the music, the dance, etc., and an orgy frequently tops off the religious festivity.]

I should add here that the sinister atmosphere that permeates "La comparsa," along with the comparison cited earlier between the dancers' glassy eyes and shiny knife blades, reflects the fear that gatherings of Afro-Cubans were natural hotbeds for criminal activities. In this sense, Pichardo Moya's poem also evokes the so-called *brujo* scare of the early twentieth century that was characterized by highly exaggerated and widely publicized reports of criminal acts that were blamed on practitioners of Afro-Cuban religions. One of the most famous cases, to which Ortiz dedicates considerable space in his study, was the alleged kidnapping and murder in 1904 of a white girl named Zoila Díaz. According to most published versions of the incident, Zoila's murder and others like it were carried out by *brujos* who needed a child's heart and blood to concoct certain magical potions (104).[7] Ortiz supports claims that such crimes were relatively commonplace in the Cuban countryside where *brujos* were believed to be especially savage (105). To corroborate his observations he cites newspaper reports from throughout the island on nearly fifty crimes that were allegedly committed by practitioners of Afro-Cuban religions between 1902–1906.[8]

In short, given the widespread prejudices against *brujos* and their alleged immoral and criminal behavior, Pichardo Moya's attention to the mysterious and seamy qualities of traditional *comparsas* can hardly be taken to be a revaluation of a lost or forgotten African tradition as one critic has implied (Mansour 118–19). It seems fair to say that Pichardo Moya—echoing the ethnographic and criminological writings of Ortiz and Castellanos, as well as the type of biases that were commonly spread by the sensationalist press—was more interested in calling attention to Havana's black underworld than he was in extolling the positive contribution of Afro-Cubans to the society of the young nation.

In her brief analysis of "La comparsa," Vera Kutzinski makes note of what she sees as "one of the most striking absences" in the poem; that is "direct references to skin color or other familiar racial markers" (181). While this observation is not altogether inaccurate, it is important to point out that the poem does contain many obvious references to the African origins of the *comparseros*. For example, when describing the old sorcerer, the poetic voice refers to the equatorial jungle and warring tribes of his homeland. Later in the poem the speaker describes a group of Afro-Cuban men as having "torsos de caoba" [mahogany chests], which is a clear allusion to their dark skin. Even though she does not elaborate, Kutzinski is right on the mark when she later adds that "it was quite unnecessary for [Pichardo] to resort to physical description to identify the dancers as Afro-Cuban" (*Sugar's Secrets* 181). Indeed, given that so many white Cubans were opposed to traditional African-derived *comparsas* and therefore loath to take part in them, contemporary readers would have automatically envisioned black Cubans as the participants in Pichardo's sinister spectacle. Moreover, even though a considerable number of whites were involved in Afro-Cuban religions, the predominant view of the day was that enchantment, sorcery, and mysterious rituals, like those described in "La comparsa," were products of "savage" African traditions.

The notable absence in "La comparsa" of the types of racial and ethnic markers—"negro," "prieto" [dark-skinned], "pardo" [dark]; "Yoruba," "Congo," "Carabalí"—that are so commonly employed to underscore blackness in the *poesía negra* of the 1920s and 1930s may seem surprising to many readers. However, Pichardo Moya's numerous evocations of witchcraft and strange religious rituals certainly would have been sufficient to convince his readers that the protagonists of his poem were Afro-Cubans. Moreover, they would have conjured very clearly the widespread fear and suspicion of Afro-Cuban religions and other cultural manifestations during the years following the Racist Massacre of 1912. We must keep in mind that Pichardo's poem predates Afrocubanismo by over a decade, and it thus was not a product of the same political agendas that underpinned this important cultural movement. The poets of

Afrocubanismo emphasized the blackness and African origins in their poems for various reasons. Kutzinski observes, for example, that by doing so they turned popular African-derived cultural manifestations into "signifiers of the desire for cultural and political independence" from the United States (*Sugar's Secrets* 15). Duno-Gottberg, for his part, convincingly argues that these poets appropriated blackness as a means to assimilate and control Afro-Cubans and their influence on a nation in search of its identity (85–100).

Detractors of cultural manifestations such as *comparsas* and *congas*—and Pichardo Moya was apparently among them—believed that they had no place in a nation that was aspiring toward Western traditions and cultural manifestations, and in this sense the undertones of "La comparsa" foreshadow opinions of the likes of Alberto Arredondo, who would argue some twenty years after the publication of the poem that *comparsas* were demeaning throwbacks to a "defeated" era that only served to promote negative and degrading stereotypes:

"A nuevos tiempos, nuevas canciones." Y las comparsas, como libre expresión popular, como incontrolado arrollao de masas, como carnaval criollo, tuvieron su tiempo, su hora, su momento. . . . No hay que olvidar, tampoco, que las comparsas con libres "arrollaos" . . . están íntimamente vinculados con lo colonial y lo negro. (*El negro en Cuba* 136–37)

["To new times, new songs." And *comparsas*, as examples of free popular expression, as uncontrolled *arrollao* of the masses, as *criollo* carnival, had their time, their hour, their moment. . . . We must not forget, either, that *comparsas* with free *arrollaos* . . . are intimately associated with the colonial period and with blackness.]

In sum, while the modern reader might expect a poem about a carnival procession to evoke vibrant images of pleasure, merriment, and vitality, Felipe Pichardo Moya's poetic rendition of a traditional *comparsa* comes across as something more akin to a menacing ritual. With its sinister undertones and imagery, "La comparsa" echoes the atmosphere of suspicion and condemnation that reigned in Cuba for years after the Racist Massacre of 1912. Moreover, it can also be read as a response to the incidents of violence among Afro-Cuban participants during the tragic carnival processions of March 5, 1916. When considering this text the reader should bear in mind that it corresponds to a time when racial tensions in Cuba were running high and *comparsas* themselves were the subject of a heated social and cultural debate in Havana and other cities throughout the nation.

But to appreciate fully the meaning and significance of "La comparsa," the reader must also take into account that it was dedicated to Fernando Ortiz, who by 1916 had written two important studies on the Afro-Cuban underworld in Havana in which he delved into what he referred to as the "mala vida" of Afro-Cubans, and argued that Cuban blacks could be freed from their criminal inclinations, "brutal superstitions," "primitive psychology," and "primitive morality" only through guidance by whites and exposure to a "superior civilization" (*Los negros brujos* 16–17, 25–28). Even a cursory reading of Pichardo Moya's poetic rendition of an Afro-Cuban carnival procession reveals that it echoes several aspects of Ortiz's studies, but especially his strong prejudices against Afro-Cuban superstitions and religious practices, and his disparagement of African-derived cultural manifestations such as traditional carnival ensembles.

2

Carnival and Ñáñiguismo

Poetic Syncretism in Alejo Carpentier's "Juego santo"

> Desde la noche de Reyes
> al Martes de Carnaval,
> iban saliendo en comparsas
> los ñáñigos a bailar.
>
> [From the night of Kings
> to the Tuesday of carnival,
> the *ñáñigos* came out
> in *comparsas* to dance.]
>
> Alfonso Camín, "Carnaval en la Habana"

Alejo Carpentier's fame as a novelist, essayist, and short story writer has largely overshadowed the handful of poems inspired by African-derived cultural traditions that he wrote during the early years of his career. These foundational—though by now nearly forgotten—texts testify to Carpentier's early fascination with African-derived culture in Cuba at the same time that they represent significant contributions to the budding literary movement associated with Afrocubanismo, of which Carpentier was a founding member. Carpentier often downplayed the importance of his poems, and he stressed that because most of them were written for musical scores they did not qualify as poetry in the strictest sense of the term. In one interview conducted decades after the publication of his earliest poems, for example, Carpentier made the following observation:

> Sé que me han incluido en antologías de poesías, pero las piezas allí reproducidas son en realidad las letras escritas para compositores de música . . . respeto mucho a la poesía. Creo que es la suprema expresión literaria. Pero no soy poeta. (Arias "Habla" 40)
>
> [I know that they have included me in poetry anthologies, but the pieces reproduced in them are really lyrics written for composers of

music . . . I respect poetry very much. I think it is the supreme literary expression. But I am not a poet.]

Notwithstanding such personal opinions, Carpentier's contemporaries did not necessarily agree with his frank assessment of these early pieces. Ramón Guirao (1908–1949), for example, observed in his seminal anthology, *Órbita de la poesía afrocubana, 1928–1937* [Trajectory of Afro-Cuban Poetry, 1928–1937], that Carpentier, along with José Zacarías Tallet and Guirao himself, was one of the founders of the avant-garde poetic movement associated with Afrocubanismo (52). In his anthology Guirao included two of Carpentier's best-known poems, "Liturgia" [Liturgy] and "Canción" [Song]. In the short bibliographical piece that introduces his own poems in the anthology, Guirao is careful to point out that his "Bailadora de rumba" [Rumba Dancer] first appeared in print on April 8, 1928 in *Diario de la Marina* and that Tallet's, which one critic has recently referred to as the first nationally recognized poem of Afrocubanismo (Moore, *Nationalizing Blackness* 200), was not published until August of the same year. However, he gives no dates for Carpentier's two contributions, the speculation over which has at once led to considerable debate and several careless errors. For example, Emilio Ballagas (*Mapa* 142) and Enrique Noble (39) mistakenly note that "Liturgia" was originally published in *Revista de Avance* in 1927 (it actually appeared in that magazine in September 1930)[1], while Klaus Müller-Berg states that the poem's first publication was in Emilio Ballagas's *Antología de la poesía negra hispanoamericana* [Anthology of Spanish-American Black Poetry] in 1935 (1030). Hilario González seems to set the record straight by pointing out in his 1983 essay "Alejo Carpentier: precursor del 'moviemiento' afrocubano" [Alejo Carpentier: Precursor to the Afro-Cuban 'Movement'] that "Liturgia" and "Canción" were both written in 1927 and published in the Parisian magazine *Genesis* in July, 1928, one month before Tallet's "La rumba" (11–12).

In 1927 Carpentier also wrote two lesser-known poems, "Marí-Sabel" and "Juego santo," both of which were set to music by Cuban composer Alejandro García Caturla in November 1929 and published a year later, in November 1930, under the title *Dos poemas afro-cubanos* (*Deux poèmes afro-cubains*) [Two Afro-Cuban Poems] (figs. 2.1, 2.2). As Hilario González has correctly pointed out, all of these poems, and a handful of others that Carpentier published during the same period, are anticipatory

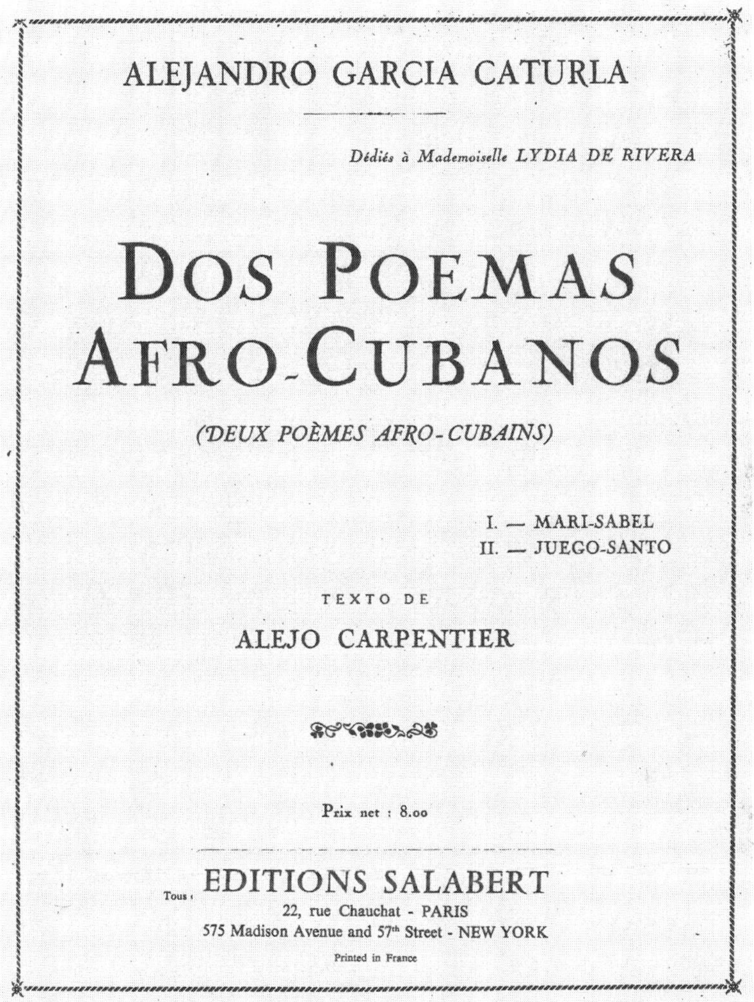

ALEJANDRO GARCIA CATURLA

Dédiés à Mademoiselle LYDIA DE RIVERA

DOS POEMAS AFRO-CUBANOS

(DEUX POÈMES AFRO-CUBAINS)

I. — MARI-SABEL
II. — JUEGO-SANTO

TEXTO DE

ALEJO CARPENTIER

Prix net : 8.00

EDITIONS SALABERT

Tous

22, rue Chauchat - PARIS
575 Madison Avenue and 57th Street - NEW YORK

Printed in France

FIGURE 2.1. Title page to original edition of *Dos poemas afro-cubanos,* which contains Alejandro García Caturla's musical scores for Alejo Carpentier's poems "Juego santo" and "Marí-Sabel." (Image courtesy of Biblioteca de la Universidad de Puerto Rico, Río Piedras. Used by permission of the Fundación Alejo Carpentier, Havana.)

FIGURE 2.2. First page of Alejandro García Caturla's musical score to "Juego santo." (Image courtesy of Biblioteca de la Universidad de Puerto Rico, Río Piedras. Used by permission of the Fundación Alejo Carpentier, Havana.)

of the poetry of a similar vein that Nicolás Guillén, Emilio Ballagas, and so many others would publish during the boom of Afrocubanismo in the 1930s (12).

Despite his later claims that his poetry was of little significance, Carpentier at times made much of his role in the foundation of this cultural and literary movement. For example, in an article titled "El recuerdo de Amadeo Roldán" [Reminiscence of Amadeo Roldán], a homage to this great Cuban composer, professor of music, and violinist, that he published in *Carteles* on June 4, 1939, Carpentier remarked that he and Roldán (1900–1939) had begun to collaborate by the mid-1920s, and were thus the true pioneers of Afrocubanismo. He stresses, however, that in those earliest years the movement suffered from an "infantile sickness":

> Aún Guillén no había publicado sus admirables poemas negros; aún andaban lejos las magníficas antologías de Ballagas y Guirao; aún no salían comparsas a las calles, con beneplácito de la Comisión del Turismo. Unos honestos señores con barbas espirituales habían decretado que todo lo africano era tabú, por popularacho, bárbaro, estruendoso, etcétera. Los poetas jóvenes, los pintores jóvenes, presentían ya que iban a ser los artesanos conscientes de una necesaria revisión de valores, pero las obras estaban en período de gestación . . .
>
> Roldán y yo, acompañados de unos pocos hombres que opinaban como nosotros, conocimos por aquel entonces un período de "enfermedad infantil" de Afrocubanismo. Devorábamos los libros de Fernando Ortiz. Cazábamos ritmos a punta de lápiz . . . ¡Abajo la lira, viva el bongo! (133–34)

[Guillén still hadn't published his admirable black poems; the magnificent anthologies of Ballagas and Guirao were still a long way off; *comparsas* were still not going out into the streets, with approval of the Tourism Commission. Some honest men with spiritual beards had decreed that all things African were taboo, since they were low class, barbarous, deafening, etcetera. The young poets, the young painters, sensed in advance that they were soon going to be the artisans who were mindful of a necessary revision of values, but the works were in a period of gestation . . .

Roldán and I, accompanied by a few men that thought like us, recognized back then the period of "infantile sickness" of Afrocubanismo. We devoured the books of Fernando Ortiz. We pursued rhythms with our pencil points... Down with the lyre, long live the bongo!]

From an Outsider's Point of View: Carpentier's *Comparsa Ñáñiga*

While Ramón Guirao and José Zacarías Tallet may indeed have been the first Cuban writers to poeticize the traditional rumba, Carpentier was the first among the poets of Afrocubanismo to focus on sacred Afro-Cuban rituals, and to attempt to interpret the esoteric rites of the Abakuá secret society. In "Liturgia," for example, Carpentier offers a dynamic and highly stylized vision of the culmination of a *ñáñigo* initiation ceremony. In "Juego santo," through an act of poetic syncretism, he melds two public spectacles that had long been associated with the Abakuá brotherhoods: semipublic, sacred processions that were performed as part of *ñáñigo* initiation ceremonies, and so-called *comparsas ñáñigas*, which first emerged during nineteenth-century Día de Reyes celebrations, and eventually became integrated into traditional carnival festivities in the twentieth century. In his 1878 painting, *Fiesta ñáñiga* (fig. 2.3), Cuban painter M. Puente depicts a group of *ñáñigos* in the streets of Havana, performing many of the same acts that Carpentier describes in "Juego santo." Other images of *ñáñigo* processions, such as a well-known illustration from Roche y Monteagudo's study (fig. 2.4), also reflect certain aspects of the scene that Carpentier describes in his poem.

Though the poem evokes a sacred rite more than it does the profane *comparsa*, Carpentier employs several key images—such as the *farola*, the *baile de la chancleta* [wooden sandal dance], and the *diablito*—that are intimately related to the traditional Afro-Cuban carnival ensembles and the festivities in which they participated. It is important to stress here that Carpentier's poetic melding of a sacred Abakuá procession and a secular carnival *comparsa* is understandable given that the *ñáñigos* had long been associated with the latter spectacles. Indeed, the members of the Abakuá secret society were perhaps best known among nineteenth- and early twentieth-century Cuba not for their esoteric rites and rituals, but

FIGURE 2.3. M. Puente, *Fiesta ñáñiga*, 1878. El Museo de Bellas Artes Havana. Procession of members of an Abakuá lodge on Día de Reyes. Note, from left to right, the *íreme* or *diablito* greeting two women, the man striking the metal bell [*ekón*] with a stick, and the man playing the tall cylindrical drum [*bonkó enchemiyá*]. Also note the scarves worn by most of the *ñáñigos* in the procession. All of these are prominent images in Carpentier's "Juego santo." (Photo courtesy of University Press of Mississippi.)

FIGURE 2.4. Abakuá procession from a mixed-race lodge. (From Roche y Monteagudo, 1925.)

rather for their public appearances during Día de Reyes celebrations, and later in the street processions that emerged during the carnival season in the late nineteenth and early twentieth centuries. It should be noted here that many of the most widely known twentieth-century *comparsa* ensembles—such as "La Culebra" and "El Alacrán"—were largely made up of members of Abakuá lodges.

As readers of Carpentier's early work already know, carnival celebrations and related events make their appearance in many of the author's writings from the 1920s and 1930s. Both "Liturgia" and "Juego santo" contain explicit references to carnival, for example, as does Carpentier's experimental ballet *La rebambaramba* (1927), which according to the author himself was inspired by French artist Pierre Toussaint Frédéric Mialhe's well-known painting of an Afro-Cuban Día de Reyes celebration (see fig. 0.1). Likewise, in his first novel, *Écue-Yamba-Ó* (1933), references to carnival and *comparsas* abound. In Chapter 21, for instance, a Lucumí exslave describes the typical Día de Reyes festivities, and recites for Menegildo the chant that accompanied a traditional dance for killing snakes. In Chapter 27, Menegildo philosophizes on Cuban political corruption and recalls the political *comparsas* or *chambelonas* of his hometown, in which blacks paraded through the streets in order to drum up support for political candidates.

Notwithstanding the obvious limitations of Carpentier's experience with and knowledge of the Abakuá brotherhoods—many of whose secrets, such as the form and appearance of the sacred *ékue* drum, were not revealed to outsiders until at least the late 1920s (Cabrera, *La sociedad* 12)—it is important to note that he made a concerted effort to understand the society and its arcane traditions. Indeed, in his early career Carpentier underscored his considerable firsthand experience with Abakuá rituals and the celebrations and processions associated with them. In "El recuerdo de Amadeo Roldán," for example, Carpentier noted that he and his collaborator went to great lengths to attend the semipublic components of *ñáñigo* initiation ceremonies: "Apenas sabíamos que un juramento ñáñigo iba a tener lugar en las cercanías de La Habana, abandonábamos cualquier compromiso . . . para asistir a él" (134). [We had hardly found out that a *ñáñigo* initiation was about to take place in the outskirts of Havana, and we bailed out on any commitment . . . in order to attend it.] Likewise, in *La música en Cuba* [Music in Cuba] (1946), Carpentier calls attention to the fact that he had witnessed *ñáñigo* initiation ceremonies many times

(261), but he also admits that it was difficult to get accurate information about them:

> In the first place, if one does not have informants who are intelligent and trustworthy, it is impossible to find out when and where a religious ceremony or a profane drumming session will be held. In the second place, because the true *ñáñigos*—that is, the most interesting ones—ascertained on many occasions, are opposed to having their musical rituals notated or taped, since they view these acts as a profanation of their secrets. In the third place, a researcher's interest quickly awakens the greed among people who ... scheme up some kind of a charade in exchange for a few coins. (261)[2]

Nearly twenty years later, in his essay "Problemática de la actual novela latinoamericana" [Problematics of the Contemporary Latin American Novel] (1964), Carpentier again stressed that his deep interest in the Abakuá in the late 1920s and early 1930s had inspired him to attended "innumerable ritual ceremonies," which served in large part as the basis for his first novel *Écue-Yamba-Ó* (12). Though Carpentier makes no direct reference to his poems in this important essay, his admission that the knowledge he had acquired from his firsthand experiences at *ñáñigo* rituals was superficial and insufficient certainly applies to them as well:

> Pues bien: al cabo de veinte años de investigaciones acerca de las realidades sincréticas de Cuba, me di cuenta de que todo lo hondo, lo verdadero, lo universal, del mundo que había pretendido pintar en mi novela había permanecido fuera del alcance de mi observación. Por ejemplo ... ciertas prácticas iniciacas ... me habían sido disimuladas por los oficiantes con una desconcertante habilidad. (12–13)

> [Well then: after twenty years of research on the syncretic realities of Cuba, I realized that all of the profound, the true, the universal, things of the world that I had pretended to describe in my novel had remained beyond the reach of my observation. For example ... certain initiation rites ... had been dissimulated to me by the officiants with disconcerting skill.]

Readers of "Juego santo" with a basic understanding of Abakuá rites will note how Carpentier's firsthand experiences at *ñáñigo* rituals and celebrations did not necessarily make for compelling or accurate poetic renditions of them. At the same time, however, we must keep in mind that in Carpentier's day few outsiders had access to the secrets of the esoteric rites, and did not necessarily understand the meanings of their key terms. To be sure, many Abakuá terms, whose definitions are by now widely known or at least easily accessible, were used very loosely and gave rise to considerable confusion in 1920s Cuba. The title of the poem we are considering here is a case in point, as it is not entirely clear how Carpentier is using the term "juego." David Brown has noted that "juego" can be understood to mean three different things "in the Afro-Cuban idiom": a "rite" or "ritual"; a "set," as in a "set of *batá* drums"; or, as it applies to the Abakuá secret brotherhoods, "the membership group of a single Abakuá lodge, consisting of 25 fundamental officers (*plazas*) followed by other initiated members (*obonekues*)" ("Afro-Cuban Festival" 70). It is important to stress that the first definition given here is not typically employed when referring to the Abakuá. Nonetheless, some experts have used the term "juego" to refer more generally to dances, ceremonies, and performances related to the *ñáñigos*. For example, in *Los instrumentos de la música afrocubana* [The Instruments of Afro-Cuban Music], Fernando Ortiz observes that the name of the *Biapá* drum of the *ñáñigo* orchestra seems to have derived from the Efik noun *akpá*, "which means 'dance' or 'juego'" (Vol. 2, 91). He similarly notes that "*ebonkó* . . . means 'juego' or dance of *Egbó*" (Vol. 2, 91). According to his usage of the term, Janheinz Jahn (who depends heavily on Ortiz throughout his study) would have us believe that "juego" was used by the Abakuá to mean "performance." "When all of the preparations are in order," he writes of an Abakuá initiation ceremony, "three persons step out in front of the temple and the performance, the 'Juego,' can begin" (*Muntu* 70).

This leads us to two fundamental questions that arise for readers of "Juego santo": how is Carpentier using the term "juego," and what exactly is he describing in the poem? It is my opinion that Carpentier, in an act of poetic syncretism, intentionally describes several things at once, all of which are related in varying degrees to the Abakuá secret society. First, certain parts of the poem clearly evoke his personal observations of the public rites and rituals that were performed as part of Abakuá *plantes* [ceremonies], though several inaccuracies that we will discuss later suggest that like many outsiders, Carpentier did not always understand what he was witnessing. Carpentier's references to the "ecón" and "bonkó" in the first and last stanzas, for example, evoke a typical sacred procession in which the musicians of the Abakuá orchestra, along with several Abakuá *plazas* (dignitaries) and *íremes*—more commonly known as *diablitos*— file through the semipublic courtyard of the Abakuá lodge, and sometimes embark on brief public sojourns through nearby streets (Brown, *Light Inside* 59, 185). Brown notes that Alejo Carpentier attended many such events, during which he would have observed other public activities associated with the ceremonies, some of which are also evoked in "Juego santo," such as the chanting of prayers, the dancing of the *íremes*, the chalking of *anaforuana* [sacred drawings] in the courtyard, the ritual cleansings of the initiates, the sacrifice of the goat, and the preparation of the communal meal (Brown, *Light Inside* 185).

In addition to specific sacred components of the Abakuá ceremony, Carpentier also seems to be describing certain aspects of the unofficial festivities that often took place in the courtyards of Abakuá lodges. The field notes taken by American folklorist and anthropologist Harold Courlander (1908–1996) during an Abakuá society meeting in 1941, describe a scene that is typical of what Carpentier would have witnessed:

> Most of the people present were not *ocobíon* (brothers) and could not enter [the temple]. For them as for me, the evening was a kind of fair or festival. Under one of the two palms which stood in the court a group of men pressed closely around the drummers and singers . . . There were four of them, who stood facing one another. One beat on a long goatskin drum called a *boncó*, . . . The others played small, shallow drums known as *encómo*, . . . Later a man with a bell joined the drummers. This instrument was played inverted, and struck with a long bolt. *Banká*, they called it. It was hand-made, of two pieces of shaped metal fastened by two rivets.
>
> One of the singers close to the drums broke into dance in the yard-square "court"; it was a jerky mimicry of something I could not identify. The drummers beat hard and the singers clapped hands. There was hardly room for the dancer to turn around, but he gave an astonishing performance. (464–65)

A number of images in Carpentier's poem suggest a scene very similar to the one described here by Courlander, most notably his evocation of the *bonkó* drum and the *ekón*, the clapperless bell that Courlander refers to as a *banká*. In "Juego santo" Carpentier also makes reference to a "Rumba en tumba," which, like the "jerky mimicry" that Courlander describes, is probably a reference to a performance of *rumba columbia*. This dance, which is performed by a single man, is inspired by the rituals of the Abakuá (Orovio, *Cuban Music* 191), and it is often performed as part of the secular festivities that form during their *plantes*. It should be noted that it would not necessarily have been clear to outsiders which activities were official components of an initiation ceremony or other rite and which were not, just as many of those witnessing the related festivities would not have known the names of the instruments. This may explain why Carpentier seems to meld the components of the sacred ceremony with those of the secular festivities, and also why some of the instruments that he names in the poem are not related in any way to the Abakuá brotherhoods.

Finally, Carpentier also describes, in the third and fourth stanzas, what we might call a *comparsa ñáñiga*. Though such spectacles were quite different from the sacred processions of the *ñáñigos*, and not directly related to Abakuá *plantes*, Carpentier's depiction of a *comparsa* in "Juego santo" is understandable. Indeed, sacred Abakuá processions and traditional Afro-Cuban carnival ensembles share many characteristics in common, and could easily have been confused by an outsider. Carpentier may also have been inspired by early writings of Fernando Ortiz, in which the latter underscored the relationship between Abakuá processions and traditional Afro-Cuban carnival celebrations, and noted that Abakuá *juegos* often sponsored their own *comparsa* ensembles (*La antigua fiesta* 31). Ortiz describes such *salidas*, or public appearances, of the *ñáñigos* as follows:

> Además de figurar en sus ritos críticos y los parcialmente públicos, los íremes salían antaño en los carnavales barrioteros de la Habana colonial, por mero divertimiento... En 1880, al acabarse la esclavitud en Cuba, fueron proscriptos los ñáñigos... y vedadas sus ceremonias y diversiones; pero desde la gran persecución colonial de los ñáñigos éstos siguieron funcionando clandestinamente hasta 1909, cuando el gobierno liberal de José Miguel Gómez les dio licencia para "salir a la calle" con sus "diablitos." Recordamos la salida de los abakuá del "Juego" Biabanga, del barrio de los Sitios. Iban nada menos que seis "diablitos" bailando... Con los "diablitos" iba el "tambor de orden" o Empegó y la orquesta de la "potencia." Como una semana estuvieron saliendo comparseando, desde el medio día a la mañana siguiente, por dicho barrio y sus aledaños. Luego esas comparsas ñáñigas se prohibieron... (*Los bailes y el teatro* 185)

[In addition to taking part in their most important rituals and the semipublic ones, in days gone by the *íremes* came out in neighborhood carnivals of colonial Havana, for mere diversion . . . In 1880, at the end of slavery in Cuba, the *ñáñigos* were outlawed . . . and their ceremonies and diversions were prohibited; but they continued to function clandestinely from the great colonial-era persecution of the ñáñigos until 1909, when the liberal government of José Miguel Gómez gave them license to "go out in the street" with their "diablitos." We remember the appearance of the Abakuá of the Biabanga "Lodge," from the neighborhood of Los Sitios. No less than six "diablitos" went about dancing . . . With the "diablitos" went the "drum of order" or Empegó and the orchestra of the "potencia."[3] For nearly a week they came out performing their *comparsas*, from midday until the following morning, around the aforementioned neighborhood and its surroundings. Later those *comparsas ñáñigas* were prohibited . . .]

Notwithstanding the notable similarities between the *íremes* in Abakuá processions and those that appear in carnival *comparsas*, it is important to stress that these two types of public performances are not the same thing even if they were conceived as such by many outsiders.

In many ways "Juego santo," like "Liturgia" and *Écue-Yamba-Ó*, is significant as a very early example of how Afro-Cuban cultural expressions, and more specifically, the Abakuá brotherhoods became "a key symbol for the *Afrocubanistas* . . . who sought to define a national culture" (Miller 168). As David H. Brown has pointed out, during the early decades that correspond to Afrocubanismo many Cuban artists and intellectuals "celebrated the figures of Santería, Abakuá, Carnival, and other popular figures and forms as markers of a complex modern *cubanidad*, wrought through the blending of cultures and histories" (*Light Inside* 174). Though Carpentier himself would later refer to this aspect of the movement as "el falso concepto de lo nacional" [the false conception of nationhood] (qtd. in Leante 63) that he and other intellectuals of his generation had at the time, he also admitted that turning to certain manifestations of Afro-Cuban culture (especially as he had done in the late 1920s) communicated a combative and rebellious attitude.

It is indeed quite noteworthy that Carpentier focused so much of his early work on the rites and rituals of the Abakuá, especially since they had been subjected for decades to massive government-backed propaganda campaigns that aimed to discredit them as dangerous, illicit organizations that sprung from the dregs of Cuban society. In his 1882 book *Los criminales de Cuba* [The Criminals of Cuba], Havana police chief José Trujillo y Monegas, in a chapter titled "Los ñáñigos," discusses at length the brutal violence and acts of revenge committed by members of the Abakuá brotherhoods (367–68). Trujillo y Monegas stresses, furthermore, that disputes between rival Abakuá lodges were often settled during public festivities, such as during Día de Reyes festivals or during the carnival season (368). Likewise, police investigator and criminologist Rafael Roche y Monteagudo and forensic pathologist Israel Castellanos both sought to demonstrate—often through decidedly unscientific methodology—that the Abakuá brotherhoods were criminal organizations guided by principals of revenge, intimidation, and savage violence.[4] Castellanos's belief that *ñáñigos* were born criminals with natural homicidal tendencies is reflected in categorical statements that are scattered throughout his writings, such as the following: "El ñáñigo, que es agresor por excelencia, verdadero criminal jurado ... tiene la hegemonía en la delincuencia más brutal: el homicidio" [The *ñáñigo*, who is an aggressor par excellence, a true sworn criminal ... reigns supreme in the most brutal form of delinquency: homicide.] (*Medicina legal* 11); "Slavery left Cuba two types of negro criminality: fetishism, which on several occasions has led to the murdering of white women, and the 'ñáñiguismo' [sic]: a criminal organization employing the knife as a means of settling grudges" ("Evolution of Criminology" 227). Roche promoted a similarly debasing image of the members of the Abakuá secret society by stressing that the slightest disagreements between *juegos* inevitably led to deadly confrontations:

> Cuando existen divergencias en dos juegos, los miembros de ambos bandos se preparan para matar a cualquiera de los que componen la potencia a que pertenece el ofensor de manera que muchas veces transita pacíficamente una persona por la calle, e inopinadamente recibe una puñalada, casi siempre mortal, como inferida por una mano experta ..." (2nd ed., 66)

> [When divergences exist between two *juegos*, the members of both factions prepare themselves to kill any of those that make up the *potencia* to which the offender belongs, in such a way that many

times a person walks peacefully along the street, and he unexpectedly receives a stab, almost always mortal, as if inflicted by an expert hand ...]

An illustration from *La policía y sus misterios en Cuba* epitomizes Roche y Monteagudo's opinion of *ñáñigos* as violent murderers (fig. 2.5). In it, a giant *íreme* points an accusatory finger at a man who is being shot by two Afro-Cuban gunmen.

It should be repeated here that there is, in fact, more than a grain of truth in observations like those of Castellanos and Roche y Monteagudo, which portray the Abakuá secret brotherhoods as violent criminal gangs. Indeed, the following comments by one of Lydia Cabrera's *Abakuá*

FIGURE 2.5. "Armed dispute between the *ñáñigo* lodges Muñangas and Taiba in the [Havana] neighborhood of Jesús María in colonial times." The image of the enormous *íreme* pointing his finger as if orchestrating the act of revenge reinforces the reputation of these figures as intimately linked with violence and bloodshed. (From Roche y Monteagudo, 1925.)

informants evoke many similarly damaging images of violent confrontations involving members of *ñáñigo* brotherhoods from the mid-nineteenth century through the early decades of the twentieth:

> Pero la verdad es que a partir de esa fecha [1860s] empezaron las rivalidades y los matados, y lo del ñañiguismo se puso feo. . . . ¡Antes, qué buenas pendencias y qué odios a muerte! Los ñáñigos de San Lázaro se enfrentaban y se iban a las manos con los de Jesús María: se abrían las navajas: y eso duró hasta el gobierno de Gómez. ¿Que un ñáñigo del barrio de Colón apuñaleaba a uno de Jesús María? Todos los de Jesús María tomaban represalias. Como es natural, tenían que vengar al hermano . . . eran guerras con sangre de barrio contra barrio. (*El monte* 197)

> [But the truth is that from that date forward the rivalries and the killings began, and that business of *ñáñiguismo* got ugly . . . What great brawls and what hatred to the death there were back then! The *ñáñigos* from San Lázaro confronted and went hand to hand with those from Jesús María: the pocketknives were opened: and that lasted until the government of Gómez. And if a ñáñigo from the neighborhood of Colón stabbed one from Jesús María? All of those from Jesús María took reprisals. It's only natural, they had to take revenge for their brother. . . . they were bloody wars of barrio against barrio.]

Even if this statement demonstrates that the reigning fear of the violence associated with *ñáñiguismo* in the early twentieth century was justifiable, however, it is also important to keep in mind that Castellanos and Roche unnecessarily intensified such fears by suggesting that all members of the Abakuá brotherhoods were violent criminals. What is more, while Cabrera's informant observes that such violence had abated considerably by the time of the administration of José Miguel Gómez (1909–1913), outside "experts" on the Abakuá secret society and Cuban newspapers continued to disseminate debasing images of the *ñáñigos* as innate criminals well past that date. Indeed, Octavio di Leo is incorrect to note that by the time Carpentier penned his first novel the Abakuá secret societies were no longer the objects of criminological studies (100–01).

In fact, in *Écue-Yamba-Ó*, Carpentier himself reinforces notions of *ñáñigo* criminality by associating them with "knifings and murders," as Matibag notes (134). However, we must not forget that much of the action of Carpentier's first novel coincides with the period that Cabrera's informant discusses. And to his credit, Carpentier does avoid such associations in his poems and essays that deal with the Abakuá.

Among the early poems of Afrocubanismo, "Juego santo" is one of the most esoteric, with its profusion of Abakuá terms and references to rituals that most contemporary outsiders would not have understood completely. This poem stands out among those considered in the present study—and indeed among the poems of Afrocubanismo as a whole—for its lack of descriptions of Afro-Cubans. The poet refers to only two protagonists of the Abakuá procession—an anonymous "congo" dancer and a "diablo" (a reference to a costumed *íreme*)—and he offers no physical descriptions of them. Like most of Carpentier's early poems, which Frank Janney correctly describes as "formalistic orchestrations of sound, striking for their hieratic seriousness" (71), "Juego santo" reflects Carpentier's deep interest in music and focuses almost exclusively on the instruments that the Abakuá protagonists are playing and the sounds that they produce, as can be seen in the first two stanzas:

> Ecón y bongó,
> atabal de timbal,
> ecón y bongó,
> timbal de arrabal.
> Rumba en tumba,
> tambor de cajón.
> ¡Qué le zumba!
>
> Ecón con ecón,
> timbal y bongó,
> tambor de cajón. (218)

Like a musicologist who has taken incomplete notes during his fieldwork, the poetic voice essentially provides us with a list of percussive instruments, some of which have no real connection to Abakuá rights or to the so-called *comparsas ñáñigas* that marched through Havana's working-class neighborhoods at various times throughout the year. These opening lines of "Juego santo" are short on semantic content and lack the vivid descriptive qualities that characterize so many of the poems of Afrocubanismo.

The poem's deliberate abstruseness echoes to a certain extent the mysteries of the esoteric rites that it attempts to depict, and only readers with at least a very basic knowledge of Abakuá processions and musical instruments can extract any real meaning from the poem.

As can be inferred from the repeated references to them, the *ecón* and *bongó* are the key instruments in the typical Abakuá orchestra. The first of these (sometimes spelled *ekón*) cannot properly be referred to as a *cencerro*, as Carpentier defines it in the glossary to *Écue-Yamba-Ó* (222), since it lacks the clapper that characterizes such bells. The *ekón* is a hollow instrument made of roughly triangular iron plates welded or riveted together at the sides, which are attached to a wooden handle. It is beaten with a stick or metal bolt to produce a sound similar to that of a cowbell (Ortiz, *Instrumentos* Vol. 1, 271; Orovio, *Cuban Music* 73, Courlander 465).[5] It is fitting that the *ekón* is the first instrument mentioned in the poem, since it is played by the *Moruá* to "command" or "direct" the ñáñigo orchestra (Ortiz, *Instrumentos* Vol. 2, 83), and "to call forth spiritual energy" (Brown, *Light Inside* 46). Though these "bells" would not typically have been played in *comparsas ñáñigas*, Ortiz has noted that in the carnivals of the first decade of the twentieth century, Afro-Cubans often went through their neighborhoods in *comparsas* led by a masked figure who would hit a frying pan with a stick, "in the same way that the *ñáñigos* played the African-derived instrument known as an ekón" (*Los bailes y el teatro* 188).

The *bongó* that Carpentier repeatedly mentions in "Juego santo" should not be confused with the ubiquitous Afro-Cuban instrument, which consists of two small drums joined together by a wooden frame. Instead, Carpentier is referring to the *bonkó enchemiyá* (*bonkó*, for short, but also commonly called *bongó*), a single-headed, conical drum that stands about a meter high.[6] The *bonkó* is musically the most important of the Abakuá drums—many of which are rarely played due to their highly symbolic importance—and along with other percussive instruments, it provides the sound that animates the Abakuá processions and ceremonies that take place outside of the group's private ritual spaces (*Instrumentos* Vol. 2, 80, 83, 91). In addition to its musical function, the *bonkó* is the drum that "speaks" to the *íreme*. It is worth noting here that even though his use of the term is ambiguous, Nicolás Guillén also evokes the *bonkó enchemiyá* and the Abakuá secret society in his poem "La canción del bongó" [The Song of the Bongo], in which the poetic voice is actually a drum that "speaks" to its audience.

In both Abakuá processions and carnival parades, which Carpentier melds at times in the poem, the *diablito* has no voice and carries no instrument other than the ritual bells (*enkaniká*) that are tied around his waist and ankles. In Abakuá ceremonies the *íreme* responds to the drumbeat and the prompting speech and gestures of the *Moruá Yuansá* with symbolic pantomimic movements, dance steps, bodily contortions, and struck poses (Ortiz, *Instrumentos* Vol. 2, 93; Brown *Light Inside* 121). A similar dance was performed by the *diablitos* that took part in the carnival processions.

The other drums that Carpentier mentions in the opening stanzas of the poem—*atabal, timbal, tambor de cajón*—might have been played by outsiders gathered in the public courtyards of the Abakuá lodge, but they are not traditional components of Abakuá processions or *comparsas ñáñigas*. It is possible that the common drums that Carpentier mentions in his poem simply reflect the fact that he—like most outsiders of his day—was not yet familiar with the names of the other three drums that were played by an Abakuá orchestra. These drums are known both by the general name of *enkómo*—which Harold Courlander uses in his field notes quoted above—and their individual names: *biankomé, obiapá,* and *kuchi yeremá* (Ortiz, *Instrumentos* Vol. 2, 82, Sosa Rodríguez 179).[7]

At first glance, the reference to rumba, a secular musical genre with no religious significance, might seem out of place in the context of the sacred procession that Carpentier describes. Indeed, the *bonkó* and other Abakuá drums are not normally sounded for secular diversion since doing so would constitute a profanation of the sacred organizations (Ortiz, *Instrumentos* Vol. 2, 81). However, as Sublette has noted, "rumberos have from the beginning been identified with Abakuá . . . and the Abakuá metal bell called the *ekón* plays the same rhythm as that played by the claves in guaguancó" (267). But it is most likely the *rumba columbia* that Carpentier had in mind when he wrote his poem, and perhaps even witnessed as the Abakuá procession filed around their semipublic courtyard, as this particular dance "is inspired by rituals observed by Abakuá and Ñáñigo secret brotherhoods" (Orovio, *Cuban Music* 191). Moreover, the *tambor de cajón* that Carpentier mentions is typical of the percussive instruments of *rumba columbia*, which, unlike the eroticized *rumba guaguancó*, traditionally involves a man dancing alone.

The *tumba* in the first stanza evokes an Afro-Cuban drum commonly associated with the traditional Afro-Cuban *conga* processions of Santiago, but the same term was also employed quite commonly in Carpentier's day to signify the sensual movements of the rumba dancer, and it is likely that Carpentier is using it here in this sense. The appearance of *rumba*, *tumba*, and *zumba* in the same stanza evoke popular expressions like the following one that Ortiz cites as an example of this meaning: "esa rumba tiene un tumbaito que le zumba" (Ortiz, *Instrumentos* Vol. 2, 130). Like many of the poets of Afrocubanismo, Carpentier may also have been influenced by popular nineteenth-century *guarachas* such as "Rumba criolla," whose catchy refrain reads as follows: "Sólo me gusta en la rumba, / El roce del tumba-tumba." The final lines of the same composition contain a similar expression that conjures the erotic connotations of "tumba": "Las mujeres bailan la rumba . . . / Porque con el tumba-tumba / De la rumba, tumbarán" (*Guarachas antiguas de Cuba* 30).

In the third and fourth stanzas of "Juego santo" Carpentier depicts certain secular diversions that were characteristic of *comparsas ñáñigas*, but not necessarily of Abakuá processions:

Por calles de Regla
lleva la comparsa
juego santo
en honor de Ecoriofó.

Farola en alto,
anilla de oro,
chancleta ligera,
pañuelo bermejo . . .

As we have seen, the *farola* is a key element of traditional Afro-Cuban *comparsas*—especially those of Havana—in which these large lanterns that were elaborately decorated with group-specific insignia were skillfully wielded by a *comparsero* who moved them in time with the music (see fig. 1.2). The reference to the *chancletas* recalls the heelless wooden sandals that were worn by members of many *comparsa* troupes, who, in a dance called the *baile de la chancleta* "move[d] their feet rhythmically substituting their foot stamps for the drum beats" (Brea and Millet, "Glossary" 184). Finally, the "pañuelo bermejo" evokes the colorful silk scarves that were worn by both *comparseros* and certain members of the Abakuá brotherhoods. Examples of this emblematic carnival accessory can be seen in Heriberto Portell Vilá's 1948 painting *Comparsa* (fig. 2.6).

FIGURE 2.6. Heriberto Portell Vilá, *Comparsa*, 1948. Note the *pañuelos*, the *diablito*, and the *farolas*, all of which are depicted in Carpentier's poem. (Image courtesy of Elliot Klein. Used by permission.)

The scarves worn by members of the latter group are described in the following passage from Ortiz's essay "La 'tragedia' de los ñáñigos" [The 'Tragedy' of the Ñáñigos]:

> El *Enkríkamo*, el *Mosongo* y otros llevan sendos pañuelos de seda de vivos colores a la cintura, al cuello, atravesado al pecho y a veces a la cabeza con dos de sus puntas sueltas y ondulantes al frente y las otras dos atadas en la nuca." (83)

[The Enkríkamo, the Mosongo, and others wear lively colored silk scarves around the waist, and neck, crossing over the chest, and at times around the head with two of the points loose and hanging over the forehead and the other two points tied together at the nape.]

Carpentier's usage of "juego" in the third stanza conveys the notion of a "rite," "ritual," or some sacred performance that the members of the *comparsa* are acting out as part of their routine, rather than a membership group of a specific Abakuá lodge. Though we have noted that this definition of "juego" is not the one most typically associated with the Abakuá, it is not uncommon to see the term employed in this way. The reference to "Ecoriofó" is significant as it explicitly links this particular *comparsa* to the Abakuá brotherhoods. Indeed, three *juegos* of white *ñañigos*, Ekório Efó Ita, Ekório Efó Taibá, and Ekório Efó Tercero, which were established in the 1870s (Miller, *Voice* 110) were among several that were accused of illicit activities by Havana police and forced to disband and hand over their sacred drums and other items in January 1889. These particular *juegos* were well known to outsiders in the early decades of the twentieth century largely because their run-in with Havana authorities was chronicled in detail in Roche y Monteagudo's *La policía y sus misterios en Cuba*, which was already in its third, expanded edition by the time Carpentier penned "Juego santo" (2nd ed. 71–74). The evocation of these particular Abakuá lodges during the *comparsa ñáñiga* serves to reflect the nonconformist and revolutionary attitudes that Carpentier saw in his own embracing of the *ñáñigos* and their widely denigrated and almost universally misunderstood traditions. Moreover, the fact that these *juegos* were made up primarily of white members would seem to suggest a sort of celebration—not unlike those heard in certain popular songs written by Abakuá-member musicians like Ignacio Piñeiro (leader of the Septeto Nacional), and Agustín Gutiérrez (of the Sexteto Habanero)—that extols those members of the brotherhoods who had worked to universalize the secret society and turn it into a "model for integration" (Miller, *Voice* 110).[8]

As the poem's fourth stanza clearly indicates—with its references to ritual animal sacrifices, and to the emergence of the *íreme*—certain parts of "Juego santo" are more evocative of an Abakuá ceremony than a carnival *comparsa*.

Ataron el chivo,
mataron el gallo,
asaron cangrejos,
sacaron el diablo . . .

Here Carpentier makes reference to the traditional offerings of a goat and a rooster, central components of Abakuá initiation ceremonies that are often performed in the courtyard. In the hours before the initiation begins, the goat, called *mbóri*, is taken to a public space or *isaroko*, outside of the *fambá* where it is tied to a tree to await its sacrifice. According to Lydia Cabrera, once the goat is purified and consecrated, it represents and substitutes the human victim in the Abakuá rite. By way of its blood, the initiates realize spiritual union with divine and ancestral forces (*La sociedad* 19). Because the *mbóri* represents "the symbolic substitute" of Sikán, the first Abakuá initiate, its skin is seen as a condensation of "the Abakuá myth-history, liturgy, principal narrative, characters, and socio-ritual hierarchies." The skin of *mbóri* is highly revered as a "sacred medium within the society" and as an embodiment of the spirit of Sikán, and is therefore used in the fabrication of all Abakuá drumheads (Brown, *Light Inside* 70).

Roosters—but never hens, since they represent the feminine—are present throughout Abakuá initiation ceremonies, and have various purposes. The blood of the sacrificial rooster, *nkíko*, serves a vital role in ritual cleansings, for example, and its flesh is an integral part of the sacred meals that "feed" drums, ceremonial objects, and the participants in the ritual. Brown explains that while alive "*nkíko* epitomizes garrulous speech . . . [but] *nkíko* as sacrificed is silent, and placed atop the silent *sese*" (*Light Inside* 76), the most sacred of Abakuá drums, which Carpentier mentions in the poem's final stanza. The sacrificed rooster can often be seen dangling by its feet from the waist of the *íreme* as he performs a ritual dance, an image that has been immortalized by Víctor Patricio de Landaluze's illustration *El ñáñigo* (fig. 2.7). This iconic image, which was published in 1881 in Antonio Bachiller y Morales's *Tipos y costumbres de la isla de Cuba*, has since been copied and reappropriated by countless individuals, from criminologists, to artists, to poets of Afrocubanismo.

The reference to the roasted crabs is puzzling since neither the members of the Abakuá society nor the practitioners of any of the Afro-Cuban religions kill or eat crabs as part of a sacred rite because the general belief is that since they walk backwards and sideways, anyone who consumes them will suffer reverses or fail to advance in life (Klein). Lydia Cabrera makes the following observation concerning the use of crabs by Afro-Cuban *brujos*:

> Como el cangrejo "camina para atrás," parece que a cada paso que avanza retrocede, es uno de los instrumentos que más le sirven al brujo para "atrasar" y provocar desgracias irreparables. (*Los animales* 76)
>
> [Since the crab "walks backward," it seems like with each step that it advances it moves back, it is one of the instruments that best serves the *brujo* to "set back" and provoke irreparable disgraces.]

72 · Carnival and National Identity in the Poetry of Afrocubanismo

FIGURE 2.7. Víctor Patricio de Landaluze, *El ñáñigo*. From *Los tipos y los costumbres de la isla de Cuba*, 1881. (Image courtesy of Boston Public Library.)

It is interesting to note that in "Liturgia," Carpentier also evokes the image of the crab:—"salió el diablito /—¡cangrejo de Regla!—/ saltando de lao" (77). In these lines Carpentier refers to the dancing *íreme* as the "Crab of Regla," presumably because his swift lateral and backward movements resemble the unique manner in which crabs advance. Given the negative connotations of crabs among many Afro-Cubans, however, this image of the dancing *íreme* is not particularly fitting.

An early manuscript version of "Juego santo" (fig. 2.8), which is held by the Fundación Alejo Carpentier in Havana, indicates that Carpentier's depiction of key components of an Abakuá ritual in the fourth stanza was problematic. Indeed, it is the only stanza that reveals substantive changes. The original version, which is crossed out and corrected in Carpentier's hand reads: "Asaron el gallo / ataron el chivo / mataron cangrejo / sacaron el diablo." Carpentier's wavering over the placement of "asaron" [they roasted] and "mataron" [they killed] suggests to me two things: on

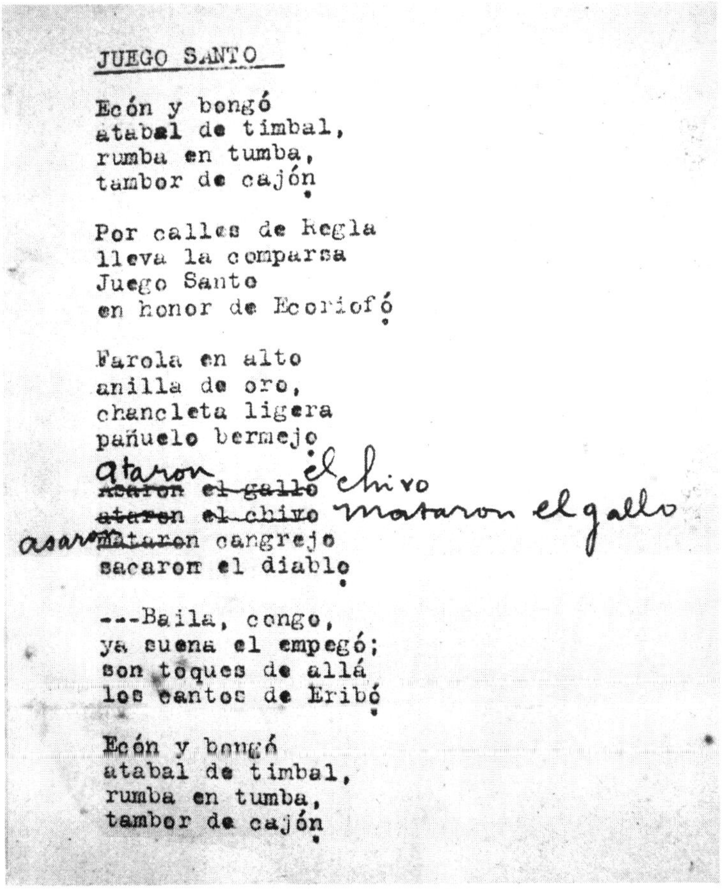

JUEGO SANTO

Ecón y bongó
atabal de timbal,
rumba en tumba,
tambor de cajón.

Por calles de Regla
lleva la comparsa
Juego Santo
en honor de Ecoriofó.

Farola en alto
anilla de oro,
chancleta ligera
pañuelo bermejo.
~~asaron el gallo~~ ataron el chivo
~~ataron el chivo~~ mataron el gallo
asaron ~~mataron~~ cangrejo
sacaron el diablo.

---Baila, congo,
ya suena el empegó;
son toques de allá
los santos de Eribó.

Ecón y bongó
atabal de timbal,
rumba en tumba,
tambor de cajón.

FIGURE 2.8. Early manuscript version of "Juego santo" (1927) with excisions and corrections in the author's hand. (Used by permission of the Fundación Alejo Carpentier, Havana.)

the one hand, Carpentier was not entirely familiar with the process involved in the sacrificing of the rooster in the Abakuá ceremony, and, on the other, he seems to have had a specific image in mind when referring to the crab(s)—perhaps something he had seen in the semipublic courtyard—but was not sure how to describe it or what its relationship might have been to the ceremonies he had witnessed.

The final line from the fourth stanza ("sacaron el diablo") recalls "Liturgia" as it evokes the appearance of the *íreme*, a masked entity with supernatural powers who emerges from the secret space of the temple "to dance and perform ritual duties" (Brown, "Glossary" 45). In one such sacred rite the *diablito* debates between the voice of *Ékue* (known as *úyo*), who calls him to his invisible realm, and the "rhythmic conjurations" of the *bonkó* drum, which draws him toward the world of the visible (Ortiz, *Instrumentos* Vol. 2, 92).

The penultimate stanza of "Juego santo" is the one that most obviously brings the reader into the realm of an Abakuá ritual (and, by extension, out of that of traditional Afro-Cuban carnival processions) through its invocation to two of the secret society's most sacred drums: the *empegó* and the *sese eribó*.

¡Baila, congo,
ya suena el empegó!
Son toques de allá,
los cantos de Eribó

The appearance of the Congo dancer seems incongruous since the Abakuá were not typically associated with Bantu Africans, the ethnic groups that hail from present-day Congo, but rather with the Carabalí from southeastern Nigeria and western Cameroon. This is not to say that Afro-Cubans of other ethnic origins did not become members of Abakuá lodges—indeed the society was open to blacks of many backgrounds as well as to whites, mulattoes, Chinese immigrants, etcetera—but rather, that "congo" is not the most fitting ethonym in this particular context. Moreover, we should stress that in Cuba, so-called Congos are associated with the practices of Palo Monte (Mayombe), not Abakuá.

The reference to the *empegó*—also *mpegó*—is somewhat misleading as it suggests that this is a musical drum, to the beat of which the members of the Abakuá brotherhoods dance. In fact, this sacred instrument is known as the drum of authority and justice, and though it is "regularly tapped

FIGURE 2.9. Sese Eribó (or *senseribó*), the most sacred of the Abakuá drums. (From Roche y Monteagudo, 1925.)

to call attention" (Brown, *Light Inside* 94), to impose silence (Cabrera, *Anaforuana* 22), and to bring an end to ceremonies, it is never played musically. The *mpegó* belongs to the scribe of the *juego*, also called *Mpegó*, and it is he who sounds this sacred drum to enforce order both inside the *fambá* and outside of its sacred space during various ceremonies (Brown, *Light Inside* 94–95; Ortiz, *Los Bailes y el teatro* 192–93, 197). Likewise, the poetic voice's invocation of the "cantos de Eribó" can also be taken as a contradiction of sorts, since the sacred drum that he evokes is purely ceremonial: technically it has no voice because it is never beaten. The *eribó*—variously referred to as *sese eribó, senseribó,* or *sese*—is a decorated, plumed drum that belongs to the *Isué* or "bishop" of the *juego* (fig. 2.9). It is only removed from the Abakuá altar for rites of consecration, initiation, and other sacred ceremonies, and the *Isué* carries it near the front of Abakuá processions. Though some members of the *juego* may dance around it and sing to it as it is carried along, the drum itself always remains silent. Carpentier certainly would have had many opportunities to see examples of these sacred drums given their important role in the public phases of certain Abakuá *plantes*, though it is conceivable that he had limited knowledge of the drum's purpose and symbolism when he wrote "Juego santo" in 1927.

It is important to note—as Carpentier himself does in the glossary to *Écue-Yamba-Ó* (222)—that even though the term "Eribó" is often employed alone to refer to one of the sacred Abakuá drums, it (much like "Ékue") is also used to refer to an abstract entity or maximum divinity of the Abakuá for whom the drum in question is a symbolic representation. It is said that while Ékue represents the father figure of the Abakuá, Eribó symbolizes the mother (Ortiz, *Instrumentos* Vol. 2, 97; Brown, *Light Inside* 75). With this in mind, it is also possible that Carpentier is not referring to the "cantos" or sound of the *sese eribó* in his poem, but rather to the chants that are being sung in honor of the metaphysical entity, the sacred mother, that the drum represents.

There are two principal types of *sese* drums, known as the *sese de copón* (goblet-shaped *sese*), and the *sese de kankamo* (an open-bottomed cylindrical version), both of which feature four feather plumes, known as *plumeros*. The first of these is often referred to as the "forma criolla" because it is said to have emerged only after the reformist innovations introduced to the Abakuá society by the mulatto priest Andrés Petit in the 1860s.[9] The drum's similarity in shape to a chalice, which many experts see as a concrete reflection of the Catholic elements that Petit introduced, has led to comparisons between the *sese eribó* and the Holy Sacrament on church altars (Roche, 3rd ed. 33, Ortiz, *Instrumentos* Vol. 2, 97–98; Cabrera, *Sociedad* 148; Brown, *Light Inside* 73, 104). Brown has noted that in an act of "syncretistic mimesis" (a term he borrows from Ortiz), "the 'Creole' *sese de copón* tactically took on the mask of *Copón Divino* (divine goblet)" with the onset of intense police persecution of the Abakuá society in 1875 (*Light Inside* 104).

This detail is especially interesting in the context of "Juego santo" since it brings to mind the fact that largely due to the phenomenon of religious syncretism that was so prevalent in Cuba, many similarities existed among the public festivities—such as Día de Reyes, Holy Week, Corpus Christi processions, Abakuá sacred processions, and carnival *comparsas*—that were celebrated in the streets of the nation's cities at various times of the year. Ortiz reports, for example, that the Día de Reyes festivities were typically referred to as the festival of *diablitos* "because, on looking for a name, the whites found in the motley costumes of the Africans, in their leaps and capers, their horns and masks, certain analog with the devil masks accompanying the old Catholic processions of Corpus Christi in Cuba, as in Spain and other countries" ("Afro-Cuban Festival" 21).

An early nineteenth-century description of traditional Corpus Christi festivities by Emilio Bacardí—with its masked figures, gigantic snakelike creature, and African chants and drumming—calls attention to at least the superficial similarities that linked these processions with Día de Reyes festivities as well as with modern Afro-Cuban carnival *comparsas*:

> In the procession different masks and figures appeared, representing angels, devils, gypsy men and women, lions, tigers, and above all a gigantic snakelike figure called the dragon. All these *comparsas* had their own dances; in both the general procession and the festival celebrated over an eight-day period, different busts of saints were carried and some of these were preceded by African chants, drumming and timbrels. (qtd. in Carpentier, *Music in Cuba* 93)

Ortiz's frequent observations about the connections that existed among these traditions (see "Los viejos carnavales" 203, "Afro-Cuban Festival" 21) and Bacardí's vivid description of the "*comparsas*" that he observed during the Corpus Christi processions are significant in the context of "Juego santo" because they call attention to the tendency among both nineteenth-century and modern audiences to use the term *comparsa* to refer to any number of public spectacles that involved costumed figures and African-derived dancing and music. In short, the common ground shared by all of these public festivities could at least in part account for Carpentier's decision to meld in his poem—through an act of poetic syncretism—certain aspects of sacred Abakuá rites and rituals with those of secular Afro-Cuban *comparsas*.

In obvious ways, Carpentier's "Juego santo" evokes many of the same traditions and contains images similar to those found in the other poems that are considered in this study. Moreover, like many of the poems of Afrocubanismo that would be published in the years to come, Carpentier's poetic recreation of Afro-Cuban rituals and traditions that had long been denigrated by Cuban government officials and the white, middle-class majority serves as a reminder that despite their exoticism, profusion of stereotypes, and inaccurate representations of African-derived cultural manifestations, many poems of this important artistic movement symbolized the combative spirit of their authors. As Carpentier put it in a response to a question about his early poems in a 1960s interview, writing *poesía negra* implied a desire to celebrate traditions despised by the bourgeois. Demonstrating an interest in black culture, Carpentier argued, signified a nonconformist and revolutionary attitude (qtd. in Arias 52). Another poem of Afrocubanismo that evokes sacred Afro-Cuban rituals at the same time that it reveals the poet's treatment of racial issues as a form of rebellion against the social and intellectual mainstream is Nicolás Guillén's widely anthologized, but little understood "Sensemayá: canto para matar una culebra," which is the subject of the next chapter.

3

Carnival and Afro-Cuban Ritual in Nicolás Guillén's "Sensemayá: canto para matar una culebra"

> va la comparsa ondulando
> como si fuera un majá
>
> [The *comparsa* moves
> as if it were a *majá*]
>
> Alfonso Camín, "Carnaval en la Habana"

> Algunas representaciones pantomímicas . . . las reprodujeron los negros en Cuba, como parecen demostrarlo los tradicionales bailes de "matar la culebra". . . que fueron usuales en las fiestas callejeras del "Día de Reyes" y en las carnavales comparsas afrocubanas que en parte sustituyeron aquella saturnal africana que ya se ve desvaneciendo por el desprecio que suele merecer en Cuba lo raigalmente folklórico, a causa de malhadados prejuicios.
>
> [Some pantomimic representations . . . are reproduced by the Cuban Negroes, as the traditional dances for "killing the snake" would seem to demonstrate. These were typical in the street festivities of "Día de Reyes" and in the Afro-Cuban carnival *comparsas*, which in part substituted that African saturnalia that is now disappearing because of the disdain that deeply rooted folklore tends to incur in Cuba, as a result of unfortunate prejudices.]
>
> Fernando Ortiz, *Los bailes y el teatro de los negros*

A study of representations of Afro-Cuban carnival traditions in Cuban poetry would be incomplete without a thorough examination of Nicolás Guillén's widely read and anthologized "Sensemayá: canto para matar una culebra" (1934). I will begin this chapter with a discussion of past readings of the poem, focusing mainly on (mis)interpretations of its key terms, the significances of which are essential to its overall meaning. I will then examine the relationship between "Sensemayá" and nineteenth-century celebrations of Día de Reyes, and demonstrate that Guillén's poem is also intimately related to traditional twentieth-century Afro-Cuban *comparsas*, which many experts consider to be the modern offspring of the former (Orovio, *El carnaval habanero* 9, Ortiz, *La antigua fiesta* 20 n. 13,

"Viejos carnavales" 214).[1] More specifically, I will argue that "Sensemayá" can be read as a carefully constructed response to the many bans that were enacted against Afro-Cuban carnival processions during the early decades of the twentieth century.

While the act of killing the snake in "Sensemayá" can certainly be seen as a re-creation of traditional chants for killing snakes, I contend that it is also a metaphor for the government's efforts to eliminate carnival processions and other Afro-Cuban cultural manifestations in Cuba, such as the rites and religious practices associated with Palo Monte (Mayombe) and the Abakuá secret society. This latter claim might seem implausible to some modern readers, but when we consider the meaning of the chant that is repeated throughout the poem ("Mayombe—bombe—mayombé!") and uncover the latent connection that links the image of the snake wrapped around a tree—one of the central images in "Sensemayá"—to a well-known symbol of the birth of Ñáñiguismo, this reading is quite seductive. Finally, in the conclusion I posit that by "killing" the snake in their carnival celebrations, Afro-Cubans were not acting out a ritual elimination of evil, but rather were taking part in an act that for them symbolized the creature's rebirth and guaranteed its survival. These ideas will be discussed at length in due course, but first a detailed discussion of past interpretations of some of the key terms found in "Sensemayá"—most of which have confounded readers and critics since its first publication in *West Indies, Ltd.* in 1934—is in order.

"Sensemayá": Still Misunderstood After All These Years

"Sensemayá" is arguably Nicolás Guillén's most widely read, recited, and anthologized poem, and it is therefore hardly surprising that over the past seventy-five years it has been the subject of numerous critical appraisals of widely varying quality and focus.[2] Brief, superficial folkloric readings of the poem are especially common, and shaky explanations of the poem's title and key vocabulary far outweigh convincing interpretations of them.[3] Many critics have essentially disregarded the deep significance of the poem's celebrated chant by referring to it as "apparent nonsense lines" (Smart, *Nicolás Guillén*, 37), a collection of "made-up words known as *jitanjáforas*" (Branche 178), "nonsense words and onomatopoeia" (L. Williams 18), "a verse . . . of purely euphonic values" (Augier, *Nicolás Guillén*

141, "Inscripción" 270), "terms without logical meaning," and "irrational utterances" (Ruffinelli 47, 48).

This tendency to downplay or overlook the significance of the repeated chant in "Sensemayá" is particularly perplexing, since the terms "Mayombe," "mayombé" (which is not a simple rhythmic variation, as we will see below), and "bombe" are loaded with meanings that are essential to the poem. On the one hand, *Mayombe* clearly evokes the Bantu-speaking cultures of central Africa, and specifically the coastal regions of what was then the French Congo. More importantly, however, *Mayombe* refers to what one expert has called the "most African and least syncretized" of the three principal *ramas* [branches] of Palo Monte (Klein). The term *mayombé*, which many have read as a mere variant of the former, actually signifies the *mayombero* himself, the priest, sorcerer, or ritual doctor. Indeed, the following chant (oral versions of which Guillén may have known), which was transcribed by Lydia Cabrera in *El Monte*, clearly demonstrates that *mayombé* essentially amounts to a shortened version of *mayombero*:

> Mayombé fué bueno en Guinea
> ¿Cuando viene?
> Ya tá puntando la Nganga
> . . . .
> Mayombé bueno en Guinea
> abre camino
> en todo lo lao
> ¡Mayombero abre camino! (129)

All of these details are especially important in the context of my contention that the killing of the snake in "Sensemayá" can be interpreted as, among other things, a metaphor for government efforts to eliminate Afro-Cuban religious practices. Indeed, the *mayomberos*—who were condemned as incarnations of "la mala vida cubana" in Fernando Ortiz's *Los negros brujos*—were widely associated with the dark arts, witchcraft, and cultural and moral degeneration (Ayorinde 18). As David Brown has noted, from the end of the nineteenth century well into the twentieth, *mayomberos* "were special targets of ferocious police raids intended to stamp out brujería" and were perceived to be widely responsible for "social 'delinquency' in general, and the ritual murder of white children for their blood, in particular" (*Santería* 57).

The fact that so many modern critics have essentially disregarded the crucial importance of *Mayombe* and *mayombé* (*mayombero*) in their readings of "Sensemayá" is hard to explain, as these terms have been familiar in Cuba since long before Guillén wrote his poem. Moreover, since the early decades of the twentieth century, those unfamiliar with Afro-Cuban religions would have had easy access to definitions and discussions of Palo Mayombe and the related *mayombero* (inaccurate as some of them may be) in works such as Ortiz's *Los negros brujos* and *Glosario de afronegrismos* (1923), Roche y Monteagudo's *La policía y sus misterios en Cuba* (1908, 1914, 1925), and Rómulo Lachantañeré's two major studies on Afro-Cuban religions, *¡¡Oh, mío Yemayá!!* [Oh, My Yemayá!](1938) and *Manual de santería* [Manual of Santería] (1942).[4] With the exception of Roche y Monteagudo's study, all of these works have been available to modern critics in reprints for some time. I should add that the same terms or slight variations of them are defined (again, somewhat inaccurately in most cases) in the glossaries of several of the major poetry anthologies associated with Afrocubanismo, as well as in those of anthologies published in the last few decades.[5] Finally, the terms in question are also defined or discussed—often at considerable length—in many contemporary books on Afro-Cuban religions.[6]

Some widely read critics, such as Vera Kutzinski, Antonio Benítez-Rojo, and Josaphat Kubayanda, have correctly argued that these seemingly innocent *jitanjáforas* are actually terms that are essential to the overall meaning of the poem. For example, Kutzinski's brief explanation of Mayombe—even if it is not entirely accurate—clearly separates her pioneering analysis of "Sensemayá" from many previous studies that essentially ignore the term. Kutzinski paraphrases Ortiz by noting that "Guillén's use of 'mayombe' derived from the Cuban *mayombero*, which, according to Fernando Ortiz, is the name for an Afro-Cuban conjuror (brujo) from the Congo region" (*Against* 139). In fact, Mayombe is not derived from *mayombero*, but rather, as we have seen, it is the very root of the latter term, and also signifies the actual "brujería negra" that this figure practices.

For his part, Benítez-Rojo correctly demonstrates how Mayombe carries the reader back and forth between Cuba and Africa. As he puts it, "the word 'Mayombe' carries us to Bantu culture and alludes to magical practice . . . to look for its locus in Africa" (297). "Nevertheless," he adds, "having invested the popular dance of the killing of the snake with African ritual, Guillén's poem returns to Cuba, to the Día de Reyes" (*Repeating*

Island 297–98). Finally Kubayanda, whose study of "Sensemayá" is brief but enlightening, posits that Guillén's poem represents "a reenactment of a magical snake rite of the Cuban Mayombe sect . . . of Central African Bantu origin" (105), but he also overlooks the deep significance of Guillén's daring invocation of this religion and its representative figure, which were widely maligned icons of fear in early twentieth-century Cuba.

The possible meanings of "bombe" have been largely overlooked by literary critics, most likely because this particular term is not defined in Fernando Ortiz's *Glosario de afronegrismos*, nor is it found in any of the glossaries of the major anthologies of *poesía negra*. Antonio Olliz-Boyd and Eugenio Matibag are among the very few who have given this question any real thought, but neither provides a convincing explanation. Olliz-Boyd's definition of *bombe* in his unpublished 1974 dissertation reads as follows: "The typical drum of almost all African cultures is called a 'bombo' or a 'bomba.' An adjustment of this African word to Spanish morphology produces the verb 'bombar' to play the drum. The command form of bombar would be bombé [*sic*]" (188). Olliz-Boyd's first claim is very problematic, especially because he does not support it with a single example of an African drum called by these names—even though there are several (see Ortiz, *Instrumentos* Vol. 2, 36–37)—but more importantly because he also ignores well-known meanings of "bomba" and "bombo" in the Hispanic Caribbean: for example, *bomba* is an Afro–Puerto Rican musical genre and dance as well as the name of a drum played in it. And though Ortiz notes that he had heard "bomba" used in Santiago de Cuba to refer to drums in a generic sense, he stresses that such was no longer the case (*Instrumentos* Vol. 2, 37).

Likewise, although "bombo" was sometimes used interchangeably with "bomba" to refer to the Puerto Rican music and drum referred to above, most experts agree that in Cuba the term denotes a bass drum of the same name, which is of European, not African, origin (Ortiz, *Instrumentos* Vol. 2, 37; Orovio, *Cuban music* 31; Roy 239). The second part of Olliz-Boyd's explanation seems especially contrived. On the one hand, the verb "bombar" does not exist in Spanish. On the other, in the opening lines of his poem Guillén is invoking the *mayombero* and his witchcraft, not calling him to play the drums. Matibag's explanation of "bombe" is similar to the one offered by Olliz-Boyd. It is also unconvincing largely because he offers several possibilities without explaining how they are related to the specific Cuban context (the chant for killing a snake) of Guillén's poem.

"*Bombé* [sic]: a popular Antillian black dance, such as the *Bombé serré* of Martinique; or, a personalized drum of Ghanaian origin . . . ; or a dance such as the *bomba* held on Sundays, with rhythm by a lead dancer, with spectators singing responses in chorus, playing two drums and two maracas, and beating on a bench with two sticks" (158). Such explanations fail to answer an obvious question: Why did Guillén use "bombe" if he meant something else, such as "bombo," "bombé," or "bomba?"

My own sense is that "bombe" has a hidden (and specifically Afro-Cuban) significance that is revealed only by its relation to the other words in the chant, and is reinforced by the very title of the poem. I think "bombe," in combination with the "mayombé" that follows it, is an invocation of the *majá*, the Cuban boa that is held sacred by every Afro-Cuban religion and cult, is a faithful guardian of the *santero* and the *mayombero brujo*, a bodyguard of priests and priestesses, and is present (either in body or spirit) at *plantes, bembés, toques*, and other similar celebrations (Cabrera, *Animales* 12–13, 16). Let me explain. As a friend and expert in Afro-Cuban religions reminded me, the *majá* is referred to by various names in the Bantu language spoken in Cuba. In her *Vocabulario Congo*, for example, Cabrera lists *mboma, bomboma, bumbema*, among others, as variants of the name for this sacred snake. The last name refers specifically to the Majá de Santa María, the largest of the Cuban boas, and the one most commonly linked to the Yoruban deity Yemayá. What I posit here is that the *majá*, known for its slyness, is hidden in the poem but appears when the words in the chant flow together, as they would when repeated rapidly. This could produce, with a simple shifting of the hyphens, the following: Mayombe—bombema—yombé. While the resulting "bombema" does not precisely match any of the variations of the name of the *majá* cited by Cabrera, its similarity to the last two mentioned above is striking: indeed, it is a combination of the first half of one and the second half of the other. It is entirely conceivable that Guillén purposefully melded the names in order to produce a more sonorous and consistent chant, or he might have even confused them and come up with "bombema" by accident.[7] As for the leftover "yombé," it is the name of a specific ethnic group from the Mayombe region of the French Congo, and as such its presence here would make perfect sense.

If the name of the *majá* is indeed hidden within this chant, as I posit here, this trick by the author reflects the common Western depiction of the snake as a sneaky and deceptive creature, at the same time that it plays the notion of name taboo, which Fernando Ortiz discusses in *La antigua fiesta afrocubana del Día de Reyes*. In this important study, which Guillén clearly knew and which likely inspired "Sensemayá," Ortiz notes that among primitive cultures it is common that what is feared is not named, and he cites traditions from Spain, Italy, and India that lead the superstitious to substitute a name like "the pest" or "the beast" for "snake" (43).

The namesake of "Sensemayá" has also been subjected to invented, inadequate, confusing, and unsubstantiated explanations. One of the earliest and most elaborate can be found in Manuel Cuéllar Vizcaino's little-known 1935 article "La leyenda de Sensemayá," which was published in the short-lived Afro-Cuban monthly *Adelante*. The author claims that the legend, which tells of a mysterious woman who responds to the magical name Sensemayá and saves a boy from the grips of a serpent-like creature, supposedly came directly "from the lips of Lucumís," that Cuéllar had met at a Cuban sugar plantation. However, in an article published nearly two decades later, Cuéllar admitted to having fabricated the story, and stressed that the name was of Guillén's invention.[8]

In more recent publications, such as Enrique Noble's 1973 anthology *Literatura afro-hispanoamericana* [Anthology of Afro-Hispanic-American Literature], Sensemayá is defined as an "onomatopoetic word with musical and sorcerous connotations" (47). Though this definition is not completely off track, Noble, like so many other critics before and after him, does not venture to discuss the term's possible origins or its specific meaning. Likewise, in one of the few decent annotated editions of Guillén's poetry, Luis Íñigo Madrigal—in a footnote to the poem—essentially strips Sensemayá of its deeply Cuban significance, at the same time that he overly simplifies the term by defining it as a "*jitanjáfora* with African resonances" (95 n. 5). Armando González-Pérez offers a typically insufficient explanation of the meaning of Sensemayá by calling it an "onomatopoeic word with great musicality and magical power, which repeated constantly provides a hypnotizing effect on a serpent that one wishes to kill" (*Acercamiento* 171). Valdés-Cruz similarly contends that Sensemayá is a magic word, the frequent repetition of which brings about the death of the snake (*Poesía negroide* 76).

One particular gloss of Sensemayá, which appears in footnotes to the poem in several popular college-level textbooks that have been published or reedited in recent years, is as intriguing as it is confusing. It states that Sensemayá is a goddess represented by a serpent in "one of the Afro-

Cuban religions." However, the editors of the textbooks in question do not specify which Afro-Cuban religion, nor do they indicate the source of this elusive information.[9] Antonio Benítez-Rojo similarly speaks of Sensemayá as a "serpent-god" (not a goddess) (*Repeating Island* 297), but does not explain the origins of the name. In his 1996 book *Afro-Cuban Religious Experience*, Eugenio Matibag, who incorrectly states that Guillén's poem first appeared in *Motivos de son* in 1930, offers a similar definition of Sensemayá, but does not expound sufficiently. According to him the term is related to the Kikongo language, and refers to "a spirit represented at times by a snake" (158). Though he is correct to state that only "a reader familiar with the vocabulary" of the poem can appreciate its meaning, he suggests his own uncertainty about the meaning of Sensemayá—as he does about "bombe"—by failing to explain how or why he arrived at his own definition of it.

I find it especially telling that in his article, "La religion en la poesía mulata" [Religion in Mulatto Poetry] (1937), Fernando Ortiz—who was at the time the foremost expert on so-called *afrocubanismos*—suggests that Sensemayá is the name of the snake (159), but then neither offers an explanation of the term's meaning nor discusses its possible etymology. Ortiz's notable lack of commentary on the term indicates to me that he, like most contemporary readers of Guillén's poem, was not sure what to make of it. Like Ortiz, Vera Kutzinski suggests in her enlightening analysis of Guillén's poem that Sensemayá is a proper name, which refers to the snake, but she does not elaborate (*Against* 143).

I believe that Sensemayá is a term of Guillén's invention that is meant to evoke the image of the snake on the one hand, and to underscore the poem's crucial links to Afro-Cuban cultural and religious practices of various origins on the other. First of all, the term shares very obvious phonetic similarities with Yemayá, and can thus be seen as an evocation of this important Yoruban *orisha*, goddess of the seas and divinity of motherhood who is widely known and recognized throughout Cuba. Such a theory is made all the more plausible when we take into consideration the fact that Yemayá is intimately related to the snake (and more specifically to the Majá de Santa María whose Cuban Bantu name is invoked in the repeated chant), the aspects of which she assumes in one of her many *caminos* (Cabrera, *Los animales* 13). The term *camino* as used here refers to the different manifestations or avatars of the *orishas*. Some *orishas*, such as Yemayá, have several *caminos*, others have only one. We should note, moreover, that in her name as well as in the title of Guillén's poem, we once again find that the name of the snake (*majá* = mayá) is craftily conjured, but not explicitly stated.[10] It is worth adding here that Yamayá is frequently spelled with a "j" by African authors, such as Femi Ojo-Ade, who writes of Marcelino Arozarena's positive evocations of "Yemajá, Ogun, and other gods" (53).

The meaning of the first half of "Sensemayá" is not quite so clear, but there are a number of possibilities. Antonio Olliz-Boyd offers one of the most interesting explanations, even if it is not completely convincing. He posits that it evokes "Sansa," a word of apparent Congolese origin that means "Providence" (190).[11] However, Olliz-Boyd does not demonstrate that such a term was known or used by speakers of Cuban Bantu, nor does he explain how or where Guillén might have come up with the word.[12] Moreover, using such logic we could also posit that Guillén had any of a number of terms from the Bantu language spoken in Cuba in mind: *sense* [deer], *sanse* [fish], *sensa* [visitor], or *sansi* [crab], among others that can be found in Cabrera's *Vocabulario congo* (272–73).

My own sense is that the meaning of *sense* can be explained by its evocation of an Abakuá term that was very widely known in Cuba in the 1930s, but was often erroneously linked by several leading "experts" on Afro-Cuban religions to so-called *brujería*. Indeed, Guillén's *sense* could be a reference to the *sése eribó*, the most sacred of the ritual drums of the *ñáñigos*. His variation with an "n" is not at all arbitrary, as it is easily explained by the fact that this sacred instrument was commonly referred to by outsiders as *senseribó* in the early decades of the twentieth century, and it appears as such in many literary and musical compositions associated with Afrocubanismo.[13] But it is also possible that Guillén was influenced by the incorrect usage of *senseribó* in texts such as *Los negros brujos* and *La policía y sus misterios en Cuba*, the first of which Guillén was reading when he composed "Sensemayá." In his study Ortiz explains that practitioners of *brujería* used this term to bring an end to the "epileptic fits" brought on by spiritual possession. "Para que cece el ataque, se tocan los tambores . . . [y] se grita al paciente repetidas veces, hasta que cece: *senseribó, senseribó, epé mancoó*" (94, emphasis in the original) [In order to bring an end to the attack, the drums are played . . . [and] they scream at the patient various times until it ceases: *senseribó, senseribó, epé mancoó*.] For his part, Roche y Monteagudo, probably borrowing directly from Ortiz, also claims that this chant was sung to bring an end to the "attacks" of spirits (2nd ed. 108). Even though it is not likely that the Abakuá term *senseribó* was actually used in such a context, the fact that two of the leading authorities of the day on Afro-Cuban religions and rituals claimed that it was could explain Guillén's inclusion of "sense" in his invented chant for killing a snake. In any case, all of the interpretations of the term "Sensemayá" that I address here imply that it is a term of Guillén's invention. Moreover, it seems clear to me that this key term can and should be understood as a symbolic melding of words of various African origins and meanings, which would corroborate claims made by others that this particular poem "pulls together different African experiences" (Kubayanda 105) and combines sounds with distant geographical referents and words inspired by diverse African languages (di Leo 96).

"Sensemayá" and Afro-Cuban Carnival

In "La religion en la poesía mulata," a forty-page article published in *Estudios Etnosociológicos* in 1937, Fernando Ortiz mentions only a handful of the poems of Afrocubanismo, and he discusses only two by Nicolás Guillén: "Sensemayá" and "Balada del Güije" [Ballad of the River Spirit]. Ortiz considers both of these poems to be fine illustrations of how so-called *poesía mulata* reflects both the "religious emotions" of Afro-Cubans and the "rudimentary" nature of their rituals (158, 160). In his musings on the first of these poems, Ortiz posits that since there are no harmful species of snakes in Cuba that would necessitate such "defensive conjurations" as that depicted in "Sensemayá," Guillén's poem seems more like an aesthetic revival of an African tradition than a Cuban one (160). Nonetheless, he establishes an important connection between "Sensemayá" and an African-derived cultural manifestation that was performed by Cuban slaves.

> El "matar la culebra" ha sido tema y nombre de un baile y canción que fue muy popular entre los festivales de los negros habaneros del siglo pasado, en su famoso saturnal del Día de Reyes, como luego, en sus esparcimientos carnavalescos. Y ya entonces debió de ser traído de África, como un rito procesional de purificación colectiva, paralelo al de matar al dragón sagrado, que aún sobrevive en los carnavales europeos, y el de pasear el monstruo de la *tarasca* en las procesiones del Corpus Christi. (160)

["Killing the Snake" has been the theme and the name of a dance and a song that were very popular during the festivities of Havana Negroes of the last century, during their famous Saturnalia of Día de Reyes, and later, in their carnival diversions. And before that it must have been brought from Africa as a processional rite of collective purification, parallel to the killing of the sacred dragon, which still survives in European carnivals, and the parading of the serpent-like monster in the processions of Corpus Christi.]

Only a handful of literary critics—most notably Vera Kutzinski and Antonio Benítez-Rojo—have revisited this key relationship between "Sensemayá" and the Afro-Cuban ritual dance that was traditionally performed by slaves when they were symbolically freed each year on Día de Reyes.[14] I should point out, however, that neither Kutzinski nor Benítez-Rojo mentions Ortiz's article, and it is therefore not clear that they were even aware that he had noted this crucial connection between "Sensemayá" and Afro-Cuban carnival traditions back in 1937.

That so few critics have examined, or even noted, the relationship between "Sensemayá" and Día de Reyes is especially surprising given that in a published interview with Angel Augier from the early 1960s, Guillén explicitly linked his poem to the "cantos para matar culebras" that were traditionally performed on that day by Afro-Cuban slaves. Kutzinski and Benítez-Rojo have rightly argued that Guillén's remarks—which they both cite in their studies, and I cite again below—offer crucial clues as to how to read and interpret "Sensemayá":

Recuerdo el día que lo compuse: 6 de enero de 1932, Día de Reyes. Yo estaba enfermo, en cama y vivía en un hotel habanero de la calle de San Rafael. El ocio forzado dio tal vez alas a mi pensamiento, que voló hacia mi infancia. Desde niño, en mi Camagüey natal, resonaba en mí una canción de negros, una canción popular, hecha también para matar una culebra: "Sámbala, culembe, sámbala culembe, sámbala culembe..."[15] ¿Cómo, por qué me venía esto a la memoria entonces? Acaso porque había estado leyendo páginas de Don Fernando Ortiz, sobre los negros brujos; tal vez por el prestigio del día, la evocación de lo que fue bajo la colonia, en Cuba, el Día de Reyes. El día esperado, el único, el grande, el magnífico día en que los esclavos negros recibían de sus amos blancos permiso para que cada cual se sintiera en su país y cantara en el seno de su familia y de su tribu y adorara a sus dioses y volviera a ser vasallo de su rey. (qtd. in Augier, *Notas* I, 112–13)

[I remember the day I wrote it: January 6, 1932, Día de Reyes. I was sick in bed and living in a Havana hotel on Calle San Rafael. Perhaps the enforced inactivity gave wings to my thoughts, which flew back to my childhood. Since my childhood in my native Camagüey, a Negro song resounded within me, a popular song that was also composed for killing snakes: "Sámbala, culembe, sámbala culembe, sámbala culembe . . ." How, why did this come to my mind at that moment? Perhaps because I had been reading pages by Fernando Ortiz, on the black *brujos*; perhaps because of the prestige of the day, the evocation of what once existed under colonial rule, in Cuba, "Día de Reyes." The longed-for day, the one, the great, the magnificent day when the black slaves received from their white masters permission for each one to feel like he was in his homeland and to sing amidst his family and his tribe and worship his gods and be once again the vassal of his king.]

In her lucid reading of the poem, Kutzinski emphasizes that Guillén's observations here attest to the fact that "Sensemayá" is clearly not the simplistic folkloric poem that "most critics have made it out to be" (*Against*, 136), but rather a pivotal text in his oeuvre that can be read on multiple levels. On the one hand Kutzinski observes that through its intimate link with Afro-Cuban Día de Reyes celebrations, this poem serves to keep alive a lost tradition by recreating "an ancestral ritual designed to reaffirm and strengthen the slaves' ties with their African heritage" (*Against* 140). On the other hand, she posits that the poem's invocation of a specific African-derived ritual—the traditional "canto para matar la culebra"— underscores on an allegorical plain Afro-Cuban resistance to slavery during colonial times and, by extension, Cuban resistance to U.S. imperialism in the early years of the Republic (*Against* 140–44, "Miraculous Weapons" 148). Benítez-Rojo, who acknowledges that his reading of the poem is similar to Kutzinski's, interprets the snake-killing dance in "Sensemayá" as an "exorcising [of] ritual violence to prevent social violence," and he adds that the death of the snake (which he refers to as a sacrificed god) "narrated in the present, is indefinite, continuing as long as racial inequality persists" (*Repeating Island* 299).

I agree with many aspects of Kutzinski and Benítez-Rojo's readings of "Sensemayá," but my own reading of the poem relies on several important points that neither critic explores in his/her respective studies, and which critics before and after them have also largely ignored. Most importantly, I believe that Guillén is not only invoking Afro-Cuban Día de Reyes celebrations in "Sensemayá," but also their twentieth century offspring: traditional Afro-Cuban *comparsas* and *congas*, which had been banned in Havana for nearly two decades when he penned "Sensemayá." We should recall here that the *comparsas* of the early twentieth century often included variations of the traditional snake dances that Guillén so fondly recalls in his poem. For example, as Alejo Carpentier notes in *Music in Cuba*, these carnival processions had specific themes such as "a snake, represented by a huge figure held on high by an expert dancer, [which] served as a focal point for dancing and singing." Echoing Guillén's recollection of the chants he heard in Camagüey during his youth, Carpentier adds that the *comparseros* would pretend to "kill the snake" and chant: "Mamita, mamita,/ yen, yen, yen:/ que me mata la culebra,/ . . . Mírale los ojos que parecen candela; / mírale los diente,/ que parecen filé" (260). I would add here that much like Carpentier's poems on Afro-Cuban themes—especially "Liturgia" and "Juego santo"—Guillén's "Sensemayá" evokes several other African-derived traditions that were maligned at the time, and it can thus be seen as an expression of his defiance of the prevailing opinion among middle- and upper-class whites and blacks alike that *comparsas*, *congas*, and many other manifestations of Afro-Cuban dance, music, or rituals should be outlawed or eliminated.

In her study of "Sensemayá," Kutzinski makes no reference at all to traditional twentieth-century Afro-Cuban carnival ensembles. Benítez-Rojo does make such a connection, but his comments are not completely accurate. As he puts it, "In 1932, when Guillén composed 'Sensemayá,' the Africanized carnival of Día de Reyes had ceased to exist; it had been prohibited in 1880 . . . Nevertheless, the Negroes of Havana had managed to put their dances into the whites' carnival. And, organized in *comparsas*, or carnivalesque troupes of musicians and dancers, they continued to dance through the streets of the city" (299). The problem with Benítez-Rojo's observation is that it does not stress the important fact that Guillén wrote "Sensemayá" in the midst of the repressive regime of Gerardo Machado, during which traditional Afro-Cuban *comparsas*, *congas*, and similar public displays of Afro-Cuban music and dance were officially banned in

Havana and many other Cuban cities, just as they had been many times since the final decades of the nineteenth century. As Maya Roy has noted, these bans were enacted during the Machadato with the aim of suppressing activities "that might give rise to opposition on the part of those social strata most adversely affected by the government's policies and it rampant corruption. As it happened the principal players in the carnivals were precisely the former slaves and their descendants, the mulattos and the poor white people who lived side by side on the outskirts" (36).

Those Afro-Cubans who did manage "to dance through the streets" of Havana, as Benítez-Rojo puts it, during the carnival seasons of the era either did so in open defiance of the bans, or were compelled to perform in "de-africanized" ensembles that were highly regulated by city officials. Keeping these details in mind, it is very significant that Guillén penned "Sensemayá" precisely during a time when traditional Afro-Cuban *comparsas*—much like the Día de Reyes festivities that had been banned decades earlier—were basically things of the past.

It is important to stress here, as those familiar with his work already know, that Guillén not only celebrated the importance of the African components of the "Cuban cocktail," as he playfully referred to his nation's collective identity in the prologue to *Sóngoro cosongo*, but also outspokenly criticized those who refused to acknowledge the profound "injection" of Africanness that flowed through the veins of Cubans of all classes and colors ("Prólogo" 10). In an article titled "¡Negra, mueve la cintura!" [Black Woman, Shake Your Hips!], for example, Guillén reiterated his opinion that African elements could be appreciated in all Cubans and in all aspects of Cuban culture, citing the popular *conga* as an example: "Cuando pasa una conga, 'arrollando,' arrastra consigo hombres y mujeres de todo color, pero cuyo denominador común es la poderosa influencia del ancestro africano, heredada o adquirida" (22) [When a *conga* passes by, 'arrollando,' it drags with it men and women of every color, but whose common denominator is the powerful influence of the African ancestor, inherited or acquired.] However, later in the same essay he ridiculed Cuba's middle-class majority—both white and colored—for their hypocritical views toward such African-derived cultural manifestations, noting that the same individuals who couldn't resist shaking their hips to the "devilish rhythm" of the *conga* had no problem condemning these spectacles when in the company of their "equals" (22).

Such comments underscore Guillén's opposition to campaigns to prohibit *comparsas, congas, rumba, son*, and so many other unique manifestations of the nation's African heritage. An article titled "Cada año es carnaval" [Every Year is a Carnival] that Guillén published some years later in the Havana weekly, *Bohemia*, also underscores his disagreement with the bans against Afro-Cuban carnival celebrations in the early decades of the twentieth century. In the opening paragraphs of this essay Guillén bemoans the drawn-out demise of these colorful spectacles in Havana, and he mocks those who disparage traditional *comparsas* as atavistic throwbacks to the slave era:

> la famosa fiesta ha ido apagándose entre nosotros y hoy es apenas un opaco dibujo de lo que ataño fuera alegre, ingenua y policromada calcomanía ... Nuestro carnaval se muere, con los miembros rígidos y los ojos muy abiertos, como atacado por una serpiente venenosa ... [Las] mismas comparas están siendo educadas como señoritas de casa particular. Cuando se las ve en el desfile, se comprende con un poco de tristeza que ellas han surgido de una circunstancia en cierto modo "académica," y que están preparadas para portarse bien en sociedad. ... Las comparsas—no lo olvidéis—tienen sus enemigos; hay mucho espíritu "fisto" que las considera una vergüenza, un motivo de sonrojo, y como parte de tradiciones que arrancan de los no muy lejanos días esclavistas. (44)

> [the famous fiesta has gradually been erased among us and it is today scarcely an opaque sketch of what was, back in the good old days, a cheerful, innocent and multicolored decalcomania ... Our carnival is dying, with its rigid extremities and its eyes wide open, as if attacked by a venomous serpent... [The] *comparsas* themselves are being educated like high-class little ladies. When one sees them in the parade, he understands with a bit of sadness that they have emerged from a somewhat "academic" circumstance, and that they are prepared to behave well in society... *Comparsas*—and don't you forget it—have their enemies; there are plenty of feisty souls that consider them to be an embarrassment, a cause for blushing, manifestations of traditions that hark back to the not-so-distant days of slavery.]

In the same essay Guillén laments the fact that "with the swipe of a pen" government officials of earlier decades (he is obviously referring to

Machado and other officials of his administration) were essentially able to wipe out what had once been spontaneous, invigorating, and, most importantly, authentic African-derived cultural traditions.

Such opinions serve to support my contention that "Sensemayá" can be read on one level as a defense of traditional Afro-Cuban *comparsas* and *congas*, and, on another, as a lightly veiled criticism of the government-led campaigns that pushed for their demise. Moreover, if we consider the fact that many of the poems of *West Indies, Ltd.* contain "indictments against the abuses and injustices to which the people of the Antilles—and particularly Cubans and Blacks—are collectively subjected" (Márquez 21), it makes sense that this poem, which so many critics have incorrectly read as a playful piece of folklore, would also contain a response to specific injustices levied against Afro-Cubans.

While Guillén's reference to *Los negros brujos* in his interview with Angel Augier might be taken as a tacit nod to Ortiz's highly unfavorable assessment of everything from *brujería*—embodied in the figure of the Mayombe witchdoctor—to traditional Afro-Cuban *comparsas* in that work, my own sense is that Ortiz's negative attitude toward African-derived culture in that and other early works served as a catalyst for Guillén's defense of them. Indeed, by poeticizing the figure of the Mayombero—who Ortiz considered to be among "the most repugnant and harmful figures of the Cuban criminal underworld" (185) and Rafael Roche y Monteagudo accused of "employing the viscera of children to cure his clients" (2nd ed. 254)—and celebrating the traditional snake chants that were associated with the Día de Reyes festivities and the modern day carnival *comparsas* that Ortiz and many others had maligned as symbols of African primitivism and backwardness, Guillén, like Carpentier before him, was carrying out an act of literary rebellion against Cuba's cultural mainstream.

We should recall that in *Los negros brujos*, Ortiz implicitly links the image of the snake—which is so prevalent in Guillén's poem—to the supposed atavistic characteristics of *comparsas*. He refers to a well-known, early twentieth-century ensemble called "La Culebra" as an example of how the "savage" names chosen for the Afro-Cuban carnival ensembles reflected the "primitive psyche" of their African members (60). This is quite significant in light of my contention that "Sensemayá" can be read as a reaction to both prevailing attitudes about Afro-Cuban *comparsas* and *congas,* and to the official bans that were enacted against them. Indeed, on an allegorical plane, the act of killing the snake in "Sensemayá" can be seen as an elimination of these spectacles and the "atavistic" African-derived cults and religions that were so frequently associated with them.

If these ideas seem contrived, I invite the reader to recall that, on the one hand, Día de Reyes festivities, *comparsas*, and *congas* have traditionally been associated with snakes in Cuban literature, folklore, music, and popular discourse. On the other hand these carnivalesque processions of Afro-Cubans had long been associated with *ñáñiguismo*—embodied in the prominent figure of the *diablito*—and with the superstitions, possessions, and other "dark" practices of *brujería*. All of these points are clearly illustrated in several poems that are considered in the present study. Pichardo Moya, for example, explicitly links his poetic recreation of an Afro-Cuban carnival ensemble to a serpent and, by extension, to slave-era "bailes y cantos de culebra." Moreover, he repeatedly links the *comparsa* and its members to the so-called Afro-Cuban underworld of black magic and sorcery. Likewise, we will see in Chapter 4 that in "Comparsa habanera," Emilio Ballagas also associates an Afro-Cuban *comparsa* with a snake ("Con su larga cola de culebra va. / Con su larga cola muriéndose va / la negra comprasa del guaricandá") and with the ritualistic possessions and "backward" superstitions of Afro-Cuban religions. Traditional *comparsas* are intimately associated with the image of the sacred Cuban boa in Marcelino Arozarena's "La comparsa del majá," which is discussed at length in Chapter 7. This poem's title and the snake dance that it recreates evoke the crucial links between modern-day *comparsas* and Día de Reyes "cantos y bailes de culebra."

"Sensemayá" and Ñáñiguismo

The invocation of the *mayombero* in "Sensemayá" clearly establishes a connection between Guillén's poem and the practices of Palo Mayombe that were much despised at the time. My suggestion that the killing of the snake in "Sensemayá" also alludes to official efforts in the early decades of the twentieth century to stamp out *ñáñiguismo*, however, may seem implausible to many modern readers, especially since, to the best of my knowledge, no other literary critic has put forth such a theory. However, there are a number of factors that lend credibility to this argument. First of all, we must reiterate that *comparsas* were widely associated with *ñáñiguismo* throughout the early decades of the twentieth century. Ivor Miller notes in his recent study, *The Voice of the Leopard*, for example, that "Although not originally Carabalí, many Havana comparsa traditions acquired a pronounced Abakuá profile. Abakuá leaders played key roles in the early-twentieth-century comparsas. This is to be expected, because many barrios had their own Abakuá lodge, itself defined as a tierra (territory) that was significant to the identity of many barrio residents... In the ethos of the participants, the carnival comparsas seemed to take on the role of a nation-group during nineteenth-century Three Kings' Day"(162).

Miller points out, moreover, that the majority of the directors of the *comparsas* were Abakuá members, and that the rhythmic influence from the Abakuá has had a profound impact on *comparsa* music (163).

Perhaps most important, however, in terms of "Sensemayá" and its evocation of *ñáñiguismo*, is the symbolism of one of the poem's central images—the snake wrapped around a tree (not a "stick," "pole," "staff," or "stalk" as this key term is variously translated by critics and translators).[16] Indeed, even though Vera Kutzinski is correct when she insists that "This emblem is the clue to 'Sensemayá,'" her interpretation of it as a metaphor for the Aesculapian staff—the universally recognized "idiomatic signature of the medical profession"—overlooks the image's implicit evocation of specifically Afro-Cuban symbols (*Against* 138–39).[17]

I do not believe that the Aesculapian staff is the icon that Guillén had in mind when he wrote "Sensemayá," even if this image is implicitly evoked. It should be pointed out here that while "stick," "pole," "staff," and "stalk" may be acceptable translations for "palo" in some instances, none of these works in the context of "Sensemayá."[18] This key term, when used in a ritual sense in Cuba—and especially in relation to Palo Mayombe and Abakuá—evokes the many trees that are sacred to the adherents of each group, such as the ceiba and the royal palm. Moreover, sacred connotations aside, the most common meaning for "palo" in Cuba, and throughout the Hispanic Caribbean for that matter, is "tree." Kutzinski's use of "pole" in her English-language translation of "Sensemayá" and Benítez-Rojo's rendering of the term as "staff" (*Repeating Island* 297) are both inaccurate, as they fail to capture the implicit sacred connotations of "palo" as it relates to Afro-Cuban rites and rituals.

Kutzinski's explanation of the image of the snake wrapped around the "stick" or "pole" is certainly not completely off the mark, but in her attempts "to establish a link between Greek, West African, and Afro-American mythologies" Kutzinski overlooks a fundamental Afro-Cuban link

Cuadro que simboliza el nacimiento del ñañiguismo en el Africa Occidental, junto al río "Oldán-Ororó", donde se descubrió el misterio de Ecue.

FIGURE 3.1. "Scene that symbolizes the birth of Ñáñiguismo in West Africa, beside the 'Oldán-Ororó' River, where the mystery of Écue was discovered." The snake wrapped around the tree "symbolizes the healing arts and divination . . . [and] is associated with Nasakó, known in Abakuá mythology as a Kongo diviner" (Miller, *Voice* 52). This image is clearly evoked in Guillén's "Sensemayá." (From Roche y Monteagudo, 1925.)

to this ancient Greek symbol: a well-known iconographic representation of the birth of Ñáñiguismo (reproduced in many studies on the subject), which features the image of a snake wrapped around the trunk of a royal palm tree (fig. 3.1).[19] It is not a mere coincidence that this image recalls the universal symbol for medicine given that the snake in it—known in the Bríkamo language of the Abakuá as Ñangabión—"is the inseparable companion of Nasakó," the ritual doctor or sorcerer of the Abakuá hierarchy (Brown, *Light Inside* 56) and "symbolizes the healing arts and divination" (Miller, *Voice* 52).

This brings us to another important oversight in Kutzinski's reading of "Sensemayá." Though she is on the right track when she alludes to the relationship between the term *Mayombé* (the Afro-Cuban *mayombero*, or witchdoctor) and the image of the snake wrapped around the *palo* (*Against* 139), Kutzinski overlooks the connection between Guillén's poem and Ñáñiguismo. Indeed, the *mayombero* that Guillén explicitly invokes in the celebrated chant of his poem does not only allude to the Palo

Mayombe priest, but also to Nasakó, who shares much in common with the witchdoctors of Congo origin, as Brown explains:

> Often ranked among the fundamental plazas, the Nasakó is the only officer who is not sworn into the Abakuá lodge through the same initiation ceremonies as the other plazas. Nasakó is considered a Congo sorcerer, a *brujo*. He is specially consecrated in a formal ceremony and conducts much of the lodge's most critical ritual work, but technically he is separate from the baroko fundamento. His "attributes," the *mañongo umpabio* [sacred pot with a mix of rooster's blood and herbs] and the divining equipment, correspondingly, are identified with the "Congo" nation, not the "Carabalí." Indeed, his ritual toolkit, along with his herbal *wemba* [purifying herb] and *mokuba* [herbal liquid] . . . , are analogous in form and substance to the ritual media of the Palo Monte priest (*palero, mayombero, ngangulero*), which, in effect, he is. (*Light Inside* 63)

In *The Voice of the Leopard*, Ivor Miller similarly states that Nasakó is "known in Abakuá mythology as a Kongo diviner" and he adds that "In twentieth-century Cuba, Abakuá selected to receive the title Nasakó were often Tata Nkisi (leading practitioners of Palo Monte, a Cuban-Kongo system). In both Cuban systems the serpent is known as a protector of fundamentos. Given the closely related philosophies from regions of the Cross River to the Congo River, it was obvious that in Cuba the Abakuá and the Kongo healing systems would have led to their cross fertilization" (52).

In addition to the iconic representation of the birth of Abakuá (which, according to Rafael Roche y Monteagudo, was drawn by an eighty-six-year-old African informant), certain *anaforuana*, or sacred ideographic drawings, that belong to the *brujo* Nasakó depict the image of the palm tree and the snake Ñangabión, and by extension "recall the universal symbol for medicine" (Brown, *Light Inside* 56). One such Abakuá ideogram appeared in all three editions of Roche y Monteagudo's study (fig 3.2), and several others, variations of which Guillén had likely seen, are reproduced by Lydia Cabrera (fig. 3.3, 3.4). Much like these sacred ideograms, the image invoked in the line in question from Guillén's poem ("la culebra viene y se enreda en un palo" [the snake comes and wraps itself around a tree]) references the birth of Ñáñiguismo, the sacred healing powers of Nasakó, and the *mayombero* with whom this figure shares so much in common.

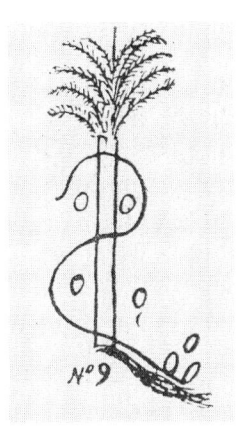

FIGURE 3.2. Sign of Nasakó depicting the snake, Ñangabión, wrapped around the palm tree. Abakuá chalk drawings, known as *firmas* or *anaforuana*, like the one depicted here (as well as those depicted in Figs. 3.3 and 3.4) may also have inspired the central image of the snake wrapped around the tree in Guillén's poem. (From Roche y Monteagudo, 1925.)

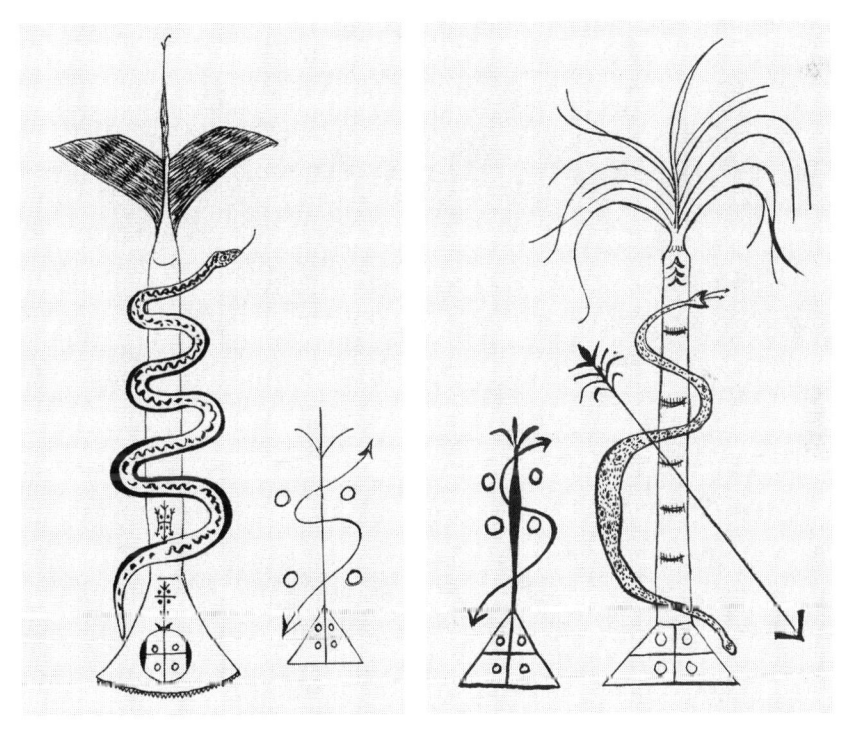

Left: FIGURE 3.3. Sign of Nasakó. These images are less abstract examples of *anaforuana* that represent the snake Ñangabión wrapped around a palm tree. (From Cabrera, *Anaforuana* 224.)

Right: FIGURE 3.4. Sign of Nasakó. (From Cabrera, *Anaforuana* 224.)

In light of these details it can be convincingly argued that the act of killing the snake in "Sensemayá," in addition to suggesting a symbolic eradication of *comparsas*, can be taken as a metaphor for official attempts to do away with Mayombe and Abakuá, for which the snake itself is a prominent symbol. The following lines of Guillén's poem lend themselves to such a reading:

> Tú le das con el hacha, y se muere:
> dale ya!
> No le des con el pie, que te muerde,
> no le des con el pie, que se va!
>
> Sensemayá, la culebra,
> sensemayá.
> Sensemayá, con sus ojos,
> sensemayá.
> Sensemayá, con su lengua,
> sensemayá.
> Sensemayá, con su boca,
> sensemayá!
>
> La culebra muerta no puede comer;
> la culebra muerta no puede silbar:
> no puede caminar,
> no puede correr!
> La culebra muerta no puede mirar;
> La culebra muerta no puede beber;
> No puede respirar,
> no puede morder!
>
> ¡Mayombe—bombe—mayombé!
> SENSEMAYÁ, LA CULEBRA.
> ¡Mayombe—bombe—mayombé!
> SENSEMAYÁ, NO SE MUEVE.
> ¡Mayombe—bombe—mayombé!
> SENSEMAYÁ, LA CULEBRA.
> ¡Mayombe—bombe—mayombé!
> ¡SENSEMAYÁ, SE MURIÓ...! (28–29)

When taken literally these lines simply state the obvious: killing the snake stops it from hissing, slithering, drinking, or biting. However, on an allegorical plane we see the desired consequences of the elimination of those Afro-Cuban cultural manifestations that the snake represents. For example, the definitive elimination of *comparsas* and *congas* would mean that they could no longer menace Cuban society with their strident chants, lubricious, snake-like line dancing, copious drinking, and allegedly aggressive disposition. The same can be said, to be sure, of the processions, communal rituals, initiation ceremonies, chants, dances, etcetera that were performed by the practitioners of Afro-Cuban religions or the members of the Abakuá secret society.

Guillén's metaphor of extermination in "Sensemayá" is actually not entirely original, as it recalls similar metaphors that prominent intellectuals had used to express their desire to rid Cuban society of everything from *comparsas*, to *brujería*, to *ñáñiguismo*. We have already seen how Ortiz argued that the first step in the battle against *brujería* was "the elimination of *brujos*" (193), and how he specifically referred to the *comparsa* known as "La Culebra" in a chapter in which he promoted the eradication of such emblems of Cuba's atavistic Afro-Cuban traditions. In Chapter 1 we also noted that in several of his editorials written during the heated *comparsa* controversy of 1916, Ramón Vasconcelos had essentially advocated the "killing" of *comparsas* and many other Afro-Cuban cultural manifestations with categorical statements: "How does one combat the illness? . . . I think that the infirm does not have a cure. Extinction is the surest approach ("Comparsas" 4); "Dead dog, no more rabies." ("Dos letras" 4).

It is worth a brief digression here to note that Guillén's *Motivos de son*, which had been printed in *Diario de la Marina* on April 30, 1930, provoked rather harsh and retrograde criticism from Vasconcelos, first in a personal letter dated May 18, and then in a published review in the same newspaper, which appeared in print on June 6.[20] Though Vasconcelos had significantly toned down his assaults on Afro Cuban cultural manifestations by the 1930s, one still senses the lingering prejudices and insecurities that led him to criticize Guillén's *son* poems with observations like the following:

La Habana le ha dado [a Guillén] su malicia y su manía de filosofar las trivialidades del barrio bajo. . . . eso es lo que canta Guillén y esto es lo que tiene cantores de sobra entre la gente de "cumbancha" que pone a San Lázaro detrás de la puerta y se da baños de albahaca para alejar la mala suerte ... [Guillén] debe universalizar su verso y su idea en vez de meterlos en el solar para que brinquen al son del bongó. (4)

[Havana has given to Guillén its wickedness and its compulsion to philosophize the trivialities of the lowly barrio ... that is what Guillén sings and it is what has more than enough singers among those partiers who put St. Lazarus behind the door and take basil baths to ward off bad luck ... Guillén should universalize his verse and his thought instead of sticking them in the urban patio so that they dance to the bongo.]

Guillén in turn responded to Vasconcelos in both a personal letter—dated June 5, the day before Vasconcelos's review appeared in print—and in an editorial titled "Sones y soneros," which was published in the *Diario de la Marina* on June 15. Though both of the young poet's responses to the well-known journalist, historian, and politician were somewhat tentative, he reminded Vasconcelos that the *son* was Cuba's most representative musical genre and intimated that he had chosen to celebrate Havana's so-called street culture as an act of defiance against the current tendency "to think with imported ideas" (*Epistolario* 38). It follows, then, that when Guillén penned "Sensemayá" two years later he was again acting in defiance of those Cubans who, like Vasconcelos, still promoted the nation's strong ties to Western European and North American culture and thought, at the same time that they pushed to abolish those cultural forms that were not favored by the mainstream.

Killing the Snake as an Act of Cultural Renewal

According to Lydia Cabrera, it is widely believed among members of the Abakuá secret society that in addition to being a faithful companion of the witchdoctor Nasakó, the snake Ñangabión was the first to sound the sacred Ékue drum by slithering over its goatskin head, and he therefore became inextricably linked with the Divine Voice (Cabrera, *Animales* 19). Moreover, as we have already seen, the snake—or, more specifically, the *majá*—is also the companion and "bodyguard" of the Santero and the

Mayombero *brujo*, and is considered the protector of both Abakuá and Congo fundamentos (Miller, *Voice* 52). Cabrera explains that precisely because the snake is so revered among practitioners of Afro-Cuban religions and members of the Abakuá secret society, that they would never unnecessarily deprive one of its life (*Animales* 16). This brings up an obvious question: why would the poetic voice encourage the killing of the snake ("Tú le das con el hacha, y se muere: /dale ya!" [You strike him with the ax, and he dies: / strike him now!]) as part of what is clearly meant to be an Afro-Cuban ritual? The answer, I think, can be found by uncovering a trick that Guillén is playing on his readers, which is informed by age-old African beliefs concerning the regenerating powers of the snake.

In his reading of "Sensemayá," Benítez-Rojo posits that the ritual killing of the snake with the blow of an ax was an act of "channeling the violence of the White against the Black through the death of a scapegoat. In reality, the snake-killing was an exorcism of slavery" (298). Again, without necessarily refuting other aspects of Benítez-Rojo's intelligent reading—which very much rings of Ortiz—I would argue that the snake is not a scapegoat at all, but rather a sacred symbol of the strength, perseverance, and enduring nature of Afro-Cuban religions and other African-derived cultural manifestations in Cuba, such as the *comparsas* and *congas* that have persevered despite being banned (eradicated) many times.

Having read the works of Fernando Ortiz, Guillén was clearly familiar with the commonly held notion that the snake that was "killed" in the Día de Reyes processions and later in the carnival *comparsas* was a symbol of evil that was destroyed in "a rite of collective purification like those classified as 'expulsions of the devil'" (*La antigua fiesta* 42–43). But he must also have been familiar with notions such as the following expressed by Ramiro Guerra:

> El cristianismo hizo fuerte énfasis en borrar—aunque no pudo—todo símbolo de las antiguas religiones, a las que llamó paganas. Éste es el caso de la conversión del reptil sagrado en animal maldito. . . . Así la ceremonia de "matar la culebra" comienza a surgir y repetirse en el folklore Americano y caribeño como una destrucción del mal, cuando en la realidad sus ejecutantes están cumpliendo el milenario rito mágico de la continuación de la especie por su muerte anual. (141–43)

[Christianity made a great effort to erase—even though it couldn't—all symbols from old religions, and those that it considered pagan. Such is the case of the conversion of the sacred reptile into the accursed animal . . . Thus the ceremony for "killing the snake" begins to emerge and repeat itself in American and Caribbean folklore as the destruction of evil, when in reality its performers are fulfilling an age-old magic rite of the continuation of the species by way of its annual death.]

Kubayanda has likewise noted that "the serpent in Africa and other ancient (pre-Christian) civilizations, is a sacred creature symbolizing renewal, fertility, growth, and wisdom" (105), a belief that carried over into all Afro-Cuban religions.

The act of cutting the snake in half with an ax in "Sensemayá" does not necessarily bring about its death, then, but rather sets the stage for its regeneration, just as the chopping of the snake in the *canto para matar una culebra* was repeated year-after-year in a symbolic act that coincided with the return of each new carnival season. As Lydia Cabrera explains with the help of a quote from one of her informants, the *majá*—the specific species of snake that is implicitly conjured in the title of Guillén's poem as well as in the poem's celebrated chant—is widely believed to possess special regenerative powers:

Por su parte el Majá conoce una yerba para curar . . . o rehacer sus semejantes. "Cuando alguien parte en dos el cuerpo de un machetazo, la planta que él conoce une los pedazos y el Majá recobra la vida entero y bien soldado." (*Animales* 17–18)

[For its part, the *Majá* knows of an herb that cures . . . or re-makes its fellow beings. "When someone chops its body in two with a blow of a machete, the plant that it knows unites the pieces and the boa returns to life in one piece and well mended."]

In the first published version of *El Monte* (1947) Cabrera makes a similar observation about this particular snake's regenerative abilities:

El majá es tan buen yerbero, aseguran [mis informantes], que si alguien lo corta en dos con un machete y lo deja en el campo abandonado, no tardará en aparecer otro majá con una yerba en la boca, que él solo conoce y que tiene la propiedad de revivirlo y de unir el cuerpo que el acto separó. (qtd. in Cabrera, *Páginas sueltas* 317–318).

[The *majá* is such a good herbalist, my informants tell me, that if someone cuts it in two with a machete and leaves it abandoned in the field, another *majá* will not delay in appearing with an herb in its mouth, which only he knows and has the ability to revive and to reunite the body that the act separated.]

I do not think it is mere coincidence that the snake in Guillén's poem happens to be hiding in "la yerba" (which can mean either "herb" or "grass") when it is struck by the ax ("La culebra se esconde en la yerba / caminando se esconde en la yerba" (27)), as it is there that it will find the elixir that will bring it back to life. In short, it seems that "killing" a snake by chopping it in two with the blow of an ax would not bring about its definitive death, but rather, would guarantee its renewal. Could it be possible, then, that what many have seen as a symbolic ritual killing inspired by a long-running carnival tradition is actually a subversive trick (like the name of the snake hidden in the chant or in the title of the poem) that only audience members familiar with certain Afro-Cuban terms or beliefs will understand? Indeed, if we choose this reading, the snake in Guillén's poem is not a scapegoat (Benítez-Rojo) or an enemy force (Augier), but a secret ally. Those who took part in the pantomimes certainly realized that the meaning of killing the snake would have depended on the audience.

Colonial-era whites as well as most modern observers of European descent would have recognized in this carnivalesque snake-killing ritual the annual collective purification rites that had been passed down from pagan rituals to their own carnival and Corpus Christi traditions, as Ortiz himself posits in several essays (see *La antigua fiesta* 35, 43; "Viejos carnavales" 205, *Los bailes* 118). The snake's death, then, might have been interpreted as a symbolic exorcism of the devil, the execution of an evil creature, or a warding off of bad luck or malevolent spirits. However, for the Afro-Cuban performers and observers familiar with African serpent cults and their various Afro-Cuban versions, the ritual "killing" of the snake might just as well have been a form of deception. Instead of a rite of elimination or purification that culminated in the eradication of a common Christian symbol of the devil, they were acting out a symbolic regeneration of one of their most sacred manifestations of divine power. By extension this sacred rite—as well as Guillén's poem that depicts it—also spoke to the perseverance of Afro-Cuban cultural manifestations in the face of the concerted attempts by successive Cuban administrations to get rid of them.

Perhaps Fernando Ortiz himself may have been underscoring his own ignorance on such a matter when he wrote in 1920 that "los afrocubanos *al matar la culebra*, realizaban inconscientemente un rito ancestral, arraigadísimo en casi todos los pueblos y continentes" (*La antigua fiesta* 43, emphasis in the original) [the Afro-Cubans *upon killing the snake*, fulfilled unconsciously an ancestral ritual, deeply rooted among almost all peoples and continents.] It seems to me that Ortiz—who had a tendency to explain African-derived rites and rituals in terms of similar ones from the Western tradition—underestimated here the astuteness of the Afro-Cuban performers, and therefore failed to realize that by "killing" snakes in their carnival celebrations, they were not performing rituals of exorcism, but rather acts that symbolized rebirth and continuation through death. Such acts represented, as Kubayanda has correctly noted, "the moment of rededication to a higher order of things, and a moment of dialogue with the Infinite represented by the Snake itself" (105).

I agree with Vera Kutzinski that the carnivalesque ritual that is depicted in Guillén's poem "had distinct subversive undertones, at least from the perspective of the blacks" (*Against* 140). I also concur with her opinion that this deceptive act is reminiscent of the famous execution of Makandal in Alejo Carpentier's *Reino de este mundo* [The Kingdom of This World] given that it probably would have outwitted most of Guillén's readers (141–42). As Kutzinski sees it, Guillén's poem "is not just a ritual killing of a snake, but in fact the same sort of metamorphosis Carpentier describes in connection with Makandal's death ... the serpent's death, like Makandal's, is a transformation that signals the triumph of the poem, not over death in general, but over slavery and cultural imperialism" (142). Rather than a metamorphosis, however, I choose to view the "killing" of the snake by chopping it in half—a pantomime that has been repeated over and over throughout the history of this carnival tradition—as an act of symbolic renewal in which the figure of the snake is not so much transformed, but rather given the strength that assures its continuation and reappearance in future rituals.

Such constant regeneration of the snake—and by extension of the carnival traditions and rites that it clearly represents—does indeed suggest a symbolic triumph, but not just over death and cultural imperialism as

Kutzinski implies. Guillén's poem also represents a subversive message of triumph over the efforts made from within Cuba and by Cubans themselves to eliminate many of the nation's most valuable and enduring African-derived traditions. And even though Benítez-Rojo may have been correct to surmise that "the importance of 'Sensemayá' is more cultural than political, more anthropological than ideological, more mythological than historical" (*Repeating Island*, 300), it is important not to overlook how the poem's invocation and tacit celebration of Día de Reyes festivities, modern Afro-Cuban carnival traditions, and related religious and cultural practices, pulls it away from the folkloric and brings it squarely into the realms of social and political resistance.

4

"Comparsa habanera," Emilio Ballagas's Emblematic Contribution to Afrocubanismo

> "Comparsa habanera" contains almost all of the motifs of Ballagas's *poesía negra*. It is filled with visual and auditory effects, with folklore and superstition, with music, rum, and sun. Star fruits are there and the Negress is there. Atavism and ritual enter: the shouts are Yoruba songs. The mystery and superstition of Changó cloud the scene and candles must be lit to ward off the shades of death.
>
> Wilfred Cartey, Black Images

Since its first appearance in *Cuaderno de poesía negra* (1934), Emilio Ballagas's "Comparsa habanera" has been one of the most widely celebrated and anthologized poems of Afrocubanismo. To this day it is considered by many critics to be emblematic of this important cultural and literary movement that ostensibly aimed, among other things, to displace racial prejudices and misconceptions of African-derived traditions by celebrating their contribution to Cuban culture, and by emphasizing "the unity of blacks and whites in the forging of the Cuban community that was culturally mulatto" (Davis 78).[1] Ballagas reflected this idea in the introduction to his *Antología de la poesía negra hispanoamericana* (1935), in which he insisted that he and other cultivators of such poetry in Cuba were joining in a common cause with the nation's black population. As he put it, "en la actualidad . . . se va más directamente al negro, haciendo causa común con él y participando en sus problemas vitales y aventuras artísticas" (18) [Presently . . . we are approaching the Negro more directly, entering a common cause with him and participating in his essential problems and his artistic adventures]. At the same time Ballagas suggested that the works in his anthology of seventeen Hispanic poets attested to the burgeoning desire, especially in Cuba, to understand and embrace

African-derived customs and cultural manifestations.[2] As he saw it, the poets whose works he had anthologized—most of whom were white men like himself—aimed to replace stereotypical and artificial depictions of blacks, which the *costumbristas* of the nineteenth century had propagated, with accurate depictions of the most "substantial" and "authentic" characteristics and traditions of Cuba's black population. He summed up his opinion about Cuba's contribution to American *poesía negra* as follows:

> En Cuba . . . hasta hace poco tiempo, el negro no había sido objeto de una auténtica curiosidad científica y estética. Los dibujantes y escritores costumbristas de nuestras generaciones precedentes tomaban al negro como objeto gracioso y exótico . . .
>
> Esa etapa superficial en que sólo se atendía al reflejo monstruoso del negro en el aspecto falaz de la criatura ha dejado lugar a otra etapa de más profundo sentido en que la atención al afrocubano se produce de un manera opuesta a la anterior. Ahora se va en busca de lo más característico y substancial del individuo afrocubano: se va, con lente certera, a su psicología, pero sobre todo—y aquí la importancia del movimiento revalorizador actual—se va al negro y a lo que le atañe con una ansia comunicativa que no había existido hasta ahora. (17)

> [In Cuba . . . until a short while ago, the Negro had not been the object of authentic, scientific and aesthetic curiosity. The *costumbrista* artists and writers of our preceding generations took the Negro as a comical and exotic object . . .
>
> This superficial era during which attention was paid only to the monstrous image of the Negro and the deceitful aspect of caricature, has ceded to a new era of more profound meaning in which attention is being paid to the Afro-Cuban in an opposite manner than before. Now one goes in search of the most characteristic and substantial aspects of the Afro-Cuban individual: one goes after, with an accurate lens, his psychology, but above all—and herein lies the importance of the present revitalizing movement—one approaches the Negro and all things related to him with a communicative desire that had not existed previously.]

In his introduction to *Órbita de la poesía afrocubana 1928–1937*, Ramón Guirao expressed a similar view. As he saw it,

La poesía afrocubana . . . entraña ya un acercamiento sincero, un deseo de acortar distancias, de salvar obstáculos que, por razón económica más que color o matices, impedían la simpatía y la fraternidad. Este es a nuestro juicio el valor fundamental de la poética negra. (xviii-xix)

[Afro-Cuban poetry . . . entails a sincere meeting of minds, a desire to shorten distances, to eliminate obstacles, which, for economic reasons more than colors or shades, impeded sympathy and fraternity. This is in our judgment the fundamental value of black poetics.]

In the brief introduction to *Mapa de la poesía negra americana* (1946), which was published long after the heyday of the *afrocubanista* movement, Ballagas acknowledged that much of the so-called *poesía negra* of the Americas was little more than "artificial fabrication," but he insisted that the predominant tenor of the poems in his anthology was sincere and authentic (9). It is likely in part due to Ballagas's claims and similar ones made by other poets and academics of that generation that "critics have tended to assume that the purpose of *poesía negra/mulata* in Cuba was to humanize racial stereotypes by replacing them with more positive, purportedly realistic, portraits of the local black population" (Kutzinski, *Sugar's Secrets* 154).

Observations in early essays by critics Guillermo de Torre "Literatura de color" [Literature of Color] (1937) and José Juan Arróm "La poesía afrocubana" [Afro-Cuban Poetry] (1942) are emblematic of the opinion, which became increasingly widespread in the 1930s and 1940s, that *afrocubanista* poets (unlike European artists and intellectuals of the same era) had been largely successful in their efforts to offer genuine portrayals of African-derived cultural manifestations. Echoing Ballagas—who had complained that the "tired European" saw the black man as "a thing of the jungle and virgin nature" and turned him into a subject of "turistic art" ("Introducción" 13)—Guillermo de Torre claims that *negrismo* in Europe was little more than an ephemeral fad with no real substance. In Cuba, however, the movement had come to represent a genuine desire to revalue African-derived traditions (8). In his words, "La literatura cubana . . . no se avergüenza de estas notas—y estas motas—de color. Al contrario, tiende desde hace unos pocos años a reivindicarlas dándolas su justo y original valor" (9) [Cuban literature . . . is not ashamed of these notes—and these motes—of color. To the contrary, it has tended for the last few years to vindicate them by returning to them their original value].

José Juan Arróm, a prominent Cuban intellectual and professor of literature, expressed a similar view in his 1942 essay "La poesía afrocubana":

> La moda negrista, sin embargo, tuvo vida muy distinta en Europa a la que ha llevado en Cuba. Allá eran arios sorprendidos quienes veían las cosas africanas con la momentánea curiosidad del turista ...
>
> En Cuba, por el contrario, lo negro tenía raigambre de cuatro siglos. El cubano blanco no veía en el negro al africano con collares de dientes de cocodrilo, sino a otro cubano, tan cubano como él, ciudadano de la misma república que juntos habían forjado a fuerza de machetazos.... Ambas razas se fusionan en lo artístico, como ya lo habían hecho en lo económico y político, para producir esta modalidad literaria. (392–93)

[The *negrista* mode, however, had a very different life in Europe than the one it led in Cuba. Over there they were surprised Arians who saw African things with the monotonous curiosity of a tourist ...

In Cuba, on the other hand, things related to the Negro had four centuries of roots. The white Cuban did not see the Negro as an African with necklaces made of crocodile teeth, but as another Cuban, just as Cuban as himself, citizen of the same republic that together with him had fought by the force of machete blows ... Both races became fused in the arts, as they had already done in the realm of economics and politics, to produce this literary modality.]

Arróm's idealistic view of racial, economic, and political harmony in Cuba and his evocation of the image of white and black soldiers fighting side-by-side as equals in the Cuban wars of independence are far cries from reality, as most modern readers of his essay will realize. Indeed, despite such claims by Arróm and others who suggested that the poetry of Afrocubanismo somehow represented the nation's victory over racism and inequality, Cuba's population was deeply divided well into the twentieth century. Aline Helg puts it succinctly by noting that "There were two social groupings distinguished from each other by physical appearance, and one group was dominant over the other. The barrier maintaining this hierarchy was founded on physical differences characteristic of continental space (Europe versus tropical Africa), including skin color, hair texture, and facial features, as well as on cultural differences such as social customs and religious beliefs" (*Rightful Share* 12–13).

Though Arróm may have indeed been correct to observe in the early 1940s that with each passing day whites and blacks in Cuba were becoming "more united in color and feelings," he seems to turn a blind eye to the fact that most of the poetry of Afrocubanismo reinforced the very evident racial hierarchy in Cuba that Helg refers to. It should be noted, moreover, that Arróm's opinion that the poetry of Afrocubanismo "Consiste ... en ver las cosas desde el punto de vista del negro, estar profundamente ligada a la música, los ritmos y los sentires del Afro-Cubano" (393) [Consists ... in seeing things from the Negro's point of view, in being profoundly connected to the music, the rhythms, and the feelings of the Afro-Cuban] fails to reflect the fact that much—if not the majority—of the poetry of the movement clearly represents views of outsiders who were largely unsuccessful in their attempts to understand and penetrate the Afro-Cuban world that they supposedly strived to re-create.

Ballagas apparently envisioned his own *poemas negros* as sincere celebrations and accurate portrayals of the contributions that Afro-Cubans had made to the culture of the young Republic, but his poems and many others of the movement were motivated by a hidden agenda of sorts, which Kutzinski describes as follows:

> rather than being an image renovation, and a largely failed one at that, Afro-Cubanism was an attempt at making poetry a stage for nationalist discourse, not by turning it into a platform for political slogans but by tapping specific cultural institutions with a long history of resilience: the syncretic forms of Afro-Cuban popular music and dance became the new signifiers of the desire for cultural and political independence. (*Sugar's Secrets* 154)

We should note that for the most part the poets of Afrocubanismo—with certain exceptions in the cases of Nicolás Guillén, Regino Pedroso, and Marcelino Arozarena—did not tend to express in their poetry any real connection with Cuba's black population and their cultural manifestations or a genuine concern for the rampant social and economic hardships that plagued Cubans of color. As Richard Jackson aptly puts it, "negrist poetry was about Blacks but not for them or directed to them" ("Afrocriollo" 8). We should add, moreover, that the *negrista* poets rarely made reference in their poetic renditions of Afro-Cuban religious rites and performances to the controversies that surrounded them, such as the campaigns against *brujería* and *ñáñiguismo*, the prohibitions of various African-derived instruments, or the multiple bans enacted against traditional *comparsas* and *congas* during the early decades of the Republic. Indeed, though many of the best-known poems of Afrocubanismo—such as José Zacarías Tallet's "La rumba," Ballagas's "Comparsa habanera," or Ramón Guirao's "Bailadora de rumba" (1934)—were ostensibly conceived as sincere embraces of Afro-Cubans and their various contributions to the nation's identity, they were not always motivated by genuine admiration or by deep knowledge of Cuba's black citizens and their religious and cultural manifestations. The case of Tallet's poems is especially noteworthy in this respect, since, as the well-known story goes, he was moved to compose "La rumba" not so much by his own desire to celebrate black culture or his knowledge of it, but because a friend bet him that he could not write a decent poem that incorporated the now famous "Mabimba, mabomba, bomba y bombó."

In many cases poems that supposedly embodied the author's solidarity with Cubans of color actually reflected sociopolitical concerns of a different ilk. On the one hand, they revealed an ever-increasing desire to express the "new sense of populism and pride" that followed the 1933 revolution against Machado, whose administration had long been associated with acts of cultural repression such as the banning of African-derived musical instruments and traditional *comparsas* (Moore 81). On the other hand, in the wake of the abrogation of the Platt Amendment in 1934, *afrocubanista* depictions of black cultural traditions can also be construed as attempts to further disassociate Cuban society and culture from the deeply engrained racism that reigned in the United States, and also from the imperialistic ambitions of the colossus of the North. Along the same line of thinking, Jackson has noted that many *negrista* poets—and especially those in Cuba—sought "strength and identity in the Black who seemed untouched and certainly unbowed to the U.S. presence." By essentially turning Afro-Cubans into "cultural heroes at home," Jackson argues, the poets rejected "the foreign interference of culture imported from the United States and the 'Yankee peril' associated with it" ("Afrocriollo" 7).

Reflecting a similar attitude in a 1937 letter to the mayor of Havana that called for the official reinstatement of *comparsas* in the Cuban capital, Fernando Ortiz underscored what he and many other intellectuals saw as a need for a new sense of national pride, which he felt could be manifested through the celebration of autochthonous cultural traditions such as traditional *comparsas*:

> Los cubanos debemos de vivir para nosotros mismos, de acuerdo con nuestra propia conciencia, sin sentir ese deprimente "complejo de inferioridad," heredado de la época colonial y esclavista . . . Los cubanos sabemos de sobra cuán frecuentemente somos denigrados todos, negros, blancos y mestizos, sin distinción y en conjunto, por ciertos extranjeros . . . alegando pretensiones de una mítica superioridad nórdica, o aria, o rubia, o celeste, o infernal . . . despreciando lo nuestro sólo por ser popular, modesto, imperfecto o traído por grupos distintos a los de la casta favorecida. . . . ("Las comparsas populares" 136–37)

> [We Cubans should live for ourselves, according to our own conscience, without feeling that depressing "inferiority complex," that we inherited from the colonial and slave era . . . We Cubans know full well how frequently all of us—whites, blacks and *mestizos*, without distinction and all lumped together—are denigrated by certain foreigners . . . who lay claim to mythical Nordic, Arian, blond, heavenly, or infernal superiority . . . disdaining what is ours only because it is popular, modest, imperfect or brought by groups who are different from the favored caste . . .]

But it is important to point out here, as Duno-Gottberg has convincingly argued, that Ortiz is not simply expressing in such statements a desire to unify a fragmented nation. Rather, he, like many of the poets of Afrocubanismo, also sought to contain and control certain Afro-Cuban traditions by assimilating them into the cultural mainstream (136–37, 144).

"La comparsa conga"—The Africanization of Havana's Carnival

In view of the fact that Emilio Ballagas included "Comparsa habanera" in both of his well-known anthologies of *poesía negra*, it seems safe to presume that he viewed the poem as an example of his own concerted attempts to offer genuine portraits of Afro-Cubans and to depict faithfully their contributions to the Republic's identity and culture. It may seem curious to the modern reader that Ballagas chose to place "Comparsa habanera" in the first section of *Antología de la poesía negra hispanoamericana*, titled "Evocaciones" [Evocations]. Indeed, the other four poems included there—"El grito abuelo" [The Grandfather's Cry] by José Manuel Poveda (Cuba, 1888–1926), "El buque negrero" [The Slave Ship] and "El candombe" by Idelfonso Pereda Valdés (Uruguay, 1899–1996), and "Pueblo negro" by Luis Palés Matos (Puerto Rico, 1899–1959)—evoke in very obvious ways images of the relatively distant past, such as the legacy of slavery or the ancestral homelands of Latin America's black populations (109). However, we must bear in mind that "Comparsa habanera" was written and published during a period in which these traditional Afro-Cuban carnival ensembles were also essentially things of the past. Indeed, they had been subjected to official prohibitions in Havana for nearly two decades by the time Ballagas wrote the poem.[3] Moreover, given that Ballagas was born in 1908, that traditional *comparsas* were officially banned in Havana by 1916, and that he did not move to the Cuban capital until 1928, it is entirely possible that Ballagas had never even witnessed a traditional Afro-Cuban carnival procession in the Cuban capital. I would also add here that by grouping "Comparsa habanera" with poems that focus on the direct connections of black Hispanic Americans with Africa, Ballagas simply called attention to the "Africanness" of traditional carnival celebrations in Havana, which is precisely what had led Cuban officials to ban them in the first place.

This notion that Ballagas conceived of his *comparsa* as an evocation of the African origins of its participants is bolstered first by the inclusion of "African sounding" words and expressions in the opening stanzas, and later by the repetition of terms that refer to their black skin ("parda," "negro"), as well as vocabulary that suggests African ancestry ("congos," "yorubas"). From the opening stanzas it becomes plainly apparent that even if Ballagas aimed to offer a sincere portrait of a traditional Afro-Cuban carnival ensemble, his poem actually reflects contemporary prejudices against *comparsas* and *congas* by presenting patently stereotypical, one dimensional images of the black participants and the African-derived expressions, dances, music, rituals, and superstitions that were associated with them. Indeed, "Comparsa habanera" shares much in common with many of the poems in *Cuaderno de poesía negra*, which Duno-Gottberg correctly refers to as "epidermic" explorations of a black "way of being," poems centered on the exterior, on gestures, on exotic sound, and on skin color (89).

In terms of its prevailing tone, Ballagas's poem comes across as a decidedly less sinister depiction of a black carnival procession than Felipe Pichardo Moya's "La comparsa." Moreover, its catchy rhythm—which led many critics to share Cintio Vitier's opinion that its verbal orchestration was among the richest that the *afrocubanista* poetry movement had to offer ("Introducción" 21)—contrasts sharply with most of the other carnival poems that are considered in the present study.[4] Despite the many merits of "Comparsa habanera," however, Ballagas's dependence on trademark stylistic devices of *afrocubanista* poetry—a profusion of *jitanjáforas* and the exaggerated recreation of Afro-Cuban speech, for example—embody, at least to a certain extent, the poet's flawed conception of authenticity. The inauthentic aspects of many of Ballagas's poems are reinforced in the various glossaries to his anthologies of *poesía negra*, in which he indicates that most of the apparently African words in his poems are his own "intuitive" creations. Though they were meant to lend rhythm and realism, from a modern perspective Ballagas's fanciful *jitanjáforas* call attention to the minimal semantic content of many of the verses in his poems, which he openly admitted, but did not see as problematic from a poet's perspective. In an essay from the 1940s, Ballagas defended his frequent use of nonsensical, African-sounding words with the following observation:

> Pero tampoco tiene significado el canto del ruiseñor y nos agrada. Ofrece estímulo al oído y a la imaginación. Nos hace saber que el hombre no es todo lógica y reflexión racional; que lo primitivo, que es energía, forma parte también del organismo mental del hombre civilizado. (qtd. in Rice 105)

> [But the nightingale's song also has no meaning, yet it pleases us. It offers stimulus to the ear and to the imagination. It lets us know that man is not all logic and rational reflection; that the primitive, which is energy, also forms a part of the mental organism of the civilized man.]

Ballagas's observation is problematic for two reasons. On the one hand, it implicitly links Afro-Cubans to the realm of instinct and the animal world. On the other, it demonstrates the poet's flawed logic. Indeed, simply because one does not understand the nightingale's song does not mean that it has no significance. In the same way, African words, or even the sounds that evoke them, have meaning, but only to those who understand them. This is clearly illustrated in our discussion of Guillén's "Sensemayá" in Chapter 3. It is very important to add here that many of the terms that Ballagas defined in his glossaries as "nonsense words," or words with strictly onomatopoeic values, actually had well-known meanings, which often served to underscore pejorative and stereotypical images of the black protagonists, as I demonstrate later in this chapter.

Even though there are obvious differences between "La comparsa" and "Comparsa habanera," I feel, nonetheless, that Ballagas's poem echoes to a certain degree Pichardo Moya's portrayal of the *comparsa* as a purely African-derived phenomenon that adds little of value to the nation's supposed cultural mix. In both poems, for example, the black performers are presented as eccentric participants in a public spectacle that attracts the curious yet more "civilized" gaze of the white poet/spectator, but does not include any white performers. The following stanzas are illustrative of this point:

La comparsa del farol
ronca que roncando vá.
¡Ronca comparsa candonga
que ronca en tambor se va!

Y . . . ¡Sube la loma! Y ¡dale al tambor!
Sudando los congos van tras el farol.
(Con cantos yorubas alzan el clamor.)
Resbalando en un patín de jabón
sus piernas se mueven al vapor del ron.

Con plumas plumero
de loro parlero
se adorna la parda
Fermina Quintero.
Con las verdes plumas
del loro verdero.
¡Llorando la muerte
de Papá Montero!

La comparsa del farol
ronca que roncando vá.
Ronca comparsa candonga

bronca de la cañadonga . . .
¡La conga ronca se vá!

Se vá la comparsa negra bajo el sol
moviendo los hombros, bajando el clamor. (np)[5]

Ballagas's unequivocal depiction of the *comparsa* as a black phenomenon appears to contradict a contention made three years after the poem's publication by Fernando Ortiz, who argued that "las comparsas no son de negros, ni de blancos, ni de mestizos. En ellas entran todos los colores y tradiciones acumulados en nuestra masa popular" ("Las comparsas populares" 138) [*comparsas* are not made up solely of blacks, nor whites, nor *mestizos*. All of the colors and accumulated traditions of our popular masses enter into them]. Much like other contemporary poems about Afro-Cuban carnival ensembles, Ballagas's text belies Ortiz's idealistic view of the *comparsa* as a symbol of Cuba's "profuse cultural heterogeneity" ("Las comparsas populares" 138). This is not to say, however, that the absence of white participants from Ballagas's "comparsa conga" is inaccurate. To be sure, it reflects a reality that Ortiz seems to have evaded: that is, that whites and blacks rarely performed together in the same *comparsas*. Alberto Arredondo would later deride Ortiz's unrealistic vision of the *comparsa* in an inflammatory editorial in *Adelante*. As he put it, the white men—namely Ortiz and other members of the *Sociedad de Estudios Afrocubanos*—who so passionately pushed for the reinstatement of Afro-Cuban *comparsas* would never have considered being seen "arrollando" in public with their black fellow citizens ("El arte negro" 6).

Especially during the early decades of the Republic, when "successive governments repressed anything that might give rise to opposition" from the country's Afro-Cuban contingent, white Cubans were encouraged to form their own carnival celebrations that would not mix with those from the black neighborhoods (Roy 37). "White carnival," as it was commonly known, was officially sanctioned and typically sponsored by manufacturers of cigarettes or alcoholic beverages. It included ornate decorated carriages (fig. 4.1), automobiles, and *carrozas* [floats] and carnival processions that often included whites in blackface or dressed in drag (fig. 4.2). The processions were characterized by carefully choreographed dances and the music was typically played on European-derived musical instruments.

FIGURE 4.1. Elaborately decorated carnival carriage transporting high-society white children, ca. 1920. Note the carnival "king" and "queen" seated in the top row. Photographer unknown. (Author's collection.)

FIGURE 4.2. Postcard depicting an automobile festooned with what appear to be "flowers" made of pantyhose, carrying men in drag (ca. 1915). (A. Otero, Cienfuegos. Author's collection.)

The members of the *comparsa* in Ballagas's poem are also far removed from the idealistic image of black Cuban brothers—"as Cuban as [the white man] . . . citizens of the same republic"—that Arróm spoke of in his essay "La poesía afrocubana" (393). Their difference is underscored most obviously by the fact that they are repeatedly referred to as "congos." This particular Afro-Cuban ethnic identifier, which refers to Afro-Cubans with roots in the Bantu-speaking areas of West Africa, is used frequently in the poetry of Afrocubanismo, and it should be stressed that in the early decades of the twentieth century, the religious cults that were typically associated with the Congos were viewed "as synonymous with both cultural and moral degeneration" (Ayorinde 18). The poetic voice also repeatedly refers to the carnival procession itself as "la comparsa negra" or "la comparsa conga," monikers that automatically remove whites from the picture. The term "conga" was used frequently by the poets of Afrocubanismo to signify many things, including a barrel-shaped drum of African origin with an open bottom, a percussive musical ensemble in a carnival procession, and carnival processions that originated during the slave era.[6]

Perhaps more than anything else, though, the black performers in Ballagas's poem are divorced from the white majority by the frequent and extraneous references in "Comparsa habanera" to Afro-Cuban religious rituals, superstitions, and "primitive" beliefs, which had long served to justify the prevailing prejudices against Cubans of color. In the following stanzas, for example, Ballagas, who—despite claims to the contrary by some critics—had limited firsthand experience with African-derived rituals, parodies the possession of an Afro-Cuban subject by a conjured spirit.[7]

"A'ora verá cómo yo no yoro.
(Jálame lá calimbanyé . . .)
Y'ora verá como yombondombo
(Júlume la cumbumbanyé.)"

El santo se va subiendo
cabalgando en el clamor

"Emaforibia yambó.
Uenibamba uenigó."

¡En los labios de caimito,
los dientes blancos de anón!

This scene, as well as another similar one that follows later in the poem and is discussed below, typifies what Coulthard has described as the "voodooesque possessions" that can be found in many poems of Afrocubanismo (94).[8] Even though Ballagas claims in his glossary to *Cuaderno de poesía negra* that the abundant "African-sounding" words such as those found in the lines cited here are used "intuitively" for their onomatopoeic value, there is no denying that their presence in this scene makes a ridiculous caricature out of an Afro-Cuban religious rite. Moreover, certain words that Ballagas passes off as playful *jitanjáforas*—such as "jálame" above, and "candonga" and "matonga" later in the poem—would have been recognizable to many readers of the poem for their negative connotations. Indeed, in the popular discourse of Cuba "jalarse" means "to get drunk," but also "to masturbate." The other two terms, which Ballagas uses to describe the *comparsa*—and by extension its black members—have several possible meanings. For example, "candonga" is sometimes used to signify "whore," but more frequently denotes one who is lazy or given to avoiding work. Moreover, this term is similar to "candanga," which according to Ortiz comes from the Congo term, *kundanga*, for "stupid" or "foolish" (*Glosario* 94). In the case of "matonga," the first word that springs to mind is "matón," which means "thug" or "lout," and immediately evokes the violence that was so intimately associated with Afro-Cuban carnival ensembles during the early decades of the Republic. On the other hand, this term again recalls a similar one—"matunga"—that was often used to refer to a weak or sickly person, but also denoted "el animal que por su mal estado es conveniente matarlo" [the animal that, because of its poor health, should be killed] (Ortiz, *Glosario* 316).

Ballagas parodies the sacred moment of the "subida del santo" [arrival of the saint] later in the poem in two stanzas that are written in an exaggerated *bozal* speech, which serves as another marker of the African origins of the poem's protagonists.

"Apaga la vela
que'l muelto se vá.
Amarra el pañuelo
que lo atajo ya.

Y ¡enciende la vela
que'l muelto salió!
Enciende dos velas
¡Qué tengo el Changó!"

The final line marks the climax of the ritual, and indicates the possession by the spirit of Changó, the Lucumí *orisha* of thunder and lightning who is known for his bellicose and capricious temperament. The summoning of Changó in this poem is especially symbolic since—like Papá Montero, who is mentioned in the previously quoted stanza—he was often equated, especially by outsiders, with "a macho womanizer, a brawler whose weakness for sex and drums has led to his stereotyped identification with feckless, party-loving blacks" (Ayorinde 12).

Ballagas's descriptions of possessions in "Comparsa habanera" are problematic for two reasons. On the one hand, they are extraneous because they bear no obvious relationship to traditional *comparsas*. Even if it is true that *comparseros* would sometimes "fall into a convulsive ecstasy and lose control of their mental capacities," as Valdés-Cruz claims (*Poesía negroide* 81, my translation), possession by spirits was certainly not an essential component of authentic Afro-Cuban carnival processions.[9] On the other hand, the references to such possessions implicitly and unnecessarily reinforce negative stereotypes of Afro-Cubans by linking them and their already controversial *comparsas* and *congas* to precisely the types of rituals and religious practices that the majority of middle- and upper-class Cubans found repugnant, strange, and threatening. In this sense, "Comparsa habanera" seems to reflect Juan René Betancourt's opinion that instead of promoting positive images of Afro-Cubans, most of the poetry of Afrocubanismo served to denigrate "the black man, his gods, and his religion" (*El negro* 127).

Though it could be argued that Ballagas largely avoids sinister descriptions of the possessed, such as the "temblor epilepsial," "furia demoníaca," and "rapto de locura" in Pichardo Moya's "La comparsa," it is also true that the allusions to spiritual possession in his poem would have immediately conjured up such images among Cuban readers in the 1930s. To be sure, those Cubans who had no direct experience with Afro-Cuban religions often came to "understand" them through unreliable and often demeaning written descriptions such as those found in the anonymously published pamphlet *La brujería y los brujos de Cuba* (1900) (fig. 4.3) or

FIGURE 4.3. Anonymous pamphlet, *La brujería y los brujos de Cuba* (1900). In the Introduction, the author claims that this is the first book of its kind to be published in Cuba. Though the pamphlet is dedicated almost entirely to Afro Cuban practitioners of *brujería*, the cover illustration depicts the iconic image of the witch as a white woman wearing a black hat and cloak and riding on a broomstick. (Author's collection.)

in more widely disseminated works like Roche y Monteagudo's *La policía y sus misterios en Cuba* and Ortiz's *Los negros brujos*, the latter two of which were still considered authoritative texts on Afro-Cuban *brujería* when Ballagas penned his poem.

In his study Roche included the type of alarmist descriptions—such as that of the "subida del santo" cited below—that led so many Cubans to fear African-derived religions and their practitioners:

> Una de esas ceremonias a la que dan nombre de bajar el santo o subirse el santo a la cabeza, da la medida del religioso fervor de la brujería. Para formarse una idea, es necesario haber visto de cerca los movimientos de todas las articulaciones, las horribles muecas producidas por la contracción de los músculos del rostro, los saltos violentos y desordenados a que se entregan los cofrades, una especie de rabia creciente, muy parecida a la embriaguez alcohólica. (2nd ed. 107)

> [One of those ceremonies, which they call the descending of the saint or the ascending of the saint to the head, gives a good measure of the religious fervor of *brujería*. In order to form an opinion about it, it is necessary to have seen up close the movements of all of their joints, the terrible grimaces produced by the muscular contortions of their faces, the violent and disorderly leaps that the members perform, a kind of increasing fury, very similar to drunkenness.]

For his part, Ortiz also presented disparaging descriptions of the rite of spiritual possession in *Los negros brujos,* and he offered a similar explanation for the phrase "subirse el santo a la cabeza." He suggests that it derived from the common expression "subirse el alcohol a la cabeza" [the ascending of alcohol to the head] given the supposed similarities between the "epileptic" fits of the possessed and the unrestrained behavior of drunks (93).[10] This interesting detail brings to mind another aspect of "Comparsa habanera" that is typical of *poesía negra*: the portrayal of blacks as drunken revelers who lose control of themselves as they dance and shake wildly to the incessant beat of drums. Such an image can be seen in the following lines from "Comparsa habanera": "¡Los diablitos de la sangre/ se encienden en ron y sol"; "sus piernas se mueven al vapor del ron"; "Ronca comparsa candonga / bronca de la cañadonga"; "La comparsa . . . de negros mojados en ron." Similar images of intoxicated black performers can be found in many poems of Afrocubanismo, such as Nicolás Guillén's widely anthologized "Canto negro," in which a black rumba dancer literally becomes lost in his drunken stupor: "En negro canta y se ajuma, / el negro se ajuma y canta, / el negro canta y se va" (80).[11]

The modern reader of "Comparsa habanera" must be sure not to overlook the fact that Ballagas twice refers to the "diablitos de sangre," which Moore renders as "blood-brother devils" in his English-language translation of the poem (240). Though Brown has pointed out that the term *diablitos* "came to refer in Cuba to virtually all individual carnival figures in the 'African' manner (for example, decked out with horns, wooden masks, and vegetable matter)," Ballagas is clearly referring here to the carnival version of the *íremes* of the Abakuá brotherhoods, whose status as black devils "located them as evil, atavistic figures opposed to true religion and Cuban social order" (Brown, "Glossary" 63). Moore's translation is not necessarily off the mark in its evocation of the fraternal bonds that link Abakuá initiates, but I think the modifier "sangre" also implies the more sinister notions of violence and savagery that were associated with these figures that were almost universally reviled and aggressively persecuted in Cuba during the early decades of the twentieth century. By connecting the *diablitos* to blood and alcohol in the same breath, Ballagas conjures up defamatory descriptions of *ñáñigo* carnival masqueraders like the following one by Ramón Meza y Suárez that Fernando Ortiz quoted in his widely read 1920 study on Día de Reyes festivities in Havana:

> En el ñáñigo se extremó toda la grosera y bárbara imaginación de las tribus africanas. Institución, signos, trajes, todo era en alto grado repugnante. Eran de ver . . . aquellas agrupaciones *ahitas de aguardiente y sangre de gallo*. (qtd. in Ortiz, *La antigua fiesta* 12, emphasis added)

> [In the *ñáñigo* all of the coarse and barbarous imagination of the African tribes was carried to the extreme. Their institution, signs, outfits, everything was highly repugnant . . . Those groups of men, drenched in liquor and rooster blood, were really a sight to see.]

Despite the fact that the *diablito-íreme* is not referred to in any of the other poems in *Cuaderno de poesía negra*, this figure clearly signified for Ballagas an embodiment of Afro-Cubanness. Indeed, why else would he have chosen as the illustration for the cover of his book a striking image—by

FIGURE 4.4. Cover of the first edition of Emilio Ballagas's *Cuaderno de poesía negra*, 1934. This image, by Cuban artist Domingo Ravenet, depicts an *íreme* holding an *itón* (cloth-covered wand) and *ifán tereré* (little broom), two key implements for carrying out his sacred duties in the Abakuá secret society. (Author's collection.)

the Spanish-born Cuban artist Domingo Ravenet (1905–1969)—of a hooded *íreme* grasping his *itón* [cloth-covered wand] and *ifán tereré* [little broom], two key implements for carrying out his sacred duties in the Abakuá secret society (fig. 4.4)? In my mind, this simple drawing, which is overlapped by the book's title and the author's name, speaks volumes about Ballagas's personal conception of Afro-Cubans and the type of image that best represented them.

This brings to mind the fact that in addition to the written descriptions of Afro-Cubans and their rites and rituals, like those found in the studies by Roche y Monteagudo and Ortiz, visual depictions of them also served to reinforce certain negative stereotypes. The illustrations in *Estampas afro-cubanas* (1939), a striking publication that contains reproductions of six giant, Afro-Cuban-inspired paintings by the Spanish-born painter Fernando Tarazona, are illustrative of this point. Tarazona, who was perhaps the first painter to turn Afro-Cubans into his principal subject matter, explains in the introduction that each image is accompanied by "a brief explanation in writing of the African ceremony . . . [that] shows clearly that the paintings are based on reality, and gives the correct interpretation of the scene, showing the climax of the most vivid, colorful and interesting part of these weird ceremonies of the strange Afro-Cuban cults" (n.p.).[12] However, just as so many poems of Afrocubanismo misrepresent African-derived cultural manifestations and religious practices, Tarazona's paintings offer similarly distorted depictions and "eroticized versions of Afro-Cuban religiosity" (Ayorinde 59). In "The Saint's Protégé," for example, Tarazona depicts the possession of an Afro-Cuban woman (fig. 4.5). Surrounded by seven Afro-Cuban drummers, the naked woman is lying on her back with her legs bent, arms spread, and mouth wide open. This provocative image clearly suggests sexual climax as much as it depicts a sacred rite of spiritual possession. Moreover, Tarazona's written description of the scene, which echoes those of Roche and Ortiz, serves to promote the negative stereotypes that one notes in the painting:

> Among the Afro-Cuban Fetishists there is a so called religious festivity in which the maniacal celebrations are climaxed in such a state of frenzy, [sic] that some member usually falls in a sort of cataleptic fit. This is looked upon by the Fetishist as the supreme moment of the festivities as it foretells the "arrival of their Saint."
>
> . . . .

The spirit is elevated at the same time as the rhythm. The clamor of drums summons the ghosts of the jungle to take part in the magic sound . . . The pitch has reached its greatest height, the exaltation its climax; and the sacred and erotical [sic] dance has been transformed into a fury. It is rather an exaltation of madness when some one, often a woman, faints and falls down, twisting about in violent, apparent epileptical convulsions [sic]. It is just then that the saint comes down. (n.p.)

Later in the same description, most of which is borrowed from Ortiz's *Los negros brujos* (see 93–94), Tarazona notes that in the background of this scene "the singers repeat the ritual phrase: 'Senseribó, Senseribó, epé mancoó! epé mancoó!'" This observation is illustrative of the tendency among outsiders from many different disciplines—including many of the poets of Afrocubanismo—to group together unrelated Afro-Cuban rites and rituals. Indeed, the chant that Tarazona cites is in the Bríkamo language of the Abakuá, and would not have been uttered in the context that he describes. In short, it is important to consider "Comparsa habanera" and other poems of Afrocubanismo that depict scenes of spiritual possession or other sacred rituals in light of the many sensationalistic and misleading written and illustrated depictions of them.

In regard to Ballagas's apparent parody of certain Afro-Cuban religious rites in "Comparsa habanera," it seems especially significant that the poet describes the route of this specific *comparsa* as one that brings it into contact with several places that evoke Christianity and Catholicism: the plaza in front of Havana's Catholic Cathedral, a street (San Juan de Dios) that bears a Christian name, and an alley behind an unnamed Havana church. On one level, this "African" presence near Christian hallowed ground could be taken as a metaphor for religious syncretism in Cuba, which reflects the notion of Cuba as "a meeting place for African gods and Catholic saints" (Ayorinde 21). On another level, however, the proximity of the "comparsa conga" to sacred sites could also be seen as a metaphor for what many Cubans saw as the threats that profane *comparsas, congas,* and other similar African-derived cultural manifestations posed to the white/Christian religious establishment in Cuba.

Another aspect of "Comparsa habanera" that is in keeping with the common tendencies among the poets of Ballagas's generation is his depiction

FIGURE 4.5. Fernando Tarazona, *La ahijada del santo* [The Saint's Protégé], 1936. The text that accompanies this decidedly stereotypical image of an Afro-Cuban ritual reads: "This is the moment the painter describes when the young woman is caught up by the spiritual trance making her initiation into the secret cult. She has been favored by the Saint—now she can wear the necklace used by the faithful which an old woman puts around her neck" [*sic*] (Tarazona n.p.). (Image courtesy of Fine Arts Library, Indiana University, Bloomington Campus.)

of Afro-Cuban men as essentially physical beings who are driven by uncontrollable sexual urges.[13] The following portrait of a *comparsero* who is literally moved to a state of "fury" by a combination of the intensifying beat of the drums and his sexual desires—is a case in point:

Y la mira el congo, negro maraquero;
suena la maraca. ¡Y tira el sombrero!

Retumba la rumba
hierve la balumba
y con la calunga
arrecia el furor. (n.p.)

The key word here is "calunga," which Ballagas defines in *Cuaderno de poesía negra* as an erotic desire intensified by a long period of sexual repression.[14] With this provocative image of an aggressive, sexually starved black man, Ballagas does little more than reinforce prevailing fears of the unbridled and threatening sexuality of Afro-Cuban men. Aline Helg has pointed out that this fear was "embodied in the male images of the black beast and black rapist of white women," and she further notes that in the early decades of the Republic—and especially in the wake of the Racist Massacre of 1912—many Cubans firmly believed that "if Afro-Cubans were left unchecked, they would supposedly regress to animality" and force themselves on white maidens (*Our Rightful Share* 18). Duno-Gottberg has pointed out that such fears were still prevalent in the 1930s, and he cites the following 1933 declaration from the Cuban Ku Klux Klan: "the negro at this time . . . has been increasing like a malignant plague, demanding rights which he has carried to the extreme, SUCH AS THE POSSESSION OF WHITE WOMEN" (114, emphasis in the original). Viewed in its proper context, then, it is hard to imagine what redeeming quality Ballagas's image of a black man pushed to a state of sexual fury could possess.

In terms of common stereotypes of Afro-Cuban women during the same period, Helg discusses widespread notions of "the lust of women of African descent" ("Black Men" 590) and of "the seductive *mulata* and lustful *negra*, a fantasy that freed white men from the guilt of rape or sexual oppression and transformed them into victims of Afro-Cuban women" (*Our Rightful Share* 18). The highly eroticized, hip-swinging *negras* and *mulatas* that populate so many poems of Afrocubanismo clearly served to bolster such negative perceptions of Cuban women of color. And even though such images of Afro-Cuban women are not the focus of "Comparsa habanera" (as they are in other Ballagas poems such as "Rumba" and "El baile del papalote") the black females that do make an appearance in the poem are cast in one-dimensional molds. One such example is "la parda Fermina Quintero," who files by in a suit adorned with brilliant green parrot feathers.

In addition to the implied comparison between Fermina's crying and the annoying chattering of a parrot, the speaker also insinuates her ignorance by expressing surprise that she is mourning the "death" of Papá Montero, the legendary figure from Havana's Afro-Cuban underworld who was immortalized in widely popular *sones*, such as Eliseo Grenet's "Papá Montero" and María Teresa Vera's "Los funerales de Papá Montero" [Papá Montero's Funeral]. Papá Montero also made an appearance in a handful of early poems of Afrocubanismo, most notably in Nicolás Guillén's "El velorio de Papá Montero" [Papa Montero's Wake](1931), but also in Alejo Carpentier's "Liturgia" and "Canción" (1928), in which he is referred to as a "ñáñigo chébere" and "chébere congo" respectively. Ballagas's reference to Papá Montero is, in its own right, significant in terms of the poem's promotion of stereotypes given that in the best-known versions of his legendary exploits he is variously described as a womanizer, a heavy drinking *cumbanchero* [partier], and a knife-wielding *chévere* [well-dressed man, but also a ruffian]. It is important to point out here that the term "chévere," which appears often in *poesía negra*, has always had positive connotations among the Abakuá, as "it derives from *Ma'chébere*, a title of the Abakuá dignitary Mokongó" (Miller, *Voice* 36). To be sure, even in modern Cuba—and in many regions in Latin America—this term still denotes positive notions such as "fashionable," "good looking," or "cool." However, in early twentieth-century Cuba, *chévere* carried many negative meanings that reflected the general sentiment that *ñáñigos* were inherently violent, knife-wielding criminals.[15] Such negative characteristics are embodied in the refrain that many of the above-mentioned compositions share: "¡zumba, canalla y rumbero!"

Other female participants in Ballagas's *comparsa* are presented as temptresses who, through their sensual dancing, entice the male *comparseros* as well as the curious male onlookers—such as the poetic voice—who gaze upon them as they pass by:

> Bailan las negras rumberas
> con candela en las caderas.
> Abren sus anchas narices,
> ventanas de par en par
> a un panorama sensual . . .

Carlos E. Polit misreads this stanza—as well as many similar verses in the poems by Luis Palés Matos, Emilio Ballagas, Nicolás Guillén, and Manuel del Cabral that he analyzes—by citing it as an example of how in *negrista* poetry the sexuality of women of color "is invariably exalted and dignified" (44). Likewise, referring specifically to these lines, José Juan

Arróm—author of some of the most patently racist commentaries on *afrocubanista* poetry—made the following observation:

> Para [los negros cubanos], amor es reproducción. . . . Creerlos inmorales porque en su composición hay más de carne que de espíritu, es llamar inmoral al pájaro que se reproduce libremente en el bosque . . . La influencia telúrica de sus llanos incendiados de sol los ha hecho como son, apasionados sin refinamientos, desbordantes del vigor progénico de los trópicos. (399)

> [For Cuban Negroes, love is reproduction . . . To think they are immoral because in their composition there is more flesh than soul is to call immoral the bird that reproduces freely in the forest . . . The telluric influence of their sun-drenched plains has made them the way they are, passionate without refinements, overflowing with the progenic vigor of the tropics.]

To this observation Arróm added that modern audiences should not be scandalized by verses such as those cited above since they capture the Afro-Cubans' "natural" and "biological" way of expressing their sexuality, which, he contended, white Cubans had learned to depict with subtleties and euphemisms (400). In addition to reflecting the typical mentality of contemporary white Cuban intellectuals, Arróm's comments are also significant because they implicitly distance Afro-Cubans—and by extension the *comparsa* itself—from the white majority by linking their idiosyncrasies to the "burning plains" of Africa.

A Hidden Political Message?

I have argued elsewhere that in "Comparsa habanera," Emilio Ballagas evades the heated sociocultural debate that surrounded *comparsas* and *congas* and the bans against them that were firmly in place when he penned the poem.[16] However, further consideration of the poem's final two stanzas has led me to believe that Ballagas may indeed have had the *comparsa* controversy in mind when he wrote "Comparsa habanera" in the early 1930s, even if he didn't explicitly refer to this contentious issue in his poem. In the lines in question the poetic voice describes the *comparsa* as it marches away and eventually disappears into the darkness of the Havana night:

Con su larga cola, la culebra vá.
Con su larga cola, muriéndose vá.
la negra comparsa del guaricandá.

La comparsa perdiéndose vá.
¡Qué lejos!. . . . lejana. . . . muriéndose vá.
Se apaga la vela; se hunde el tambor.
¡La comparsa conga desapareció!

The reference to the *culebra* is especially significant as it evokes not just the name of one of the most popular and well-known *comparsa* troupes of the early decades of the twentieth century, but also the very image of traditional Afro-Cuban carnival ensembles, which were commonly associated with snakes in the literature, music, and popular discourse of the day. This image also conjures up the traditional chants for killing snakes, which played such a prominent role in the Día de Reyes celebrations of nineteenth-century Cuban slaves, but had all but ceased to exist by the time Ballagas penned his poem.

In these stanzas the speaker again stresses the blackness of the *comparsa* with the terms "negra" and "conga," and adds that its members hail from the "guaricandá," or lower classes. In other words, the "comparsa conga" that is described in the poem is just the type of African-derived cultural manifestation that had been the source of so much controversy during the early decades of the Cuban Republic. It could be argued that the allusions to the death and disappearance of the *comparsa* may simply be meant to suggest that the Afro-Cuban carnival procession described in the poem is fading from view as it moves farther away from the speaker's point of observation, but an alternate reading is also possible. Indeed, by repeating the notion of a dying *comparsa*—which is reinforced by the images of the snuffed-out candle and the vanishing drum in the poem's final stanza—and then ending the poem with its definitive disappearance ("¡La comparsa conga desapareció!"), the poetic voice might also be alluding to the actual demise of traditional Afro-Cuban carnival processions in Havana.

Argyll Pryor Rice has correctly pointed out that Ballagas purposefully avoided social and political problems in his *poesía negra* because he felt that dwelling on such issues only served to obscure the essential aspects of the Afro-Cuban soul that he aimed to depict (97). Likewise, Kutzinski refers to Ballagas's "belief in the existence of 'pure poetry,' unaffected and thus uncontaminated by sociopolitical issues" (*Sugar's Secrets* 157), and she cites the following lines from his introduction to *Mapa de la poesía negra americana* to support her observation: "Nuestra actitud hacia la poesía negra no es la del etnógrafo ni la del sociólogo, mucho menos la del político" (*Mapa* 8) [Our attitude toward *poesía negra* is not that of an ethnographer nor a sociologist, and much less that of a politician]. The possible sociopolitical subtext to "Comparsa habanera," a poem that is in so many ways a typical example of *poesía negra*, may therefore seem out of place or uncharacteristic. Though Nancy Morejón does exaggerate when she speaks of Ballagas's "marcadísmima ambición social" [very noteworthy social ambition] (*Nación y mestizaje* 88), it is important to keep in mind that some of his *poemas negras* ("Elegía de María Belén Chacón" and "Actitud" for example) do reveal in subtle ways the poet's social-mindedness. At the same time, much like "Comparsa habanera," they also exude the superficiality that characterized so much of the poetry of Afrocubanismo.

Traditional Comparsas as Slave-Era Throwbacks

Given the rarity of *Cuaderno de poesía negra* and *Antología de la poesía negra hispanoamericana*—both of which were published in very small editions that were never reprinted—most modern readers of "Comparsa habanera" know the poem through versions published in more readily available anthologies, such as Ballagas's *Mapa de la poesía negra Americana* (1946), Idelfonso Pereda Valdés's *Lo negro y lo mulato en la poesía cubana* (1970), or Jorge Luis Morales's *Poesía afroantillana y negrista* (1976, 1981, 2000), just to name a few. What many modern readers and critics do not realize is that these, and many other anthologies, include a truncated version that leaves out twenty-seven lines from the original 1934 edition of the poem.[17]

Many of the omitted lines evoke to a much greater extent than the rest of the poem, the sinister undertones that dominate Felipe Pichardo Moya's "La comparsa." Take, for example, the following lines:

Los gatos enarcan
al cielo el mayido.

Encrespan los perros
sombríos ladridos.

Se asoman los muertos del cañaveral.
En la noche se oyen cadenas rodar.
Rebrilla el relámpago como una navaja
que a la noche conga la carne le raja.
Cencerros y grillos, güijes y lloronas:
cadenas de ancestro . . . y . . . ¡Sube la loma!
Barracones, tachos, sangre del batey
mezclan su clamor en el guararey.

Con luz de cocuyos y helados aullidos
anda por los techos el "ánima sola."
Destrás de una iglesia se pierde la ola
de negros que zumban maruga en la rumba.

The predominance of images and terms that recall slavery and *brujería* in these stanzas reinforces the notion that Ballagas saw *comparsas* as peculiar spectacles that embodied both the innate superstitions and the cultural backwardness of the Afro-Cuban participants. The references to animals are illustrative of this point as they are all significant in terms of their obvious evocation of the witchcraft and magic that so many Cubans associated with the nation's black population. Cats are widely recognized in the Western tradition as the quintessential allies and protectors of witches, and according to the author of *La brujería y los brujos de Cuba*, no accredited witch can function without one (21). Lydia Cabrera explains that it is commonly held that cats are in cahoots with the devil, and she adds that the black cat is indispensable "in the black magic of the Congos," as it is a principal ingredient of the Mayombero's *nganga judía*, a magical potion whose purpose is to cause harm (*Animales* 110–11). Cabrera also reports that dogs are known to bark at the malevolent spirits that inhabit some individuals (*Animales* 184), which suggests a possible motive for Ballagas's inclusion of this detail just before the emergence of the spirits of the African slaves. The *cocuyos* or fireflies—which light the path for the *ánima sola*—also emphasize the atmosphere of mystery and superstition that imbues the final stanzas of "Comparsa habanera." In some regions of Cuba it is believed that fireflies are souls from Purgatory or spirits of the dead, and practitioners of *brujería* have been known to use them as vehicles to send curses to distant enemies, as Cabrera has noted: "Para enviar lejos un hechizo ... se toma al Cocuyo y se le dice: 'Cocuyo ve a casa de Fulano'" [To send a curse far away ... one takes the firefly and says to him: 'firefly, go to the house of so-and-so'] (*Animales* 86).

The symbolic importance of the *cocuyo* is reinforced through the other spirits that seem to be conjured by the ritualistic drumbeats of the passing *comparsa*: deceased slave ancestors, whose rattling shackles add to the cacophony of the *comparsa*; *güijes* and *lloronas*, evil river spirits believed to bring bad luck; and the *ánima sola*, a soul from Purgatory, which was typically identified with the *orisha* Eleguá in Afro-Cuban rituals. The sudden emergence of these spirits indicates the culmination of the carnival procession at the same time that it directs the reader's attention to the "naïve superstitions" of Cubans of color. The *güije*—derived from the indigenous term *jigüe* by metathesis—is a malevolent river spirit that, according to the most popular versions of the legend, takes on the form of a dark-skinned Indian dwarf or a naked "negrito brujo" (Ortiz, *Glosario* 252). According to Guirao, the appearance of the *güije* was considered to be an omen of an impending calamity (*Órbita* 192), but these malevolent spirits were also known for their trickery and devilish antics. Given that traditional *comparsas* were associated with rowdy behavior and wanton violence, the *güije's* emergence from the tumult of the procession can easily be construed as a metaphor for the fear that many Cubans had of such spectacles and of large crowds of Afro-Cubans in general. The reference to the *llorana* is somewhat less fitting in the context of the Afro-Cuban carnival, as the legends associated with this river spirit in the form of a woman in mourning are not particularly well known in Cuba, and the spirit itself is not associated with any of the Afro-Cuban religions. The "ánima sola" is invoked to ward off evil, but Ballagas notes in the glossary to *Cuaderno de poesía negra* that the mere utterance of the term was enough to drive Afro-Cubans to shout out in fear: "¡Sola vaya!" [Sola, be gone!]. According to Fernando Ortiz, fetishes of the *ánima sola* were often hung from the doors of the homes of practitioners of Afro-Cuban religions to bar the entrance of evil spirits (*Los negros brujos* 73). The *marugas* used by the *comparseros* in Ballagas's poem are also symbolic of their fear of the supernatural, since these primitive maracas were allegedly employed most often in Afro-Cuban rituals to chase away malevolent spirits (Ortiz, *Los negros brujos* 92).

It is not entirely clear why these lines were excised from several post-1937 versions of "Comparsa habanera." For lack of more convincing explanations, I would posit that Ballagas was motivated to truncate the poem by the lively debate over *comparsas*—to which we have already alluded several times—that played out among members of the *Sociedad de Estudios Afrocubanos* (of which Ballagas was a founding member), Havana's mayor, and the members of *Adelante*. In his well-known response to the mayor, who had solicited feedback on a plan to legalize *comparsas*, Fernando Ortiz underscored the importance of embracing *comparsas* as symbols of Cuba's distinctive, mixed-race identity. He argued, moreover, that traditional *comparsas* should not be seen as purely African-derived traditions, since they embodied the cultural heterogeneity that made Cuba unique.

Ortiz also emphasized the need for a stronger sense of national pride, which, he implied, could be expressed through unique Cuban cultural traditions such as *comparsas*. Despite his push for their reauthorization, however, Ortiz stressed the need for "a stable system of regulation" that would serve to transform *comparsas* into a valuable social and cultural institution ("Las comparsas populares" 141). Once *comparsas* were officially reauthorized in February 1937, white intellectuals began to take credit for having "saved" them from extinction. José Antonio Fernández de Castro, a prominent member of the white cultural mainstream and the *minorista* generation, put it this way:

> Afortunadamente y debido a una campaña estética dirigida por Fernando Ortiz y secundada por E. Roig de Leuchsenring y otros intelectuales blancos, estos espectáculos tan típicos y bellos, han vuelto a reproducirse en nuestras calles y paseos habaneros. ("La literatura" 11)

> [Fortunately, and thanks to an aesthetic campaign directed by Fernando Ortiz and backed by E. Roig de Leuchsenring and other white intellectuals, these beautiful and typical spectacles have again begun to be produced in our Havana streets and promenades.]

In light of these details, I would argue that by 1937 Ballagas felt compelled to revamp his poetic rendition of a traditional Afro-Cuban carnival procession to make it more compatible with the evolving vision of *comparsas* as valuable vehicles for the expression of national pride and cultural autonomy. By cutting the slavery-associated images, as well as many of those that most patently evoked African-derived witchcraft and superstitions, Ballagas effectively toned down a poem whose original version evoked too many of the shameful legacies of the colonial era that Ortiz, the members of the *Asociación de Estudios Afrocubanos,* and many black and mulatto intellectuals wished to eradicate.

According to Emilio Roig de Leuchsenring, the highly regulated carnival celebrations of 1937 exemplified how spectacles whose atavistic qualities had in the past evoked the repugnance of so many Cubans could be "elevated" to the level of admirable folkloric art by stripping them of their most patently African-derived elements ("Las comparsas" 149). An editorial published in *Diario de la Marina* on February 14, 1937 expressed a similar sentiment. In it the unnamed author marveled that despite the fact that over 100,000 spectators crowded the streets of Havana to watch the first *comparsas* of the carnival season file by, no incidents of violence, lewdness, or immoral behavior had been reported. Like Roig de Leuchsenring, this author stressed that careful organization, strict police observance, and the eradication of certain unsavory African elements had elevated traditional *comparsas* to a new level of respectability:

> es satisfactorio observar que la magnífica organización dada a ese espectáculo produjo los mejores resultados, pues lo que en otros tiempos constituyera motivos de preocupación para las autoridades, ya que siempre los choques de las comparsas—con su intromisión de ñáñiguismo—significaban epílogos trágicos, fué anoche una fiesta de simple regocijo . . . las comparsas realizaban sus maniobras y sus bailes . . . en forma que no podía herir los sentimientos de la decencia. ("Las comparsas" 1)

[It is satisfying to observe that the magnificent organization of that spectacle produced the best results. Indeed what in other times constituted motives for preoccupation for the authorities, since the confrontations between comparsas—what with the interference of *ñáñiguismo*—used to signify tragic epilogues, last night was a fiesta of simple joy ... the *comparsas* acted out their maneuvers and their dances ... in a way that could not offend our senses of decency.]

It seems clear from such opinions that it was widely accepted among the Cuban majority that the regulations imposed on *comparsas* after they were officially reinstated in 1937 were meant to de-Africanize them and—as Ramón Vasconcelos put it—to diminish the likelihood of their degeneration into "celebrations of *ñáñiguismo*" ("Al margen" 34). Ballagas's decidedly toned-down version of "Comparsa habanera" may indeed reflect the ever-increasing push among middle-class Cuban intellectuals in the mid-1930s to civilize traditional *comparsas* by shifting the focus from their most "primitive," slavery-associated characteristics to their latent potential to inspire a sense of national pride and to reflect Cuba's distinctive cultural legacy. As we have seen, however, even in its truncated version, Ballagas's widely anthologized poem still exudes ambivalence toward Afro-Cubans and their culture. On the one hand its vibrant rhythm and colorful images seem to be in keeping with the ostensibly festive nature of carnival, and they suggest, at least on a superficial level, a celebration of Afro-Cubans and their cultural legacy in the young Republic. On the other hand, Ballagas's stereotypical depiction of the black *comparseros*—who are marked by their exaggerated *bozal* speech, ignorance, primitive superstitions, drunkenness, and unrestrained sexuality—belies his claims that his *poesía negra* embodied the desire among *afrocubanista* poets to replace negative portrayals of black Cubans by authors of previous generations with sincere and authentic images. In short, the post-1937 version of "Comparsa habanera," even with its reduced number of images associated with *brujería* and absence of direct references to the shameful legacy of slavery, still echoes the prevailing sentiment in Havana in the mid-1930s that African-influenced cultural manifestations would only be fully accepted as "vital" and "beneficial" components of Cuba's evolving national identity if they were tailored to fit the tastes and standards of the white, middle-class majority.

5

Drumming Up the Black Vote

Chambelonas and Cuban Electoral Politics in José Zacarías Tallet's "Quintín Barahona"

> A los partidos oficialmente reconocidos les conviene mucho la supeditación de la masa negra. Por ello seguirán con el hombre de color el mismo procedimiento que hasta aquí: Buenos ofrecimientos que siempre . . . serán olvidados a la hora del cumplimiento.
>
> [The submission of the Negro masses serves the purposes of the officially recognized parties. For that reason with the man of color they will follow the same procedure as they have until now: great offerings that will always . . . be forgotten at the hour of fulfillment.]
>
> Juan Marinello "Acción y omission"

> El más genial de los políticos había sido aquel futuro representante que repartía tarjetas redactadas en dialecto Apapa, prometiendo rumbas democráticas y libertad de rompimientos para ganarse la adhesión de las Potencias ñáñigas. ¡Votad por él . . . !
>
> [The most brilliant of the politicians had been that future representative who handed out cards written in the Apapa dialect, promising democratic rumbas and freedom to celebrate their rituals in order to win over the loyalty of the Ñáñigo *potencias*. Vote for him . . . !]
>
> Alejo Carpentier, *Écue-Yamba-Ó*

From a political standpoint, the concerted efforts made by Cuban politicians to ban or eliminate supposedly backward Afro-Cuban customs and traditions presented them with a significant conundrum: how to uproot or contain African cultural influences while at the same time courting the support of black men who had recently been granted the right to vote. As Alejandro de la Fuente has noted, Afro-Cubans represented nearly one third of the voting population by 1907, and the mainstream Cuban press warned that there were "'too many' to be ignored by candidates. No matter what their personal feelings and prejudices, political figures were forced by universal male suffrage to pay at least lip service to the ideal of an inclusive republic . . . in other words, Cuban politicians could not afford to be racist" (58). The great hypocrisy of many administrations was revealed by their courting of the black vote and promotion of certain causes dear to Cubans of color in order to advance their own political agendas at the same time that they condemned and outlawed certain African-derived music and dance, religious practices, and other cultural manifestations. For example, David Brown has noted that because of the ever-increasing "visibility, economic power, and voting-block influence of the Abakuá by the early 20th century, candidates for local office began to court the votes of Abakuá constituencies. Political messages in the Brícamo language appeared on handbills" and "innumerable greased hands" enlarged Abakuá coffers (*Light Inside* 32).[1] De la Fuente has similarly noted that "presidential and congressional candidates made Afro-Cuban societies an unavoidable stop on their tours," and he adds that "in their quest for votes" politicians even visited associations such as the Abakuá brotherhoods despite the fact that they were widely reputed to be hotbeds of criminal activity (162).

Cuban president José Miguel Gómez was known for aggressively soliciting the black vote by visiting Abakuá lodges and using Afro-Cuban symbols during his political rallies (Ayorinde 52), and he was vehemently derided by his conservative opponents for failing to condemn *ñañiguismo*. Gómez was also among the first to drum up the black vote by hiring traditional Afro-Cuban carnival ensembles to play in his electoral campaign. However, during his administration there was an aggressive fight against *comparsas* and *congas* and other cultural manifestations associated with them. Furthermore, it should be pointed out that it was during his presidency that the Partido Independiente de Color was banned, political organizations based on race were outlawed, and more than three thousand black Cubans lost their lives during the Racist Massacre of 1912. Gerardo Machado also hired Afro-Cuban *congas*, and he provided considerable financial support to certain Afro-Cuban cults during his electoral campaign (Thomas 683, Ayorinde 52). He was also well known during the early years of his presidency for "pro-black" policies: he granted land and funds to black organizations such as the Club Atenas, signed a law that turned the date of Antonio Maceo's death (December 7) into a national holiday, opposed the formation of a chapter of the Ku Klux Klan in Camagüey, and appointed blacks and mulattos to prominent positions in his administration (de la Fuente 92, 163, Bronfman 136–37). At the same time, however, he signed legislation in 1925 that banned the playing of "drums or musical instruments of African flavor" in public and prohibited, under threat of strict penalties, traditional *comparsas* and *congas*, all "Lucumí-style dances . . . and any other ceremonies contrary to morality and good customs" (qtd. in Moore 231).

Among the most obvious and prevalent forms of political exploitation of Afro-Cubans and their culture during the formative years of the Republic was the hiring of Afro-Cuban carnival ensembles during electoral campaigns. Indeed, despite official prohibitions of the most traditional forms of these masqueraded carnival troupes, many candidates—and most notoriously those from the Liberal Party—hired groups of Afro-Cuban dancers and musicians as a means to "drum up support," as Sublette puts it (322), for their campaigns. In his first novel, *Écue-Yamba-Ó*, Alejo Carpentier devotes a chapter to this divisive tradition among Cuban politicians, and wryly describes, through the recollections of one of the black protagonists, the advent of political *comparsas*—known as *chambelonas* among the liberals and *congas* among members of the conservative party—in the early decades of the twentieth century:

> Cierto candidato había tenido la inefable idea de entronizar el espíritu de la conga colonial en sus fiestas de propaganda. De este modo, cuando el mitin era importante y la charanga de la tribuna de enfrente comenzaba a sonar antes de tiempo, el orador tenía la estupefacción de ver a su público transformado en una majadera de rumberos, mientras sus palabras se esfumaban ante una estruendosa ofensiva de: ¡Aé, aé, aé la Chambelona! Los electores recorrían toda la calle principal en un tiempo de *comparsa arrollada*, y regresaban a escuchar otro discurso, abotonándose las camisas. (114, italics in the original)

> [A certain candidate had had the infallible idea to enthrone the spirit of the colonial conga in his fiestas of propaganda. Thus, when the meeting was important and the orchestra on the speaker's platform across the way began to play too early, the speaker would be amazed to see his public transformed into an annoying mob of rumba dancers, while his words faded away in the midst of a resounding offensive of: ¡Aé, aé, aé la Chambelona! The voters traversed the entire

main street to the tempo of a *comparsa arollada*, and they returned to listen to another speech, while buttoning their shirts.]

Carnival and Politics: the Case of "Quintín Barahona"

In this chapter I will discuss the contentious issue of the hiring of political *comparsas* by white politicians in the context of José Zacarías Tallet's "Quintín Barahona" (1935), which deals directly with this long-running tradition among Cuban politicians. This lengthy poem is one of just two that Tallet (1893–1989) wrote on Afro-Cuban themes, both of which were published in Ramón Guirao's *Órbita de la poesía afrocubana* in 1938. As has been the fate of many of Tallet's poems, "Quintín Barahona" has been largely overshadowed by the critical attention that has been showered on "La rumba." This important poem first appeared in print in the Cuban literary magazine *Atuei* in August 1928, and has been variously referred to as the "first nationally recognized *afrocubanista* poem" (Moore 151), and the poem "that established the rumba dancer as a standard poetic figure" (Claudette Williams 52). "Quintín Barahona," on the other hand, has been the subject of little more than passing references in critical studies, and is virtually unknown among modern readers.[2] It is, nonetheless, a fascinating and alluring poem, and its frank treatment of the sociopolitical plight of Afro-Cubans makes it a relatively rare example of an *afrocubanista* poem in which substantive issues outweigh the requisite stereotypical images of blacks and their cultural traditions.

Before discussing the sociopolitical themes in "Quintín Barahona," it is important to underscore the fact that the poem is not without the racial stereotypes that typify much of the poetry of Afrocubanismo. In the first place the poem's namesake is repeatedly referred to with derogatory terms like *comebola* [stupid or gullible person], or, most notably, as a *negro ripiera* [black rogue, lout, or scoundrel]. The importance of the latter term is underscored by the fact that all publications of the poem subsequent to its first appearance in Guirao's 1938 anthology appear under the title "Negro ripiera." The poem's black speaker also makes much of Quintín's fat lips and big mouth when criticizing him for blowing his cornet and singing in support of a white politician. The most notable stereotype in "Quintín Barahona" is the parody of the broken Spanish spoken by uneducated and lower-class black Cubans. The highly exaggerated *bozal* speech of the black poetic voice somewhat diminishes the poem's social and political punch since it is hard to overlook its implicit racist undertones.

Nonetheless, unlike many other poems about carnivals, *comparsas*, and *congas*, demeaning references to drunkenness, unbridled revelry, and raucous dance and music are all but absent from Tallet's poem. Likewise, stereotypical descriptions of the Afro-Cuban protagonist are limited, and take a backseat to more meaningful issues such as the exploitation of Afro-Cubans by white politicians, the long and shameful legacy of electoral corruption in Cuba, and the apathy and lack of political awareness among black voters.

In the opening stanzas the anonymous—though presumably Afro-Cuban—poetic voice introduces us to Quintín, a black cornet player who, as we learn later, has been recruited by local government officials to take part in a political *comparsa* during the electoral campaign:

Su bemba de negro congo
se prolonga, se prolonga
y se pone ancha y dorá
cuando e negrito pilongo,
Quintín,
nieto de la negra conga,
se pega su conettín
y resopla de beddá. (68–69)

Here, and throughout the poem, the black onlooker refers frequently to Quintín's thick, "Congo" lips, which are significant not just as markers of his Africanness, but also as the key instruments, so to speak, of his profession as a cornet player and singer. As he watches Quintín pass by, the speaker seems to focus on his lips, which stretch and pucker as he blows his horn, and then later open wide as he shouts the lines of "La chambelona." Quintín's emaciated and lanky black body—the poetic voice twice refers to him as a "negrito pilongo"—is also significant since it suggests that his hunger may be a motive for his participation in the political *comparsa*.

The description of Quintín as a "nieto de la negra conga" can be read in two ways. On the one hand the poetic voice could be referring to the Congolese origins of his grandmother. On the other hand, in a reading that works well in the context of a poem about a black man who performs in a political rally for white politicians who want his vote, "la negra conga" may also refer to these traditional carnival processions that originated from African slave celebrations and were banned repeatedly in the early years of the Republic for their supposed primitive qualities. Though it is important to point out that the political *comparsas* of the conservatives were often referred to as *congas*, the speaker here is certainly not suggesting that Quintín should be playing his cornet for the opposing political party.

Indeed, the poetic voice seems to imply that Quintín is completely uninterested in politics, and that while he blasts his cornet he is absorbed in thoughts of an entirely different nature:

¿Po qué tú mira pa sielo
y pone lo sojo en blanco
y te queda como lelo
y suda tinta? Sé franco ...

¿E que tu bemba dorá
ta resando a Obatalá? (69)

Unlike many other poems of Afrocubanismo, in which references to blackness do little more than conjure up racial stereotypes and prejudices, those in "Quintín Barahona" are essential to the poem's political message. Here it is clear that the speaker is trying to understand why Quintín, whose dark skin he accentuates by noting that his sweat looks like black ink as it rolls down his body, would betray his African origins by taking part in what essentially amounts to a bastardization of a traditional carnival procession. It seems unlikely to him that Quintín—who appears to be totally absorbed in the music and dance could actually enjoy playing his cornet for white politicians. He therefore posits that he must be secretly paying homage to *Obatalá*—one of the most important deities of the Yoruba pantheon who is at once the god of creation and overseer of the activities of all other divinities—as he marches down the street. Along the same line of thinking, the reader can surmise that the speaker's interrogation of Quintín is motivated by the fact that he knows that he is a practitioner of Santería, and therefore has no business associating with the same white politicians who disparage his religious beliefs and cultural traditions.

The speaker realizes, moreover, that Quintín knows nothing about Cuban politics, and that he has no reason to perform for the benefit of the Liberal Party candidate—or any other politician for that matter. When he asks Quintín, "¿Po qué tú toca en la fietta / si tú no ere liberá?" (69), and later inquires, "¿tú no piensa dentro e guíro / po quién tú ba i a botá . . . ?" (72), the speaker is not so much questioning his party affiliation, but rather is underscoring his own opinion that Quintín has never cared about politics, and that the politicians have likewise never cared about him. At the same time he is emphasizing how white Cuban politicians are exploiting Afro-Cubans and their culture with the sole purpose of winning votes. To emphasize Quintín's ignorance the speaker insists that he doesn't even understand the significance of the song that he is singing:

Tú no piensa en ná,
en la fietta liberá,
cuando tu bemba gritona
canta, negrito Quintín:
"Yo no tube la cupitta
ni tampoco la cuppona,
¡aé, aé, aée La Chambelona!"

By the time Tallet penned his poem, "La Chambelona" had long been associated with Liberal Party political campaigns and the Afro-Cuban *comparsas* that played for them. There is some dispute as to when "La Chambelona" was composed and when it was first employed to drum up black support for white political candidates, but it is generally agreed that it first became well known when the Liberal Party used it during the 1916 electoral campaign to hurl insults at the incumbent conservative, Mario García Menocal.[3] The following verses from a popular 1916 version of the tune serve to underscore how "La Chambelona" was employed to ridicule the opposition candidate and the policies of his administration:

El rey de España mandó un mensaje,
diciéndole a Menocal:
"Devuélveme el caballo
que tu no sabes montar."

A pie, a pie, a pie,
a mi pueblo le da pena.
A pie, a pie, a pie,
los timbales ya no suenan.[4]

As Robin Moore reports, the first stanza refers to a horse that the king of Spain gave to Menocal during his first term, but on a metaphorical level the horse "represents the country, while jokes about Menocal's inability to ride allude to his decreasing popularity and assumed failure in the election campaign" (77). In Alejo Carpentier's *Écue-Yamba-Ó*, the narrator suggests that the popular phrase "¡A pie!" [On foot!] synthesized the democratic spirit of the Liberal Party at the same time that it served to oppose the Conservative Party's chant of "¡A caballo!" [On horseback!] (130). The second stanza can be read as an allusion to the widespread prohibitions against Afro-Cuban instruments and traditional *comparsas* that were enacted during Menocal's administration.

Shortly after seizing power in the fraudulent elections of November 1916, Menocal, who was not amused by such gibes against him, prohibited the playing of "La Chambelona" (Sublette 322). However, the ban was of little use since the song's constant repetition during the 1916 campaign guaranteed its nearly mythic fame. Indeed, "La Chambelona" became so loaded with symbolic importance that a civil uprising in February 1917—which was led by José Miguel Gómez and other members of the Liberal Party who sought to win back power that the conservatives had recently wrested from them in the fraudulent election—came to be known as the Chambelona Revolution.

With the passing of time and the comings and goings of new candidates, the lyrics of "La Chambelona" inevitably changed to reflect relevant political issues, but its melody and its principal purposes—to promote political agendas and ridicule the opposition candidate—remained constant.[5] By 1935, the year that Tallet penned his poem, "La Chambelona," along with the myriad social and political implications that the popular song implied, was familiar to virtually every Cuban citizen of voting age. At the same time "La Chambelona" and the political *comparsas* associated with it came to be viewed with scorn by many leading Cuban intellectuals who considered them to be crude symbols of government hypocrisy and exploitation of the lower classes, as well as artless versions of traditional Afro-Cuban carnival processions.

According to Alberto Arredondo, Cuba's political history is full of examples of "disgraceful *congas*" being turned into tools of electoral exploitation by "unscrupulous strongmen" (*El negro en Cuba* 134). In an article written in the mid-1930s Emilio Roig de Leuchsenring followed a similar vein by criticizing political *comparsas* for their vulgarity and total lack of folkloric elements. Like Arredondo he saved his harshest criticism for the white politicians who had used them for years to further their own agendas:

> chambelonas se sacan año tras año a las calles habaneras por políticos y gobernantes, en la creencia de que así mejor engañan al pueblo con esos falsos y explotadores halagos de democracia. ("Dos actualidades" 44)

> [*chambelonas* are brought out into the Havana streets year after year by politicians and government officials, in the belief that by doing so they can better deceive the people with those false and exploitative blandishments of democracy.

Finally, in his 1937 letter to Havana mayor Antonio Beruff Mendieta, in which he argued for the relegalization of traditional Afro-Cuban *comparsas*, Fernando Ortiz ridiculed Cuban politicians for condemning traditional *comparsas* as atavistic Afro-Cuban rituals at the same time that they hired *chambelonas* and *congas* to promote their political agendas.

> [Las comparsas] tuvieron años de libertad; pero la política se mezcló en sus festejos, y el problema de si se permitían o no se convirtió anualmente en juego de intereses políticos. Así conservadores como liberales, ayudaban o reprimían esas expansiones populares, según el criterio cambiadizo de sus conveniencias circunstanciales.
>
>   Y son bien notorios y repetidos los casos de que esa misma política que prohíbe a veces las comparsas, calificándolas de resabio inculto . . . organice para sus propagandas electorales, multitud de *chambelonas*, congas, y otras músicas vulgares y de escasísimo arte. ("Informe" 13, italics in original)

> [*Comparsas* had their years of freedom; but politics got mixed up in their festivities, and the problem of whether they should be permitted or not turned into an annual game of political interests.

Conservatives as well as Liberals, helped to repress those popular pleasures, according to the ever-changing criteria of their circumstantial expedients.

And there have been many notorious cases in which the same politicians that prohibited *comparsas*, classifying them as uncultured vices . . . have organized for their electoral propaganda great numbers of *chambelonas*, *congas*, and other vulgar music of scant artistic value.]

In his poem Tallet clearly suggests that *chambelonas* are offensive spectacles that lack artistic merit, but he focuses mainly on the more significant issue of how these political *comparsas* embody the legacy of exploitation of Cuban blacks by white men in power. In one brief stanza, for example, the poetic voice calls attention to the fact that many politicians literally tried to buy the black vote by paying token fees to the musicians, and he reminds Quintín that he is only "supporting" the Liberal Party candidate because he is being paid to do so: "Tú piensa en la do peseta / que te ban a dá" (70). And later in the poem Quintín himself confirms that he participates largely for the money, which he spends at campaign parties held at the Liberal headquarters. Quintín's admission is significant since it reinforces the notion that Afro-Cubans are being recruited and paid not for their own benefit, but for that of the candidate. Indeed, the money paid to the black participants in the *chambelona* is essentially returned to the coffers of the candidate who knows that the tasty treats at the parties will be as hard to resist as the pocket change.

It is worth pointing out here that enticing potential black voters to participate in political *comparsas* with promises of money and food was a common practice throughout Cuba during the early years of the Republic. And while many Cubans—such as Fernándo Ortiz and Ramón Vasconcelos—criticized the politicians for exploiting the Afro-Cuban population, many others felt that the latter group was equally to blame. In a scathing editorial published in the Santiago newspaper *El Oriental* in July 1924, for example, Pablo W. Guerra ridiculed that city's black population for using Cuban politics as a pretext to fill their empty bellies and line their pockets with money from the national treasury:

El carnaval político tiene sus comparsas que al compás de la "conga" van "arrollando" sin importárseles otra cosa que ver su abdomen lleno de buenos manjares y los bolsillos repletos del oro que lleva el pueblo trabajador a las cajas del Tesorero. (325)

[The political carnival has its *comparsas*, which to the beat of the "conga" go about "arrollando" without caring about anything but seeing their bellies full of treats and their pockets replete with gold that the hard working public brings to the Treasurer's cash boxes.]

In his very brief commentary on Tallet's "Quintín Barahona," Jorge María Ruscalleda Bercedóniz follows a similar line of thinking by suggesting that Quintín is presented as an opportunist who only cares about money (406). However, this interpretation seems to give little weight to the fact that Quintín is a poor and hungry black man in 1930s Havana, and that for most individuals like him, even a few cents would have been hard to resist. Indeed, the real opportunists are not the black musicians, but rather the white politicians who offer them money and food in exchange for a vote precisely because they know that they will not be able to refuse.[6] Moreover, they also realize that much of the money will be returned to their own coffers.

Another important sociopolitical problem that Tallet introduces in "Quintín Barahona" is that of government exploitation of Afro-Cubans during the Wars of Independence. The poetic voice implies that this mistreatment simply carried over into the present as evidenced in the *chambelona* that he is witnessing. In what seems like an attempt to at once awaken Quintín's political consciousness and his sense of dignity and to convince him not to take part in the political *comparsa*, the speaker reminds Quintín of the suffering and disillusionment endured by his grandfather, an ex-slave and decorated war veteran, and his father, who apparently was killed during the Racist Massacre of 1912:

Tu abuelo fué negro eclabo
y compró su libettá:
bino de e monte hecho cabo
y con un braso na má.

Tu padre, e negro Facundo,
botó por José Migué,
y a e lo botaron de e mundo
cuando [a] Etenó Iboné. (70)

The reference in the first of these two stanzas to Quintín's grandfather evokes the long legacy of racism and exploitation endured by so many Cubans of African ancestry; first as slaves, and then as second-class citizens of the Republic who, despite their indispensable services to the nation in the Wars of Independence, remained marginalized in all spheres of Cuban society. Aline Helg has pointed out that during these conflicts, "Afro-Cubans' *expectations* regarding their position in the *future* increased dramatically. Many viewed their contribution to the struggle against Spain as an outstanding effort that called for proportionate reward when independence was achieved... Thus, after 1902 their sense of injustice arose from their ability to compare the rewards they received with those of other groups" (*Rightful Share* 12, emphasis in original). Despite promises by politicians and government officials that the lots of Afro-Cubans would improve with independence, such was not the case, as Louis A. Pérez has pointed out. In fact, "Conditions for Afro-Cubans did not materially improve with the establishment of the republic," but rather "seem to have actually deteriorated." According to Pérez, even blacks who had risen to high ranks in the war were victims of job discrimination, were systematically excluded from the rural guard and the police force, and rarely found employment in civil departments of government (*Cuba Under* 147-48)

In Tallet's poem, then, the fate of Quintín's grandfather epitomizes the great disillusionment faced by many black soldiers who had sacrificed so much for Cuba's freedom but received little in return for their defense of the nation after the establishment of the Republic. According to the poetic voice's cynical vision, Quintín's grandfather, who had achieved the rank of corporal in the army, had nothing to show for his distinguished military career but a missing arm. Likewise, the speaker in the poem also underscores how Quintín's father became an unwitting victim of governmental deception and institutionalized racism. Despite his support of liberal presidential candidate José Miguel Gómez, for whom he cast a vote in the 1908 campaign, Quintín's father was killed four years later by Cuban government troops—who were under Gómez's leadership—during the Racist Massacre of 1912. It is important to repeat here that throughout his presidential run Gómez was well known for his concerted efforts to court black voters. Christine Ayorinde has noted, for example, that Gómez aggressively solicited Afro-Cuban votes by hiring black *comparsas* and frequently "visit[ing] the black societies and us[ing] Afro-Cuban symbols in rallies" (52).

Paradoxically, Gómez also went to great lengths to quash attempts made by Afro-Cubans to organize politically outside the realm of the traditional two-party system. Shortly after the establishment of the Partido Independiente de Color by Evaristo Estenoz and Pedro Ivonet, President Gómez worked to discredit the party and its leaders since they posed a great threat to the Liberal Party's considerable sway over the Afro-Cuban electorate. When Estenoz refused to dissolve the PIC, Gómez's administration responded by arresting and jailing him and then drawing up legislation known as Morúa's Law that outlawed the formation of racially exclusive political parties. In order to further derail the black opposition, the Gómez administration engaged in "strong antiblack propaganda" and revived damaging stereotypes "of the black rapist and of a Haitian-style revolution." According to Helg, such repression was not just aimed at the members of the PIC, but also at other blacks who were reminded that white tolerance had it limits and that they should therefore "stay in their places" (*Rightful Share* 165, 184).

In February 1912 Estenoz, who had been released from prison after serving six months of his sentence, warned President Gómez to repeal Morúa's Law or risk a rebellion by PIC members and supporters. When Estenoz's demands were not met by their April 22 deadline he, Pedro Ivonet, and several hundred supporters led an uprising that met with fierce repression from the Cuban army. In a span of several months Cuban troops, under the leadership of Gómez, massacred thousands of blacks, many of whom were innocent citizens—like Quintín Barahona's father— who had supported his administration and had no connection to the rebels other than the color of their skin.

In the second stanza quoted above, Tallet plays on the Spanish homonyms "votar" [to vote] and "botar" [to kick out, throw out, but here used figuratively to mean "to kill"], to underscore the notion that by voting or getting involved in the political establishment during such turbulent times Cuban blacks risked becoming victims of a deeply corrupt system. Indeed, despite their support for José Miguel Gómez—who had so enthusiastically courted them—Quintín's father and many other Cuban blacks ended up becoming casualties of governmentally sanctioned violence. As Louis Pérez points out, the events of 1912 revealed not just "the depth and breadth of social tensions in the early republic" but also how "in every sense, the republic betrayed the hopes of Afro-Cubans" (*Cuba Under* 151).

With the historical backdrop of 1912 in mind, the speaker reminds

Quintín that public involvement in Cuban politics is a risky business that may very well turn him into an unwitting victim like his father and grandfather: "Tú ere negro ripiera, / siempre ha bibío en solá, / ¿qué impotta que tú te muera / po tocá / en la fietta liberá?" (7). It is worth adding that these cautionary words to Quintín can also be seen as a reflection of the fact that political *comparsas* from opposing sides sometimes met in the streets and became involved in violent confrontations, as Virtudes Feliú Herrera has pointed out (*Carnaval cubano* 22). Later, when the deeply disillusioned speaker insists that Quintín Barahona is nothing but a black Cuban ("Tú ere . . . / negro cubano na má") he at once underscores the relative worthlessness of blacks in Cuban society and the fruitlessness of their involvement with the nation's major political parties. Indeed, he insists that even large-scale black support of white presidential candidates—he refers to the case of Ramón Grau San Martín as a concrete example—has no real effect since campaign promises to Afro-Cubans are always broken:

Y cuando se fué Machao
y bino Grao
con su sincuenta po siento,
tu salite entusiammao,
metiendo biento y má biento
con tu bemba amoratá
pegá contra e conettín,
pa gritá:
"¡Sube la loma Sanmattín!"
Totá, pa ná.

Se fué Mongo,
tu bemba de negro congo
ya no lo pué saludá;
y su sincuenta po siento
no te dió na;
to fué cuento,
cuento e camino na má.[7] (71)

In September 1933, after the military coup that brought about the ouster of Gerardo Machado, Ramón Grau San Martín was named Cuba's provisional president, an office that he would hold only until January 1934. Espousing nationalistic reform, Grau, who had made apparently sincere attempts to appeal to Afro-Cuban voters, proclaimed a socialist revolution and enacted sweeping changes in every sphere of Cuban society under the battle cry of "Cuba for Cubans." In addition to demanding U.S. abrogation of the universally hated Platt Amendment, "the provisional government committed itself to economic reconstruction, social reform, and political reorganization" (Pérez, *Cuba* 268): the traditional political parties were dissolved, a department of labor was created, an eight-hour workday was established, a minimum wage was set for sugarcane cutters, interest rates were slashed, women were given the right to vote, maternity leave was mandated for working mothers, etcetera. One of the most notable reforms enacted by Grau's administration—and the one that the speaker in "Quintín Barahona" directly refers to—was the "Ley del cincuenta por ciento" [The Fifty Percent Law], which mandated that at least 50 percent of employees of the nation's industries and commercial enterprises had to be native Cubans.

This significant piece of legislation was especially attractive to disenfranchised Afro-Cubans who saw it as a harbinger of greater employment opportunities for them in all sectors of the Cuban economy. In his 1939 book *El negro en Cuba*, Alberto Arredondo recalled the great significance of the pro-labor reforms enacted by Grau, stressing—as Tallet does in his poem—that the 50 Percent Law was especially enticing to Cuban blacks:

> Inmediatamente que se promulgó esa ley, los negros cubanos la acogieron con calor. Si no llenaba plenamente sus justas ambiciones, por lo menos constituía un indiscutible paso de avance hacia la eliminación del prejuicio y de la discriminación y hacia la ocupación de miles de individuos que estaban sin trabajo. (145–46)

> [Immediately after this law was put into effect, Cuban Negroes took to it enthusiastically. Even if it didn't completely fulfill their just ambitions, at least it constituted an indisputable step toward the elimination of prejudice and discrimination and toward the employment of thousands of individuals who were without work.]

Despite their initial enthusiasm, Afro-Cubans soon learned that the 50 Percent Law would not live up to their expectations. As Arredondo observed some six years after the passage of the law, prejudice and discrimination were still major problems, and relatively few blacks had found gainful employment since the passage of the law. Citing an example of hundreds of foreign-born street car operators who were forced to give up their jobs, he notes that not a single position was given to a black worker because white Cuban women balked at the idea of coming into contact with black hands when paying their fares (*El negro en Cuba* 157–58).

In Tallet's poem, the speaker conjures up the deep disillusionment felt by blacks who had expected to find employment under the new legislation. The image of Quintín blowing his cornet with ever increasing vigor ("metiendo biento y más biento") as he marches in support of Grau and his reformist agenda, then, suggests the inevitable deflation of their hopes. On another level, Quintín's blowing can be seen to symbolize the "hot air," so to speak, of politicians who during their electoral campaigns had made many bold promises that they either could not or would not keep. In the case of Grau San Martín, the desire to better the lot of Afro-Cubans may have been genuine, but his term came to an end in just four months, and unemployment and discrimination would hinder the progress of Afro-Cubans for years to come. In Tallet's poem, we learn through the speaker that Quintín, like so many Afro-Cubans of the era, is still without work, and that his enthusiastic support of Grau and his 50 Percent Law had therefore been for naught.

Despite his suggestion that Afro-Cuban involvement in Cuban politics is fruitless and even risky, the speaker in "Quintín Barahona" ridicules black men like Quintín who make a mockery out of the electoral system in Cuba by having no clear political ideology and not even bothering to learn anything about the candidates that they "support." Referring to a line from a 1916 version of "La Chambelona," he ridicules Quintín for his gullibility and ignorance:

> tocando tu connetín
> hasiéndote e comebola
> tú canta pa tí en la chola,
> Quintín:
> en la fietta liberá:
> "Apiaso me dió boteya
> y yo boté po Barona." (70)

The speaker implies here that Quintín doesn't even understand what he is singing about. The lines in question refer to the hotly contested and controversial mayoral elections in Havana in 1916, the year that "La Chambelona" was incorporated on a wide scale into the fabric of national politics.

During their respective campaigns liberal candidate Manuel Varona Suárez, who won handily but amid much controversy, and his Conservative Party opponent, Leopoldo Aspiazu, were reported to have taken part in a shameless political game of buying and selling votes. It should be noted that the presidential elections of the same year were also marred by corruption and controversy. As Clifford L. Staten puts it, Mario García Menocal "won an election in which more votes were cast than the number of people who were eligible to vote" (51).

According to Moore, this excerpt from a 1916 version of "La Chambelona" attests to "the common practice of candidates buying the votes of the working classes with the promise of *botellas* or government jobs under their administration" (77). This observation, however, is inaccurate, since "*botellas*" does not refer to government jobs for the working classes, but rather to sinecures, or governmental "soft jobs" that had no real responsibilities but came with significant financial benefits. Such "jobs," which were handed out to people with important political connections and not to the working class, were a disaster for the Cuban economy and for the government since they depleted much-needed funds at the same time that they endangered the positions of many legitimate government employees. This tradition of "*botelleros*" handing out cushy jobs is said to have originated during the administration of José Miguel Gómez, but hit its peak during the vastly corrupt administration of Mario García Menocal (1913–1921). According to Alejandro de la Fuente, "the secretary of the treasury estimated in 1921 that about 15 million pesos were paid annually for such jobs, an amount that represented more than 40 percent of what the state paid for 'real' employees. In other words, botellas were equivalent to the annual average salary of 19,000 additional employees" (130).

By including these lines twice in his poem Tallet at once alludes to the deeply corrupt nature of the electoral process in Cuba and calls attention to the ironic outcomes of the game of buying political support: on the one hand, the "influential" white voters take the soft jobs from one candidate and then vote for another, and on the other, the poor black voters take money from the same politicians and then don't vote at all. Both scenarios make a travesty of the political system at the same time that they perpetuate the cycle of corruption. As we learn in the final stanzas of the poem, in which Quintín assumes the poetic voice, he accepts payment from a white politician to play his cornet in a political *comparsa* and the subsequent festivities at the Liberal Party headquarters, but never bothers to exercise his right to vote in the elections.

> Yo toco mi conettín
> en la fietta liberá,
> pero a desí la beddá,
> Quintín
> ¡subuso! no bá a botá . . . (72)

It is worth pointing out here that black nonparticipation in Cuban elections was not always a symptom of apathy or ignorance on their part, as it seems to be with Quintín Barahona. Indeed, some prominent black leaders discouraged Afro-Cubans from taking part in any type of political activity. Around the same time that Tallet published "Quintín Barahona," black journalist and intellectual José Armando Pla, for example, discouraged Afro-Cuban involvement in the political process until significant racial vindication had become a part of programs of the major political parties in Cuba. He argued, moreover, that only through total abstention of black voters would white leaders in Cuba realize just how important Afro-Cubans were to the political, social, and economic future of the nation (qtd. in Marinello 7). Much like Tallet, who seems to be advocating a black political consciousness in "Quintín Barahona," fellow *minorista* Juan Marinello criticized Pla's controversial opinions in a 1936 article published in *Adelante*:

> Yo creo que este punto de vista es equivocado. . . . Las posturas negativas determinan a la larga la desmoralización del grupo que las adopta. Predicar abstencionismos a una masa que tiene el retraso natural de sus esclavitudes seculares es enterrarla en un derrotismo del que será difícil levantarla cuando llegue el día de las energías decisorias. (7)

> [I believe that this is a mistaken point of view. . . . In the long run negative postures bring about demoralization of the group that adopts them. To predicate abstention to a group that suffers from the natural setback of their age-old slaveries is to bury that group in a defeatism from which it will be difficult to escape when the day of decisive strength arrives.]

It would seem that it is precisely the sort of defeatism that Marinello speaks of in his article that has lead Quintín Barahona not just to forgo his own right to vote, but also to view the political process with indifference. His apathetic outlook is clearly reflected in his frank admission that his "support" of the Liberal Party candidate has nothing to do with politics at all, but rather boils down to a matter of necessity, since the nominal fee that he is paid is just enough for a meal to fill his hungry belly.

> Yo tumbo la do peseta
> en la fietta
> de e pattío liberá;
> tengo la frita segura
> mientras dura
> la campaña eletorá.
> y cuando miro pa e sielo
> y me pongo como lelo
> tocando La Chambelona,
> pienso en mi guira pelá:
> "¡Apiaso me dió boteya
> y yo boté po Barona!"
> Eso na má.
>
> Yo soy Quintín Barahona,
> negro cubano na má. (72–73)

Here Quintín essentially underscores his ignorance of the current political situation in Cuba by admitting that as he sings "La Chambelona" he thinks of nothing but a few lines that hark back nearly twenty years to the hotly contested 1916 campaign for mayor of Havana. It is also significant that in the poem's final lines Quintín not only offers an apolitical justification for participating in the *chambelona*, but also admits that he—like so many of his fellow Afro-Cubans—accepts his subservient role in Cuban electoral politics as a natural consequence of his blackness. Since he is "nothing but a black Cuban" with empty pockets and an empty belly, he sees no reason why he shouldn't milk the system that has always exploited him by accepting money from a politician for whom he has no intention to cast a vote.

In this important and socially progressive poem, Tallet clearly criticizes such political apathy, which was not uncommon among the increasingly disenfranchised Afro-Cuban population in the 1930s. However, instead of the political abstention and disaffiliation from all of the nation's political parties that some leaders in the Afro-Cuban community—such as José Armando Pla—advocated, Tallet seems to be suggesting in his poem that Cuban blacks need to become informed and actively involved in the electoral process. It would be an exaggeration to suggest that Tallet is advocating Afro-Cuban militancy since he does not explicitly invoke such an idea in the poem, but it does seem reasonable to posit that Tallet would have agreed with black intellectual and sociologist Gustavo E. Urrutía, who insisted that Afro-Cubans needed to express their political ideals more actively and openly if they ever wanted to see the changes that they so longed for. As Urrutía put it in an article written in the early months of 1935:

> Los negros deben militar en todos nuestros partidos políticos, pero desde cada uno deben emplear la fuerza de sus votos para hacer cumplir la igualdad de oportunidades que les garantizan y constitución y las leyes vigentes. (qtd. in Llarch 11)[8]

> [Blacks should militate in all of our political parties, but from each one they should use the force of their votes to bring about the fulfillment of the opportunities that the constitution and the current laws guarantee them.]

More than anything, though, the image of an ignorant and sycophantic Afro-Cuban who plays his cornet in the *chambelona* underscores the idea—which was especially prominent in certain poems by Tallet's fellow poets Regino Pedroso and Marcelino Arozarena—that Afro-Cubans would gain little ground in their struggle for political, economic, and social equality by currying the favor of white politicians who had little real concern for such issues.

6

"La conga prohibida"

Felix B. Caignet's Response to Carnival Controversy in Santiago de Cuba

> *Qué noche para gozar señores,*
> *que la conga se soltó.*
>
> [*What a night to enjoy folks,*
> *the conga has been let loose.*]
>
> Ignacio Piñeiro, "Noche de conga"

> *el arrollao de la conga criolla se arrastra las muchedumbres en gozo anestesiante de sus angustias neuróticas.*
>
> [the collective dancing of the *conga criolla* pulls along with it the crowds whose delight numbs their neurotic anguish.]
>
> Fernando Ortiz *"Los factores humanos de la cubanidad"*

Though Felix B. Caignet (1892–1976) is not well known among modern students and critics of Afrocubanismo, his poems were very familiar to audiences throughout Latin America during the height of the movement thanks in large part to Eusebia Cosme (1911–1976), the famed *declamadora* of *poesía negra* and dear friend of Caignet, who included many of his poems in her widely popular recitals. Indeed, from the late 1930s through the mid-1950s many of Caignet's poems—"Coctel de son" [Son Cocktail], "Un despojo" [A Plundering], "El bongosero" [The Bongo Player], "¡Soy maraquero!" [I am a Maraca Player], "Ña Josefa mi abuela" [Ña Josefa, My Grandmother], "Diente de coco" [Coconut Tooth], and "La conga prohibida" [The Forbidden Conga]—were prominently represented in her repertoire. In a typical recital Cosme performed between fifteen and twenty poems, and often included two or three by Caignet. A perusal

Teatro Municipal

EMPRESA JUAN LUCAS Y CIA.

TEMPORADA POPULAR

DE

EUSEBIA COSME

RECITALES DE

POESIA NEGRA

VIERNES 24 DE ABRIL DE 1936 - - A LAS 9 DE LA NOCHE

FIGURE 6.1. Program for an April 1936 recital of *poesía negra* by Eusebia Cosme. (Eusebia Cosme Papers. Manuscripts, Archives, and Rare Books Division. Schomburg Center for Research in Black Culture. The New York Public Library.)

of programs of her recitals from 1936—the year that Caignet arrived in Havana with his poems in hand—to the mid-1950s reveals that Nicolás Guillén is the only Cuban poet that Cosme recited more frequently than Caignet (fig. 6.1).[1]

Despite the fact that Caignet's poems were recited often, their relative anonymity among modern readers is understandable since many of them were not available in print until the publication of his only book of poetry, *A golpe de maracas* [To the Beat of the Maracas], in 1950. It is likely because of their belated publication in this small, privately printed edition (fig. 6.2), that Caignet's poems have appeared in very few anthologies of *poesía negra*, and that his name has not been widely associated with Afro cubanismo.[2] Other factors also help to explain Caignet's virtual exclusion from the annals of so-called black poetry in Latin America. First, Caignet never really considered himself to be an accomplished poet. In fact, he gave most of the credit for the popularity of his verse to Cosme, for whom

FIGURE 6.2. First edition of Felix B. Caignet's only book of poetry, *A golpe de maracas: Poemas negros en papel mulato* (1950). The cover illustration is by Caignet. (Author's collection.)

he wrote several of his poems. The following passage from a 1936 letter to the famed *declamadora* clearly underscores Caignet's debt to Cosme:

> En tí Eusebia palpita algo que no palpita frecuentemente en los artistas nuestros: y ese algo es tu cubanismo, no en la forma vulgar de una banderita y un himno, sino el cubanismo puro, espontáneo, que surge de tu arte pleno de personalidad. De ahí que yo diga siempre, haciéndote justicia, que el 90 por ciento del mito de mis versos está en tu interpretación. Yo francamente soy un diez por ciento de poeta. ¡Mis versos lo son cuando los dices tú! (Caignet, "Letter")

> [In you Eusebia pulsates something that does not pulsate frequently in our artists: that something is your Cubanness, not in the common form of a little flag and a hymn, but a pure, spontaneous Cubanness, that surges from your art that is full of personality. That is why I always say, giving you your just deserts, that 90 percent of the myth of my poems is in your interpretation of them. Frankly, I am just ten percent poet. My verses are verses when you recite them!]

It is also important to point out that whatever fame Caignet's comparatively scant poetic production—just over twenty poems—achieved through recitals by Cosme was almost entirely eclipsed by the international fame of his radio soap operas. *El Derecho de nacer* [The Right to Be Born], for example, first aired in April 1948, and nearly twenty years later was still being hailed by the likes of Carlos Fuentes as "the most faithful reflection of a certain sentient and immediate reality in Latin America" (47). I should add, moreover, that Caignet also became a celebrity and a household name throughout Latin America through the scores of hit songs, such as "Te odio" [I Hate You], "Ratoncito Miguel" [Little Mouse Miguel], and "Frutas de Caney" [Fruits of Caney] that he penned, and even today he is, for good reason, much more widely recognized as a songwriter than a poet. One final factor that may partially account for Caignet's traditional exclusion from the literary group associated with Afrocubanismo is that he wrote and first disseminated his poems in Santiago de Cuba, where he lived from 1897–1936, and not in Havana where the movement flourished. Moreover, he did not tend to associate with literary circles, and, as we have seen, even though he brought his poems with him when he moved to Havana in March 1936, they were not published in book form until fourteen years later.

Caignet as Social Poet: A Brief Overview

Caignet's eastern Cuban roots make his poems especially interesting, since they are among a very small minority of poems associated with Afrocubanismo that focus on that region and its unique African-derived customs and traditions. Moreover, Caignet's poetic treatment of traditional *congas, tumbas francesas, son,* rumba, and other forms of Afro-Cuban music and dance in Santiago attests to the widespread condemnation that such cultural manifestations received throughout the nation during the early decades of the twentieth century. Several of Caignet's politically oriented poems deal with specific forms of Afro-Cuban music and dance and the controversies that surrounded them during the period that he lived and worked in Santiago. For example, in "El bongosero" Caignet alludes to the bans that were placed on bongo drums in various Cuban cities through the voice of a black bongo player and member of a sextet, who declares that to be deprived of his beloved drum would amount to losing his only source of income and, by extension, his very reason for living. A brief reference to a presumably white American tourist who gets drunk on Cuban rum and wildly dances to the drumbeat underscores the poet's sardonic indictment of the two-faced nature of official attitudes toward Afro-Cuban music, which was condemned by government officials as offensive at the same time that it was promoted by them to draw tourists to the island. In this poem Caignet also satirizes the common phenomenon of the racist American tourist who only dances to music played by black musicians when he is intoxicated and far away from home, where associating with blacks would have been unseemly.

Echoing the social undertones of Nicolás Guillén's "Maracas" (1934), which glorifies poor, black musicians who show pride in their culture, the Afro-Cuban protagonist of "¡Soy maraquero!" proclaims that he is proud to play maracas even if his profession implies a lower social status or brings disdain from the "refined" elements of Cuban society.

> ¡A mucha honra lo tengo:
> soy maraquero!
> Soy maraquero
> y eso no quita para que yo sea
> al mismo tiempo que maraquero,
> caballero.

Pero...
si para ser caballero,
tengo que tirar,
botar,
o dejar de tocar
las maracas...
¡Ah!... entonces,
sí que no quiero
ser caballero. (41)

Like the bongo—though to a lesser extent—maracas were also prohibited by some government ordinances since they were widely considered to fall into the very broad category of "instruments of African nature," which were banned by several decrees in the 1910s and '20s in Havana, Santiago, and other cities. In addition to being essential to many genres of Afro-Cuban music, maracas were also employed by black *brujos* in their dances and religious practices, and it was thus often assumed that they came from Africa. However, as Ortiz has pointed out, even though the maraca is one of the most universal of "primitive" instruments, its name is of Arawak origin and Cuban versions of the instrument are native to the Caribbean (Ortiz, *Glosario* 311–12, my translation). This fact is important in the context of Caignet's poem since it suggests that the poet is celebrating not just Afro-Cuban music, but also the important indigenous influence on twentieth-century popular culture in Cuba.[3]

In one of his most scathing poems, "¡Que muera er son!" [Down With the Son!], which also rings of Guillén's early poetry in its condemnation of blacks who refuse to embrace their own cultural heritage, Caignet repudiates those Afro-Cubans who disparage their traditions or pretend to be "refined" like some of their white counterparts. In this poem, which is accompanied by an illustration by Caignet of a pretentious-looking black man dressed in a fine light-colored suit and hat and smoking a cigar (fig. 6.3), the speaker insists that he detests the coarseness and vulgarity of black slum culture and instead prefers reading and writing and dancing the waltz. However, his purposefully exaggerated *bozal* speech suggests his own lack of refinement and education, and thus underscore his hypocritical opinions about his fellow Afro-Cubans. To emphasize his supposed aversion to African-derived traditions he says that he avoids contact with Afro-Cuban music and dance, but especially son, which he sees as a backward cultural manifestation that hampers the advancement of blacks in Cuban society:

> no soy negro de cumbanchas
> de'sos negros
> tocadores de bocú...
> ....
> Yo no voy a la fietta que hay ahora
> Pol no bailar er son;
> Er son e'mu grosero e'mu oldinario.
> ....
> Hay que ir pa'lante,
> adelantar la rasa
> pa no quedalnos
> dentro del cajón. (71–72)

It should be pointed out that even though the theme of the controversial *son* makes this poem applicable to virtually any area of the nation in the early years of the Republic, the reference to the *bocú*, a long,

FIGURE 6.3. This illustration by Felix B. Caignet accompanies his poem "Qué muera er son," in *A golpe de maracas*. The poem and the image mock Afro-Cubans who shun their culture and traditions in favor of "blending in" with the white, middle-class mainstream. (Author's collection.)

single-headed drum used in the traditional *congas* of Santiago de Cuba, places us squarely in eastern Cuba. The poetic voice's implied distaste for Santiago's traditional Afro-Cuban carnival ensembles is significant since such groups, like those in Havana, were widely seen as symbols of African backwardness, and were subjected to numerous bans and prohibitions throughout the early decades of the twentieth century.

Given that the *son* is widely believed to have been born among the Afro-Cuban slaves of Oriente province, the cry of "Down with the son!" by a black man from Santiago is highly ironic and suggests that Caignet's main targets in this poem are not high-society whites, but rather certain members of the growing black and mulatto middle class who increasingly rejected their cultural roots since they viewed them as impediments to their future equality with Cuban whites. In many ways Caignet's poem echoes opinions of other promoters of Afro-Cuban culture—such as Rosendo Ruiz, an Afro-Cuban composer and Santiago native—who expressed their frustration over the ever-increasing tendency among black Cubans to denigrate African-derived music and dance. In an interview with Nicolás Guillén, for example, which was published in January 1930 in the Havana daily *Diario de la Marina*, Ruiz made the following observation concerning black Cubans who rejected their rich cultural legacy:

> El negro cubano... vive al margen de su propia belleza. Siempre que tenga quien lo oiga, abomina del son, que hoy tanto tiene de negro; denigra la rumba, en cuyo ritmo cálido bosteza el mediodía africano, y cierra los ojos, como para que no le descubran un destello de comprensión, frente al profundo requerimiento del bongó, con su voz grave del abuelo. (qtd. in Augier, *Notas para un estudio* 114)

> [The Cuban Negro... lives on the margin of his own beauty. Whenever someone is within earshot, he hates the son, which today shows so much Negro influence; he denigrates the rumba, in whose warm rhythm the African midday yawns, and he closes his eyes, as if to make sure no one will discover the twinkle of understanding, before the profound behest of the bongo, with its serious voice of a grandfather.]

Guillén himself also criticized two-faced Afro-Cubans who condemned African-derived music and dance in public while embracing them in private, such as in his 1931 poem "La canción del bongó," in which the poetic voice (the bongó itself) mourns "Habrá quien llegue a insultarme, / pero no de corazón; / habrá quien me escupa en público, / cuando a solas me besó..." (78). Likewise, in a 1949 article Guillén made the following observation about attitudes of middle-class Cuban blacks toward traditional *comparsas* and *congas*: "nunca falta descendiente de mandinga o carabalí que las vea de reojo, maldiciéndolas en público mientras por dentro se le va el corazón tras el ritmo de la tambora" ("Cada año" 44) [there is always some descendent of Mandinga or Carabalí who looks askance at them, speaking badly of them in public while his heart beats to the rhythm of the bass drum].

Another irony to which Caignet clearly alludes in "¡Qué muera er son!" is the fact that *son* was extremely popular among both blacks and whites in the 1920s and '30s despite—or, perhaps, precisely because of—official condemnation of it. Indeed, as Robin Moore has noted, *son* actually became more popular among the white elite as condemnation of it by members of the black and white middle class increased. Moore summarizes this emblematic example of social hypocrisy in early twentieth-century Cuba as follows: "Paradoxically, the very fact that middle-class society as a whole continued to condemn son music and to discourage its performance in public areas seems if anything to have increased its appeal for many of Cuba's elite" (100). Indeed, even the supposedly vulgar nature of the dance that the speaker in Caignet's poem condemns served to stir up interest among the rich and powerful since, as Moore notes, "A perception of son music as an overtly sexual dance attracted them" (100).

"¡Viva la conga!"

Among the many *afrocubanista* poems that deal with Afro-Cuban carnival celebrations, Felix B. Caignet's "La conga prohibida" is the only one that explicitly refers to and denounces governmental prohibitions of traditional *congas* (and by extension, other related traditions such as *comparsas* and *tumbas francesas*) during the early decades of the Cuban Republic. By focusing specifically on the official bans placed on *congas* in Santiago de Cuba during the 1920s and 1930s, Caignet also distinguishes himself as the only *afrocubanista* poet who poeticized the unique carnival celebrations from Cuba's eastern region during the height of the movement.[4]

In terms of its treatment of traditional Afro-Cuban carnival troupes, "La conga prohibida" differs from other poems that deal with a similar subject largely because its aim is to satirize the rampant social and political hypocrisies in Santiago de Cuba, rather than to present an exaggerated sketch of a *conga* and its Afro-Cuban participants. The reader of Caignet's poem will notice that it offers no descriptions of the black musicians and dancers, and contains very few references to the actual carnival celebration. Nonetheless, it is important to stress that, like Tallet's "Quintín Barahona," "La conga prohibida" is written in an exaggerated—though to a lesser extent—*bozal* Spanish that makes it clear that the speaker is meant to be an uneducated, lower-class black man. But like the black speaker in Tallet's poem, the voice of "La conga prohibida" is one of protest, and we are thus less likely to read the broken Spanish as a purely superficial poetic device.

Though they have some characteristics in common, there is a considerable difference between the poetic voices in "Quintín Barahona" and "La conga prohibida." Tallet's Quintín, for example, is a lone black speaker who directs his complaints and criticisms to another black man, who is both apathetic and unintimidating. The first-person plural voice in Caignet's poem, on the other hand, addresses a more threatening collective Afro-Cuban audience at the same time that it showers accusations upon the white government officials who have enacted the ban on traditional *congas*.

> ¡Qué balbaridá, Dio mío!
> A donde bamo'a paral . . . ?
> A lo negro no han dejao
> lo blanco sin calnabal.
> La conga ettá prohibía,
> dice un bando milital . . .
> Quien no tenga traje'seda
> Se queda sin calnabal . . .

There are a number of important issues in these opening lines that deserve comment. For instance, Caignet's use of the popular expression, "¡Qué barbaridad!"—which loosely translated means something along the lines of "What an outrage!" or "How scandalous"—is very significant. On the one hand, through this popular expression the speaker directly condemns the official bans enacted against traditional *congas*. On the other, if we take the expression for its literal meaning, Caignet's black voice turns the tides, so to speak, by pointing out the "barbarity" of the white leaders—both in terms of their cruel act and their uncivilized behavior—who have abused their authority by depriving the black population of Santiago of their beloved carnival celebrations. It is also noteworthy that Caignet's collective poetic voice explicitly turns the *conga* controversy into an issue of whites against blacks by suggesting that while the former wield the power and make the decisions, the latter suffer the consequences and have no authority to change them. The black speaker's lament ("¿A dónde bamo'a paral . . . ?" or "What will become of us?") concerning the future of Santiago's black population and their traditions, is like a call to action to all Afro-Cubans to put a stop to the exploitation or risk the demise of their culture at the hands of the white decision makers.

Caignet's "La conga prohibida" is at once a celebration of traditional Santiago *congas*—which Bettelheim has referred to as the most quintessentially African and Santiaguero of carnival groups ("Carnival in Santiago" 98, 104)—and a blunt condemnation of the hypocrisy of official attitudes toward them. The exact historical reference in Caignet's poem is most likely the 1935 edict penned by Santiago's military supervisor, Lieutenant Angel Pino y Águila, which was published on the front page of Santiago newspaper *Adelante* on June 24 of that year. This official military decree expressly banned *congas* and their collective dances, known in Santiago as "arrolladeras," and stipulated that carnival processions that were not "perfectly dressed and organized" would be subjected to strict penalties (16).

Despite its apparent historical context, "La conga prohibida" can also be read on a broader level as a reaction to the long-running controversy that had surrounded traditional *congas* for decades in Caignet's native Santiago. In her two-volume compendium of original documents related to carnival celebrations in Santiago de Cuba from the colonial times to the eve of the Cuban Revolution, Nancy Pérez-Rodríguez provides complete transcriptions of dozens of official decrees that banned *congas* either implicitly (by forbidding certain types of drums or costumes, for example) or explicitly (by directly referring to them, such as in 1935). A 1907 decree, for example, allowed certain types of carnival processions but expressly forbade "African drums and dances" as well as "Cabildos llamados 'de congos'" (vol. I, 175). Though "Cabildo" was most commonly used to denote Afro-Cuban mutual aid societies of the nineteenth century that were grouped according to their native nations and worked to preserve and transmit important manifestations of their cultures, the term was also used to refer to the traditional Afro-Cuban carnival troupes of Santiago de Cuba (Brea and Millet, *Glossary*, 180). On June 20, 1919 the Santiago newspaper *El Cubano Libre* published on its front page an edict from Mayor José Camacho Padro. Though there was no specific mention of *congas*, the edict set forth to ban permanently from Santiago's carnival celebrations all African dances and the accompanying "indecorous contortions," and it imposed strict regulations on the types of costumes that could be worn (244–46). In his brief introduction to the decree, Mayor Camacho Padro made the following statement, which clearly alluded to the *congas* that had traditionally paraded through Santiago's streets during the summer carnival season:

> Próximamente celebrará nuestro pueblo su clásico carnaval. El grado de cultura que hemos alcanzado, nos obliga a renunciar de una vez por siempre a las viejas y malas costumbres que . . . exteriorizan los que no titubean en ofender la moral pública con cantos brutales y contorsiones deshonestas, todo acompañado de música salvaje, impropia de sonar en oídos civilizados. (Camacho Padro 244–45)

> [Shortly our city will celebrate its classic carnival. The level of culture that we have achieved obligates us to renounce once and for all the outdated and bad habits that . . . are displayed by those who do not hesitate in offending public morals with brutal chants and indecent contortions, all accompanied by savage music, which is ill-suited to sound in civilized ears.]

Several times in the 1920s Santiago's mayor and Machado supporter, Dr. Desiderio Arnaz (father of drum-beating Desi Arnaz Jr. of *I Love Lucy* fame), enacted bans that more specifically targeted traditional *congas*. In his well-known edict from 1925, for example, which was published in the Santiago daily *La Independencia*, he condemned African-derived *congas* at the same time that he differentiated them from Santiago's high-society and supposedly European-derived *comparsas* and *paseos*. Like Mayor Camacho Padro before him, Arnaz sought the permanent eradication of *congas* from his city's carnival celebrations, as the following resolution illustrates:

> HE RESUELTO: Primero: Prohibir irrevocable, definitiva y terminantemente en los próximos días de carnaval y sus vísperas las

comparsas conocidas con el nombre "Congas," quedando vigentes las autorizaciones . . . para las comparsas que, trajeadas con uniformidad y decencia, ofrezcan la impresión agradable de un positivo y honesto divertimiento. (336)

[I HAVE RESOLVED: First: To prohibit irrevocably, definitively, and categorically in the upcoming days of carnival and evenings before *comparsas* known as "Congas," while the authorization . . . of *comparsas* that, outfitted with uniformity and decency, offer a pleasing impression of a positive and honest diversion will remain in place.]

In the main text of his edict Arnaz virulently condemned *congas* as "humiliating spectacles" and "inexplicable regressions . . . to the dark past," and he argued—quite ironically given his city's large Afro-Cuban population—that they were contrary to the traditions of the "patriotic and cultured city of Santiago de Cuba." Leaving no room for doubt as to the target of his diatribe, he offered the following description of a "typical" Afro-Cuban *conga*:

Me refiero a la "conga" ese conjunto estridente de tambores, sartenes y alaridos, a cuyos sones recorren las calles de nuestra urbe muchedumbres epilépticas, andrajosas y semidesnudas que, entre contorsiones lúbricas y brutales movimientos, irrespetan a la sociedad, ofenden la moral, desconceptúan nuestras costumbres, nos rebajan a los ojos del extranjero y lo que es más grave, contagian con el ejemplo a menores de edad . . . (337)

[When I say "conga" I am referring to that strident group of drums, frying pans, and shrieking, to whose sounds shabby-looking, semi-naked, epileptic crowds, performing lubricious contortions and brutal movements, file through the streets of our city, disrespecting society, offending our morals, discrediting our customs, lowering us in the eyes of foreigners and, most serious of all, infecting minors with their bad example.]

Arnaz's implication that *congas* brought white (or European-derived) customs into disrepute clearly underscores the fact that he and his supporters viewed the perennial controversy over these African-derived carnival troupes as a battle between white civilization and black backwardness. The speaker in Caignet's poem reflects this notion when he complains that "A lo negro no han dejao / lo blanco sin calnabal." His lament is especially significant in the context of the many bans that specifically targeted *congas* because such prohibitions never applied to the popular *comparsas* and *paseos* favored by high-society whites, which consisted of elegant costumes, carefully choreographed dances, and decorated automobiles. When the speaker of "La conga prohibida" complains that Santiago's carnival is only open to those with fine silk costumes, then, he is clearly alluding to strict resolutions, like the one cited above, that demanded that participants in carnival celebrations be decently and uniformly dressed. Given that the city's poor black population could not typically afford the silk fabrics and the carnival attire that were sold in specialty shops throughout Santiago, these stipulations effectively barred their legal participation.[5]

As the poem progresses, the defiant speaker begs an explanation—presumably from someone who has voiced their moral opposition to the *conga*—for the paradoxical attitudes of government officials, who stigmatize *congas* as damaging to Cuban society but fail to take into account that these cultural manifestations enjoy widespread popular support:

¿Y qué daño hase la conga?
Bamo . . . dígame, ¿qué daño?
Si cuando el bocú resonga
y repiquetea el caldero,
la coquilla de la conga
etremese al pueblo entero:

The derisive question posed here by the black poetic voice implies that official attitudes toward Afro-Cuban *congas* serve to hide a secret attraction to them. Despite their supposed moral objections, the speaker suggests, many opponents of the *congas* find the clanging of metal pans and the strident beat of the *bocú* drum—an emblematic element of Santiago *congas*, which one especially vehement critic referred to as "a war drum in the flesh of the devil" (Raigada 48)—hard to resist. Indeed, the following comments taken from a 1931 editorial in the Santiago daily *El mundo* epitomize the double-faced nature of high-society attitudes toward traditional *congas* in eastern Cuba in the early decades of the twentieth century:

No está bien... [ese] desfile impúdico e insolente, esa masa humana a medio vestir, contorsionándose frenéticamente y sudando acres olores. Eso hay que exterminarlo de una vez. Pero uniformado, en bandas por la propia indumentaria y sin el gesto generoso, que no hace falta para bailar esa música mágica, que hasta el pudibundo y férreo hombre de levita y cuello alto, bastón y calzonete, hace sacudir levísima pero perceptiblemente los hombros, mientras los labios critican lo que el cuerpo pide... hay que permitirla. (Acha 9)

[It is not acceptable... that indecent and insolent parade, that half-dressed human mass, bending their bodies frenetically and sweating acrid odors. That has to be exterminated once and for all. But uniformed, in groups with proper attire and without the excessive gestures, which are not necessary to dance that magic music, that makes even the prudish and stiff man in a frockcoat and high collar... shake very lightly, but perceptibly his shoulders, while his lips criticize what his body begs for... we have to permit that.]

In Caignet's poem, the speaker's implication that traditional *congas* were extremely popular among many sectors of Santiago's population is actually very accurate. As Brea and Millet have observed, there was such widespread public support of traditional *congas* that local authorities in Santiago de Cuba found it nearly impossible to enforce the bans against them, and they were sometimes forced to annul them altogether ("Acerca de" 112).

Toward the end of the poem Caignet reinforces this notion with a truly defiant condemnation of the high-society whites and government officials who publicly disdain *congas* while embracing them in private:

¿Pol qué no dejan al pueblo
que cante y vaya'rroyal?
¡Ah... ya sé! Polque la conga,
según disen los mayore,
resulta un baile inmoral.
¡Eso sí que hase grasia!
¡Hablal de moralidá!
y con conga... arroyando,
se telminan casi siempre
la fietas de sosiedá!

Indeed, despite condemning the dancing associated with traditional *congas* as lewd and immoral, many high-society whites could not resist the catchy *conga* rhythms or the temptation of grabbing a partner by the waist and forming a giant, snake-like *conga* line—in the street, a ballroom, a private home—and dancing until the small hours of the morning. Nicolás Guillén criticized such hypocrisy in a 1941 article in which he complained that "mientras la burguesía mueve las caderas en Nueva York o en La Habana, al ritmo endiablado de la conga, murmora para su clase: '¡Estos negros, no sirven más que para bailar!'" [while the bourgeois moves its hips in New York or Havana, to the bedeviled rhythm of the conga, he murmurs to the members of his class: 'These Negroes, they are good for nothing but dancing!'] ("Negra, mueve" 22). The great popularity of the *conga* among upper-class Cuban whites has also been noted by modern critics and historians. For example, Antonio Benítez-Rojo has pointed out that the "contagious conga rhythm" became so popular that it began to be danced in the most sophisticated nightclubs of Havana and even in the homes of the very wealthy ("Música y literatura" 4). In his recent book on the history of carnival in Havana, Helio Orovio similarly makes reference to the hypocritical nature of the private carnival balls of high-society *habaneros*, which often ended with the same traditional *conga* rhythms that many of the partygoers would have publicly condemned:

> No nos engañemos, casi siempre estos carnavales exclusivistas y sofisticadas terminaban . . . arrollando y fiestando de lo lindo en el mismísimo Paseo del Prado. O descargando en uno de los clubes *non sanctos* de Centro Habana. (*Carnaval habanero* 17–18)
>
> [Let's not kid ourselves, the exclusive and sophisticated carnivals almost always ended up . . . dancing collectively and partying marvelously on the Paseo del Prado itself. Or getting down in one of the forbidden clubs in central Havana.]

In another act of defiance, the poetic voice in Caignet's poem expresses his support of traditional *congas*—which he proudly associates with the black lower class—and explicitly denounces (as Tallet had done a year earlier in "Quintín Barahona") the two-facedness of white politicians who condemn traditional *congas* on the one hand, and recruit them to drum up the black vote during their electoral campaigns on the other:

¡La conga! ¡Biba la conga!
¡La conga, con su alegría, la conga que huele a grajo,
la conga del pueblo bajo
sin social hipocresía!
¡la conga que noj pelmiten
pa'nuncios eletorales,
y ahora noj quitan la conga;
¡noj dejan sin calnabale!

One of the most notable qualities of Caignet's poetic representation of a traditional *conga* is that it lacks sensationalistic descriptions of the black participants and is almost entirely devoid of negative stereotypes. Even though it could be argued that the speaker's reference to the body odor, and his equation of the *conga* to the lower classes reflect negatively on these quintessentially Santiaguero carnival troupes, these observations must be read in their proper context. The mention of "grajo," for example, may bring to mind Tallet's decidedly sensationalistic description of two Afro-Cuban dancers in "La rumba," since the speaker in that poem uses the same term to refer to the body odor of the black dancers. However, whereas the description provided by Caignet's black *conguero* is brief and frank, in Tallet's poem the voice of the white outsider dwells on the "primitive" aspects of the rumba and describes a whole slew of smells— "olor de grajo" [smell of body odor], "olor de selva" [smell of the jungle], "olor de hembra" [smell of a woman], "olor de macho" [smell of a man], "olor de solar urbano" [smell of an urban patio], "olor de rústico barracón" [smell of a rustic barracks]—that conjure up images of Afro-Cuban backwardness, explicit sexuality, inequality, and slavery. Likewise, when the black speaker in "La conga prohibida" describes the *conga* as a lower-class phenomenon, he is merely reflecting the historical divide that existed between white and black carnival celebrations in eastern Cuba.

In Santiago de Cuba there were traditionally two distinct carnival celebrations: the winter carnival and the summer carnival. As Bettelheim points out, the former was held during the Lenten season and was highly organized, private in nature, and sponsored by exclusive Santiago social organizations and clubs. Given its association with Spanish, rather than African heritage, winter carnival was nicknamed "carnaval de blancos Cubanos" [White Cubans' Carnival]. Summer carnival, on the other hand, which coincided with the celebration of the feast day of St. James (Santiago) on July 25, originated in the slave era, involved primarily the black working class, and was commonly referred to as "carnaval de las clases bajas" [carnival of the lower classes] ("Carnival" 105).

Carnival celebrations were suspended during the political upheaval of the early 1930s, and the tradition of winter carnival was abandoned thereafter. However, high-society whites quickly carved out their own niche in the summer festivities, and even worked to usurp the tradition by lobbying for the total prohibition of traditional Afro-Cuban *congas*, which had always been kept at a distance from the high-society *comparsas* and the balls and dances organized by exclusive clubs or commercial sponsors during winter carnival.

When Caignet's speaker alludes to traditional *congas* as being free of social hypocrisies, he may also have been referring to the ever-increasing commercialization of carnival in Santiago thanks to the strengthening influence of large corporations under white ownership like Edén Tobacco and Bacardí Rum. Indeed, by the mid-1930s when summer carnival celebrations were reauthorized, what had once been a tradition marked by the joyful and sincere celebration of Afro-Cuban culture that involved largely the black lower class, was forever metamorphosed not only by strict government controls, but also by the aggressive marketing campaigns of businesses owned largely by members of the white upper class. For example, the 1935 summer carnival celebrations, which may have served as the inspiration for Caignet's "La conga prohibida," were sponsored by Edén Tobacco, which in full-page newspaper advertisements invited all Cubans to take part in tournaments with cash prizes that ranged from $10 to $100. But instead of enriching Santiago's carnival traditions—as such companies would have liked to see it—they detracted from their authenticity and progressively diminished the importance of their African roots by offering prizes for such things as "the comparsa that dedicates the best song to Edén," "the student group that dedicates the best bolero to Edén," or the "mask decorated with the most original Edén-themed advertisement."[6]

When reading "La conga prohibida" it is also important to keep in mind that while so many poems about rumbas, *comparsas*, and *congas* are filled with gratuitous references to drunkenness, witchcraft, and lascivious behavior, Caignet avoids such images altogether and instead focuses on the *conga* as a joyful and sincere expression of Afro-Cuban tradition, a concrete example of the exploitation of lower-class blacks by powerful white men, and as an instrument of social protest. The poetic voice's cries of "¡Biba la conga!" are quite significant in that they call attention to the *conga's* potential as a weapon of resistance against the oppression of Afro-Cubans and their culture. Indeed, it was not unheard of for *congas* to defy and even mock the bans that were enacted against them. Rafael Brea notes, for example, that in response to the 1919 edict by Santiago mayor Camacho Padro, an Afro-Cuban *conga* from the predominantly black neighborhood of Los Hoyos marched through the streets ridiculing the mayor's decree with the following lines: "Camacho no quiere conga Africana / y yo vengo con mi trombón / hasta que me dé la gana ... ¡Bon! ¡bon! ¡bon!" [Camacho doesn't want African conga / I'll come with my trombone / As long as I feel like it ... Bon! bon! bon!] ("Un día en San Juan" 64).[7] The following year many *conga* troupes again defied the ban, as reported in the following passage from an article published in *La Independencia* on July 26:

> A pesar del bando prohibitivo, las tumbas resonaron con intensidad por todas partes, incluso en los lugares más céntricos y transitados. Y junto con el ronco y selvático son de la tumba africana la conocida "arrolladera" lució sus contorsiones. (Pérez-Rodríguez I, 254)

> [Despite the prohibitive edict, everywhere the drums sounded with intensity, even in the most centrally located and traveled places. And along with the roar and wild sound of the African drum the well-known "arrolladera" showed off its contortions.]

The sole reference to political *congas* in "La conga prohibida" is brief, but its strategic placement near the middle of the poem reinforces its essential role in Caignet's condemnation of the hypocrisies of Cuban politicians and government officials who denigrated Afro-Cuban traditions and ignored the social injustices faced by Cuban blacks even as they pretended to be their advocates during the electoral campaigns. As if to stress his indignation in the face of such double standards, the poetic voice mocks the type of dismissive attitudes that Afro-Cubans often confronted in their dealings with the middle-class white majority and with the white men who wielded the power: "¡Sufre, negro, / date un trago, / y anda ... acuétate a dolmil!" Indeed, despite their best efforts to become fully integrated

Cuban citizens, blacks in Oriente, like their counterparts throughout the island, continued to be courted to cast votes for white politicians or perform music and dance for American tourists or high-society Cubans, at the same time that they continued to be disenfranchised from the nation's political, social, and economic spheres.

During a 1972 interview with Orlando Castellanos, which was broadcast over Cuban radio, an eighty-year-old Felix B. Caignet made a statement that served to confirm what many of his contemporaries had already alleged; that is, that this famous composer of popular music, author of internationally celebrated radio soap operas, and occasional poet was largely uninterested in national politics: "Soy muy cubano, cubano nada más. Nunca he tenido un puesto en el gobierno, nunca voté, lo que me exonera de responsabilidades; no he sido político porque no me ha gustado la política" [I am very Cuba, nothing but Cuban. I have never had a government job, I never voted, which exonerates me from responsibility; I have never been a politician because I don't like politics] (Orlando Castellanos 23). Caignet's declaration is a bit misleading, however, since it would seem to suggest that like many of the members of the *afrocubanista* movement this author failed to address important political issues in any meaningful way in his poetry. However, even a cursory reading of the twenty poems that make up *A golpe de maracas* reveals that far from coming across as apolitical, Caignet directly addressed many pressing social, economic, and political matters in the majority of his poems.

"La conga prohibida" is especially noteworthy in this respect since in this poem Caignet openly criticizes a number of pressing social and political controversies that underscored the ongoing struggles of Santiago's black population to become integrated into mainstream society. On the one hand, Caignet levies an attack against the white middle and upper classes for publicly denouncing traditional Afro Cuban carnival celebrations in Santiago as immoral spectacles at the same time that they imitate them in their own private parties and balls. On the other hand, Caignet's poem represents a harsh indictment of the widespread hypocrisies of Cuban government officials who enforced strict bans against *congas* during carnival season, while actively seeking them out at election time. In "La conga prohibida," a marginalized Afro-Cuban cultural manifestation comes to emblematize the lot of the majority of Afro-Cubans who, four decades after their decisive role in the liberation of Cuba from Spanish rule, were still little more than marginalized citizens controlled and manipulated according to the whims of the power-wielding white majority. Perhaps the poetic voice of Caignet's "Lamento veterano" [Veteran Lament] expresses this notion most succinctly with the following passionate expression of his disillusionment with the lot of early twentieth-century Afro-Cubans:

> ¡Ay, Dio mío!
> ¡La cosa que 'tan pasando!
> Luchal tanto, peleal tanto
> pa' conseguí la libeltá . . .
> y totál ¿pa qué?
> ¿Pa qué? ¡Pa ná!
> Ay, mi generá Maseo,
> quien te lo jiba a desí!
> ¡Ma' bale que te haiga muelto
> que bel a tu Cuba así! (39)

7

Representations of Afro-Cuban Carnival in Three Poems by Marcelino Arozarena

> *¿No somos más que rumba,*
> *lujurias negras y comparsas?*
>
> [Are we nothing more than rumba,
> black lewdness and *comparsas*?]
>
> Regino Pedroso, "Hermano negro"

> *río ante el negro tumulto de las comparsas*
> *desorbitadas*
>
> [I laugh at the black tumult of excessive
> *comparsas.*]
>
> Marcelino Arozarena, "La canción del orate"

In a 1971 interview with Adolfo Suárez, the Afro-Cuban poet Marcelino Arozarena (1912–1996) noted that since the early years of his literary career he had been turned off by the tendency among the poets of Afrocubanismo to present images of Cubans of color that seemed more like caricatures than genuine portraits. As he put it, "cuando cundió la moda— luego modo—mucha gente tomó las cosas por el carapacho, por lo exterior; trataron de ver solo el lado pintoresco y de exagerarlo al estilo del teatro vernáculo" [when the fad—and later mode—began to proliferate, many people saw things only for their carapace, their exterior; they only attempted to see the picturesque side of things and they exaggerated in the style of the *teatro vernáculo*] (Adolfo Suárez 11–12). In the same interview Arozarena commented that during the height of Afrocubanismo in the 1930s he aspired to elevate blacks and their various cultural manifestations in his poetry, and made every effort to avoid the type of superficial and sensationalistic portrayals of Afro-Cubans that he found in poems by key figures of the movement such as Ramón Guirao, José Zacarías Tallet, and Emilio Ballagas (12).

These comments, which were made by Arozarena nearly four decades after he published his first *poemas negros*, are somewhat misleading and ironic for two reasons. First, even a cursory reading of many of Arozarena's early poems reveals that they are filled with the type of shallow images of Afro-Cubans and their cultural manifestations that he supposedly tried to avoid. Secondly, in the same interview that he implicitly takes issue with the exoticism of "La rumba," Arozarena admits his debt to certain aspects of Tallet's poem, which is very clear in "Caridad" (1933), "La comparsa del majá" (1936), "Liturgia etiópica" (1936), and other early poems. Moreover, it is important to add—and this is a point that Arozarena does not mention in the interview with Suárez—that the original version of the last of these poems, which is one of his most superficial and stereotypical, actually bears a dedication that reads: "a José Zacarías Tallet en honor de su 'RUMBA'")[To José Zacarías Tallet, in honor of his Rumba] (fig. 7.1).[1] What this suggests to me is that Arozarena's supposed aversion to sensationalistic portrayals of Afro-Cubans, which he underscored in his 1971 interview, was a product of hindsight that developed later in his poetic career.

In his recent book, *Writing Rumba: The Afrocubanista Movement in Poetry*, Miguel Arnedo-Gómez focuses much-deserved attention on Marcelino Arozarena's underappreciated poetry. He examines in depth several of the poems that Arozarena wrote during the height of Afrocubanismo, and stresses their profound "symbolic dimension" and deep connections to Lucumí lore and cultural traditions (157). In his analysis Arnedo-Gómez emphasizes that "Arozarena's poetry certainly reflects a profound knowledge of Afro-Cuban culture," and to underscore his point he adds that Arozarena "made use of a much larger array of Afro-Cuban cultural traditions" and dealt with a greater number of *orishas*—or Yoruban deities—than other *afrocubanista* poets did (157–58).

In a similar manner, Miriam DeCosta-Willis, one of only a few critics who have written serious academic essays on Arozarena's life and writings, has observed that Arozarena's poems are "profoundly African in their form, content, and sensibility," and adds that the Cuban poet "always treated [African culture] with seriousness and profundity" ("Journey" 12–13). The same critic has insisted that while "Guillén underscored the plastic or exotic elements of black life" such as song, dance, and ritual, "Arozarena almost always subordinate[d] these elements to his message" ("Black song" 351).

La Litúrgia Etiópica

*A José Zacarías Tallet
en honor de su "RUMBA"*

Sobre la liturgia pura del etiópico ancestral
tonante toque en tumulto tam tam tam-tamborilea;
no hay un viro
ni hay un giro
en que no bulla la bulla de la bacha que emborracha
diluída en la guaracha de la timba del solá.
¡Tiempla los cueros, José Caridá!,
llama a tu ecobia que baile el bembé,
que mueva la grupa,
que estire los pies,
que salte,
que grite,
se agache, se pare y se vire al revés.
 Lasciva, rugiente, se ríe Mersé;
desencaja la cintura,
y la apura con bravura en tam-tambaleante paso
que es en su ebúrnea canela
mórbida y vibrante estela de lujuriante sopor.
En torpe rebambaramba de aguardiente y de sudor,
tonante toque en tumulto tam tam tam-tamborilea.
Entona su canto José Caridá;
lamiendo la bemba vigila a Mersé,
y en tanto cansado y sudado cantaba el bembé
pensaba orgulloso:
"Tu paso sabroso que mata, mulata,
lo está protegiendo Babayú Ayé".
Violentamente vibrando sobre el parche que se parte
ecos secos repercuten su macámbica genial:
    "Teberé, monina, teberé;
    que sabroso baila mi ecobia el bembé"
y no hay bulla que no bulla de esta bacha que emborracha
diluída en la guaracha de la timba del solá.
¡Tiempla los cueros, José Caridá!;
llama a tu ecobia que baile el bembé,
que mueva la grupa,
que estire los pies,
que salte,
que grite,
se agache, se pare y se vire al revés.
Lasciva, rugiente, se ríe Mersé
y mientras la mulata su cuerpo menea,
tonante toque en tumulto
tam tam tam-tamborilea
sobre la liturgia pura del etiópico ancestral.

Marcelino Arozarena

FIGURE 7.1. First appearance of Marcelino Arozarena's poem "La liturgia etiópica" (*Adelante*, Nov. 1936). Note the dedication: "A José Zacarías Tallet en honor de su 'RUMBA'" [To José Zacarías Tallet in honor of his 'Rumba']. (Evergreen State College Library.)

Femi Ojo-Ade has similarly contended that "even more than Guillén, Arozarena shows a profound knowledge of African culture . . . Yemaja, Ogun, and other gods are positively evoked in Arozarena's works. The sublimity, absent from the poetry of others before him, is restored to African religious feeling" (53). And in his landmark study, *The Black Image in Latin American Literature*, Richard L. Jackson—who dedicates just over a page to Arozarena's oeuvre—stresses two major points about his poems: first, that they demonstrate that Arozarena was "well-grounded in African and Afro-Cuban culture," and second that they "are remarkably consistent in their characteristic expressions of the poet's pride in his blackness and in his African heritage" (123–24). Finally, in a largely biographical article, Georgina Arozarena Himely and Celia Pinto observe that Arozarena's poetry "always moves toward deep reflection" and demonstrates his "unremitting commitment to his race" (9).

All of these comments by critics of Marcelino Arozarena's poetry share a quality that is typical of the relatively scant body of contemporary studies on this important Afro-Cuban poet: that is, they offer a somewhat distorted and one-sided view of his poetic production. It is not my goal in this chapter to question Arozarena's knowledge of or commitment to Afro-Cubans and African-derived cultural traditions, nor to suggest in any way that he was not a great social poet and defender of his race. Rather, I aim to demonstrate through close readings of three of his poems that find their inspiration in traditional Afro-Cuban carnival celebrations, that Marcelino Arozarena's multifaceted poetic images of Afro Cubans and their cultural manifestations were not consistently positive or profound, and thus do not lend themselves to facile description and clear-cut categorization.

As I have argued in an earlier article, an examination of Arozarena's early poetry reveals that nearly half of the dozen or so works that he wrote during the 1930s are archetypal of the poetry of Afrocubanismo in terms of their essentially shallow portrayal of Cubans of color (especially women) and African-derived music, dance, and religious rituals. On the other hand, the remaining poems from the same period turn Afro-Cubans and their various cultural practices into springboards for the communication of profound social and political messages. These latter poems serve to justify the many comparisons that have been made between Arozarena's verse and the great sociopolitical poems of his fellow Afro-Cuban poets Regino Pedroso and Nicolás Guillén (Anderson, "Inconsistent Depictions").

I should stress that I agree with some of the above-cited critics in terms of their appraisals of Arozarena's most patently social-minded and militant poems from the 1930s, such as "La canción del estudiante pobre" [The Song of the Poor Student] (1934), "Canción negra sin color" (1935), "Justicia" [Justice] (1935), and "Evhoé" (1936). However, I also feel that certain claims made by some of them—that the "profound" African roots of "Caridá" suggest that Arozarena "may have intended his ode to [Oshún] to be understood only by other Lucumí" (Arnedo-Gómez 160); that "Caridá" and "Liturgia etiópica" exemplify Arozarena's "antipathy to sensationalized and exotic verse" (DeCosta-Willis "Journey" 13); that "La comparsa del majá" demonstrates the poet's vast knowledge of Afro-Cuban culture (Jackson 124)—are misleading. Indeed, the latter three poems—the last of which will be discussed at length in this chapter—are among Arozarena's most superficial, and they reveal that he, like many of the other poets of Afrocubanismo, was not always successful in his attempts to steer clear of racial stereotypes and cultural exoticism.

After a brief examination of two of Arozarena's best-known poems from the 1930s, "Caridá" and "Liturgia etiópica," which will help to put the other poems examined in this chapter in their proper context, the remainder of the chapter will be divided into three parts, each of which corresponds to a different carnival-inspired poem. In the first two of these sections, I examine poems that Marcelino Arozarena penned during the waning years of the Afrocubanismo craze of the 1930s, "La comparsa del majá" (1936), and "La conga" (c. 1937).[2] In my discussion of the first poem, which has been referred to by various critics as an authentic text with deep African roots, I demonstrate that despite its evocation of the long-standing tradition of carnival rehearsals in Cuba, "La comparsa del majá" essentially trivializes these spectacles by turning them into a lightly guised pretext for sexual conquest.

"La conga" melds two major trends in Arozarena's verse at the same time that it reveals seemingly conflictive images of a specific variety of traditional carnival ensemble. On a purely superficial level, "La conga" comes across as typical of Marcelino Arozarena's early poems as it contains many negative images of these traditional Afro-Cuban carnival ensembles and their black participants. I argue, however, that Arozarena's unfavorable depiction of a typical *conga* is a key to the poem's sociopolitical message: that is, that *congas*, like other publicly performed Afro-Cuban cultural manifestations, have a largely negative impact on Cubans of color because they at once serve to justify prejudices and divert the attention of Cubans of color from more pressing social, economic, and political issues. In my examination of "La conga" I also posit an alternate—though not necessarily incompatible—reading of the poem by suggesting that the traditional *conga* can be taken as a symbol of Afro-Cuban resistance to centuries of racial prejudice and social injustice.

Finally, in the third part of the chapter I consider "Carnaval de Santiago" (1953), which like "La conga" offers a largely unfavorable image of traditional carnival celebrations and presents them as obstacles to Afro-Cubans' struggles for equality in Cuba. First published in the Havana daily *Hoy* on July 26, 1953—"a fortunate coincidence" of dates according to Arozarena (Adolfo Suárez 14)—this poem about the carnival celebrations of eastern Cuba is imbued with a militant revolutionary message, which evokes Arozarena's most accomplished social poems of the 1930s at the same time that it reflects the country's mounting struggles against the tyranny of the Batista regime.

Several of Arozarena's most widely anthologized poems epitomize in many ways my contention that much of his early verse offers predominantly shallow images of black Cubans and African-derived cultural manifestations. Arozarena's first published poem, "Caridá," originally appeared in the Cuban periodical *El Mundo* in 1933. It has since become one of Arozarena's best-known works largely because it has appeared in most of the important anthologies of *poesía negra*,[3] but also because it was among the favorites of Eusebia Cosme's repertoire of *poemas negros*, and she recited it in the majority of her public performances.

Several aspects of this poem belie claims by modern critics that it stands out for its profound treatment of Afro-Cuban music and dance. In terms of the poem's reinforcement of stereotypes, the negative terms used to portray the *mulata* rumba dancer—who is not actually present but rather conjured by the poetic voice who laments that this seductive temptress has not shown up to dance with him—are especially noteworthy. Through the eyes of this frustrated man, Caridad is recalled as a sensual, manipulative temptress who is bewitched by the strident drumbeat of rumba rhythms. The male poetic voice describes her as "fleshy" and "tasty" like a piece of fruit, and he delights in her "sweetness" and her "sugary blood," all of which suggest that he sees her as an object of his sexual appetite. According to Claudette Williams, the speaker's supposed amorous feelings suggest that he "views the dancer not merely as a sexual sensation but also as an individual with whom he can engage intimately" (62). By deemphasizing the obvious vulgar elements of the poem and downplaying Arozarena's patently one-dimensional depiction of Caridad as a coquettish reveler and object of sexual desire (not love), Williams is able to call attention to what she refers to as "an alternative to the exotic veneer" of other *negrista* poems, that is Arozarena's supposedly unique "sensitivity to the African origins of the [rumba] dance" (63).

It is somewhat ironic that Fernando Ortiz, who was certainly not known for keen literary analysis, is one of the few critics of "Caridá" who seems to have noticed that the poem is marked by strong erotic undertones. In an article published in *Revista Bimestre Cubana* in 1935, Ortiz devotes much space to what he correctly identifies as an apparent obsession among *negrista* poets with the female backside, and he makes the following observation: "A veces esta metáfora nalgar tan resobada en los versos blanquinegros, se complica con apicarados sentidos eróticos, como al referirse Marcelino Arozarena, en sus rimas a *Caridá*, a 'su grupa mordisqueante y tentadora del amor'" ("Versos mulatos" 328) [Sometimes this buttock metaphor, so hackneyed among whitish-black poems, is complicated with mischievous erotic meanings, as when Marcelino Arozarena refers, in his rhymes to Caridad, to 'her nibbling rump, temptress of love'"]. Far from criticizing Arozarena and his contemporaries—he also cites lines from Luis Palés Matos, José Zacarías Tallet, Emilio Ballagas, Ramón Guirao, and Vicente Gómez Kemp—for their propensity to focus on the buttocks of their black female subjects, Ortiz defends such images as authentic representations of the inherent sensuality of Cuban women of color:

> Este concepto estético de la negra nalguda y la atracción sensual de la mulata nalgueante no son tornadizo capricho de una moda chabacana, ni desenfadada travesura de poetas picarescos ante la mujer morena, sino imposición del realismo descriptivo de su anatomía y del vivo erotismo de la ondulante carnalidad de sus traseras pulpas. . . . Los poetas antillanos, al dar expresión realista

a sus impresiones sensitivas de la hembra africanoide, han tenido que emplear los mismos elementos plásticos que los artistas de hace milenios ante la hembra negra o negroide y sus pomposas protuberancias. (328)

[This concept of the black woman with prominent buttocks and the attraction of the big-bottomed *mulata* are not fickle caprices of a vulgar fad, nor is it unabashed naughtiness of mischievous poets dealing with the dark-skinned woman, but rather an imposition of realistic description of their anatomy and of the lively eroticism of the undulating carnality of their pulpous backsides. . . . Antillean poets, by giving realistic expression to their sensitive impressions of the Africanoid woman, have found it necessary to employ the same plastic images as the artists from thousands of years ago when faced with the black or dark-skinned woman and her sumptuous protuberances.]

Miguel Arnedo-Gómez likewise justifies Arozarena's vulgar description of the female dancer's "nibbling" and "trembling" haunches by defending it as an accurate reflection of Yoruba culture, in which "animal comparisons . . . do not have the same derogatory connotations that they do in western culture" (120). He goes on to insist that certain aspects of *afrocubanista* poetry—he specifically refers to the portrayal of Caridad's buttocks—that "feminist critics" have viewed "as products of their author's sexist imaginations" are often examples of "the poetry's utilization of actual Afro-Cuban cultural elements" (122). Later in his study Arnedo-Gómez recognizes the "openly erotic tone" of "Caridá" (159), but he also insists that the appearance of Oshún in the poem "subverts dominant representations of women as sexual objects by introducing the connotations of love that are attached to this orisha" (163). Echoing Janheinz Jahn's reading of the poem in *Muntu* (95), he adds, quite unconvincingly, that Caridad's name—which comes from the Latin *caritas*, or "love"—also serves to soften the poem's strong sexual undertones. Moreover, Arnedo-Gómez insists that by imbuing "Caridá" with an erotic subtext, Arozarena "secured its publication by making it popular with whites" and thus surreptitiously "introduced important Afro-Cuban religious notions into dominant culture" (161).

Much like "Caridá," "Liturgia etiópica" (1936) reveals how the use of

African-derived vocabulary and the description of Afro-Cuban religious rites or dances do not automatically make for a profound poem. Moreover, this early poem—which, we should recall, Arozarena originally dedicated to José Zacarías Tallet and his poem "La rumba"—also echoes its better-known predecessor by focusing largely on the figure of a *mulata* dancer, who is portrayed as a sensual temptress and inflamer of the carnal desires of the black male spectator. Arnedo-Gómez correctly observes that Arozarena's description of the female dancer as lascivious in "Liturgia etiópica" exemplifies the "conception of female sexuality as inevitably leading to the sexual act" (163). Despite Arozarena's apparent attempts to imbue his poem with authentic African-derived imagery and vocabulary, the supposed spiritual dimensions of "Liturgia etiópica" are largely overshadowed by the stereotypical portrayals of Mersé and José Caridad, her male, bongo-playing counterpart.

As is the case with many of the poems that Arozarena wrote in the 1930s, a female Afro-Cuban dancer becomes the central focus of the poet's depiction of African-derived dance and ritual. In her discussion of poetic representations of Cuban women of color in *poesía negra*, Vera Kutzinski makes just a passing reference to "Liturgia etiópica," but she correctly indicates that the poem is very typical of such verse in terms of its stereotypical representation of the *mulata* (*Sugar's Secrets* 186). According to Kutzinski, the *mulata* is depicted in many poems of the movement as "little more than a body inscribed with and subjected to male desire, sexual and political" (174). To be sure, much like Caridad before her, Mersé is presented through the eyes of the mythically lustful black man who sees her as a tempting object of his carnal fantasies. The *mulata* dancer so excites José Caridad that he licks his lips as he stares at her—"lamiendo la bemba vigila a Mersé" (152)—apparently in anticipation of satiating his sexual appetite. The negative undertones of the language used to describe both Mersé and her dancing—"lasciva" [lascivious], "rugiente" [raging], "mórbida" [morbid], and "lujuriante" [lewd]—effectively turn her into an archetypal symbol of what Kutzinski has referred to as "the mulata's imputed sexual pathology" (196).

The Seductive Snake: Cultural Stereotypes in "La comparsa del majá"

Arozarena's best-known poems from the 1930s were first made available to large audiences through recitations by Eusebia Cosme, and then through their publication in Ramón Guirao's important 1938 anthology, *Órbita de la poesía afrocubana, 1928–1937*. One such poem is "La comparsa del majá," which, along with "Caridá" and "Liturgia etiópica," also detracts somewhat from Arozarena's reputation as a social poet who rejected sensationalistic images of Afro-Cubans and descriptive exoticism. This important early poem portrays the black subjects and their carnival dance in a very superficial manner, at the same time that it evades the pressing sociocultural debate that had surrounded *comparsas* since the early years of the Republic. Though I argue later that Marcelino Arozarena probably supported some aspects of the bans of *comparsas* and *congas* that had been in place for nearly twenty years by the time he penned "La comparsa del majá," it still seems fair to say that his shallow treatment of such a politically charged subject represents something of a missed opportunity for a poet who is widely considered among contemporary critics to have been one of the great voices of social and political militancy of his day.

In *Lo negro y lo mulato en la poesía cubana*—one of very few critical studies that even makes reference to "La comparsa del majá"—Idelfonso Pereda Valdés offers a somewhat confusing analysis of this carnival-inspired poem. Early in the study he notes that Arozarena's poem evokes a Voodoo snake ritual (22), which, he argues, reflects the profound African vein that runs through Arozarena's poetry. However, he later remarks that "La comparsa del majá" is actually reminiscent of Ballagas's "Comparsa habanera" in terms of its "peripheral" treatment of African themes (49). Pereda Valdés's observations bring to mind two important points. On the one hand, he is correct to concede that the poem does not reflect Arozarena's West African roots in a profound way. I would add, in fact, that "La comparsa del majá" is Arozarena's most superficial poem in terms of its treatment of Afro-Cubans and their rich cultural traditions. On the other hand, while Pereda Valdés may be correct when he claims that "La comparsa del majá" is reminiscent of a Voodoo ritual, he fails to stress that it more accurately reflects the snake dances that had been part and parcel of Afro-Cuban carnival celebrations since the slave era.[4] It is true that these pantomimic dances, in which participants pretended to kill a giant serpent, were widely accepted to be "offshoot(s) of a Dahomey snake cult that still persists in Haiti" (Carpentier, *Music in Cuba* 260). However, Arozarena's poem is clearly rooted in an essentially Afro-Cuban carnival tradition, and its title, moreover, comes from a well-known *comparsa* troupe of the same name, which was known for its pantomimic portrayal of a young girl being attacked and "bitten" by a snake (Ortiz, "Viejos Carnavales" 213).

The *majá* (Cuban boa) of the title evokes not just the traditional "bailes de matar culebras" but also the serpentine lines of dancers that slithered through the streets of Havana during carnival celebrations. The refrain of Arozarena's poem—"saca la cabesa / güébbela a sacá /q'aquí biene rebalando / la compassa del majá" (147)—alludes to these traditional dances in which participants grab the person in front of them and swing their hips and heads from side to side while shuffling around like a giant snake. Despite its evocation of traditional carnival dances, it is important to point out that "La comparsa del majá" does not portray an actual carnival procession, but rather a rehearsal that takes place in a private location instead of on a public thoroughfare. To reflect this important aspect of the poem, Arozarena eventually changed its title to "Ensayando la comparsa del majá," and it has since appeared as such in many collections of *poesía negra* as well as in both editions of *Canción negra sin color*.

Referring to the rich tradition of rehearsing for *comparsa* competitions in a nostalgic article published in *Bohemia* in 1949, in which he expressed his longing for the days when carnival represented a truly joyous and authentic celebration of African-derived culture in Cuba, Nicolás Guillén wrote the following:

> Cuando se las comienza a ensayar, lentamente, ya anticipan cierto aire de bullicio y gozo previo, que cuajará más tarde en un jubilo de arte mayor. De repente, una noche, en las cercanías de marzo o febrero, nos ocurre ir por una calle oscura y apartada... ¿Y ese tambor? ¿Y ese cántico que se estira dulzón bajo las estrellas? ¿Y ese coro de voces femeninas, sostenido por el vozarrón de los baritones?... Allí está un grupo de hombres y mujeres que todavía vestidos "de paisano," ensayan los pasos iniciales de lo que va a ser la comparsa cuando desfile ante el Alcalde, allá en el Malecón. ("Cada año" 44)

> [When they begin to rehearse them, slowly, they bring forward a certain air of foregone bustling and enjoyment, which will come together later in the joyfulness of high art. Suddenly, one night, around February or March, it occurs to us to go to a dark and out-of-the-way street... And that drum? And that canticle that stretches

out sweetly under the stars? And that chorus of feminine voices, held up by the deep voices of the baritones? ... Over there is a group of men and women who, still dressed like "peasants," rehearse the initial steps of what will be the *comparsa* when it parades in front of the Mayor, over there on the Malecón.]

According to Cristóbal Díaz-Ayala, planning and organizing *comparsas* was a complicated business, and the rehearsals would often begin several months before the onset of carnival season. He points out, moreover, that it was important for each *comparsa* company to scout out a location for their rehearsals that would not be accessible to members of other carnival troupes for fear that they might copy their dance steps or their original musical scores ("De congas" 31). In this sense, Arozarena's poem, which apparently takes place in just such a "secret" location, reflects a long-standing Cuban carnival tradition. However, the rehearsal evoked in the revised title of the poem is not one that involves the entire ensemble, but rather it is a private encounter between an unnamed woman and man, members of the same troupe, the latter of whom uses the rehearsal as a pretext to seduce her. Even if "La comparsa del majá" does evoke a hallowed Afro-Cuban carnival tradition, it is fraught with stereotypical images that end up casting it in a largely negative light.

In the opening lines of "La comparsa del majá" the black poetic voice initiates his seduction of Encarnación by trying to lure her away from a *bembé*, an informal ritual celebrating the Yoruban deities. The speaker also begs Encarnación to try to shake off the effects of a curse, which apparently has prevented her from rehearsing with him for the upcoming *comparsa* competition:

Encarnasión!!
Suetta e cajón que cansatte sacudiendo e bembé;
suetta esa murumba que te come e pié;
suéttala,
suéttala,
suéttala yá,
a vé cómo nos sale la compassa del majá.
. . ..
Eh!
Saca e pié,

como si tubiera romatismo e la sintura
y te asuttara un majá;
un majá de sabrosura que te muedde las caderas:
no las muebas,
no las muebas,
dentro de esa masa llebas la fiebre de mi cansión. (146–47)

Several aspects of "La comparsa del majá" belie contentions by modern critics that Arozarena offered consistently profound portraits of Afro-Cubans and their culture. For example, much like Ballagas does in "Comparsa habanera," Arozarena introduces black witchcraft and the implicit superstitions associated with it in the opening stanza of the poem but never contextualizes these references in any way. For example, the "murumba"—a harmful curse resulting from brujería—that has possessed Encarnación has no apparent ritual significance in the poem.[5] Instead, it is presented as an obstacle that has hampered the black speaker's attempts to lure the *mulata* dancer away from a communal *bembé* so that he can seduce her in private through an erotic, secular dance. In this context, the image of the *majá* is especially significant given that according to an Afro-Cuban legend cited by Lydia Cabrera, this Cuban snake inspired violent amorous passions. According to one of Cabrera's sources, "el Majá enseñó a los hombres a procrear con un baile muy bonito que consistía en mover frente a frente la cintura hasta que al son de la música las parejas se acoplaban" [the Majá taught men how to procreate with a very pretty dance that consisted in moving the hips face to face until, to the sound of the music, the couples mated] (*Animales* 19). The poetic voice's reference to Encarnación's rheumatism is also noteworthy in the context of this poem about a carnival snake dance, since the fat from a *majá* is reportedly used by practitioners of Afro-Cuban religions to cure this and other related ailments of the muscles and joints (Cabrera, *Animales* 18; Roche, *La Policía* 2nd ed. 111).

Though "La comparsa del majá" does manage to steer clear of the stereotypical images of drunkenness, strident music, and wild revelry that characterize other Cuban poems that portray traditional *comparsas* (including some by Arozarena himself), this is probably best explained by the fact that this particular poem depicts a rehearsal by just two dancers rather than an actual carnival celebration. Nonetheless, even as "La comparsa del majá" echoes an Afro-Cuban myth of the *majá* as a provoker of amorous passions that most outsiders would not have known, it also projects a decidedly demeaning image of a lustful black man and his attempted sexual conquest of a coquettish *mulata* dancer, the latter of whom is predictably reduced to a formidable pair of swinging haunches. True to the genre, Arozarena's poem is marked by suggestive language and lightly veiled double entendres that most readers would have had no problem understanding. The succulent Cuban boa ("un majá de sabrosura") that bites at the mulata's gyrating hips, for instance, is an obvious phallic symbol that imbues the poem with strong erotic undertones. When the poetic voice first begs Encarnación to stop swinging her hips, and then announces that between them she carries the fever of his song, we can easily detect a metaphor for sexual penetration.

Those who fail to see the vulgar subtext in the lines cited above will have a harder time ignoring the more explicit scene that the poetic voice describes in the stanza that immediately follows:

Encarnasión!!
Yo boy detrá de tu cueppo con mobimiento oppotuno.
Si no miran de frente a los do,
paresemo uno;
si no miran de lao,
oh!
no no miren de lao, por Dió![6]

The multiple exclamation points underscore the speaker's mounting excitement as he focuses on the sensual mulata's body. By expressing his hope that no one is looking at the dancing couple from the side, the nameless speaker clearly alludes to the vulgar nature of his so-called opportune movements, that is, that he is thrusting himself into the mulata's backside. This erotic subtext is reinforced several lines later when the speaker cries out to Encarnación, "me vas haciendo bagaso," a reference to the pulp that is left behind after sugarcane is passed through a press. The parallel between this image of the sugarcane and the previous representation of the speaker's phallus between the mulata's gyrating haunches is unmistakable, and it reflects Manuel Moreno Frangials's observation that "a good part of the Cuban ... sexual lexicon originated on the sugar plantations" (cited in Kutzinski, *Sugar Secrets* 191). This reading of Arozarena's poem is also consistent with a recognized tendency among *negrista* poets to draw connections between black female sexuality and sugar production. Luis Palés Matos, for example, compares a black woman's sensual swaying hips to a sugar press in "Majestad negra"—"Prieto trapiche de sensual zafra / El caderamen, masa con masa, / Exprime ritmos, suda que sangra" [Dark sugarcane press of a sensual sugar harvest / Your great haunches, mass against mass, / Press out rhythms, sweating and bleeding] (57)—while Nicolás Guillén offers a very similar image in his description of a scene of sexual conquest in "Secuestro de la mujer de Antonio" [The Abduction of Antonio's Woman]: "De aquí no te irás mulata/ . . . / aquí molerán tus ancas / la zafra de tu sudor" [From here you will not escape, *mulata* / . . . here your hindquarters will grind / the sugar harvest of your sweat] (85).

This notion that the black speaker in "La comparsa del majá" is motivated by sexual desire in his private dance rehearsal with Encarnación is further reinforced in the final stanzas, first when he begs her to cast aside her inhibitions ("deja tu cuerpo sin broches"), and later when he lets out a frustrated cry ("Ah! / No siga bailando má!!") which implies that the dancing is just a pretext for his true goal of sexual conquest.

In addition to evoking the traditional *ensayos* that took place during the months preceding the carnival season in Havana, Arozarena's poem also recalls traditional *comparsa* chants and songs for killing snakes, such as those that are collected in the section titled "Antecedentes folklóricos" in Ramón Guirao's *Órbita de la poesía afrocubana*. One composition in particular, "Ta Julia," which Guirao includes in a section titled "Cantos de comparsa," seems to have influenced the erotic undertones of "La comparsas del majá." For example, in the following verse from this anonymous eighteenth-century chant, which tells of a black slave who has been raped by an overseer, the reader will immediately note how the notion of being "frightened" by a snake is essentially equated with the act of sexual penetration:

    —Ma Rosario ta malo.
    (¡Cángala lagontó!)
    —A ve qué cosa tiene.
    (¡Cángala lagontó!)
    —Tiene barriga y doló.
    (¡Cángala lagontó!)

—Está embarasá.
(¡Cángala lagontó!)
—Culebra l'asuttá.
(¡Cángala lagontó!) (6)

"El tropelaje de ruidos": The Problematic *Conga*

In Havana traditional *congas* were constantly subjected to heated controversies, and their many detractors variously referred to them as "degrading . . . grotesque, repugnant spectacles" (spokesperson for the Comité Conjunto de Sociedades de Color qtd. in Roig de L. "Las comparsas" 149), and outdated traditions with "vulgar music and minimal artistic elements" (Ortiz, "Informe" 18).

Following a lively debate over *comparsas* and *congas* that played out for months in the pages of the Havana-based Afro-Cuban monthly *Adelante*, Tomás Acuña L'azcano, in his capacity as secretary general of the association of the same name, penned an official statement on this contentious issue in March 1938. As he and other members of the Asociación Adelante saw it, *congas* were completely devoid of artistic merit, and were nothing more than "humiliating manifestations" of Afro-Cuban backwardness (7). The members of the Asociación Adelante were especially critical of the strident percussive music and the disorderly nature of the collective dancing that typified *congas*, since they felt that these elements only served to justify prejudices and hamper black Cubans' fight for equality. Acuña L'azcano summed up this attitude with the following remark: "Jamás podrá estar identificado el movimiento reivindicador del negro con el 'arrollao' retardatorio de las congas" [The movement to vindicate the Negro will never be identified with the retarding collective dancing of the *conga*] (8). For his part, Alberto Arredondo, who clearly had a hand in the penning of the article signed by Acuña L'azcano, argued for the elimination of traditional *congas*, which he felt were detrimental to Afro-Cubans' hope for progress. As he put it:

> el desenvolvimiento ilimitado de 'Las Congas' no constituye nada útil, práctica o progresista para el sufrido negro cubano. A [su] nombre . . . se volverán a erguir las nefastas teorías de la inferioridad racial y el retraso negro. (*El negro en Cuba* 143)

[the unlimited unleashing of "Congas" does not constitute anything useful, practical, or progressive for the suffering Cuban Negro. In their name . . . the mean spirited theories of racial inferiority and Negro backwardness will again be raised.]

Given Marcelino Arozarena's widespread reputation as a champion of authentic manifestations of Afro-Cuban cultural traditions, one might be inclined to assume that he was a staunch defender of *comparsas* and *congas*. However, Arozarena was an active member of the Asociación Adelante and an occasional contributor to the publication, and he shared many of the views expressed in the journal. He probably would have agreed, for example, with Acuña L'azcano and Arredondo, who saw *comparsas* and *congas* as artistic opiates that "obscur[ed] more important issues in the clamor of bells and drumbeats" (Moore, *Nationalizing* 82).

Indeed, a reading of Arozarena's early poetry and other writings from the same period suggests that even though he was a champion of certain Afro-Cuban cultural manifestations, there were others that he saw as problematic obstacles to the social, political, and economic aspirations of Cubans of color. In the 1930s his opinions about traditional *comparsas* and *congas* seem to have been very much in keeping with those of many Afro-Cuban intellectuals who believed that true vindication for Cuba's black population would not be achieved through singing and dancing in public spectacles, but rather by taking an active part in a struggle for change. Alberto Arredondo summed up this attitude well when he wrote in a 1937 article published in *Adelante* that "[los] que quieran impulsar al negro por verdaderos caminos de renovación . . . no estrarán al lado de las comparsas" [those who want to urge the Negro toward true roads of reform . . . will not take the side of the *comparsas*] ("El arte negro" 6). In a 1935 essay, also published in *Adelante*, titled "Rebeldía paradojal" [Paradoxical Rebellion], Arozarena expressed related concerns, most notably that Afro-Cubans' alleged obsession with music and dance was undermining their efforts to gain equal footing with their white counterparts:

Mientras [el negro] vigila el momento de las REIVINDICACIONES DEFINITIVAS ahoga cualquier gesto sin madurar, en la tumultuosa algarada de sus Sones, o los estrujará en el tirabuzón gozoso de un Guaguancó sudado en aguardiente de caña! (15, emphasis in original)

[As the Negro awaits the moment of DEFINITIVE VINDICA-
TIONS he stifles any unfinished acts in the tumultuous racket of his
son, or he'll crush them in the joyful twisting of a Guaguancó while
sweating sugarcane liquor!]

A similar notion resurfaces in two militant social poems from Arozarena's early years—"Canción negra sin color" and "¡Evohé!"—both of which were penned in 1936. In the first of these two works Arozarena presents the image of the black man as seen by a typical member of the Cuban upper class or a foreign tourist. He is a musician who, while lost in the fog of drunkenness, performs his music with the sole purpose of satisfying the curiosity of the outsider who scarcely appreciates him or his culture:

Somos lo anecdótico:
Lo eternamente beodo,
de una embriaguez de látigo, de selva y de canción;
en los bares del ritmo
la rumba nos da rones batidos en cinturas
y Trópico,
el orate de las Islas Sonoras,
—charcos musicales en las amplias praderas del Atlántico—
nos envasa en vitrinas de sextetos y sones
para peinar la desmelenada curiosidad turística. (163)

According to this pessimistic viewpoint, which at once serves to dispel common stereotypes (many of which had been propagated at least in part by *afrocubanista* poets like Arozarena himself) and to underscore the need for social and political change in Cuba, Afro-Cubans have become inseparable from and dependent on the entertainment value of their music and dance. This, the poetic voice implies, has greatly hampered Afro-Cubans' struggle for equality and justice. Along the same lines, he suggests that the Cuban bourgeoisie—incapable or unwilling to grasp the bleak reality of Afro-Cuban suffering—see blacks as little more than physical embodiments of their songs:

Para los párpados preñados de imágenes burguesas
retina que no apresa la verdad raigal,
nuestra Hambre es canto,
nuestra cultura es canto;
nuestra risa, canto, y nuestra llanto,

canto, canto,
canto en negros como corcheas;
canto en negros como bueyes de penas
arrastrando su oprimida vida de carreta musical. (164)

Likewise, in "¡Evohé!," which did not appear in print until its publication in the first edition of *Canción negra sin color* (1966), Arozarena largely portrays Afro-Cuban music, song, and religious rituals as obstacles that too often distract blacks from pressing political and social issues, rather than as potential vehicles through which to achieve equality with white Cubans. The poem's title refers to the call that the Romans used to announce the Bacchanalia—ancient feasts in honor of Bacchus that celebrated hedonism and involved orgiastic rites—and it reflects Arozarena's criticism of the parallels that he apparently saw between the drunken revelry of these ancient Roman festivities and the hedonistic tendencies of Afro-Cuban dancers and musicians. At the same time, though, the title also serves as "a cry to call people together" to take part in a common cause (Larrier 57): that is, the fight for racial harmony and social justice.

In the opening stanza the poetic voice implores his fellow Cubans of color to cast aside their instruments, stop their dancing, forget about their spells and their Yoruba deities, and instead turn their attention to the pressing issues of racial injustice that were much more meaningful to the black experience of the 1930s:

¡Evohé!,
   suelta el bongó,
suelta el patín de munición de tu cintura;
suelta el gesto en espiral que te exprime el espinazo;
y sin palos de timbal,
sin jícaras de maracas,
sin manteca de corojo ni maíces del embó,
piensa un poco en SCOTTBORO [sic] y no en Ogún. (18)

Reflecting his own Marxist militancy Arozarena implies here and throughout the poem that except for the environments associated with entertainment and African-derived religions, Cuban blacks have no place of their own, and he therefore encourages them to reclaim the space in society that is rightfully theirs. Like Regino Pedroso before him—who in "Hermano negro" (1931) had written "Negro, hermano negro, / silencia un poco tus maracas. /. . . . / y escucha allá, en Scottsboro, en Scottsboro" (156-57)—Arozarena turns the infamous case of the "Scottsboro Boys" into "a rallying point for turning black attention to more serious affairs of race in the world" (Jackson, *Black Image* 123). Alejandro de la Fuente observes how in the 1930s, Cuban Communists increasingly turned to vociferous denunciations of racism in the United States "to foster anti-imperialist feelings among Afro-Cubans." In 1931, he adds, "they waged a campaign denouncing the death sentence imposed on nine blacks in Scottsboro, Alabama, as 'an assassination en masse'" (192).

This case, which is widely regarded as one of the most shameful travesties of the United States justice system, involved black youth—ranging in age from twelve to nineteen years—who were falsely convicted and sentenced to death by an all-white jury for raping two white women in 1931. Though all of the defendants were eventually pardoned, paroled, or acquitted (with the exception of one who escaped from prison in 1948), they spent years in deplorable Alabama penitentiaries. Two other Cuban poets, Mirta Aguirre and Ana González, also published poems about the Scottsboro Boys. The poems in question were both written in 1935 and likely served as sources of inspiration for the young Arozarena. In her "Scottsboro," Aguirre condemned the infamous case as "un manto de martirio y . . . vergüenza/ que cobija las dos razas" [a blanket of martyrdom and . . . shame/ that covers the two races] (121). In her "Romance negro del negro," González writes "Pobres negros de Scottsboro /. . . . . / los jueces y magistrados / los guardias y carceleros / no los encierran por malos, / ¡son negros, los nueve negros!" [Poor Negroes of Scottsboro / . . . / the judges and magistrates / the guards and prison keepers / do not lock you up because you are bad, / ¡you are Negroes, the nine Negroes!] (82).

Arozarena also evokes another of Pedroso's sentiments—"¿no somos más que rumba, lujurias negras y comparsas?" ("Hermano negro" 157)—when he suggests that African-derived music and religious rituals are of little importance if they divert the attention of Afro-Cubans from the flagrant injustices to which blacks at home and around the world were continually subjected. The poetic voice therefore insists that instead of wasting their energy singing and dancing for tourists or taking part in rituals that are far removed from the civil strife of the day, Cuban blacks would do better to lend their powerful voices to more meaningful and urgent causes:

No seas eco recortado por agria minusvalía,
y no seas sólo eco:
que tus ricas ansias mudas,
que tu voz humedecida por sonoras selvas vírgenes,
es dinamia de heroísmos,
es potencia de proclamas
y no risa de turistas en rumbática secuencia.
¡Evohé!,
 tu indigencia, tus hermanos,
son canciones en que debes aprender. (18–19)

Echoing one of the major themes of "Canción negra sin color," Arozarena underscores the untapped power of the Afro-Cuban population, but implies that change will come about only if Cuban blacks deliberately fight exploitation and injustice. It is important to stress here that Arozarena does not so much deny the value of Afro-Cuban song, dance, and ritual in these poems, but rather he suggests that their importance has been supplanted by the more pressing matters of racial prejudice and social injustice. Moreover, he implies that many African-derived cultural manifestations had been cheapened and commercialized to such an extent that they had long since lost their deeper meaning as well as their ties to their cultures of origin.

It is precisely these ideas that surface again in "La conga," in which Arozarena expresses opinions on *comparsas* and *congas* that are very much in keeping with many of those that appeared in the pages of *Adelante* in the mid-1930s. The reputation of *congas* as Afro-Cuban cultural manifestations that had served to fuel prejudices and perpetuate base notions of black cultural atavism and inferiority is clearly reflected in Arozarena's poem even as strong social undertones emerge in the final stanza. This important early text is rife with negative imagery that reflects Arozarena's own belief that certain Afro-Cuban cultural manifestations were damaging the black cause. Moreover, even a cursory reading of "La conga" reveals that despite Arozarena's supposed aversion to superficial and exoticized images of Afro-Cubans, his poetic rendition of a traditional carnival ensemble shares significant common ground with some of its decidedly sensationalistic predecessors. The following stanzas, in which Arozarena focuses on the raucous music, drunken revelers, and supposedly menacing aspects of the *conga*, are illustrative of these points.

Hiere el tumulto orquestal de mil gargantas resecas,
ebrias, agrias, duras, frías;
aleluyas de gangarrias desploman su algarabía
—latigazos en los músculos,
   tirabuzón en la piel
   y serpiente resbalosa que se sacude de sol.

Huracanes de colores—negro y rojo,
rojo y negro—
agitan sus banderolas de lasciva contorsión:
sudorosas percusiones manchan el aire de alcol
y entre los pulmones negros
ecos múltiples anudan su cansada entonación.

Parancantinquin tinquin tan
Parancantinquin tinquin tan

¡Ah!, las siluetas negras
desarticulan sus miembros en conflagración de ritmos:
ritmo en el mar de los brazos
ritmo en el pedal del pie
persiguiendo presuroso el tropelaje de ruidos
sobre las fibras sonoras del repicado tambor.

Andarines tremolando locas campanas de conga,
en su furia peligrosa,
en su litúrgica acción,
cual plumeros de estropajo sacudiendo sus cabezas
ágiles saltan los mástiles del sopor y la emoción.

Parancantinquin tinquin tan
Parancantinquin tinquin tan

Frescos trompos de mulatas son brujas y calaveras
y en medio de la balumba Barambambulla bailaba
—ojos de hogueras de soles,
   gruesos labios de lujuria guardando besos de ron. (39–40)

Arozarena's poem certainly calls into question his supposed "antipathy to exotic and sensationalized folkloric verse" (DeCosta-Willis, "Journey" 13) and avoidance of "descriptive exoticism" (Jahn, *History* 221), and it should be noted that the veritable profusion of terms and phrases with negative, destructive, or pathological undertones—"ebrias" [drunk], "duras" [rough], "frías" [cold], "agrias" [sour], "serpiente resbalosa" [slippery serpent], "huracanes" [hurricanes], "conflagración" [conflagration], "tropel" [disorderly mob], "furia peligrosa" [dangerous fury], "locas campanas" [crazy bells], "lujuria" [lewdness], "lascivia contorsión" [lascivious contortion], "cólera" [rage/cholera]—that the poet employs in his descriptions of the spectacle and its participants evoke similar aspects of "La comparsa." As we noted in our discussion of Pichardo Moya's poem, notions of the links between Afro-Cubans and certain physical and mental illnesses were largely disseminated and popularized by pseudo-scientific discussions of Afro-Cubans and their culture in widely read works by Fernando Ortiz, Israel Castellanos, and Rafael Roche y Monteagudo.

Like its precursors, Arozarena's poem dwells on aspects of traditional *congas* that the majority of Cubans considered telltale signs of their allegedly primitive or degenerate nature: the ear-piercing racket, the ritualistic dancing, the stench of sweat and alcohol, the "bewitched" *mulatas*, and the fiery eyes and "lecherous" lips of the male participants. Even the nonsensical name of the black male dancer—Barambambulla—is derogatory as it implicitly equates the black man with the repetitive drumbeat (*barambam*) and the noisy uproar (*bulla*).

The *mulata* dancers described in "La conga" are reminiscent of those in "Caridá" and "Liturgia etiópica" as they are presented in predominantly debasing terms. They are *trompos* [clumsy dancers], *brujas*, and provokers of sexual passions. Indeed, as presented through the gaze of the drunken, lustful black man they are equated to succulent treats that are fit to be devoured when our attention is called to their "teats of molasses" and "thighs of marmalade."

Arozarena's implicit association of *congas* with violence and danger is especially important in light of the ongoing campaign against them. When Havana mayor Antonio Beruff Mendieta reauthorized traditional Afro-Cuban carnival celebrations in 1937, detractors of such festivities again evoked images of violence and criminality in their attempts to convince authorities to outlaw *congas*. For example, members of the Asociación

Adelante wrote an official letter to the mayor, in which they expressed their concern that his decision could lead to unforeseen consequences, such as the formation of illicit *congas* by the city's criminal elements:

> lo que sería negativo, si en vez de comparsas bien organizadas ... se le permitiera transitar por los barrios de la ciudad, a los núcleos desorganizados, las llamadas "congas" ... pues es más que sabido que los elementos de las más bajas capas sociales aprovechan estas oportunidades para dar rienda suelta a sus vicios y bastardas pasiones. (Salas Aranda 4)

> [what would be unfortunate is if instead of well organized *comparsas* ... permission were granted for those disorganized groups, the so-called "congas," to pass through the neighborhoods ... indeed it is more than well known that elements from the lowest layers of society take advantage of such opportunities to give free reign to their vices and spurious passions.]

In a recent article on Arozarena's early poetry, I argued that the tumult, harshness, fury, and chaos that characterize Arozarena's portrayal of a traditional *conga* in the first five stanzas reappear in the poem's final stanzas as crucial components of its political subtext since they suggest the collective energy of the black participants who have turned the *conga* into an outlet for the pent up anxiety and frustration that has resulted from centuries of oppression. I posited that the poet's allusion to a palpable sense of fear among the female dancers toward the end of the poem—"brincan, / brincan / con/ mie—/ do"—materializes in the form of government riflemen who open fire on the carnival procession in the final stanza:

> Hábiles carabineros
> ametrallan sobre el parche descargas de percusión
> y al derribar el cansancio, la pimienta, y el furor
> —párpados de curva lenta
> lengua enruemada con ron—
> muere el tumulto orquestal de mil gargantas resecas.
> ¡Tropel de siglos frustrados en el aborto ancestral!

In my reading of these lines I contended that since instruments of African origin were officially banned on numerous occasions throughout Cuba, it is highly symbolic that the government riflemen open fire on the drumheads themselves. Indeed, by shooting the drums they destroy a physical symbol of Cuba's African heritage at the same time that they forcefully silence the music and singing (Anderson, "Inconsistent Depictions" 28–29). It is important to point out that such a reading reflects a historical fact: that is, that during the Machadato members of Cuba's police force would sometimes destroy African-derived musical instruments in their attempts to eradicate traditions such as *congas* and *comparsas*. According to José Millet and Rafael Brea, in Santiago de Cuba scenes such as the following one described by one of their informants were not at all uncommon:

> Machado suprimió los carnavales y todo, no había conga, ni nada. Pero aquí en Los Hoyos la gente siempre fue porfiada: sacaban las congas sin autorización. Al poco rato, venía la guardia rural y la desbarataba. ¡A fijarse, a correr, qué sé yo! Eso era un desorden; se iban los guardias y la gente volvía a sacar la conga, y venían de nuevo los guardias . . . y algunos dejaban las tumbas botadas y los guardias las rompían. (*Barrio, comparsa, y carnaval* 190)

> [Machado suppressed the carnivals and everything, there was no *conga*, nothing. Here in Los Hoyos people were always obstinate: they went out in *congas* without authorization. After a while, the rural guard came out and broke them up. To stay put, to scatter, what do I know! That was chaos; the guards left and the people came out again in their *congas*, and the guards came again . . . and some left their drums behind and guards destroyed them.]

With this historical backdrop in mind, then, the final stanza of "La conga" can also be read as an evocation of the enduring prejudices against traditional *conga*s, which take on a twofold symbolism. On the one hand they can be seen to represent the fruitless attempts by Afro-Cubans to maintain their ancestral ties with Africa and preserve their unique cultural legacy, while on the other they come to embody their resistance against attempts made to eradicate that legacy. Though I would not go so far as to refute this reading of "La conga," further consideration of this key Arozarena poem and its historical context has led me to an alternate interpretation of its conclusion, which seems every bit as plausible. Indeed, if we take into consideration Arozarena's own apparent misgivings about traditional *conga*s, which I overlooked in my earlier essay, it could be argued that the "aborto ancestral" that he refers to in the poem's final verse might actually be an evocation of the widespread notion that *congas* were cultural abominations and damaging and shameful offspring of the slave era. Such a reading implies that Arozarena shared the opinion of many fellow middle-class blacks who viewed *congas* as formidable obstacles to Afro-Cubans' ongoing struggles for social, political, and economic equality. This reading is reinforced by the repetition in the final stanza of stereotypes—harsh-sounding music and song, laziness, inebriation, lack of control—that serve throughout the poem to cast a negative light on traditional *congas* and their participants.

"El grito de mil voces": Carnival and Revolution

Arozarena's "Carnaval de Santiago" stands out among the poems considered in this study for several reasons. Most obvious among these are its later publication date and the coincidental circumstances that surrounded it. Indeed, the poem first appeared in print in the Havana daily *Hoy* on July 26, 1953, the same day that Fidel Castro and his band of rebels undertook their brazen assault on the Moncada barracks in Santiago (the Cuban army's second largest at the time) with the hopes that the dancing, drinking, and partying of the carnival celebrations the night before would serve to hamper the response of Batista's soldiers to their early morning attack. In this uncannily prophetic poem Arozarena essentially underscores how eastern Cuba's traditional carnival festivities of 1953 have become a distraction from the country's ever-mounting political tensions, and the poetic voice therefore implores the carnival participants to channel their energies toward the revolutionary struggle.

"Carnaval de Santiago" also stands out as one of the few poems that considers Santiago de Cuba's summer carnival festivities, which by the 1950s had become highly commercialized extravaganzas like the winter carnival celebrated in the capital. Despite the poem's title, strong political undertones largely overshadow descriptions of the actual carnival ensemble and its participants.

The opening stanzas of "Carnaval de Santiago" evoke in many ways the stereotypical depictions of Afro-Cuban carnival traditions that can be found in Arozarena's "La comparsa del majá" and "La conga," as well as in other Cuban carnival poems that we have considered.

SANTIAGO se despereza
al descoyuntado toser de los tambores
como un pulmón dolido de atávicos sonidos.

¡Ah!, el pensamiento suda.
La boca alegre suda su gesto de embriaguez,
y al paso atento y ágil
que calcan las canciones,
tendones de aguardiente se tirabuzonan
por descorchar el ritmo que esconden nuestros pies.

¡Ah! El pensamiento suda!
El grito de mil voces se cauja en emoción,
y hasta la vieja esquina
colgada en su pasado como un balcón de ecos
   —"un solo golpe,
   mamá;
   un solo golpe na má..."—
va anudando en caderas los cuerpos de sopor:
. . . .
Raja la voz seca
al eco espeso y duro.
Tu voz,
mi voz, ¡cien voces!
se violan en los ecos para ser sola voz. (21–22)

Arozarena twice implies in these lines that carnival celebrations in Cuba are outdated remnants of the past, first by referring to them as atavistic in the opening stanza, and then by describing the carnival procession as rounding a corner that is "suspended in the past."

Notwithstanding its evocation of many carnival stereotypes, "Carnaval de Santiago" is a very different sort of poem. Even in the lines cited above one can detect the emergence of the social and political undertones that dominate the second half of the poem. The most notable of these is the implied notion of the *conga* as a communal enterprise with great potential for uniting disenfranchised Afro-Cubans. The poetic voice of this poem is a participant in the *conga* who seems to realize as he marches along that the collective energy and unified voice of the ensemble could be put to a more productive use: instead of marching in the carnival parade, he and his fellow Afro-Cubans could be marching toward economic, social, and political justice. Once he becomes conscious of this notion, the speaker changes his tone dramatically, as can be seen in the stanzas that follow:

Una corneta en mástil
—pirata del silencio

su grito de metales
como una banderola de revolución:

¡¡Brinca, Bárbaro Babastro!!

Si la tierra que alimentas
no te quiere alimentar,
¡anímala con los pies!

Si el músculo se te oxida
Por amnesia de un quehacer,
¡anímalo con los pies!

The high-pitched, piercing sound of the *corneta china* that leads the carnival procession evokes the collective voice of the people, and the potential for change that comes through breaking the silence. By comparing this instrument, which is unique to the carnival celebrations of eastern Cuba, to "a revolutionary pennant," Arozarena suggests with uncanny prophecy that the time is ripe for change in Cuba. At the same time, he implies that revolution will require the active participation of Santiago's Afro-Cuban population.

When the poetic voice encourages the participants in the *conga* to "liven it up with your feet," he is, of course, speaking figuratively. He is not encouraging them to continue on with their carnival dance, but rather to cease dancing and lend their feet to a more noble and productive enterprise: that is to march, as it were, for change. In this regard "Carnaval de Santiago" shares much in common with some of Arozarena's early social poems—most notably "¡Evohé!" and "Canción negra sin color."

In the opening lines of the final stanza of "Carnaval de Santiago" Arozarena underscores—in much the same way that he had in his early social poems—his conviction that overemphasis on expressive culture and entertainment was highly detrimental to Afro-Cubans' struggle for equality. In "Canción negra sin color" Arozarena observed that Afro-Cubans were like "bueyes de penas / arrastrando su oprimida vida de carreta musical," and in "Carnaval de Santiago" he offers a similar image of traditional music as an embodiment of Afro-Cuban oppression: "En tambor de rumbabuena / se baña el dolor del pueblo" (23).

While reading "Carnaval de Santiago," one must keep in mind that when Arozarena penned it, Cuba was on the brink of revolution, and the author felt strongly at the time that Afro-Cubans needed to define their positions and take a stand against the Batista regime. It is very important to point out here that much like Machado before him, Batista was actually quite popular among blacks, even though he was not particularly concerned with championing their causes. Hugh Thomas has noted, for example, that Batista "gave consistent support to various Afro-Cuban cults," and he adds that many of Fidel Castro's "black or mulatto followers had been taunted by their black soldier captors at the time of Moncada for following a white leader against Batista, the friend of Negroes." "Some soldiers," Thomas continues, "expressed genuine surprise that there were any 'black revolutionaries'" (851).

These details are especially important in the context of Arozarena's poem, which was clearly written with the intention of stirring up black support for change in Cuba, and by extension for Fidel Castro and his fellow revolutionaries. Arozarena certainly could not have known about the plans for what he later referred to as "the glorious assault on Moncada" (Adolfo Suárez 14), much less that the attack would take place on the very day he published "Carnaval de Santiago." However, as a militant Marxist and champion of equality on all levels of Cuban society, he yearned for a revolution like the one that was about to get under way, and he wanted his fellow Afro-Cubans to take an active part in it. Such an opinion is clearly revealed in the following lines:

La carne que se te muere
de tanto esperar,
¡suéltala!

El alma que se te muere
de tanto soñar,
¡suéltala!

Y la voz que se te muere
de tanto callar,
¡suéltala!

Here Arozarena takes issue with the apathy and passivity of the participants in the carnival *conga*, who seem to have plenty of energy for dancing and singing, but not for fighting for their human dignity and equality. Instead of waiting for change and dreaming of a better future in silence, Arozarena prods his fellow Afro-Cubans to take a militant role in the revolution, which will assure that their legacy lives on forever: "que así carne, tu alma y voz / cuando el alma se te seque seguirán bailando solas / y hechas corazón de olas siempre ancho mar quedarán" (23). It is highly ironic that in addressing the participants in the *conga* the speaker alludes to their silence, given that such spectacles were known—and often criticized—for their strident singing and music. But the reference to silence serves to underscore the author's message that such "noise" is largely responsible for the virtual silence of Afro-Cubans in the arenas of political, social, and economic justice.

A Poet in Three Dimensions

In 1943, several years after the climax of Afrocubanismo, Marcelino Arozarena published "El antillano domador de sones" [The Antillean Tamer of Sons], a critical appraisal of the poetry of Nicolás Guillén, in the Havana cultural review *América* (1939–1958). In this important essay Arozarena claims that Guillén's approach to Afro-Cuban themes in the poems collected in *Sóngoro cosongo y otros poemas* (Havana: La Verónica, 1942)[7] can be divided into three dimensions. The first dimension, which according to Arozarena is exemplified by poems such as "Velorio de Papá Montero," "Rumba," and "Secuestro de la mujer de Antonio," is dominated by "superficial" images and "reactionary" profiles of solitary Afro-Cubans, who are presented largely in terms of their relationship to "rum, rumba, and sex." Arozarena argues that the poems that correspond to this dimension of Guillén's oeuvre are characterized by "a pleasurable flight from reality," "political blindness," and "a cover-up of the present oppression of the Negro" (37). Referring to the poems from the so-called second dimension, Arozarena contends that the black subject is merely "recuperating from his drunkenness." Even though he "begins to take note of his surroundings," he is still guided by a "broken compass" and recognizes his problems only by their "chromatic surface" (38). In poems such as "Canción del bongo," "El abuelo" [The Grandfather], and "Balada de los dos abuelos" [Ballad of the Two Grandfathers], Arozarena identifies an attempt at denunciation, but not a clear call for militancy. It is only in the third dimension, Arozarena insists, that Guillén finally "knows WHAT he is looking at and WHY he is looking at it" (40, emphasis in original). In this phase—represented by poems like "No se por qué piensas tú" [I don't Know Why you Think], "Elegía a un soldado vivo" [Elegy to the Living Soldier], and "Cantaliso en un bar" [Cantaliso in a Bar]—Guillén leaves behind his uncertainties and "unsheathes his agile machete . . . in order to open up paths to the future" (40). According to Arozarena, the black subject in this third dimension has found his voice of protest and has become part of a collective effort to bring about change in the Caribbean and around the world.

In his book *Black Images*, Wilfred Cartey upholds many of the arguments that Arozarena presented in his article on "Guillén's approach to the Negro theme," and he qualifies the text as a "fine incisive appraisal" (130). However, Jackson somewhat tentatively takes issue with Arozarena's critical approach to Guillén's early poetry. Referring to "El antillano domador de sones," he observes with a mildly accusatory tone that "Arozarena has even accused Nicolás Guillén, his fellow Afro-Cuban poet, perhaps erroneously, of perpetuating . . . negative images of blacks" (41). My own sense is that in his article Arozarena is at times overly critical of the work of his fellow poet, but he is correct to suggest that Guillén, like many poets of his day, approached "black themes" with varying degrees of profundity and offered inconsistent portrayals of Afro-Cubans and their notable contributions to Cuban popular culture.

What this brings to mind—and what Cartey and Jackson both fail to notice—is that Arozarena's deliberate division of Guillén's poetry into three dimensions (his article is subdivided by the titles "Primera dimensión," "Segunda dimensión," and "Tercera dimensión") is somewhat ironic since it serves as a model for compartmentalizing his own poetry, which is also inconsistent in terms of its representations of Afro-Cubans and their cultural manifestations. If we were to adopt Arozarena's schematic presentation of Guillén's poetic production, then, poems such as "Caridá" and "La comparsa del majá" would fit neatly into the so-called first dimension, which lacks political themes and in which blacks are portrayed as embodiments of a hedonistic world of "rum, rumba, and sex." In the second, transitional, dimension we could place poems like "La conga," which straddles a world in which blacks are portrayed through superficial and retrograde images and one in which they become embodiments of a collective will to denounce centuries of oppression and social injustice. Finally, Arozarena's best sociopolitical poems, such as "Carnaval de Santiago," "Canción negra sin color," and "¡Evohé!" belong in a third dimension in which superficial depictions of Afro-Cubans and African-derived cultural manifestations are largely overshadowed by the poet's condemnation of social injustice and his calls for militant action against its every manifestation. It should be added, moreover, that like Guillén, who in his third dimension "sailed full speed ahead toward wider horizons" (Arozarena, "El antillano" 40), Arozarena reveals in his best social poems his deep commitment to revolutionary change in Cuba, as well as his genuine desire for a brighter future for Afro-Cubans and other oppressed groups around the world.

8

An Outsider on the Inside

Alfonso Camín's "Carnaval en la Habana"

> ... *un pintor extranjero, no podría ver sin experimentar la más profunda emoción un espectáculo tan brillante, tan movido y tan nuevo para él como ... una comparsa habanera*
>
> [... a foreign painter could not witness without experiencing the most profound emotion a spectacle so brilliant, so moving, and so new for him as ... a Havana carnival]
>
> Fernando Tarazona, *Estampas Afro-Cubanas*

Some readers might question the inclusion of Spanish poet Alfonso Camín (1890–1982) in this study of representations of carnival traditions in Cuban poetry. It is important, therefore, to clarify from the outset of this chapter dedicated to his "Carnaval en la Habana" that despite having been excluded from many important anthologies of *poesía negra* and *afrocubanista*—most notably Ballagas's *Antología de poesía negra hispanoamericana* and Guirao's *Órbita de la poesía afrocubana*—Camín has been hailed by many critics as one of the initiators/precursors of these important literary movements.[1] As Valentín Tejada has pointed out, Camín's best verse found its inspiration in American, and especially Cuban, themes and motifs (695). Cuba occupies such a prominent place in Camín's poetic production largely because he resided there during his early years as a poet—1905–1918—and visited several times in the 1920s and 1930s.

Several sources give erroneous information concerning Camín's formative years in Cuba. For instance, Ruiz del Vizo (*Black Poetry* 22) mistakenly notes that he emigrated there at the age of four, when, in fact, his family arrived in Cuba in October 1905, when he was fifteen years old. Fernández de la Vega and Pamies, for their part, make no mention of Camín's early years in Cuba, and incorrectly cite 1924 as the year of his arrival in Havana. In his autobiography, *Entre palmeras: vidas emigrantes*

(1958), Camín tells of his early years working in various Havana businesses, and notes that he began his writing career in Santiago de Cuba, where he worked as a contributor to and editor of newspapers such as *El Cubano Libre* and *El Liberal*. He returned to Havana sometime in 1913, and immediately began to collaborate in *El Diario Español*, moving later to a job at *Diario de la Marina*.

Alfonso Camín and the Birth of *Afrocubanismo*

Despite their inaccurate statement that Camín arrived in Havana in 1924, Fernández de la Vega and Pamies are correct in their assertion that that year was an especially significant one in his lengthy stay in Cuba. In fact, 1924 would turn out to be a turning point in his poetic career and in the history of Cuban poetry since it was during that year, while working at the Havana daily *El País*, that Camín published an editorial in which he underscored what he saw as a pressing need for a major renovation of Cuban literature.[2] In the article the Spanish-born poet suggested that such a renovation could be achieved through the exploration of the island nation's most authentic and characteristic qualities, such as African-derived customs and traditions. As Camín points out in his autobiography, his editorial was met with scorn by both black and mulatto intellectuals— who "saw black art as something inferior" that belonged to *ñáñigos* and slum dwellers (*Entre palmeras* 563)—and it was vehemently criticized by prominent white intellectuals. According to Camín, one of his harshest critics was Jorge Mañach, who argued that it was impossible to detach from Spanish modes in the novel, the short story, and in poetry since Cuba had no real literary tradition of its own (562).[3]

It should be added here, moreover, that Mañach had a hard time conceiving of an independent space for the expression of Afro-Cuban themes, as Duno-Gottberg has noted (112). Like many other prominent Cuban intellectuals in the early 1920s, Mañach envisioned a properly constructed Cuban nation as one in which blackness would be seen as a mere accent, and not a standard measure of Cubanness.

After a drawn out polemic with Mañach, Camín writes how a truce with the Cuban intellectual and critic was brokered through their mutual friend Manuel Aznar, after which Camín tacitly agreed to drop the subject of African-inspired literature in Cuba. As Camín puts it, "ya no se habló más, ni de sobremesa ni en *El País*, de la poesía cubana o afrocubana" [no more was said, either in after-dinner conversation or in El País, about Cuban or Afro-Cuban poetry] (*Entre palmeras* 563). By 1925, however, Camín revisited the polemical subject through the publication of his poem "Elogio a la negra," which he and other critics have cited as the initiator of *poesía negra* not just in Cuba, but also throughout the rest of the Antilles.

Though Camín makes clear on several occasions that he did not aspire to be known as a "poeta afro-cubano," he resented the fact that so many practitioners of so-called black poetry seemed to forget that he was one of the original sources of the fad. In the prologue to *Carey y nuevos poemas* [Carey and New Poems] (1945)—and later in a chapter titled "Cómo nació la poesía afro-antillana" [How Afro-Antillean Poetry Was Born] in his autobiography—Camín convincingly argues that he wrote and published his first *poemas negros* before any of the other initiators of Afrocubanismo; he specifically mentions Guirao, Tallet, and Carpentier. Camín also claims to have preceded Puerto Rican poet Luis Palés Matos, who is widely hailed as having initiated the Afro-Antillean poetry movement with the publication of "Pueblo negro" [Black Town] in the San Juan daily *La Democracia* in March 1926, by putting forth the following argument:

> En 1925 escribo mi poema formal "Elogio a la negra." Inmediatamente "La negra Panchita," que publican los periódicos de España y de Cuba. "Demasajova," que remito en una postal a la amiga de Santa Clara. La poetisa negra se encarga de hacerla popular por la prensa cubana. Aparte de otros poemas de este sabor, que publico en "La Esfera" de Madrid, sale en Madrid—Editorial Renacimiento, 1926—mi libro "Carteles." En ese libro van incluidos mis primeros poemas negros.
>
> Desde ese momento ... los poetas de las Antillas, blancos y negros, todos a uno, primero en periódicos, después en el libro, comienzan a hacer versos de esa índole, con temas iguales o variados, haciendo baraja revuelta con muchas de mis palabras y no pocas imágenes. El ron de "Macorina" me lo han bebido treinta y dos veces.
>
> De ese modo nace lo que han dado en llamar ellos mismos poesía afro-cubana. (*Carey* 9–10)

[In 1925 I wrote my poem "Elogio a la negra." Immediately thereafter "La negra Panchita," which was published by Spanish and Cuban newspapers. I sent "Demasajova" in a postcard to a female friend in Santa Clara. The black poet made sure to make it known through the Cuban press. Apart from other poems of that flavor, which I published in "La Esfera" in Madrid, my book "Carteles" came out in Madrid—Editorial Renacimiento—in 1926. My first black poems were published in that book.

From that moment on . . . the poets of the Antilles, white and black, together as one, first in newspapers, later in books, began to write poems of that ilk, with the same or similar themes, turning many of my words and no small number of my images into a mixed up deck of cards. The rum of "Macorina" has been drunk thirty-two times.

That is how what they themselves call Afro-Cuban poetry was born.]

It should be noted here that "Demasajova" was published in Cuba in the second issue of *Revista de Avance* in March 1927—just over a year before the appearance of Guirao's "Bailadora de Rumba" in *Diario de la Marina*—and was accompanied by a brief note that made reference to its appearance in Camín's recently published book, *Carteles* (1926).[4] "La negra Panchita" [The Negress Panchita] was published in *Revista de Avance* in January 1928. Though Camín's foundational role in the dissemination of *poesía afro-antillana* is still not widely acknowledged, a handful of critics have convincingly supported his claim to the title of initiator of Afrocubanismo. In a 1969 essay Gastón Baquero, for example, refers to Camín as "el creador de la poesía afrocubana o afroantillana" [the creator of Afro-Cuban or Afro-Antillean poetry], adding that while Nicolás Guillén was still writing under the influence of Rubén Darío and *modernismo* in the mid-1920s, Camín was discovering the rich mine of Afro-Cuban themes and images that the future poets of the movement still disdained (240). Three years later Hortensia Ruiz del Vizo similarly contended that Camín "was the true initiator of black poetry in Cuba" (*Black Poetry* 22). In more recent studies of Camín's work, Spanish critics have underscored Camín's decisive role in the foundation of Afrocubanismo. In his introduction to a 1990 compilation of Camín's poetry, for example, Albino Suárez makes the following observation:

> Fue Camín quien, en convencimiento serio y firme, defendió el Son cubano como razón genuina del sentir nativo. Acaso Rubén Darío

escribiese antes "La negra Dominga" . . . pero, incluyendo incluso los escarceos de García Lorca, que también divagó en la poesía afrocubana, fue Alfonso Camín quien sembró la semilla y recolectó la mayor cosecha sobre el Son cubano, o la poesía Afrocubana o Negroide. (16)

[Camín was the one who, with firm and serious conviction, defended the Cuban *son* as a genuine basis of native sentiment. Perhaps Rubén Darío wrote "La negra Dominga" before . . . but taking into consideration even the amateur efforts of García Lorca, who also dabbled in Afro-Cuban poetry, it was Alfonso Camín who planted the seed and gathered the best harvest relating to the Cuban *son*, or to Afro-Cuban or Negroid poetry.]

Albino Suárez's comments echo Camín's poem "Negro," written in the 1940s and first published in *Maracas y otros poemas* (1952), in which he writes:

Negro: no te olvides mañana
que yo fui el primer pregón
negro en la tierra antillana;
que he recogido tu son
y lo eché, como un ciclón,
a correr la mar lejana.
Y hoy ya tienes tu canción. (50)

Even though Camín was excluded from the major poetry anthologies that emerged during the height of Afrocubanismo, the fact that several of his poems were de rigueur numbers in the performances of Eusebia Cosme, the famous diseuse of Afro-Antillean verse, serves as an accurate indicator of his prominence among the early promoters of the movement. Camín's "Macorina" was among the poems that Cosme recited in her public appearances in the early 1930s, and a perusal of programs from Cosme's recitals in Cuba, Puerto Rico, and the United States from the 1930s through the mid-1950s confirms that poems by Camín—especially "Macorina" and "Demasajova," but also "El tren de Cococún" [The Cococún Train] and "Elogio a la negra" [Eulogy to the Negress]—were integral numbers in her repertoire for over two decades.

Carnival is Black and White

Alfonso Camín's "Carnaval en la Habana," which offers a fascinating poetic rendition of traditional carnival celebrations in Cuba, was first published in *Maracas y otros poemas* in 1952, and was probably penned some time in the 1940s when Afrocubanismo was already on the wane. However, what interests me most about Camín's 176-line poem is not so much its relationship with Afrocubanismo or with other poems of the movement, but rather the panoramic view that it offers of Havana carnival traditions during the first half of the twentieth century. Indeed, Camín's poem illustrates the two-sided reality of Havana's carnival season: it was celebrated in very different ways and often in different locations by white Cubans and Cubans of color. Along these lines, Camín's poem can be divided into two distinct parts. In the first four stanzas he focuses on traditional Afro-Cuban carnival celebrations and the requisite *comparsas* and *congas* from Havana's lower-class neighborhoods, while in the next four he turns his attention to so-called "white carnival" with its parades of decorated automobiles, elaborate floats, beautiful carnival queens, and dances and balls in exclusive clubs and organizations.

Before embarking on our discussion of "Carnaval en la Habana," it is important to call attention to the fact that in *El carnaval habanero*, Helio Orovio does a major disservice to Camín's little-known poem by including only the first half (and making no reference to the second), and thereby giving the false impression that the Spanish author was only interested in presenting Havana's carnival as an essentially African-derived cultural manifestation. What makes Camín's poem so valuable is precisely the fact that it presents Havana carnival during the early years of the Republic for what it really was: a segregated event that rarely saw harmonious mixing along class and racial lines.

Despite the obvious differences between the first and second parts of "Carnaval en la Habana," these two halves, which delineate the nature of black and white carnival traditions respectively, are framed by the following brief stanza that introduces the poem and then is repeated with only the slightest changes at its conclusion.

> Yo no sé lo que serán
> los Carnavales en Niza,
> en Venecia, en Nueva Orleáns;

pero los cuatro domingos
de la Habana en Carnaval,
esos no hay quien los supere
ni los iguale jamás.

This stanza is significant mainly because of the implicit connection that it draws between Havana's carnival and ancient carnival traditions in Europe, which offers a stark contrast to what seem like purely African-inspired celebrations in several of the poems we have considered. At the same time, however, this stanza—with its obvious evocation of European, and especially Spanish, traditions—bears a more obvious relationship to the second part of Camín's poem than it does to the first. Camín's description, in a chapter in his autobiography titled "El primer carnaval" [The First Carnival], of a high-society carnival parade in which he had participated in the 1910s echoes many elements of the introductory and concluding verses of his poem:

Jamás yo había visto, ni tampoco he visto después, unas fiestas de Carnaval más animosas y con tan inmenso gentío. Dicen que las de Nueva Orleáns las superan y que las de Yucatán le van a la zaga . . . Pero no creo que los de Niza fuesen mejores que los Carnavales celebrados en La Habana en los primeros quince años de este siglo. (68)

[I had never before seen, nor did I ever see afterward, carnival festivities that were more lively or that attracted such immense crowds. They say that those in New Orleans are better and that the ones on the Yucatan Peninsula are right behind . . . But I don't think even those in Nice are better than the carnivals that were celebrated in Havana in the first fifteen years of this century.]

Camín's evocation of the four Sundays of carnival in the poem's opening and concluding stanzas recalls the fact that traditional white carnival celebrations of early twentieth-century Havana could be traced back to centuries-old Spanish traditions, a connection that Feliú Herrera (*Fiestas* 136), Orovio (*Carnaval* 10), and Fernando Ortiz ("Informe" 11–12, "Viejos carnavales" 205–06) have discussed at length. These festivities, which typically consisted of highly organized dances and parades that largely catered to members of the Cuban upper classes, took place on four consecutive Sundays during the Lenten season, each of which was known by a specific name that evoked various elements of the traditions.

The first of these four Sundays was known as "Domingo de la piñata" [Sunday of the Piñata], so named because on that day, after taking part in public carnival parades, members of the capital's high society attended private dances at which piñatas filled with confetti, candies, and fruits were broken to symbolize the imminent arrival of the abundances of spring. The second Sunday, "Domingo del figurín" [Sunday of the Figurine], centered on the figure of the "king of the carnival" (known in Cuba as "Rey Momo"), an embodiment of the excess and sensuality that characterize the carnival season. According to Ortiz, this male figure recalled the age-old evocation of the ever-youthful and handsome Adonis in the springtime processions and celebrations of classical Greece. Ortiz adds that the Cuban tradition of selecting a beautiful woman—the carnival queen—to represent the ephemeral pleasures of carnival time was a relatively recent phenomenon that reflected modern attitudes toward sexuality:

> Hoy día [1954], el renacimiento de la desenfrenada sensualidad y del culto a la belleza femenina y sus desnudeces ha hecho que por lo común sea "reina" y no "rey" quien represente el efímero imperio del carnaval. ("Viejos carnavales" 205)

> [Nowadays [1954], the rebirth of unbridled sensuality and the worship of feminine beauty and nudity has made it so that most commonly it is a "queen" and not a "king" that represents the ephemeral realm of the carnival.]

The third Sunday, "Domingo de la vieja" [Sunday of the Old Woman], was dedicated to the personification of Lent, typically embodied in a cardboard figure of a hideous old hag with seven legs that represented her seven-week lifespan. This figure often made its first appearance on Ash Wednesday, and was burned on Holy Saturday or Easter Sunday along with an effigy of Judas (Feliú Herrera, *Fiestas* 136–37). Ortiz notes that the destruction of this repulsive figure also evoked ancient collective pagan rites of purification meant to scare off evil spirits ("Informe" 133, "Viejos carnavales" 205). Finally, "Domingo de la sardina" [Sunday of the Sardine] brought the carnival celebrations to their official close. The sardine was an important penitential symbol in Spain, as it served as a staple of the

Lenten diet. However, given that Lent in Cuba coincided with the sugar harvest—and cane cutters needed to eat high-calorie foods—sardines had little symbolic importance there. The name of the last Sunday of the carnival season, therefore, can be seen as a passed-down Spanish tradition in name only, as many Cubans did not strictly observe Lenten fasting.

Following the poem's Eurocentric opening stanza Camín embarks on a poetic exploration of African-derived carnival celebrations, which offers a stark contrast to the Christian and pagan traditions that he has just evoked. The Afro-Cuban *comparsas*—made up of members of Abakuá *juegos*—that he describes quickly distance us from the references to Nice, Venice, and New Orleans.

> Desde la noche de Reyes
> al Martes de Carnaval,
> iban saliendo en comparsas
> los ñáñigos a bailar.
> . . . .
> oliendo a negra y a mar,
> bailando va "La Culebra,"
> bailando va "El Alacrán."

In these lines Camín presents a panoramic view of Afro-Cuban carnival traditions from the nineteenth century to the early decades of the twentieth. The allusion to Día de Reyes, for example, implicitly evokes the slave-era tradition in which blacks were symbolically freed for a day and permitted to don elaborate costumes and sing, dance, and play music in the streets of the nation's cities where they would request *aguinaldos* from wealthy onlookers. On this momentous occasion, which Ortiz has referred to as "one of the most picturesque scenes of colonial life" in Cuba, "black Africa, its people, its costumes, its music, its tongues, its song and dance, its ceremonies, its religions and political institutions, were brought across the Atlantic to Cuba, especially Havana" ("Afro-Cuban Festival" 1).

The reference to the *ñáñigos* and the carnival *comparsas* that these members of secret Abakuá brotherhoods organized also evokes a tradition that goes back to 1836, when the first Abakuá lodge was established in the working-class Havana neighborhood of Regla. As Brown has noted, from 1836 until carnival was outlawed in Cuba in 1884, each *juego* would emerge in carnival processions on January 6 (*Light Inside* 15). At the same time, in these lines Camín explicitly conjures images of early twentieth-century carnival celebrations, which were reauthorized shortly after the establishment of the Republic. La Culebra and El Alacrán were two of the best-known Abakuá-affiliated *comparsas*, the latter of which was founded in 1908 in Jesús María, a humble, working-class Havana neighborhood. El Alacrán was originally made up mostly of members of a white Abakuá lodge, but it eventually included many black and mulatto participants. Camín's allusion to this particular *comparsa* in his poem is especially significant, since it was widely associated with the violent behavior that many Cubans claimed was part and parcel of *ñáñiguismo*, and by extension the Afro-Cuban carnival processions that were widely associated with these esoteric brotherhoods. As we have already mentioned in Chapter 1, members of El Alacrán were involved in a notorious street brawl with a rival *comparsa* troupe in March 1912, which resulted in several deaths and injuries (Orovio, *El carnaval habanero*, 31–32; Moore 69–70). Camín clearly evokes the violence associated with the Abakuá in his description of the *diablito*, which comes across as a menacing character:

> Diablito cascabelero
> salta de aquí para allá;
> unas veces va adelante
> y otras veces va detrás,
> como un faquir comelumbre,
> como un Fu Manchú oriental.

It is apparent from the similes presented here that Camín, like many outsiders, misrepresented the significance of the *diablito* and his actions. For instance, by comparing the *diablito* to a fire-eating fakir, a performer of seemingly impossible feats that suggest magical powers, Camín conjures up the negative stereotype of a black sorcerer and practitioner of dark arts. The evocation of Fu Manchú is even more suggestive of the threatening character of the *diablito*. Indeed, this literary creation of English writer Sax Rohmer (1883–1959), who first emerged in the serialized novel *The Mystery of Dr. Fu Manchu* in 1912–1913, is often referred to as the archetypal criminal genius and is best known for his murderous plots. Like the *ñáñigo* figure that Camín describes, Dr. Fu Manchu was also a member of an arcane society, and he had a reputation for violence. One of the best-known descriptions of this notorious figure, which appears at the end of the second chapter of *The Insidious Dr. Fu Manchu*, clearly underscores the name's negative connotations:

> Imagine a person, tall, lean and feline, high-shouldered, with a brow like Shakespeare and a face like Satan, a close-shaven skull, and long, magnetic eyes of the true cat-green. Invest him with all the cruel cunning of an entire Eastern race, accumulated in one giant intellect, with all the resources of science past and present, with all the resources, if you will, of a wealthy government—which, however, already has denied all knowledge of his existence. Imagine that awful being, and you have a mental picture of Dr. Fu-Manchu, the yellow peril incarnate in one man. (n.p.)[5]

If Fu Manchu symbolizes the so-called yellow peril, then Camín's *diablito* can be seen, by extension, as an incarnation of the "black peril," that is, the Afro-Cuban underworld and all of the crime and violence that it implied.

Even though Camín does reinforce many negative stereotypes of Afro-Cuban *comparsas* in "Carnaval en la Habana," his poetic rendition of them also stands out as perhaps the only one that explicitly refers to their popularity with white audiences on the one hand, and their syncretic nature on the other. In the following lines, for example, Camín describes a passing group of *negras* and *mulatas* whose sensual dance attracts whites and blacks alike:

> Detrás, vestidas de rojo,
> lo mismo que un framboyán,
> vienen bailando las negras,
> sudor, cadera y compás.
> Vienen también las mulatas
> —mango, caoba y coral—
> . . . .
> Abren balcones las blancas,
> sale el tendero al portal;
> igual que antorchas al viento
> los cuerpos vienen y van;
> gritan, se alejan, se acercan,
> sigue la danza sensual
> y aplauden blancos y negros

la danza del Calabar.
Danza de Sierra Leona,
Noche, desierto, arenal;
Danza que vino del Congo, (32)

In his autobiography Camín describes his impressions of the first Afro-Cuban *comparsas* that he witnessed in Havana in the early 1910s. Though his recollections are not without a tinge of racism (he notes, for example, that he felt as if the African jungle had spilled onto the streets of Havana (63)), he speaks of the great pleasure he felt in the presence of these impressive spectacles, and he marvels at the fact that the approaching uproar of drums and *cencerros* lured folks from every walk of life out onto the street:

> la gente corría a ver aquel espectáculo, saliendo a los portales desde las casas de comercio, de los patios de vecindad . . . el bodeguero dejaba sus cuentas, el sastre su tijera, el farmacéutico su receta, el médico su consultorio, el dependiente la yarda, la clientela suspendía sus compras; la negra lavandera dejaba la batea, el zapatero su lezna [sic] y todo con gran holgorio, para ver las comparsas . . . (63)

> [the people ran out to see that spectacle, coming out to the portals from commercial establishments, emerging from their neighborhood patios . . . the grocer left behind his accounts, the tailor his scissors, the pharmacist his prescription, the doctor his office, the sales-clerk his yardstick, customers put off their shopping; the Negro washerwoman left her washing trough, the shoemaker his awl, and all with great merrymaking, to see the *comparsas* . . .]

Though he focuses here primarily on the African origins of traditional *comparsas*, the poetic voice also admits that they represent a "Mezcla de rito africano / y de catolicidad" (33), which he sees embodied in the following refrain that follows each of the six main stanzas of the poem: "*Écue, Abasí, Changó, / Ochún, Yemayá.*" Though these lines are clearly not the most apt embodiments of the syncretic nature of Afro-Cuban carnival *comparsas*, it is nonetheless worth discussing their significance. The first two terms are Abakuá names, but only the second reflects in an obvious way what Brown has referred to as the tradition of "borrowing and blending of Catholic objects within the Abakuá iconographic repertoire"

(*Light Inside* 32). The supposed syncretic nature of *Écue* is not clear, as this term has no real parallel in the Christian tradition. Though it has many possible meanings, when written with a small "e," *écue* usually refers to God's "Divine Voice," but when written with a capital "E" it signifies the secret, "hidden friction drum that reproduces the 'Divine Voice'" (Brown, *Light Inside* 36). On the other hand, Abasí, the Abakuá "Supreme Being," is a better example of religious syncretism since this figure is often represented by a monstrance and a crucifix on the Abakuá altar and in their sacred processions. We must keep in mind, however, that the addition of such Western religious symbols to Abakuá rites and rituals should not be seen simply as an indication of an encounter or symbiosis between two belief systems, but also as a strategic "response to formidable sociopolitical stress," which allowed the Abakuá to continue religious practices that had been previously considered illicit (Brown, *Light Inside* 5). Moreover, one must not lose sight of the fact that, as many experts have pointed out, Abakuá rites bear only superficial points of similarity with Catholicism (Cabrera, *Sociedad* 12; Ortiz, *Instrumentos* 2, 98, 111; Brown, *Light Inside* 31–32).

The same can be said of the creolization and syncretism that have shaped many of the rites and rituals of Afro-Cuban Santería, such as the traditional pairing of Yoruba deities with Catholic saints. Changó, Ochún, and Yemayá, for instance, are traditionally syncretized with Santa Bárbara, La Virgen de la Caridad del Cobre, and La Virgen de Regla, respectively. Though most experts agree that "Africans and their descendents 'worked out' a series of iconographic, functional, ecological, and temporal 'parallels' between gods and saints," the issue of genuine belief in such parallels—that is, "whether the saints merely 'masked' the gods or were internalized along with the Catechism"—continues to be a topic of debate (Brown, *Santería* 119).

What remains clear after reading Camín's poem is that, like the white Cuban intellectuals who began to defend *comparsas* in the 1930s as symbols of Cuba's mixed-race national identity, Camín offers a very vague illustration of their supposed syncretic nature. However, his poem stands out because it also calls attention to the fact—even if inadvertently—that Havana's carnival was a two-sided cultural phenomenon that exposed deeply engrained prejudices that divided Cubans along class and racial lines. In this sense, his poem reflects observations like the following one by Emilio Roig de Leuchsenring, which offers a typically skewed image of Havana's traditional *comparsas* as cultural manifestations that brought citizens of all classes and races together in harmonious celebration of their common *cubanía*, or active desire to be Cuban:

> ¿Qué son las comparsas callejeras de La Habana?
>
> Pues, sencillamente, la forma típica y tradicional con que los diversos elementos componentes del pueblo de esta ciudad celebran costumbres heredadas de sus antepasados. El más rico valor artístico de las comparsas, viene, desde luego, del África; pero no es exclusivamente africano, sino producto de la adaptación de los elementos africanos en nuestra tierra y de su fusión con los elementos blancos españoles y nativos y con los elementos de procedencia china. O sea, está allí el verdadero pueblo de Cuba, que no es ni blanco español sólo, ni negro africano, sólo, ni amarillo chino sólo, sino la resultante de la unión de todos esos pueblos. ("Comparsas" 150)

> [What are Havana's street-walking *comparsas*?
>
> Well, quite simply, they are the typical and traditional form in which diverse constituents of this city celebrate customs that they inherited from their ancestors. The richest artistic merit of the *comparsas* comes from Africa, to be sure; though it is not exclusively African, but rather a product of the adaptation of African elements in our nation and their fusion with white Spanish and native elements as well as with elements of Chinese origin. That is to say, we find in them the true Cuban nation, which is not just white Spanish, nor just black African, nor just yellow Chinese, but the resultant union of all of those peoples.]

Evocations of the Reemergence of Traditional *Comparsas* in 1937

In the fourth stanza of "Carnaval en la Habana" Alfonso Camín evokes the historic 1937 reemergence of traditional Afro-Cuban *comparsas* in Havana—to which we have referred various times—and the foundation of new carnival troupes in following years. Of the four troupes that Camín mentions here, three—"Los Dandys," "Las Bolleras," and "La Jardinera"— eventually achieved the enviable status of "los grandes" [the greats], that is, the most traditional and most popular of Havana's *comparsas* (Moliner Castañeda 68). There is a palpable sense of nostalgia in these lines, in which the poetic voice seems to lament the fact that the highly regulated *comparsas* that emerged in 1937 and shortly thereafter lacked the folkloric charm and authentic flavor of the Afro-Cuban *comparsas* Camín had witnessed during his early years in Havana.

> Ahora son otras comparsas
> las que por las calles van.
> La Costa de los Esclavos
> se refleja en "Los Gambá";
> negros que mueven trapiches,
> cantan, sudan sin cesar,
> temorosos al componte
> y a la voz del mayoral.
> "Dandys" de Jesús María
> con aires de Ku-klux-klan,
> ya no son lo que ayer eran
> ni echan la Habana a temblar.
> Pero vienen "las Bolleras"
> dando bollitos de pan,
> y viene "La Jardinera,"
> "La Jardinera" se va.

When the poetic voice suggests that the *comparsas* are different, he is not only alluding to the poem's opening stanzas in which he had evoked more traditional carnival troupes—such as "La Culebra" and "El Alacrán"—from the early years of the Republic, but also to the drastic changes in the Havana *comparsas* that emerged in 1937, which Israel Moliner Castañeda describes as follows:

> Se produce, al estímulo de las autoridades, una desafricanización en las comparsas tradicionales, que abarcó desde mutaciones organológicas, transposiciones conceptuales, y complejidades coreográficos, hasta cambios de nombres. Por ejemplo, Las Lucumisas comenzaron a llamarse Las Bolleras. Mientras que los elementos africanos que se conservaron fueron preservados en virtud de lo

pintoresco y llamativo para los turistas y por una espontaneidad tradicional. (67)

[The great efforts of the authorities has produced a de-Africanization of the traditional *comparsas*, which has included everything from organizational mutations, to conceptual changes, to choreographic complications, to changes of names. For example, Las Lucumisas began to call themselves Las Bolleras. Meanwhile the African elements that were maintained were conserved only by virtue of their quaintness and attractiveness and for the sake of tourists and traditional spontaneity.]

The veracity of Moliner Castañeda's comments finds support in several of the documents collected in *Las comparsas populares del carnaval habanero, cuestión resuelta* [The Popular *Comparsas* of Havana's Carnival, Problem Resolved] which was published by the Municipality of Havana in 1937. In his letter to the mayor of Havana, for example, Ortiz implicitly promotes the toning down of the African elements of traditional *comparsas*, first by stressing the need to regulate them, and then by condemning *congas* for their "vulgar music," "artlessness," and "lack of esthetic and folkloric elements" ("Informe" 18). In his contribution to this important collection of documents, Emilio Roig de Leuchsenring also hints at the "whitening" of traditional *comparsas*, inadvertent as it may have been, by supporting the push of the Comisión Asesora de Turismo Municipal to "renovate Havana carnival" by "elevating" the artistic and educational value of traditional *comparsas*, and by making them more attractive to foreign tourists. In other words, *comparsas* needed to be made less "black" ("Dos actualidades" 40–41).

The first *comparsa* that Camín refers to in the above-quoted lines is most likely "Los Gangá" (not "Gambá" as the name appears in the poem) which was established in the Havana neighborhood of Los Pocitos in 1938. Most *comparsas* of the era had specific themes, and many of them found inspiration in historical episodes from the colonial period. For example, this particular *comparsa*—whose name refers to a specific region and people of Western Africa—evoked the legacy of slavery and the arduous work on the sugarcane plantations.

Camín's description of "Los Dandys" is inaccurate because this well-known *comparsa* was from the working-class, Afro-Cuban enclave of

Belén, not Jesús María. What is more, the comparison to the Ku Klux Klan is puzzling since "Los Dandys" were primarily Afro-Cubans, and they were considered to be one of the most elegant carnival troupes of the era. Indeed, one member of the jury in charge of awarding prizes for best *comparsas* in 1939 referred to this carnival troupe as being "trajeados con la más exquisita corección anglofrancesa" [dressed with the most exquisite Anglo-French refinement] (Villoch 18). The men typically donned fine white suits, bow ties, patent-leather shoes, gloves, and top-hats, with other accents such as handkerchiefs in their breast pockets, boutonnieres of red roses in their lapels, and canes that were incorporated into their carefully choreographed dances. The women wore elegant dresses, white gloves, and tiaras or small hats. This particular *comparsa* included several famous musicians among its performers. Singer, dancer, drummer, and composer Chano Pozo (1915–1948), for example, served in its early years as the "baron" who led the troupe through the streets, and legendary trumpeter Félix Chapottín (1909–1983) functioned as the ensemble's musical director (Orovio, *El carnaval habanero* 46).

The only conceivable parallels that could be drawn between "Los Dandys" and the Ku Klux Klan are their all-white attire and the fact that the majority of the male members were also members of a secret society—in this case an Abakuá brotherhood. But it is more likely that Camín was referring either to *diablitos* from another *comparsa* or perhaps even to a group of hooded penitents taking part in the carnival parade, like those pictured in a 1946 carnival poster by Enrique Caravia (fig. 8.1), which had been commissioned by the Office of Tourism.

The *comparsa* "Las Bolleras," which hailed from the neighborhood of Los Sitios, was originally made up mostly of men who dressed in the traditional garb of female Lucumí fritter vendors, commonly referred to as *bolleras* because of the popular fried rolls that they sold. Following the reemergence of *comparsas* in 1937 the theme of this carnival troupe remained the same, but women assumed the roles of the namesake "bolleras." Emilio Roig de Leuchsenring considered this *comparsa* to be especially interesting among those that emerged in 1937 because of its evocation of this colonial-era tradition:

> Una de las más interesantes comparsas de 1937 fué la de *Las Bolleras* por su valor costumbrista y la propiedad interpretativa de las antiguas bolleras lucumís que en las calles y plazas de la Habana

cocinaban y expedían su mercancía a los transeúntes, durante la época colonial. ("Comparsas" 167)

[One of the most interesting *comparsas* of 1937 was that of Las Bolleras because of its reflection of local customs and the interpretative appropriateness of the old Lucumí fritter vendors who, in the streets and plazas of Havana, used to cook and vend their products to passersby during the colonial era.]

As they passed through Havana's thoroughfares the members of "Las Bolleras" would hand out fresh fritters—the "bollitos" to which Camín refers in his poem—to the audience and the judges. These delicacies—prepared on a small wooden cart upon which sat a gas stove and a kettle of frying oil—were a big hit with the audience members, but they sometimes had an even bigger impact on members of the jury assigned to hand out awards. For example, one juror of the 1939 competition praised the "exquisite" traditional fritters with the following words: "la nutritiva, apetitosa y democrática fritura que consoló tantas veces el hambre de los desheredados; de los cesantes; de la bohemia callejera" [the nutritious, appetizing, and democratic fritter that consoled so many times the hunger of the underprivileged; the unemployed; the bohemians of the street] (Villoch 18).

It is worth pointing out here that the refrain in Camín's poem—"Écue, Abasí, Changó, / Ochún, Yemayá"—may have been inspired at least in part by a traditional component of the performances of "Las Bolleras," whose chants and instrumentation were very much reminiscent of traditional *congas* (Guzmán Moré n.p.). At the specific moment in the carnival procession when the *comparsa* passed by the judges and the organizers of the festivities, a soloist accompanied by a *batá* drum would belt out various chants to the Yoruba deities.

The last *comparsa* to which Camín alludes, "La Jardinera," was founded in Jesús María, and made its debut appearance during the carnival season of 1938. Like many other *comparsas*, its name evokes a historical event from Havana's past: the 1926 hurricane that destroyed the main park of this working-class Havana neighborhood. The members of this carnival ensemble typically wore silk shirts and dresses with floral patterns, and they carried baskets full of carnations, roses, and jasmine, which they threw to members of the crowd as the filed by (Villoch 18). The group's

FIGURE 8.1. Carnival poster by Enrique Caravia, 1946. This original poster was one of many issued by the Departamento de Turismo del Municipio de la Habana with the aim of attracting tourists to Havana's annual carnival festivities. (Library of Congress.)

legendary theme song—the refrain of which is known throughout Latin America—refers to the great efforts that were made after the hurricane to restore the park and replant the lost trees and flowers: "Flores, flores, / ahí viene La Jardinera, / viene regando flores" [Flowers, flowers / here comes La Jardinera sewing flowers].

In the final lines of the fourth stanza Camín again suggests the universal popularity of the Afro-Cuban carnival ensembles, whose infectious rhythms inspire all of Havana to dance and cheer as they pass by:

> Toda la Habana bailando,
> toda la Habana aclamando
> ritmo, cadera y compás,
> va la comparsa marchando,
> va la comparsa ondulando
> como si fuera un majá.

As we will see in the next section, however, the three stanzas that make up the distinctive second part of "Carnaval en la Habana" effectively contradict this notion of Havana's carnival celebrations as inclusive, mixed-race spectacles by focusing on the parades and the high-society balls and dances that were strictly off limits to the majority of the city's lower classes and the members of its Afro-Cuban population.

Havana's Other Carnival

The second part of "Carnaval en la Habana" focuses on a very different type of carnival experience, which would have been enjoyed mainly by Cuba's high-society white population and well-to-do tourists from the United States, Europe, and Latin America. It is clear from the nostalgic tone that characterizes these verses that despite his apparent delight in certain aspects of the Afro-Cuban carnival traditions, Camín identified with Havana's "white" carnival and its palpable evocations of the traditions of Spain, France, Italy, and the United States, as the following lines suggest:

> Carnaval el de mis tiempos
> de la Habana en Carnaval:
> toda la Habana en colores,
> toda la Habana en tambores,

toda la Habana en fulgores,
toda la Habana en vals.

Though the repetition of "toda la Habana" here would seem to imply that this "other" Havana carnival was enjoyed by Cubans from all sectors of society, such was certainly not the case. Indeed, the "vals" in the sixth line clearly alludes to the exclusive high-society balls and private festivities that characterized "white" carnival. It should be noted, moreover, that even the so-called public events of the carnival season were often segregated according to racial and class lines, as Dennis Moreno Fajardo has pointed out:

> La división socioeconómica implicaba división . . . de diversión colectiva. . . . En los días de festejos populares, mientras el pueblo se divertía en las calles y parques, una minoría se refugiaba en los locales de sus respectivas sociedades. . . . En los festejos populares, los blancos que no pertenecían a la sociedad, se divertían separados de los negros. En las áreas de fiestas se levantaba una cerca de tela metálica para separar a unos de otros, o simplemente se usaba una soga que hacía las veces de frontera para, de esta manera, evitar el contacto entre ellos. (14)

> [Socioeconomic division implied division . . . of collective diversion . . . In the days of popular fiestas, while the people enjoyed themselves in the streets and parks, a minority took refuge on the premises of their respective societies . . . In the popular festivals, whites who did not belong to high society, enjoyed themselves separated from blacks. In the areas of the festivities a wire fence was erected to separate the two groups, or they simply employed a rope that served as a division meant to prevent contact among them.]

In the lines that follow, Camín describes other traditions—such as the crowning of the carnival queen (fig. 8.2) and the showering of confetti and streamers upon elaborately decorated automobiles and carnival floats (fig. 8.3)—that clearly underscore the differences between "black" and "white" carnival in Havana.

La Reina con sus princesas
y en su carroza triunfal,
va, desde Marte y Belona,

por todo el Prado hasta el mar.
Confetis y serpentinas
al aire vienen y van
. . . .
Blancas y en blancas carrozas,
mujeres sin antifaz,
pues que esconder esas caras
fuera pecado mortal.
Ojos que París no tiene,
Que nunca Londres tendrá,
y hay que buscar en Sevilla. (35)

A comparison between the description of the high-society carnival and that of the Afro-Cuban *comparsas* in the first part of the poem reveals some noteworthy differences. Most obviously, both the participants and the props in this carnival procession evoke whiteness, a notion that is reinforced later in the poem when the women are compared to "Blanca Nieves," and "espuma del Mar Caribe." Likewise, whereas the participants in "black" carnival are explicitly linked to Africa through references to Ethiopia, Calabar, Sierra Leone, and the Congo, the women in the "white" carnival evoke comparisons with France, England, and especially Spain.

In his description of the Afro-Cuban *comparsa*, the speaker calls attention to the sensual bodies of the black women—"las negras, / sudor, y cadera;" "los cuerpos vienen y van; / . . . sigue la danza sensual" (32)—and even notes that the *comparsas* file past "oliendo a negra" (31). The white women, on the other hand, stand out for their beautiful countenances and alluring eyes, and as they pass by the air takes on the smell not of sensual body odor, but rather of a rosebush: "va oliendo el aire a rosal" (36). Finally, in the "black" carnival the masked *diablito* conjures up the menace of a legendary criminal mastermind, while the white women are equated with fairy tale queens and princesses.

It is very interesting that in his autobiography, much like in his poem, Camín makes clear that like most middle-class white men of his time, he saw Afro-Cuban *comparsas* as formidable spectacles worth observing from a distance—"[la comparsa] se me metió por los ojos y los oídos y gocé a lo grande con aquel espectáculo" [the *comparsa* entered through my eyes and ears and I greatly enjoyed that spectacle] (64)—, but not as events in which he would have participated actively. Indeed, Camín

Reina del Carnaval.

Srta. Ramona Garcia

Left: FIGURE 8.2. Photo of a Havana "Carnival Queen," ca. 1915. Photographer unknown. (Author's collection.)

Below: FIGURE 8.3. Early twentieth-century postcard depicting a procession typical of "white" carnival, with a decorated float, automobiles covered with *serpentinas* [streamers], and well-dressed onlookers lining Havana's Malecon. The handwritten note along the top edge reads: "We were in a parade like this." (Author's collection.)

Habana: Paseo de Carnaval en el Malecon.
Carnival at Malecon Promenade.

FIGURE 8.4. Original promotional poster by Cuban artist Mario Carreño, issued by the Departamento de Turismo del Municipio de la Habana shortly after the official reauthorization of *comparsas* by Mayor Antonio Beruff Mendieta. Despite the reference to "Spanish" romance, the poster highlights many Afro-Cuban elements of Havana's carnival. The text in English suggests that the poster was designed with U.S. tourists in mind. (Library of Congress.)

expresses great surprise first when he notices that some white audience members join in the festivities, and then when he sees some white members in one of the passing *comparsas*, which a Cuban friend explains as follows: "Son juegos de ñáñigos a los cuales también pertenecen algunos blancos" [They are ñáñigo lodges to which belong some whites as well] (65). On the other hand, Camín describes at length his enthusiastic participation in a high-society *desfile de carrozas* [parade of decorated automobiles and floats], which in his mind outshines some of the most famous carnival celebrations of the United States, Latin America, and Europe.

In many ways Camín's poem—which vividly describes both "black" and "white" carnival, but tacitly elevates the latter—echoes the type of imagery that appeared in posters commissioned by the Municipal Tourist Department of the City of Havana in the 1930s and 1940s. One particular poster by Cuban artist Mario Carreño (1913–1999), which served as an announcement of the reemergence of traditional carnival celebrations in 1937, bears much in common with the themes and images in Camín's poem (fig. 8.4). This attractive poster features a title in English that reads: "FEBRUARY FIESTAS IN HAVANA / January 30 to February 28 1937." In the lower portion of the poster we find the following text, which underscores the "Spanish" (i.e. "white") elements of Havana's carnival in order to attract well-to-do tourists from the United States and Europe: "DANCE, MUSIC, HISTORICAL PAGEANTS / COLOR AND TRUE SPANISH ROMANCE / REVIVING THE GAIETY AND SPLENDOR / OF HAVANA'S GLAMOROUS PAST." Though Afro-Cuban *comparsas* and other cultural manifestations such as traditional rumba were big tourist draws throughout the early decades of the Republic, it is clear from this and other posters of the era that, despite the official reauthorization of these cultural manifestations in 1937, the Municipal Tourist Department was still loath to call too much attention at least in writing—to the African-derived elements of Havana's carnival celebrations. A promotional poster from 1937 by Cuban painter Enrique Caravia (1905–1992) is very similar to the Carreño piece in this regard (fig. 8.5). It prominently features an enticing black rumba dancer donning a see-through dress, but the text in English—which is the same as in the above example—highlights the so-called "Spanish romance" and old-world "glamour" of the carnival, while avoiding reference in writing to the reemergence of traditional *comparsas* or to other Afro-Cuban cultural elements of that year's celebrations. It is

FIGURE 8.5. Enrique Caravia's promotional poster for Havana's 1937 carnival festivities entices English-speaking tourists with the image of a buxom Afro-Cuban *rumba* dancer in a see-through dress. The text in English at the bottom right-hand corner reads: "For all information apply to the Transportation Companies, Travel Agencies, Cuban Consulates, Municipal Tourist Department (Havana City Hall) or the Cuban Tourist Commission." (Library of Congress.)

FIGURE 8.6. Carnival poster by unknown artist, 1941. Note how this particular poster avoids the Afro-Cuban elements of Havana carnival by evoking the masks worn in European cities such as Nice and Venice, or in Havana's private, high-society balls. (Library of Congress.)

Interesting to note that a 1941 poster by an unnamed artist, the Spanish text of which indicates a different target audience, avoids the Afro-Cuban elements of Havana carnival altogether by evoking the carnival masks like those worn in Nice and Venice (fig. 8.6).

As we have seen, Alfonso Camín's poem begins with a detailed description of traditional Afro-Cuban *comparsas* and the iconic figure of the masked *diablito*, which, we learn in the second stanza, is being contemplated by white women standing on balconies above the street. Carreño's promotional poster features a strikingly similar scene: the masked *diablito* in the center of the image is the obvious focal point of the carnival procession, and he, too, is being observed from above by two white women on the balcony of a Spanish-style home. Their attire evokes the references to Spanish princesses in Camín's poem. Below the elegantly dressed women, barely noticeable in the shadows of an arcade, is a wealthy-looking white couple who also contemplate the spectacle from a distance. In the foreground at the bottom right corner of the poster, suspended just above the text that evokes Havana's "Spanish romance" and "glamorous past," is an image that is clearly meant to highlight further the African elements of Havana's carnival: a polychrome, fluted drum with a sculpted anthropomorphic face. This particular image was obviously inspired by a famous *Arará* drum, which was seized by Cuban authorities from an Afro-Cuban *cabildo* in Matanzas in 1913. This drum is described by both Brown and Ortiz (*Light Inside* 178, *Instrumentos* II 16), and is currently housed in Havana's Museo Nacional where it has long been considered to be one of the jewels of the collection. However, the presence of this drum in Carreño's artistic rendering of a *comparsa* attests to the fact that like so many of the carnival poems that we have studied, it is not a fully accurate depiction. Indeed, as Brown has argued, "it is unlikely that any observer of Havana carnival or Abakuá ceremony would have seen such a drum . . . [since they] were meant to be played not singly, but in stationary drum batteries, and they remained hidden within the old, secretive Arará *cabildos* of Matanzas, Javellanos, Agramonte, and Perico one hundred kilometers to the east" of the capital (*Light Inside* 178).

In the background of Carreño's poster, the Spanish-built Catholic cathedral of Havana towers above the *comparsa* and its host of *farolas*. A white dove just under the women on the balcony, and almost touching the extended right arm of the *diablito*, echoes two notions that are implicitly expressed in Camín's poem: first, that Havana carnival is syncretic in nature, and second, that the Christian, Spanish traditions of Havana's carnival are more refined—and thus more important—than the "black" *comparsa* and the African-derived dance, music, instruments, and rituals that it implies.

The Commercialization of Carnival

One of the most unique and significant aspects of Alfonso Camín's poem is his realistic depiction of the commercialization and consumerism that increasingly dominated Havana carnival during the 1930s and 1940s. The complete absence of this theme in most of the other Cuban carnival poems that we have considered might at least in part be due to the fact that most of the poets of Afrocubanismo—in their quest to distance themselves from the legacy of colonialism by evoking uniquely Cuban cultural manifestations—were wont to avoid references that might suggest U.S. and Spanish domination of Cuba's society, culture, and economy. As a Spaniard who had essentially been excluded from the annals of Afrocubanismo, Camín had no real reason to present carnival as anything different from what it really was: a cultural phenomenon that underscored rampant racial, social, and economic inequalities and called attention to the continued foreign domination of the nation's economy.

In the following lines, Camín implicitly underscores Cuba's economic disparities by emphasizing the materialism and consumerism that eventually came to dominate Havana's white carnival:

> La carroza de "El Encanto"
> con tantas bellezas va,
> que por donde va pasando
> va oliendo el aire a rosal.
> "Crusellas y Compañía"
> perfuma el aire al pasar;
> da chocolates "La Estrella"
> y aroman el litoral
> "Villaamil," "Tomás Gutiérrez,"
> "Gener," "Punch" y "Partagás,"
> ojos de ron "Carta de Oro"
> y una flor en el ojal,
> "Bacardí" llegó de Oriente
> y es en la Habana el sultán. (36)

All of the commercial enterprises named here emphasize the exclusive nature of Havana's "other" carnival, which stands in stark contrast to the "black" *comparsas* and *congas* poeticized in poems by Pichardo Moya, Ballagas, Arozarena, and Caignet. The references to major Cuban businesses

FIGURE 8.7. Carnival float advertising Chocolates la Estrella, 1920. Photographer unknown. (Author's collection.)

such as El Encanto, Chocolates la Estrella, Crusellas y Compañía, Bacardí, and various cigar manufacturers in Camín's poem are significant for two reasons. First, their ubiquitous presence in the carnival processions demonstrates in a very concrete way how these cultural manifestations were essentially appropriated by Cuban and foreign-owned commercial enterprises, which came to view carnival as a prime vehicle for promotion of everything from fine clothing, to expensive candies, to soaps and perfumes, to alcoholic beverages (fig. 8.7).

Helio Orovio notes that by the 1940s the carnival *carrozas* were practically overtaken by Havana businesses, such as purveyors of fine clothing, who festooned their floats with advertisements and populated them with models who donned and displayed merchandise offered in the respective shops. But Orovio adds that the most elaborate floats tended to be those of the alcohol distributors, which typically included Cuba's hottest musical ensembles: Celia Cruz and the Sonora Matancera, for example, performed on the float of Cervecería Hatuey, and the Conjunto Casino promoted Cervecería Tropical (*Carnaval* 15). Others, such as the famous floats for Pedro Domecq's Brandy Fundador and that of Cervecería Polar, enticed the audience with beautiful women sitting on or standing next to massive bottles of their product (figs. 8.8, 8.9).

Second, several of the commercial enterprises that Camín refers to are also significant in the context of this poetic rendition of Cuban carnival by a Spanish author, since they were founded by Spaniards (mostly from

FIGURE 8.8. Carnival float sponsored by Pedro Domecq Brandy Fundador with women in Spanish-style dress, 1940s. Photographer unknown. (Author's collection.)

FIGURE 8.9. Carnival float sponsored by Cervecería Polar with female dancers and musical ensemble, 1956. Photographer unknown. (Author's collection.)

Catalonia) and thus underscore the continued influence of the mother country and former colonizer not just on the Cuban economy, but also on the island's society and popular culture. For example, El Encanto was owned and operated by Spanish immigrants Bernardo Solís, M. Solís Mendieta, and Aquilino Entrialgo. These prominent businessmen were also among the first Spanish members of the Institución Hispano-Cubana de Cultura, which was founded by Fernando Ortiz in November 1926 with the main objective of increasing intellectual relations between Spain and Cuba (Naranjo Orovio 9). Like many major sponsors of "white" carnival, El Encanto—which was famed as one of the world's finest department stores—appealed mainly to Cuba's upper crust and to wealthy foreign tourists. The store's prominent location on the corner of Avenida de Italia and San Rafael attracted discriminating shoppers from around the world who were lured there to purchase elegant and fashionable attire and accoutrements by catchy slogans such as: "Si quieres tener 'chic,' espiritualidad, distinción . . . no le des vueltas: lo compras en El Encanto" [If you want chic, spirituality, and distinction . . . don't put it off: shop at El Encanto](qtd. in Pancrazio 92). El Encanto was also a major supplier of carnival regalia for Havana's upper crust, and during the carnival season they—and their competitors—promoted their products through large ads in Havana's major dailies (figs. 8.10, 8.11).

In a similar manner, Crusellas y Compañía also exemplifies the lasting impact of Spanish-owned companies on various levels of Cuban society. Founded in 1866 by Catalonian immigrants and incorporated in Havana in 1914, Crusellas was a leading manufacturer of soaps, laundry detergent, perfumes, and other personal care products that were consumed by Cubans from all walks of life. Crusellas entered in a joint business venture with Colgate-Palmolive in 1929, which led to a proliferation of popular U.S. brands in Cuba. However, the agreement allowed them to continue to manufacture their own product lines, whose popularity remained high until the company was nationalized shortly after the triumph of the Revolution. In terms of its impact on Cuban society and popular culture, Crusellas y Compañía was a pioneer in radio and television advertising, and it became famous for annual contests in which winners were awarded new homes with the company's logo on the facade. This company eventually became a major sponsor and promoter of popular TV and radio programs that featured some of the country's best-known musicians and celebrities.

FIGURE 8.10. Newspaper advertisement promoting carnival attire and fabrics offered for sale at El Encanto, one of Havana's finest department stores. The image of the carnival mask and the finely dressed carnival masqueraders evokes the private carnival balls held by high-society whites. (*Diario de la Mariana*. Feb. 6, 1937. 12.)

FIGURE 8.11. Advertisement for carnival regalia at Los Precios Fijos, one of El Encanto's main competitors. This ad—with its Afro-Cuban drum and dancing *diablito*, a white woman in a carnival mask, a black man and white woman dancing together, and its promise of offering "adornments in good taste that, for very little money, will allow you to make the most beautiful costumes"—is clearly aimed at a much broader public. Note the similarities between the *diablito* and the drum on this illustration and those on the poster by Mario Carreño (see Fig. 8.4) (*Diario de la Marina* 10 Feb. 1937. 9.)

Several of the other commercial enterprises that Camín mentions as sponsors of Havana's high-society carnival also have important Spanish connections. For example, Partagás and Gener, two of Cuba's most prestigious cigar labels, were both founded by Catalonian immigrants in the mid-1800s. Likewise, Bacardí Rum was founded by a Catalonian, Don Facundo Bacardí Massó, in Santiago de Cuba in 1862. As Camín's poem indicates, this world-famous rum producer eventually moved from Oriente Province to Havana, where it became the "sultan" of Cuban rums.

As if to underscore even further the crucial Spanish component of Havana's exclusive carnival, Camín offers the following list of high-society social clubs that take part in the parade:

> Desfila el Centro Asturiano,
> el Canario y el Balear;
> desfila el Centro Gallego
> y hay Baile en el "Nacional." (36)

Here Camín also evokes the private balls that were central components of what Helio Orovio has referred to as "Havana's other carnival." Orovio specifically refers to parties that were organized by the Spanish societies to which Camín refers in his poem: "En los salones del Centro Gallego tocaban las mejores orquestas, al igual que en el Centro Asturiano ... en sus bailes sabatinos de carnaval" [In the salons of the Centro Gallego the best orchestras played, as they did in the Centro Asturiano ... during its Saturday carnival dances] (*El carnaval habanero* 17). He adds, moreover, that many other private clubs and organizations celebrated Havana's carnival seasons with exclusive galas:

> En los lujosos y amplios edificios y jardines del Havana Yacht Club, Miramar Yacht Club, Habana Biltmore, Casino Deportivo, Club Náutico, Club Comodoro, Country Club, Club de Profesionales, Casino Espanol, y en el histórico Vedado Tennis Club amenizaban excelentes orquestas ... Y se organizaban comparsas integradas por socios, que variaban cada año su temática, con bellos vestuarios, y coreografías montadas por miembros entusiastas y conocedores o por coreógrafos profesionales. (17)

> [In the luxurious and extensive buildings and gardens of the Havana Yacht Club, Miramar Yacht Club, Havana Biltmore, Casino Deportivo, Club Náutico, Club Comodoro, Country Club, Club de

Profesionales, Casino Español, and the historic Vedado Tennis Club excellent orchestras entertained . . . And *comparsas* that included members, and varied their themes each year, were organized with beautiful attire and dance routines that were put together by enthusiastic members or by professional choreographers.]

Articles in the society pages of Havana's major newspapers offered vivid descriptions of these elaborate festivities, complete with lists of the winners of *comparsa* competitions as well as hundreds of names of the high-society folks who attended the balls. A lengthy article published on February 16, 1937 in *Diario de la Marina*, is typical in its flowery presentation of an upper-class carnival ball at the Miramar Yacht Club, which it describes as "a grand social event, of extraordinary splendor and brilliance" that was punctuated by "exquisite, beautiful, floral adornments of the highest quality." The unnamed author adds with apparent pride that the radiance of the ball was greatly enhanced by the "sumptuous" regalia worn by the female attendants ("La fiesta del Miramar" 7).

Orovio's reference to the high-society *comparsas* is especially interesting because it serves as a reminder that such spectacles do not make an appearance in Camín's depiction of Havana's "white" carnival, nor are they mentioned in any other poem that we have considered in the present study. Moore has noted that "Many of Havana's middle-class and elite Cubans who had little interest in watching or participating in street parades that included Afrocuban *comparsas* and who did not condone their reauthorization [in 1937] nevertheless continued to create their own blackface groups safe within the walls of exclusive clubs" (84). It should be noted, however, that even though these high-society *comparsas* were meant to remain in the confines of their exclusive clubs, it was not at all uncommon for them to end up—perhaps after their inhibitions had been dulled by hours of revelry—in the bars and clubs of central Havana or even "arrollando" down the Paseo del Prado (Orovio, *El carnaval habanero* 17–18).

Hortensia Ruiz del Vizo's remark in a 1971 essay that Alfonso Camín was systematically excluded from the annals of Afrocubanismo out of "nationalist bigotry" makes a certain amount of sense. Likewise, she may be correct to surmise that Camín's tiff with Jorge Mañach over the Spanish poet's idea to reinvigorate Cuban literature through the celebration of Afro-Cuban themes likely had something to do with Camín's future marginalization. However, Ruiz del Vizo's suggestion that Mañach's marginalization of Camín was in large part due to his "antiespañolismo" [anti-Spanish feelings] (*Poesía* 14), is not as convincing. Indeed, Mañach was a well-known hispanophile who expressed a view in the early decades of the twentieth century that Cuba's cultural formation was incomplete and that the nation was in need of "the tutelage of a true civilization" (Duno-Gottberg 111). For Mañach the Spanish language "linked [Cubans] to an exalted historical lineage, a civilization of origin, and a great literary tradition" (qtd. in Duno-Gottberg 111).

We should add that Mañach expressed in no uncertain terms his distaste and disregard for *negrismo* as a literary and cultural movement, which he characterized as a transitory fad that reflected, more than anything else, the nation's desperate search for identity. He summed up this idea as follows in a very brief section titled "Negrismo" in his 1944 study *Historia y estilo*:

[El negrismo] traducía el designio de vincular los acentos intactos de la primitividad negra a los vacíos expresivos de la frustración cubana. Respondía así, en parte, a la angustiosa busca [*sic*] de sustancia y de peculiaridad expresiva en que andaba empeñada nuestra conciencia.... Hacía falta un estilo "cubano," y quisimos encontrarlo en el ritmo abrupto, en la elementalidad sensual, en los sentimientos y resentimientos de nuestras presencias negras ... pero en el fondo no era otra cosa que un recurso desesperado de la angustia republicana. Cuando esté cabalmente lograda, la nación tendrá en lo negro un acento, pero no una pauta. (198)

[Negrismo translated the intention to connect the intact accents of African primitivism to the expressive voids of Cuban frustration. It responded thus, in part, to the anguished search for substance and for expressive originality that our conscience had undertaken ... A "Cuban" style was necessary, and we wanted to find it in the abrupt rhythm, in the elemental sensuality, in the sentiments and resentments of our Negro existence ... but in its core it was nothing but a desperate resort of republican anguish. When it is wholly achieved, the nation will have an accent of blackness, but not a norm.]

Even though Mañach's categorical rejection of Camín's promotion of Afro-Cuban culture in 1924 seems to have been motivated more by lingering prejudices and his own discomfort with the celebration of the African elements of Cuba's national identity than by his supposed anti-Spanish sentiment, his attacks on the Asturian poet likely intensified his marginalization by other Cuban authors and intellectuals. I would add here, moreover, that it could also be argued that the most ardent promoters of Afrocubanismo—namely Ballagas and Guirao—must have felt that a Spaniard had no business claiming to be the initiator of a Cuban literary movement.

This argument would seem to find support in that fact that in his *Antología de poesía negra hispanoamericana*, Emilio Ballagas includes Federico García Lorca's "Son," a poem dedicated to Fernando Ortiz that the Spanish author wrote after "a brief stop in Cuba" in 1930 (178). In his foundational anthology, however, Ballagas does not so much as mention Camín, whose *poemas negros* were by then very well known in Cuba. It seems clear, then, as Valentín Tejada has argued, that one cannot allege that Camín was excluded from the anthology—or from the literary movement for that matter—simply because he was Spanish (697). Instead, I would argue that unlike García Lorca, whose poem was written well after the supposed foundation of Afrocubanismo by Cuban poets, and which Ballagas essentially admits is only tangentially related to the movement ("Casi como una curiosidad damos aquí estos versos" [Almost as a curiosity we include this poem here] 178), Camín had written and published more "black" poems by 1935 than most of the other major *afrocubanista* poets. He therefore held a legitimate claim to the roots of a movement that by its very nature needed to be of distinctly Cuban origin.

It is very interesting to note that it was not until 1946, a year after Camín vehemently defended his role as the initiator of Afrocubanismo in the introduction to *Carey y nuevos poemas*, that Ballagas acknowledged the Spanish poet's role in the movement by including just one of his poems, "Elogio de la negra," in *Mapa de la poesía negra americana* in a section titled "Poesía de motivo negro escrita por españoles" [Poetry of Black Themes Written by Spanish Poets]. In the brief biographical sketch that precedes Camín's poem, however, Ballagas is careful not to credit him with initiating Afrocubanismo, but rather states that he was an important "precursor" of "black" poetry in general: "En el género negro [Camín] tiene un señalado lugar de precursor y ha escrito otros poemas afros que no aparecen en la presente selección" (287) [In the black genre Camín has a distinguished place as a precursor, and he has written other Afro poems that do not appear in the present edition.]

Roberto Fernández Retamar continued in the tradition of denying Camín his rightful place as either a precursor to or initiator of Afrocubanismo by excluding his name altogether from a chapter titled "Poesía negra" in his 1954 study *Poesía contemporánea en Cuba*. In his brief chronology of the movement Fernández Retamar categorically states that *poseía negra* appeared in Cuba in 1928, and cites Guirao and Tallet as the founders of the movement (45). Like so many critics before and after him, Fernández Retamar seems to have forgotten that Camín had written and published several "black" poems before 1928, one of which— "Demasajova"—appeared in Cuba's own *Revista de Avance* in March 1927. Fernández Retamar's list of non-Cubans who had made a notable impact on the poetry of Afrocubanismo further serves to marginalize Camín from the movement for which he clearly served as a major catalyst. Indeed, the Cuban author and intellectual stresses that the movement was more profoundly influenced by Americans than by Europeans, and to back his claim he cites just three authors—Luis Palés Matos, Idelfonso Pereda Valdés, and Langston Hughes—who, in his opinion, preceded the Cubans in the cultivation of *poesía negra* (46).

Though "Carnaval en la Habana" was written several years after the climax of Afrocubanismo in Havana, this poem is, nonetheless, more than tangentially related to the movement and to the controversy that surrounded Camín's involvement in it. On the one hand, the poem serves to evoke this Spanish poet's continued interest in Afro-Cuban cultural manifestations, which he had demonstrated in his poems as early as 1925, and which clearly served to bolster interest in the subject among Cuban intellectuals in the years preceding the movement. By taking on the subject of traditional *comparsas* in the first half of "Carnaval en la Habana," Camín implicitly evokes the other carnival poems that we have considered in this study at the same time that he resurrects the notion that such texts actually owe a debt to his own pioneering efforts to celebrate the unique African-derived elements of Cuban culture. On the other hand, Camín's carnival poem also conjures up his continued bitterness about being systematically excluded from the annals of Afrocubanismo since it calls attention to the fact that the Cuban carnival, which was largely celebrated by the likes of Emilio Ballagas as a wholly African-derived spectacle, actually owed much to Spanish traditions as well. Indeed, in this compelling and realistic depiction of Havana's "black" and "white" carnivals, Camín reminds his readers that just as Afrocubanismo owed at least part of its existence to the influence of a Spanish outsider, Havana's rich carnival traditions, which were so often depicted in the poetry of the 1930s as purely African spectacles, were equally impacted by the enduring influence of Spain on Cuba's cultural legacy.

Epilogue

Carnival and Cultural Essence

> Es cierto que el arte y la literatura del Caribe han dado al mundo magníficas muestras. Pero también es cierto que las más importantes expresiones de la región son la música y la danza. Es natural, la mejor expresión de lo Caribeño es exhibicionista, densa, excesiva y transgresora, y no hay nada en el mundo que tenga la capacidad de mostrar estas propiedades como el cuerpo humano—o el carnaval, esa abigarrada aglomeración de cuerpos travestistas en movimiento, la metáfora más plena que hallo para imaginarme lo Caribeño.
>
> [It is true that Caribbean art and literature have provided the world with magnificent works. But it is also true that the most important expressions from the region are music and dance. It is natural, the best expression of Caribbeanness is exhibitionist, compact, excessive and transgressive, and there is nothing in the world that has the capacity to demonstrate these properties better than the human body—or the carnival, that multicolored conglomeration of transvestite bodies in movement, the most complete metaphor that I can find to imagine Caribbeanness.]
>
> Antonio Benítez-Rojo, "Música y nación"

The initial inspiration for this project came from my classes on Hispanic Caribbean literature and culture, in which I routinely dedicate considerable time to the poetry of Afrocubanismo. In preparation for my lectures I have read many books and essays on the poetry of this important artistic movement, and have been struck by certain themes and topics of discussion—the image of the Caribbean woman of color, the rumba, son, and other traditional musical genres, Afro-Cuban religious experience, etcetera—that have captured the attention of so many modern critics. One of the first images that struck me in my earliest experiences with this poetry was that of the Afro-Cuban *comparsa*, a spectacle that I first came to know through Felipe Pichardo Moya's "La comparsa" and Emilio Ballagas's "Comparsa habanera." Moved by personal interest, but also by a desire to add some continuity to my lectures and class discussions, it occurred to me to seek out other "comparsa poems," and to teach them as a related group of texts bound together not just by common formal and thematic elements and recurring imagery, but also by a shared history of controversy and debate.

I eventually came up with a dozen or so poems, all written by literary figures—some better known then others—associated with Afrocubanismo. Ten of those poems are studied in depth in the eight chapters that make up the bulk of the present study. Most are obvious choices whose very titles—"La comparsa del majá," "Comparsa habanera," or "La conga prohibida"—suggest their intimate relationship with and evocation of Afro-Cuban carnival traditions. At first glance some of the other poems—"Sensemayá," "Juego santo," and "Quintín Barahona"—seem less relevant, but they too deal in varying ways with traditional Afro-Cuban carnival ensembles and the national controversies and debates that surrounded them throughout the early decades of the Cuban Republic.

Though I may have covered the majority of carnival poems that were written by the major figures of Afrocubanismo, it is important to point out that there are other poems associated with this cultural movement that poeticize Cuba's rich and varied carnival traditions, but either for reasons of space or continuity I have chosen not to discuss at length in this book. In Ramón Guirao's indispensable anthology of poems on Afro-Cuban themes, for example, there are a number of carnival-related texts that merit further study. For example, though they are not poems in the strictest sense of the term, the anonymous "cantos de comparsa" that Guirao includes are essential precursors in terms of their obvious influence on some of the poems studied here—most notably Nicolás Guillén's "Sensemayá" and Marcelino Arozarena's "La comparsa del majá." But these "folkloric antecedents," as Guirao refers to them, are also interesting as literary texts in their own right.

Several other poems in Guirao's anthology touch on the topic of Afro-Cuban carnival ensembles. For example, one of Guirao's well-known *décimas* is a poetic representation of a traditional Afro-Cuban *conga*. This brief text begins with a stereotypical homage to the swaying hips and sensual backsides of the female participants in the carnival procession: "Porque al ritmo de la conga / se muevan nubes de nalgas." The strong sexual undertones of Guirao's *conga* are echoed in many images of such spectacles, such as Fernando Tarazona's painting *La conga* (Fig. o.3), which is discussed in the introduction. Though Alejo Carpentier's "Liturgia" (1927) is, above all, a poetic rendition of an Abakuá initiation ceremony, much like "Juego santo" it also evokes the carnival *comparsas* that were so intimately linked to these secret brotherhoods and sometimes even confused with the sacred processions of the *ñáñigos*. The poem's fourth stanza clearly demonstrates its melding of various related Afro-Cuban cultural manifestations:

> Aé, Aé,
> salió el diablito
> —¡cangrejo de Regla!—
> saltando de lao.
> En su gorro miran
> ojos de cartón:
> ¡brujo del Senegal,
> tabú y Carnaval! (77)

Another early poem by Carpentier, which was written in French and first published in Paris in *Poèms des Antilles: neuf chants sur des texte d'Alejo Carpentier* [Poems of the Antilles: nine Songs Based on Texts by Alejo Carpentier] (1929), also evokes traditional Afro-Cuban *comparsas*. In the following lines from Carmen Suárez León's Spanish-language translation of "Fete" ["Fiesta"], which underscore once again the importance of carnival motifs in Carpentier's Afro-Cuban inspired works, the audience is called to join in the dance of a *comparsa* troupe that files down the street:

> ¡Salgan de sus casas!
> ¡Entren el el baile!
> Sigan las farolas,
> Que cabecean en la noche. (17)

Alfonso Hernández Catá's "Rumba" (1931), shares much in common with the array of *afrocubanista* poems of the same or very similar titles—by Tallet, Guirao, Guillén, Ballagas, Antonio Portuondo, Vicente Gómez Kemp, and others—as its central motif is the sensual, lascivious black woman and her tempting dance. At the same time, however, the poem is interlaced with several references to *congas* and *chambelonas*, and many of its verses come from versions of the songs that were sung during these controversial political *comparsas*. Even one of Nicolás Guillén's best known poems,

"Canto negro," may be related to Afro-Cuban carnival, as Helio Orovio clearly suggests by including it in a short section of carnival-inspired poems in *El carnaval habanero* (136). Though Orovio does not explain his inclusion of "Canto negro" alongside other more obvious choices such as "Comparsa habanera," the chants in Guillén's poem do evoke some of those that are traditionally sung by Afro-Cuban carnival troupes. Though it may be a matter of mere coincidence, the first and last verses of "Canto negro"—"¡Yambambó, yambambé!," "¡yamba, yambó, yambambé!"—also echo a traditional chant sung in Afro-Uruguayan carnival celebrations—"Dale yambu, yumbambé"—which Guillén himself discusses in an article on carnival written years later ("Cada año" 72). In more general terms, Guillén's widely anthologized poem, with its evocation of wild dancing, raging drum beats, and alcohol certainly shares much common ground with several of the carnival poems that we have discussed in this study.

Other less-known poems that were inspired by Afro-Cuban carnival traditions, and appeared during or shortly after the craze of Afrocubanismo, also come to mind. One such text, written by the mulatto poet Gilberto Hernández Santana, and published in his collection *Semblanzas negras* (1939) [*Black Sketches*] is "Comparsa de semana santa" [Holy Week Comparsa]. This particular text is unique among those that I have encountered as it is the only one that poeticizes the particular carnival traditions of this little-known poet's native town of Santa Clara. This unique text contains vivid imagery that conjures nineteenth-century Día de Reyes festivities as well as the traditional dances of early twentieth-century *comparsas* in Havana, such as "El Alacrán" and "La Culebra." At the same time, it shares much in common with other *comparsa* poems—especially Ballagas's "Comparsa habanera"—with its profusion of African-inspired terms, references to Yoruba deities, gratuitous invocations of Afro-Cuban rituals and religious practices, and descriptions of deafening drum beats and harsh singing, as can be seen in the following lines:

> La comparsa con Obalufón
> viene con caretas
> y alacranes de cartón
> y culebras de trapo de horrendo mirar . . .
> Africa bulle
> en el estruendo con que la conga espanta

y sigue en danza con sus faroles
la comparsa bronca de Semana Santa . . .

Hay quien viene investido
de túnica de rafia; distribuye el libengue
para los profanos:
la comparsa loca clama con voz ronca:
—Bulo, Bulo, Bulo
gracia de Likundu . . . [1]
Presa de faroles prosigue la marcha
cantando
con Obafulón.
. . . .
Se rompe la bumba de la quimbisa,
Los hechiceros de la macumba
Y del candombe
buscan el mal . . .
dos pollos negros y un gato prieto
se descuartizan
en la ballunga;
y por las calles huérfanas de la luna
va la corriente
supersticiosa de la negra barahunda
presa de faroles y ebria de tambores. (55)

It is worth noting that even though Hernández Santana's poem does not address them directly, it brings to mind images of another important breed of Cuban carnival ensemble: the Band Rará, processions of Haitian laborers that formed during Holy Week in many locations throughout Cuba, but especially in the sugar-producing regions of Palma Soriano, Victoria de las Tunas, Camagüey, and Oriente. Much like the Afro-Cuban *comparsa* that Hernández Santana describes, these ensembles of Haitian sugarcane workers would file through the streets by the light of large torches "sounding their primitive instruments, dancing like 'diablitos' and singing their voodoo hymns, dressed in ragged clothing and wearing rustic masks, just as they do on Holy Thursday and Good Friday in Haiti" (Ortiz, "Viejos carnavales" 219).

Julio Ayllón Morgan's "Romance de la comparsa" [Romance of the Comparsa] is another intriguing carnival poem that, despite catching the attention of Fernando Ortiz—who praised its "descriptive value" and "artistic merit" in a letter to the author dated February 10, 1946 ("Letter to Julio" 9)—has escaped the eyes of modern literary critics and failed to make it into later anthologies of *poesía negra*. This poem first appeared in print in *Estudios Afrocubanos* in 1946, thanks to Ortiz who requested the author's permission to publish it. In the same year "Romance de la comparsa" was included in *Romancero cubano*, Ayllón's excellent collection of poems inspired by various Afro-Cuban cultural manifestations.[2] What makes Ayllón Morgan's poem especially interesting is that, despite containing many elements that are typical of poems about Afro-Cuban culture (the sensual female dancers, the lustful black men, an "epileptic" *diablito*, a menacing throng of dancers), it touches on important topics that none of the poets discussed here address, namely the economic impact of traditional *comparsas* on working-class blacks, who could scarcely afford the required regalia, and the important role of carnival as a temporary opiate for the lower-class masses. The following two stanzas from "Romance de la comparsa" are illustrative of Ayllón Morgan's original take on this popular theme:

> Macumbele, el "*abacuá*,"
> "írimo" [*sic*] de los "*biabangas*,"
> ha dejado en la repisa
> de su cuarto la "*demanda*,"
> porque costaba el disfraz
> treinta y cinco pesos plata
> y no pagó al "*encargado*"
> y se apretujó la faja
> para estrangular el hambre.
> Pero eso no importa nada,
> porque al impulso del ritmo
> que balancea la comparsa,
> Macumbele, el "*abacuá*,"
> se siente un rey negro de Africa. (48)

Here the poetic voice highlights a typical sacrifice made by a particular *comparsero*—in this case an *íreme* from an ensemble sponsored by an Abakuá lodge from Matanzas (Los Biabanga) who skips a rent payment and willingly goes hungry in order to take part in the carnival celebrations.[3] In the following stanza we are presented with a similar situation, this time involving a female participant named Macusa, whose decision to pawn household necessities in order to purchase her extravagant carnival attire has a profound impact on her family:

> Se peleó con el marido
> y la hijita anda descalzada;
> llevó a la casa de empeños
> hasta la ropa de cama;
> pero eso tampoco importa:
> con sus sandalias plateadas
> y su vestido de seda,
> en medio de la comparsa
> se siente la emperatriz
> de la ciudad de La Habana. (49)

Much like Caignet's "La conga prohibida," Ayllón Morgan's poem highlights the notion that carnival serves as an outlet through which Afro-Cubans can alleviate their suffering and channel their frustrations. But "Romance de la comparsa" stands out for its biting sarcasm, through which the author underscores the fact—often ignored by participants and observers alike—that carnival celebrations often entailed significant sacrifices and created many unrecognized problems for their predominantly working-class participants.

Carnival Poems in the Newspapers of Santiago

A veritable treasure trove of carnival poems by mostly unknown authors can be found in Nancy Pérez-Rodríguez's compendium of texts related to Santiago's carnival traditions. It includes over a dozen such poems, which were originally published in that city's newspapers during the early decades of the twentieth century. These texts deal with themes that range from outright condemnations of traditional Afro-Cuban carnival ensembles, to celebrations of Santiago's "white" carnival, to laments of and protests against government bans of Afro-Cuban music, dancing, and other activities related to the city's rich carnival traditions.

One of the most intriguing of these poems is "Versificación sobre los carnavales cultos" [Versification on Cultured Carnivals], which appeared in the Santiago daily *La Independencia* on July 28, 1916. This lengthy poem, signed with the pseudonym "Rodrigueroa," conveys the fear of Afro-Cuban crowds and public spectacles that reigned in the years following the 1912 Racist Massacre. The poem is essentially a celebration of the newspaper's publication on the previous day of an anonymous letter that called for the complete prohibition of the "brutally grotesque" and "scandalously immoral" carnival masquerades that were popular among the city's black citizens. Published in the same year as Pichardo Moya's "La comparsa," this poem similarly presents the Afro-Cuban carnival as a sinister spectacle, but it is most interesting for its unabashed moralizing and condemnation of the groups of Afro-Cuban masqueraders—commonly referred to in Santiago as *mamarrachos*—that typically danced through Santiago's streets alongside the *comparsas*:[4]

Publica la Independencia
con muchísma razón
un sensacional artículo,
que bastante aplaudo yo;
"Lo que debe (ya) prohibirse,"
epigrafa el redactor,
con un contexto juicioso
de alta moralización.

Se alude a los mamarrachos,
que son escándalo atroz
transitan por nuestras calles
con pirueta y contorsión
y las personas decentes
los rechazan con rubor
especialmente las damas
de nuestra culta Nación.

Las autoridades nuestras
deben tomar desde hoy
muy rigurosas medidas
que eviten la permisión
de esos troneras bellacos
sandungueros del bongó

al son del grito "¡Arrollando!"
con desmesurada voz. (Pérez-Rodríguez Vol. 1: 223)

Another unique carnival poem was published in the literary section of the same newspaper in August 1917, this one by an Afro-Cuban woman named Elvira Balbuena de Moro. In "Canto africano" [African Chant] Balbuena de Moro protests Santiago mayor José Camacho Padro's June 1917 ban of Afro-Cuban music and dancing from that year's carnival celebrations. The poet opens by stating that she is the daughter of slaves, for whom dancing and singing have always served as outlets for their suffering. She then expresses her disappointment with the government's decision to prohibit her and her people from participating in the city's carnival celebrations:

> Les han prohibido su canto,
> y dicen que es salvajada;
> pues bien, si es un pueblo libre
> y así en su niñez cantaba;
> ¿Por qué arrancar la alegría
> de aquellos que sienten ansias
> por la zambra de sus padres,
> que aun siendo esclavos cantaban? (Vol. 1: 239)

This fascinating composition stands out for its direct response to the government's seemingly senseless suppression of Santiago's popular carnival traditions, and it may very well be the only poem of this ilk written by an Afro-Cuban woman during the early decades of the twentieth century.

Another carnival poem titled "¡Bomba!" appeared in *La Independencia* on July 26, 1924, the day after the traditional celebrations of the city's patron saint. This composition was apparently inspired by a song of lament that the author had heard on the streets of the city the day before. It follows a brief editorial whose author, Daniel Beltrán, ridicules Santiago officials and many of the city's citizens for their opposition to Afro-Cuban carnival ensembles, and their desire to replace them with Western European–style orchestras and dances: "Oponerse a la tradición es una bellaquería que no luce a ningún santiaguero de buena cepa. . . . ¿Por qué, pues, algunos cubanos no quieren sentirse santiagueros, desean convertir esta pintoresca ciudad de suaves pendientes en una Venecia o en Niza?" ("Liborio" vol. 1: 318) [Opposing tradition is a mean trick that does not look good to any Santiago citizen of good stock... Why, then, do some Cubans not want to feel like they are Santiago citizens? Why do they want to turn this quaint city of gentle slopes into Venice or Nice?]. In the *décimas* that make up the poem that follows, Beltrán captures the spirit of resilience and rebellion that led many of Santiago's citizens of color to defy the bans against their carnival traditions:

> Nuestro pueblo así lo quiere
> y amante a su tradición,
> pone todo el corazón
> en el goce que prefiere.
> Hoy nada habrá que le altere
> ni lo abacore nada,
> y gritando entusiasmada,
> con entusiasmo sincero
> dirá: ¡Yo soy santiaguero
> que adora a su mascarada!
>
> Quien combata sin piedad
> mis honestas diversiones,
> son unos hipocritones
> que se ocultan la verdad.
> Sólo lo hacen por maldad,
> pues buscan, para gozar,
> algún oculto lugar
> y bajo de una careta,
> hacen más de una pirueta,
> sacan el pie... y a arrollar!... (Vol. 1: 319–20)

Here the poet evokes the hypocrisy of high-society whites who pretend to scorn the Afro-Cuban carnival dances, but then don a mask and join the crowds as they go "arrollando" through the streets.

Several of the poems collected by Pérez-Rodríguez present a picture of Santiago's carnival traditions as primarily geared toward the enjoyment of high-society whites. One such poem, "Himno del Carnaval" [Hymn to Carnival], which was sent to *La Independencia* on June 19, 1925 by Jaramillo Meza and Blanca Lisaza, contains verses such as the following:

Llevemos al labio
la flauta de Pan
cantamos en triunfo
del rubio Champán

Vibre la farándula
su loco clarín
que pasan del brazo
Pierrot y Arlequín

Al amor agite
su tisso de rosas
y vuelven confettis
Como mariposas. (Vol. 1: 335)

Along much the same lines, Daniel Beltrán's "Carnaval," published in *La Independencia* on January 29, 1928 also furnishes an idealized vision of high-society carnival festivities:

¡Oh mascarada loca
Que hacer ver tras la copa
Del Champán que deshace los enojos,
Ora a Julieta de ensoñados ojos,
Ora de Cleopatra de lasciva boca . . . ! (Vol. 1: 359)

The poems collected by Pérez-Rodríguez are significant in terms of their evocation of many aspects of Santiago's carnival, but especially the distinct traditions and opposing mentalities that characterized the carnival celebrations of high-society whites and working-class Afro-Cubans. My suspicion is that a careful perusal of Havana's newspapers from the same period might yield similar compositions, but again, that project will have to be undertaken at another time or by another scholar.

Carnival as Nostalgia: Poems from Exile

The important relationship between traditional carnival celebrations and Cuba's national identity is clearly evoked in another body of texts that is ripe for future study: carnival poems written after the Revolution by

Cubans in exile. What I find most intriguing about the handful of poems that I will discuss briefly here is that, despite being written in the 1960s and 1970s, they all evoke the traditional Afro-Cuban *comparsas* of earlier decades, which clearly demonstrates to me that these spectacles represented for many Cubans in exile not just iconic images of their longed-for homeland, but also important embodiments of their nation's cultural identity. In his book of collected poems, *Mi Habana . . . poemas desde el destierro* (1971) [My Havana . . . Poems from Exile], all of which were written in memory of the poet's "lost" native city, Álvaro de Villa includes an interesting poem called "La comparsa" that is typical in many ways of carnival poems by Cuban exiles. Written in Miami in March 1964, de Villa's poem recalls the excitement of carnival time in Havana through its evocation of some of that city's greatest *comparsa* troupes—Los Marqueses, La Bolleras, Los Dandys de Belén—as well as the quintessential images associated with them such as the giant *farolas*, the booming drums, and the drunken hordes of dancers. De Villa's wistful recollection of a lost tradition leads him to idealize the carnival processions, which he presents as embodiments of the nation's mixed-race identity as well as symbols of the supposed harmony of pre-revolutionary Cuba:

> La voz del cuero nos llama
> . . . .
> Uno, dos, tres
> La piel de blancos y negros
> Se confunde por los pies. (83)

The poet later speaks of the *comparsa* as a cultural phenomenon through which Afro-Cubans managed to reconcile past injustices and put aside their differences with those who had exploited and oppressed them: "[La comparsa] Supo olvidar latigazos. . . . [y] conquistar la selva / del odio para bailar" (84). In the final stanza de Villa exalts the *comparsa* as nothing less than a divine Cuban institution—he calls it a "Holy Trinity" of drum, *farola*, and dancing feet—that the exile community has lost forever (84).

Two poems by Jack Rojas also attest to the importance of carnival as a symbol of the exile's nostalgia for the homeland. In "Llora el bongó" [The Bongo Cries] and "La reina del carnaval" [The Carnival Queen], both published in Madrid in his collection of Afro-Cuban inspired poems *Tambor sin cuero* (1968)[Drum Without a Drumhead], Rojas reveals how memories of carnival provoke feelings of sadness and absence on the one hand, and joy and national pride on the other. It is worth noting here that the book's title, like many of the poems, conveys a sense of absence and lacking that mirrors the exile experience: a drum separated from its goatskin head is like a Cuban divorced from his homeland. The first poem, as its title suggests, is essentially a lament for a lost tradition, but it is also an evocation of the pain felt by the absent poet, as Ruiz del Vizo has pointed out (*Poesía* 85).

> Llora el bongó.
> Llora la tumba.
> Llora el tambor.
> . . . .
> Llora la negra.
> Sube la negra.
> Baja la negra
> en su camisón.
>
> El dale, dale de la comparsa,
> la bemba abierta del bailador,
> el negro, negro de su cubierta
> en la batea de blanco olor
> hace pensar a la brava negra
> en lo profundo de su dolor. (26–27)

Rojas's "La reina del carnaval" is characteristic of Cuban exile literature in its idealistic portrayal of the lost homeland, in this case as it is embodied in a joyful, harmonious, mixed-race carnival celebration. Though Rojas first focuses on the figure of the high-society carnival queen who rides through the streets of Havana on an elaborately decorated float, he seems most interested in images of traditional Afro-Cuban *comparsas* and *congas*, which he introduces by way of two transitional stanzas that, much like Álvaro de Villa's poem, suggest the peaceful coexistence of white and black carnival traditions:

> Delante ya va la reina,
> la reina del carnaval.
> Detrás vienen las comparsas
> con su ritmo peculiar.

Detrás van blancos y negros,
negros y blancos ya van,
van mulatos y van chinos
y va un dandy gentlemán.

For the rest of this 100-line poem Rojas recalls some of the best-known carnival ensembles of pre-Castro Cuba and then turns to the problematic *conga*, all of which he presents not only as romanticized cultural icons that united the Cuban population, but also as symbols of the nation's pride:

Los Marqueses, Las Bolleras,
La Sultana, Los Chucheros,
una tras otra aparecen
con bongoes y bongoseros.

La comparsa viene ya.
La comparsa va a pasar.
Las comparsas ya desfilan
con su ritmo sin igual

Hay jóvenes y hay más viejos.
Hay blancos y hay de color.
Y todos bailando vienen,
bailando al compás del son. (70)

Like many of the poets associated with Afrocubanismo, Rojas essentially evades the racism and controversies that enveloped Afro-Cuban carnival ensembles during the first half of the twentieth century, though his motivations for doing so are clearly different. When he refers later to traditional *congas*, Rojas suggests that one of the most important aspects of such carnival processions is their capacity to alleviate one's pain and sorrows through their unbridled singing and dancing. This, he implies, is precisely why carnival is such an important motif for the exile poets like himself who can lessen their own sadness by losing themselves, so to speak, in its rhythm: "El que en Cuba sus pesares / no los pueda terminar / es porque no se ha dejado / por el ritmo controlar" (71). Finally, in the poem's last stanza, Rojas emphasizes the carnival's role as a national symbol when he laments, in a reference to the empty parade route, that

"El Prado ya está vació / . . . pero en el Prado se queda / el alma de mi nación" (72).

Anisia Meruelo's "Estampa habanera" (1969) [Picture of Havana], written from exile in the United States, shares much in common with other carnival-inspired poems by Cuban exiles, and its title suggests how traditional *comparsas* have come to represent for those separated from the homeland a typical, evocative description of the nation's character and identity. Like the other exile poets considered here, Meruelo's reminiscence makes for a rather romanticized poetic rendition of an Afro-Cuban carnival ensemble:

Por las anchas avenidas
vi bailar unas comparsas
al son de negro bongó
y de la alegre maraca;
el cielo era cubano,
y el mar era de La Habana.
Era la reminiscencia
de una música africana
que con el rudo tambor
tomó suavidad cubana. (95)

She later speaks of the *comparsas* in decidedly sugarcoated verses—"Era toda la dulzura / del mamey y de la caña; / era toda la belleza / del monte y de la sabana" (96)—which again relate this remembered spectacle to the very essence of Cubanness. To be sure, when Meruelo recalls the *comparsa* her mind is flooded with nostalgic memories of things lost: Cuban fruits, tropical forests and fields, sunshine and clear blue skies, white sand beaches and rocky shores. When she describes a *conga* troupe passing by—with its colorful attire, catchy music, and giant *farolas*—the vision inspires the poetic voice to shout "este *era* nuestro folklore" (96 emphasis added), stressing again the sense of personal loss that recollections of traditional carnival ensembles provoke. Finally, in the poem's closing lines, Meruelo adds that like the *comparsas* that she witnessed in Cuba, "el recuerdo ha quedado / en las calles de La Habana" (97).

As Bibi Armas de Arenas explains in a brief prologue to her poem "El carnaval habanero," this nostalgic piece was inspired by her experiences in February 1977 at a carnival celebration in the Casa Cuba de Puerto

Rico. Her poem offers another interesting twist on this popular theme, as it is written from the perspective of a young girl in the Cuban countryside who dreams of witnessing Havana's legendary carnival festivities. Much like Jack Rojas, she begins with images of a beautiful carnival queen, decorated floats, and confetti, all of which recall the carnival festivities of high-society whites, but she quickly transitions into an evocation of an Afro-Cuban *comparsa*, and suggests that it is the true "carnival queen":

> Hay un ritmo que enloquece,
> con su tun-tun embriagante,
> viene arrollando triunfante;
> la reina del carnaval:
> la comparsa callejera. (94)

With a palpable sense of longing for this quintessential Cuban tradition, the poetic voice concludes with a statement that again demonstrates how for the exile poet, carnival becomes a metaphor for Cuba's national identity: "Quiero gustar del sabor / de la comparsa habanera . . . ¡será por siempre, cubana! (96).

Lyrics from Traditional Twentieth-Century *Cantos de Comparsa*

The traditional cantos de comparsa sung by twentieth-century carnival ensembles are, strictly speaking, songs rather than poems. However, they are worthy of comment here not just in terms of their obvious relationship to the poems that have been considered in this book, but also in regard to the unique ways in which they evoke the relationship between carnival and national identity in Cuba. The colorful and changing lyrics from these traditional songs—which were by and large written by Afro-Cubans and sung during their carnival performances—could be turned into the subject of a fascinating study. Robin Moore's suggestion that traditional *cantos* tended not to refer to Afro-Cuban dance or to the sensual *mulata*, but rather to "nonracial themes derived from the names of the groups in question" (80) is not wholly accurate. Indeed, even though *cantos de comparsa* do include a broad variety of themes that sometimes evoke important social issues or historical events, the lyrics to many of them do make explicit references to the dancing, partying, drinking, and general good times associated with these lively spectacles, as well as to the sensual women of color who ostensibly found them impossible to resist.[5] The following lyrics from various *cantos* from some of Havana's best-known *comparsas* demonstrate one of the preferred motifs of these traditional songs: the rebellious Afro-Cuban woman who is seduced by the irresistible *comparsa* or *conga*, and shirks her domestic duties, disobeys her parents, or even leaves her husband or children in order to join the passing procession:

> Mamá, dile a mi marido
> que estamos en carnaval
> que me voy con Las Bolleras
> y no puedo cocinar.
> . . . .
> Adiós mamá, adiós papá,
> Que yo voy con Las Bolleras. (Orovio, *El carnaval habanero* 49)

> Mamá, cuide a los niños,
> si acaso pregunta mi esposo
> usted le dice que yo fui
> con Los Componedores. (Roig de Leuchsenring, "Comparsas" 162)

> Anoche Las Guaracheras me sacaron de mi casa.
> ¡Qué modo de divertirse! ¡Se acabó lo que se daba!
> Ya no tengo ni quiero marido: me botó.
> Que yo sigo arrollando guarachera de mi amor.
> Madre mía, déjame salir que ahí viene la guarachera,
> y yo de cualquier manera me tengo que divertir. (Roig de Leuchsenring, "Las comparsas" 167)

> Qué problema me busqué con mi mamá
> porque pasó La Sultana
> y me fui al carnaval.
> Yo te prometo mamá
> que no lo hago más. (Orovio, *El carnaval habanero* 74)

In terms of their evocation of important social concerns or historical events, the traditional *cantos* of La Jardinera and Los Mambises offer illustrative examples of the variety of themes treated in these compositions. In their *comparsa* chant the members of La Jardinera do indeed "discuss tending their flower beds," as Moore puts it in his brief description of the song (80), but their widely known tune is much more than that. On the one hand, it refers to the great efforts made by the residents of the Havana neighborhood of Jesús María to restore their public park after it was destroyed by a hurricane in 1926. On the other hand, it evokes the beauty of the nation, the importance of solidarity, and the longing for peace:

> Del jardín cubano cogeremos flores
> y por siempre unidas formaremos un ramo,
> al público oyente se lo dedicamos,
> somos jardineras, flores, muchas flores.
>
> Flores, flores,
> allí viene La Jardinera,
> viene regando flores. (Orovio, *El carnaval habanero* 56)

The canto of Los Mambises evokes the battles fought by Afro-Cubans in the Wars of Independence, but it also serves as a lament over the suffering of those same soldiers who were still subjected—decades after the war—to prejudices and exploitation despite their invaluable service to the nation:

> Pobrecito mambí, anda
> por el mundo vagando,
> y la gente mirando,
> ¡Gran Dios! ¿Qué será de mí?
> . . . .
> ¡En los campos, cuánta gloria
> conquisté!
> Mi machete dondequiera
> Allí brilló
> ¡El cubano, cuánto hizo
> por darle gloria a la doctrina de Martí!
>
> Dios le dé Gloria a Maceo,
> que venimos de luchar
> y ahora somos Los Mambises,
> de la misma capital.
> ¡Gloria a Maceo!
> ¡Gloria a Martí! (Roig de Leuchsenring, "Las comparsas" 160–61)

Another *comparsa* theme song with notable social and historical significance is that of El Alacrán. The song in question dates from 1937, the year that this carnival troupe moved from Jesús María to the neighborhood El Cerro. It recounts a colonial-era legend about a slave woman who has been stung by a scorpion and the subsequent search for and killing of the creature in a cane field. But as Ivor Miller has correctly noted, it also contains an overt political message as it evokes the continued use of forced labor in Cuban sugarcane plantations (*Voice of the Leopard* 163).

> Oye colega no te asombres cuando veas,
> Oye colega no te asombres cuando veas,
> el alacrán tumbando caña,
> el alacrán tumbando caña,
> costumbre de mi país,
> mi hermano,
> costumbre de mi país,
> mi hermano.
> Sí, sí, tumbando caña. (Orovio, *El carnaval habanero* 35)

Though Miller claims that this is the most openly political *canto de comparsa* of the day, the theme song of Los Guajiros (penned by Ignacio Piñeiro in 1937) is certainly more forthright in its criticism of a number of aspects of Cuban society, from racism, to violence, to governmental corruption and civil unrest. It is made up of several *décimas*, each one of which focuses on one of the nation's many social ills. The following *décima*, for example, laments how Cuba's intimate relationship with the United States comes at a great expense to the nation's pride and wellbeing:

> No conviertas tu amor sano
> en un error lastimero,
> uniéndote al extranjero
> para matar a tu hermano;
> mira que el suelo cubano
> de nuestros padres es orgullo
> piensa bien años tras año
> no maltratar al extraño;
> pero defiende lo tuyo. (Roig de Leuchsenring, "Las comparsas" 172)

Lyrics of popular twentieth-century *cantos de comparsa* can be found in a number of sources, but two in particular are worth citing: Emilio Roig de

Leuchsenring's "Las comparsas carnavalescas de la Habana en 1937," and Helio Orovio's *El carnaval habanero*, in which the authors provide complete transcriptions of the *cantos* of Los Mambises, Los Componedores, Los Colombianos Modernos, Los Marqueses, Los Guajiros, Las Bolleras, El Alacrán, La Jardinera, Los Dandys, La Sultana, Las Guaracheras, and Los Componedores de Batea, among several others.

Afro-Cuban Carnival in Cuban Popular Music

There is scarcely space to discuss here in any depth the lyrics from the scores of *sones, danzas, rumbas,* and salon *congas* that were inspired by traditional Afro-Cuban carnival music and composed and performed in the early decades of the twentieth century by many of the nation's most talented and popular musicians. Indeed, that would be a suitable subject for another book-length study. However, I think it is important to make at least a passing reference to several of these popular songs that helped to turn Afro-Cuban carnival processions and stylized versions of their traditional music into international commercial sensations precisely during an era when *comparsas* and *congas* were banned from the streets of Havana. It is interesting to point out that while the poems of Afrocubanismo that we have discussed in this book introduced the *comparsas* and *congas* of Havana and Santiago to a relatively limited audience that was made up primarily of well-educated Spanish speakers, the numerous popular, carnival-inspired songs written during the same era reached diverse audiences all over Latin America, Europe, and the United States through live performances in nightclubs, over the radio waves, and by way of increasingly popular professional recordings.

Much like the poems of Afrocubanismo, the lyrics of most of these songs were written by middle-class white men who, as Moore puts it, "had probably never seriously considered dancing behind the Afrocuban groups that were their source of inspiration" (80). Moore has further pointed out that many of these songs offer a rather superficial portrait of Afro-Cuban performance and emphasize the "perceived carefree nature of Afrocuban culture as well as the sensuality of the *mulata*" (80). Sublette similarly opines that "the lyrics . . . of the salon conga tended to portray the exoticism of the Afro-Cuban" (408). But we must be careful not to overlook the fact that the lyrics of such songs also share in common with the poems of Afrocubanismo and the traditional *cantos de comparsa* a diversity of themes and tones that belie generalizations and facile categorization. A brief discussion of several songs will serve to illustrate this point.

The opening lines of "Cavalcada de las congas" [Cavalcade of the Congas] (ca. 1933) by Eliseo Grenet (1893–1950) focus on the carnival procession as a purely African-derived phenomenon by evoking the three principal ethnic groups with which Cubans of color are associated: Congo, Lucumí, and Carbalí. Moreover, the somber tone of the music—which for the first minute and a half consists of conga drums, a *cencerro*, and a piano—imbues the composition with a somewhat sinister air. The following lyrics are sung with a serious tone that suggests a chant or ritual:

> Alegres cumbancheros
> van los congos por allí
> y lleva su algarada
> la locura lucumí
> y dicen en su canto
> el amor carabalí. (Grenet)[6]

In the second half of the song—which includes the addition of the cheerful sound of the trumpet—the tone changes notably, and the focus shifts to a vision of the *conga* as a source of laughter, enjoyment, and, above all, love. The following line is repeated twice as the music becomes softer, suggesting that the *conga* is fading into the distance as it marches down the street: "reír, gozar, para poder amar."

A 1935 recording of "Conga de la Habana" [Havana Conga] (1935) by Eduardo "Jaruco" Vázquez—composer and trumpet player for the Lecuona Cuban Boys—features catchy lyrics that express the delight of joining a *conga* as it makes its way from a working-class Havana neighborhood to the center of the city.

> Ay sí, ay no
> con la conga
> a la Habana
> me voy.
>
> Quiero,
> bailar contigo
> en la Habana
> la conga. (Vázquez)

The lighthearted tone of the song is diminished, however, by the drunk-sounding voice of a supposedly Afro-Cuban man (identifiable by his *bozal* speech), who conveys the stereotypical image of a rowdy and lascivious spectacle through his nearly unintelligible mumbling: "Caballero . . . vacúnala, vacúnala, ya, arriba, ja, ja." Here the singer evokes the dramatic forward pelvic motion of the male dancer in *rumba guaguancó*, which signifies the moment at which the female dancer submits to his advances. The expression as used here carries an obvious sexual connotation that loosely translated means "screw her, screw her."

Despite the fact that many carnival-inspired songs of the 1930s and 1940s stand out for their stereotypical personifications of Afro-Cubans and their cultural manifestations, it is important to stress that a good number of the song lyrics inspired by *congas* and *comparsas* present these lively street processions in a rather positive light.[7] The lyrics to such songs tend to be catchy and very simple, and more often than not they exude pleasure through their allusions to the irresistible beat of the drums, the clanging of the *cencerros*, and, most importantly, the collective dancing. Indeed, it is interesting that one of the most common motifs of carnival-inspired songs of the 1920s–1940s is their celebration of the *arrollao*, despite the many contemporary campaigns to ban this supposedly offensive and uncivilized dancing. For example, in his *son* titled "Noche de conga" [Night of Conga], Ignacio Piñeiro calls attention to the great popularity of the *conga* and the collective dancing that brings pleasure to and unites people from all walks of life.

> Qué noche para gozar señores,
> que la conga se soltó.
> Por do'quiera que pasó,
> la gente le iba detrás. (Piñeiro)

Later in the same song, the soloist reinforces the point by shouting to the chorus: "la conga pasó tocando / y todo el mundo arrolló."

Likewise, in his "La conga de Jaruco" [Jaruco's Conga] (1937), Eduardo "Jaruco" Vázquez alludes to the alluring nature of the collective dance and to the irresistible rhythms of traditional carnival music without evoking any of the negative sentiments associated with such dancing:

> La conga de Jaruco,
> ahí viene arrollando.

....
con su ritmo sin igual. (Vázquez)

In a similar manner Osvaldo Estivil's "Conga de la Habana" [Havana Conga] (ca. 1940) presents a positive image of the *conga*, its music, and especially its collective dance, which is portrayed as a joyful Cuban tradition that arouses harmony and passion instead of the lewdness and uncontrolled revelry with which these spectacles were so commonly associated:

Ya se escucha la conga de la Habana
y sus cencerros ya se oyen sonar.
....
Y yo quisiera que conmigo estuvieras
y allí muy juntos siempre arrollar,
en la conga que viene alegre
dejando mi alma llena de ardor,
y sentir que eres mía negra
en la Habana alegre llena de amor. (Estivil)

It should be noted that even though the Cuban woman of color is evoked in these lines, sexual innuendos and lewd images are absent. When considered in the context of an era during which traditional Afro-Cuban *congas* and *comparsas* continued to be subjected to debate and controversy, the lyrics to these and many such songs from the same time period—especially since they were in large part written by successful and well-known members of the white middle class—can be viewed as bold challenges to mainstream prejudices and as "a step toward empowerment of black music" (Sublette 408). In terms of the salon *congas* more specifically, we should add that even as forms of stage entertainment these were daring since the conga drums themselves had been prohibited in public performances until the early 1930s, and were still widely associated in the late 1930s and early 1940s with "fractious congas of the streets and rumbas of the slums" (Sublette 408).

Another popular song from the early 1940s, "Se acerca la comparsa" [The *Comparsa* Approaches], also sheds positive light on traditional carnival processions by depicting the popular *arrollao* as a dance with a distinctive rhythm and a liberating quality, not as a wild free-for-all or a destructive force.

> Ya se acerca la comparsa
> vamos con ella a arrollar
> con la farola en la mano
> llevaremos el compás. ("Se acerca")

What sets this particular piece apart is its explicit rejection in the final verses of unfounded prejudices against *comparsas* and *congas*, which were still linked to Afro-Cuban backwardness and *brujería* by many middle-class whites and blacks alike:

> Bailaremos en la conga
> gozaremos como es.
> No para ceñir embrujo,
> pá vivirse, pá gozar. ("Se acerca")

The singer in this particular recording by the Orquesta Siboney is the inimitable Celia Cruz, who insists that the *conga* should be enjoyed just as it is, and not maligned for being something that it isn't. The final verses are especially important as they stress the mass appeal of the Afro-Cuban carnival processions and the songs that these traditions inspired, at the same time that they implicitly call the opponents of such spectacles to see them for what they really are: joyful celebrations that bring great pleasure to all of those who participate.

Much like the poems that served as the principal inspiration for this study, the poetry from Santiago newspapers, the exile poems, and the traditional *cantos de comparsa*, the popular songs and the dances associated with them attest to the fact that in Cuba "carnival has always been linked to different spheres of national culture" (Orovio, *El carnaval habanero* 20). But perhaps even more importantly the poems, cantos, popular songs, dances, paintings, posters, and ballets—among other popular art forms—that have been inspired by traditional Afro-Cuban *comparsas* and *congas* and the rich iconography associated with them demonstrate, as Orovio has pointed out, that "the carnival, the *conga*, the *comparsa*, with all their richness and local color, are interwoven into the cultural essence of the nation" (21).

Appendix: A Brief Anthology of Poems Inspired by Afro-Cuban Carnival

1) Felipe Pichardo Moya, "La comparsa" (1916)

Para el Dr. Fernando Ortiz

Por la calleja solitaria
se arrastra la comparsa como una culebra colosal.

En el silencio de la noche
hombres, mujeres, niños, cantan con un monótono compás;
los unos detrás de los otros en una fila inacabable,
van agarrados por los hombros con un temblor epilepsial.
Los ojos brillan en las órbitas
chispeando como un puñal en la siniestra oscuridad,
y los cuerpos se descoyuntan en una furia demoníaca
al impulso irresistible de los palitos y el timbal.

Por la calleja solitaria
se arrastra la comparsa como una culebra colosal.

Vienen primero los muchachos
Llevando hachones cuyas luces el viento hace temblequear;
y un gran tumulto de mujeres, con los brazos extendidos,
haciendo estremecer sus hombros y sus caderas, van detrás.
Suben las voces por encanto,
y luego vuelven a bajar;
la música, ronca y monótona, va evocando mil raras cosas
como el simún cuando remeda el estertor de algún titán,
y de los pechos que jadean
sale un soplo sibilante: ¡tal el del viento sobre el mar!

Por la calleja solitaria
se arrastra la comparsa como una culebra colosal.

Uno, dos, tres hércules
con sus trajes más chispeantes y el paso esclavo del compás
van apoyando sobre el vientre unas farolas gigantescas
que en un equilibrio penoso parecen irse a drribar.
Dan unos pasos hacia el frente,
luego dan otros hacia atrás
como un rapto de locura... Y de pronto, a un vago impulso,
atravesando las aceras como en un rápido zig-zag,
hacen temblar a las farolas
con un temblor epilepsial.

Poe la calleja solitaria
Se arrastra la comparsa como una culebra colosal.

Pasa una guardia numerosa
que va estremeciendo sus cuerpos con el más lúbrico ademán...
Cesa la música de pronto, suben las voces por encanto
cual si llegaran al final....
Es "Él" que viene: todos callan:
¡Hay un silencio emocionante, se siente el fuerte respirar:
en la cabeza de una joven, sobre el escudo legendario
lleva un simbólico animal!

En la calleja solitaria
se enrosca la comparsa como una culebra colosal.

Entre dos filas de mujeres
que se contorsionan nerviosas como mordidas por Satán,
va un alto anciano tembloroso en cuyos ojos luce el fuego
de una mirada casi irreal.
Lleva un cetro entre las manos y murmura con voz opaca
un misterioso sortilegio que sólo él puede rezar,
un misterioso sortilegio
como un rezo de ritual

que evoca la gloria del trono donde él reinaba cuando niño
allá en su selva ecuatorial,
entre las tribus de guerreros y de sagrados sacerdotes
que lo adoraban al pasar . . .

En la calleja solitaria
se enrosca la comparsa como una culebra colosal.

Bajo la luz de las farolas
se ven los torsos de caoba que el sudor hace rebrillar;
las sombras tiemblan en las casas
con un temor del más allá:
la música, ronca y monótona va evocando mil cosas raras
—tal el simún cuando remeda el estertor de algún titán—
de entre los pechos que jadean
sale un soplido sibilante como el del viento sobre el mar,
y los cuerpos se descoyunten en una furia demoníaca
al impulsar irresistible de los palitos y el timbal.

En la calleja solitaria
se enrosca la comparsa como una culebra colosal.
(Habana, Carnaval de 1916)

(from *Gráfico* 7.160 (March 25, 1916): 8.)

2) Alejo Carpentier, "Juego santo" (1927)

Ecón y bongó,
atabal de timbal,
ecón y bongó,
timbal de arrabal.
Rumba en tumba,
tambor de cajón.
¡Qué le zumba!

Ecón con ecón,
timbal y bongó,
tambor de cajón.

Por calles de Regla
lleva la comparsa
juego santo
en honor de Ecoriofó.

Farola en alto,
anilla de oro,
chancleta ligera,
pañuelo bermejo . . .

Ataron el chivo,
mataron el gallo,
asaron cangrejos,
sacaron el diablo . . .

¡Baila, congo,
ya suena el empegó!
Son toques de allá,
los cantos de Eribó

Ecón y bongó,
atabal de timbal,
rumba en tumba,
timbal de arrabal.

(from *Obras completas de Alejo Carpentier*. Vol. 1. Mexico: Siglo XXI, 1983.)

3) Emilio Ballagas, "Comparsa Habanera" (1934)

La comparsa del farol
(bamba uenibamba bó.)
Pasa tocando el tambor.
¡Los diablitos de la sangre
se encienden en ron y sol!

"A'ora verá cómo yo no yoro.
(Jálame lá calimbanyé . . .)
Y'ora verá como yombondombo.
(Júleme la cumbumbanyé. . .)"

El santo se vá subiendo
cabalgando en el clamor

"Emaforibia yambó.
Uenibamba uenigó."
¡En los labios de caimito,
los dientes de anón!

La comparsa del farol
ronca que roncando vá.
¡Ronca comparsa candonga
que ronca en tambor se vá!

Y . . . ¡Sube la loma! Y ¡dale al tambor!
Sudando los congos van tras el farol.
(Con cantos yorubas alzan el clamor.)
Resbalando en un patín de jabón
sus piernas se mueven al vapor del ron.

Con plumas plumero
de loro parlero
se adorna la parda
Fermina Quintero.
Con las verdes plumas
de loro verdero.
¡Llorando la muerte
de Papá Montero!

La comparsa del farol
ronca que roncando vá.
Ronca comparsa candonga
bronca de la canadonga . . .
¡La conga ronca se vá!

Se vá la comparsa negra bajo el sol
moviendo los hombros, bajando el clamor.
Y ¡Sube la loma! (Y baja el clamor.
Pasa la comparsa mientras baja el sol.)

Bailan las negras rumberas
con candela en las caderas.
Abren sus anchas narices,
ventanas de par en par
a un panorama sensual...

La conga ronca se vá
al compás del atabal...

¡Sube la loma, dale al tambor!
Sudando los negros van tras el farol.
(Los congos dan vueltas y buscan el sol
pero no lo encuentran porque ya bajó)

La comparsa se enciende su rojo farol
con carbón de negros mojados en ron.
La comparsa negra menéandose va [sic]
por la oscura plaza del Catedral.
La comparsa conga vá con su clamor
por la calle estrecha de San Juan de Dios.

"Apaga la vela
que'l muelto se vá.
Amarra el pañuelo
que lo atajo ya.

Y ¡enciende la vela
que'l muelto salió!
Enciende dos velas
¡Qué tengo el Changó!"

La comparsa conga temblando salió
de la calle estrecha de San Juan de Dió.
¡Clamor en la noche del ronco tambor!

Rembombiando viene
rembombiando vá...
La conga rembomba

rueda en el tambor.
La conga matonga
sube su clamor
ronda que rondando
¡ronca en tambor!

En la oscura plaza del cielo rumbea
la luna. Ye sus anchas caderas menea.
Con su larga cola de blanco almidón
vá la luna con
su bata de olán.
Por la oscura plaza de la noche vá
con una comparsa de estrellas detrás.

Y la mira el congo, negro maraquero,
suena una maraca. Y tira el sombrero!

Retumba la rumba
hierve la balumba
y con la calunga
arrecia el furor.

Los gatos enarcan
al cielo el mayido.
Encrespan los perros
sombríos ladridos.

Se asoman los muertos del cañaveral.
En la noche se oyen cadenas rodar.
Rebrilla el relámpago como una navaja
que la noche conga la carne le raja.
Cencerros y grillos, güijes y lloronas:
cadenas de ancestro . . . y . . . ¡Sube la loma!
Barracones, tachos, sangre del batey
mezclan su clamor en el guararey.

Con luz de cocuyos y helados aullidos
anda por los techos el "ánima sola."

Destrás de una iglesia se pierde la ola
de negros que zumban maruga en la rumba.

Y apaga la vela
Y ¡enciende la vela!
Sube el farol,
abaja el farol.
Con su larga cola, la culebra vá.
Con su larga cola, muriéndose vá
la negra comparsa del guaricandá.

La comparsa ronca perdiéndose vá.
¡Qué lejos!... lejana... muriéndose vá.
Se apaga la vela; se hunde el tambor.
¡La comparsa conga desapareció!

(from *Cuaderno de poesía negra*. Santa Clara: La Nueva, 1934.)

4) Felix B. Caignet, "La conga prohibida" (1936)

¡Qué balbaridá, Dio mío!
¿A donde bamo'a paral...?
A lo negro no han dejao
lo blanco sin calnabal.
La conga ettá prohibía,
dise un bando milital...
Quien no tenga traje'seda
se queda sin calnabal...
Y qué daño hase la conga?
Bamo... dígame, ¿qué daño?
Si cuando el bocú resonga
y repiquetea el caldero,
la coquilla de la conga
etremese al pueblo entero:
¡La conga! ¡Biba la conga!
¡La conga, con su alegría,
la conga que huele a grajo,
la conga del pueblo bajo
sin social hipocresía!

¡la conga que noj pelmiten
pa'nuncios eletorales,
y ahora noj quitan la conga;
¡noj dejan sin calnabale!
Me paltieron pore'leje . . .
¡Tanto como yo pensaba
que me iba a dibeltil!!
¡Sufre, negro,
date un trago,
y anda . . . acuétate a dolmil!
"Las congas están prohibidas"
dise un bando milital,
y no se puede arroyal;
quien no tenga traje'seda,
se queda sin calnabal.
¿Pol qué no dejan al pueblo
que cante y vaya'rroyal?
¡Ah . . . ya sé! Polque la conga,
según dicen lo mayore,
resulta un baile inmoral.
¡Eso sí que hace grasia!
¡Hablal de moralidá;
y con conga . . . arroyando,
se telminan casi siempre
la fietas de sosiedá!

(from *A golpe de maracas: poemas negros en papel mulato*. Havana: Casin, 1950.)

5) Alfonso Camín, "Carnaval en la Habana"

Yo no sé lo que serán
los carnavales en Niza,
en Venecia, en Nueva Orleáns;
pero los cuatro domingos
de la Habana en Carnaval,
esos no hay quien los supere
ni los iguale jamás.

Desde la noche de Reyes

al Martes de carnaval,
iban saliendo en comparsas
los ñáñigos a bailar.
Por Zanja y Carlos III,
Belascoain y Amistad;
por todas las calles viejas
que van al Parque Central,
que arrancan de la Machina
oliendo a negra y a mar,
bailando va "La Culebra,"
bailando va "El Alacrán."
Diablito cascabelero
salta de aquí para allá;
unas veces va delante
y otras veces va detrás,
como un faquir comelumbre,
como un Fu Manchú oriental;
como otro rey de Abisinia
que hace un alto en Gilbraltar,
con más talegas que Londres
y más pompas que un bajá.

Ecué, Abasí, Changó
Ochún, Yemayá.

Detrás, vestidas de rojo,
Lo mismo que un framboyán,
vienen bailando las negras,
sudor, cadera y compás.
Vienen también las mulatas
—mango, caoba y coral—
canela que ahora da Cuba
y antes la daba Ceylán.
Abren balcones las blancas,
sale el tendero al portal;
igual que antorchas al viento
los cuerpos vienen y van;
gritan, se alejan, se acercan,

sigue la danza sensual
y aplauden blancos y negros
la danza de Calabar.
Danza de Sierra Leona,
Noche, desierto, arenal;
Danza que vino del Congo,
como un clamor, sobre el mar.
Mezcla de rito africano
y de catolicidad,
se oye en los aires calientes
la frase sacramental:

   Ecué, Abasí, Changó
   Ochún, Yemayá.

Ahora son otras comparsas
las que por las calles van.
La Costa de los Esclavos
se refleja en "Los Gambá";
negros que mueven trapiches,
cantan, sudan sin cesar,
temorosos al componte
y a la voz del mayoral.
"Dandys" de Jesús María
con aires de Ku-klux-klan,
ya no son lo que ayer eran
ni echan la Habana a temblar.
Pero vienen "Las Bolleras"
dando bollitos de pan,
y viene "La Jardinera,"
"La Jardinera" se va.
Toda la Habana bailando,
toda la Habana aclamando
ritmo, cadera y compás,
va la comparsa marchando,
va la comparsa ondulando
como si fuera un majá.

Ecué, Abasí, Changó
Ochún, Yemayá.

Carnaval el de mis tiempos
de la Habana en Carnaval:
toda la Habana en colores,
toda la Habana en tambores,
toda la Habana en fulgores,
toda la Habana en vals.
La Reina con sus princesas
y en su carroza triunfal,
va, desde Marte y Belona,
por todo el Prado hasta el mar.
Confetis y serpentinas
al aire vienen y van
y hasta las velas del puerto
se ven alegres bailar.
Blancas y en blancas carrozas,
mujeres sin antifaz,
pues que esconder esas caras
fuera pecado mortal.
Ojos que París no tiene,
que nunca Londres tendrá,
y hay que buscar en Sevilla
o en la Arbia del Corán.
No va en las carrozas Momo,
sino que va Floreal
y huela toda Habana
a jazmín y a tulipán.

Ecué, Abasí, Changó
Ochún, Yemayá.

Todos los coches abiertos
al clamor de la ciudad
y todos los corazones
campanario en catedral.
La carroza de "El Encanto"

con tantas bellezas va,
que por donde va pasando
va oliendo el aire a rosal.
"Crusellas y Compañía"
perfuma el aire al pasar;
da chocolates "La Estrella"
y aroman el litoral
"Villaamil," "Tomás Gutiérrez,"
"Gener," "Punch" y "Partagás."
Ojos de ron "Carta de Oro"
y una flor en el ojal,
"Bacardí" llegó de Oriente
y es en la Habana el sultán.
Desfila el Centro Asturiano,
el Canario y el Balear;
desfila el Centro Gallego
y hay Baile en el "Nacional."
Con todo el Valle en los ojos
y el cielo de Monserrat,
Matanzas trajo a la Habana
las Cuevas de Bellamar.

Llaman la atención
y el cuerpo de Trinidad;
que ver ojos trinitarios
no es una cosa vulgar.
Panchita, que va bailando,
"Para Camagüey se va,"
pero dejando un recuerdo:
cintura, caña y palmar.

*Ecué, Abasí, Changó
Ochún, Yemayá.*

Todo el cielo de la Habana
Se viste de Carnaval:
La tarde se viste de oro,
La noche lleva antifaz

y está siempre amaneciendo
la Habana por tierra y mar.
Bien vista Blanca Nieves,
bien de luna y alquitrán,
de espuma del Mar Caribe,
de sol, de rosa y coral,
la Habana es siempre la Habana,
la Habana alegre y locuaz,
la del balcón y los brazos
abiertos de par en par
Si París vale una misa,
la Habana vale algo más;
por ser la Habana paloma;
se hizo Drake gavilán.
No muere el yanque de tedio [sic]
porque hay en Cuba un palmar
y tiene en Tampa y en Miami
la misma luz tropical.

Yo no sé lo que serán
los carnavales en Niza,
en Venecia, en Nueva Orleáns;
pero los cuatro domingos
de la Habana en Carnaval,
esos no hay quien los supere
ni los iguale jamás.

¡Ecué, Abasí, Changó
Ochún, Yemayá!

(from *Maracas y otros poemas*. Mexico: Impresora Azteca, 1952.)

6) Julio Ayllón Morgan, "Romance da la comparsa" (1946)

¡Paso, paso! que ya viene
desfilando la comparsa
como un maja voluptuoso
de liturgia milenaria.
La música toma el aire

y lo penetra y empapa
impregnando al gran gentío
que contempla la parada
con los sones elocuentes
de su verba alucinada.

Voz de mujer, tentación,
el clarinete levanta
los salmos estupefactos
de una leyenda olvidada
y responden los tambores
en masculina sonata,
arrancando un canto al coro
que va siguiendo las pautas:
ayes de angustia y lujuria
martirizando gargantas.

Lazarito y Caridad,
delante de la comparsa,
el uno con un hachón
y la otra con bata larga,
entre los dos son seis palmos
de vibraciones mareadas.
Nunca fueron al colegio
o están en el primer aula;
pero ¿que? sin saber tanto
van bailando en la comparsa
y los aplaude la gente
con frenética rociada.
Son dos principes tostados
recibiendo esclava y salva
de pólvora que las manos
homenajean admiradas.

Macumbele, el *"abacuá"*
"írimo" de los *"biabangas,"* [sic]
una epilepsia de ritmo
va floreando en la comparsa.

Las piernas son dos alambres
poderosos, donde pasan
las corrientes formidables
del rayo de Santa Bárbara,
y la cintura se pierde,
como un remolino de agua,
para después encontrarse
por una brusca parada.
Macumbele, el *"abacuá"*
"írimo" de los *"biabangas,"*
ha dejado en la repisa
de su cuarto la *"demanda,"*
porque costaba el disfraz
treinta y cinco pesos plata
y no pagó al *"encargado"*
y se apretujó la faja
para estrangular el hambre.
Pero eso no importa nada,
porque al impulso del ritmo
que balancea la comparsa,
Macumbele, el *"abacuá"*
se siente un rey negro de África.

Macusa, la de los Sitios,
desenrollando las ancas
que son el alfiletero
de setecientas miradas,
temblequeantes sobre el talle
la pulpa de dos guanábanas,
se recuesta, palpitante,
sobre el rojo de la sábana
que ha formada el misterioso
son de música africana.
Se peleó con el marido
y la hijita anda descalza;
llevó a la casa de empeños
hasta la ropa de cama;
pero eso tampoco importa:

con sus sandalias plateadas
y su vestido de seda,
en medio de la comparsa,
se siente la emperatriz
de la ciudad de La Habana.

¡Paso, paso! que desfila
por el Prado, la comparsa.
La música, en armonía
grandiosa a fuerza de bárbara,
se filtra por los pulmones
como una atmósfera rara
y hace la respiración
tomar una marcha rápida,
mientras la sangre, en las venas,
galopa desenfrenada,
y el corazón se aligera
y el cerebro se emborracha.

¡¡Paso!! que a los sones cósmicos
de la música africana,
como un majá voluptuoso,
va ondulando la comparsa.

(from *Romancero Cubano*. Havana: Rebeldía Estudiantil, 1946.)

7) Gilberto Hernández Santana, "La comparsa de semana Santa" (1935)

A Pedro Pérez García

Ya se oyen las latas,
y se siente el clamor;
Y en a vuelta de la esquina
se escucha la bumba que la voz quebranta
de la comparsa de Semana Santa.

Penetra la muerte
por la puerta del pecado que galope
vertiginoso;

retiemblan las calles
y viene el cortejo en danza
chunguendao en el Viernes Santo;
se oyen los bongoses
y el ronco clamor, de los negros congos
con Obalufón,
trayendo el libengue
entre el ruído de tambores [sic]
y van para el cabildo de la loma del Carmen
donde está el Egbó.

    Conga, malonga, con con có,
    conga, malonga, con con có,
    se escucha la lata,
    se calla la lata,
    conga, malonga, con con có.

La comparsa con Obalufón
viene con caretas
y alacranes de cartón;
y culebras de trapo de horrendo mirar...
Africa bulle
en el estruendo con que la conga espanta
y sigue en danza con sus faroles
la comparsa bronca de Semana Santa...

Hay quien viene investido
de túnica de rafia; distribuye el libengue
para los profanos:
la comparsa loca clama con voz ronca:
—Bulo, Bulo, Bulo
gracia de Likundu...
Presa de faroles prosigue la marcha
cantando la conga
con Obafulón.

    Conga, malonga, con con có,
    conga, malonga, con con có,

se escucha la lata,
se calla la lata,
conga, malonga, con con có.

Se rompe la bumba de la quimbisa,
los hechiceros de la macumba
y del candombe
buscan el mal...
dos pollos negros y un gato prieto
se descuartizan
en la bullanga;
y por las calles huérfanas de luna
va la corriente
supersticiosa de la negra barahunda
presa de faroles y ebria de tambores.

Ya se va alejando
la potencia conga
hacia el cabildo oblongo y rústico
de la loma del Carmen;
y sólo quedan los ecos de la bumba
arrastrándose por las calles
en un·son que la voz quebranta
y se pierde a lo lejos
la comparsa de Semana Santa

    Conga, malonga
    Con ... con ... cóooooo ...

(from *Semblanzas negras* Havana: Alfa, 1939.)

Anonymous Eighteenth- and Nineteenth-Century
"Cantos de comparsa"

1) "Ta Julia"

    Ma Rosario ta malo.
    (¡Cángala lagontó!)

—A be qué cosa tiene.
(¡Cángala lagontó!)
—Tiene barriga y doló.
(¡Cángala lagontó!)
—Etá embarasa.
(¡Cángala lagontó!)
—Culebra l'asuttá.
(¡Cángala lagontó!)

¿Qué diablo son ese?,
pregunta e mayorá.
Mira diente d'animá,
mira fomma ne roccá,
mira sojo d'ese nimá,
¿candela ne parese?
¿Qué nimá son ese
que ne parese majá?
Ta Juliá mimo ba matá.

(¡Báquini ba di ba yo!)
—¿Qué nimá son ese?
(¡Báquini ba di ba yo!)
—Yo coje guataca.
(¡Báquini ba di ba yo!)
—Yo coje la pala.
(¡Báquini ba di ba yo!)
—Tierra co l'asaó.
(¡Báquini ba di ba yo!)
—Ma Rosario ta buena.
(¡Báquini ba di ba yo!)
—Mañana ba trabajá.
(¡Báquini ba di ba yo!)
—Grasia ta Juliá.
(¡Báquini ba di ba yo!)
—Fué quié la mato.
(¡Cángala lagontó!)

2) "Canto para matar culebras"

    (Negrita)
—¡Mamita, mamita!
Yen, yen, yen.
¡Culebra me pica!
Yen, yen, yen.
¡Culebra me come!
Yen, yen, yen.
¡Me pica, me traga!
Yen, yen, yen.

    (Diablito)
—¡Mentira, mi negra!
Yen, yen, yen.
Son juego e mi tierra.
Yen, yen, yen.

    (Negrita)
—¡Le mira lo sojo,
parese candela! . . .
¡Le mira lo diente,
parece filere! . . .

    (Diablito)
—¡Culebra se muere!
¡Sángala muleque!
¡Culebra se muere!
¡Sángala muleque!
¡La culebra murió!
¡Calabasó-só-só!
¡Yo mimito mató!
¡Calabasó-só-só!

    (Negrita)
—¡Mamita, mamita!
Yen, yen, yen.

Culebra no pica
Yen, yen, yen.
Ni saca lengüita.
Yen, yen, yen.
Diablito mató.
¡Calabasó-só-só!

(Diablito)
—¡Ni traga ni pica!
¡Sángala muleque!
¡La culebra murió!
¡Sángala muleque!
¡Yo mimito mató!
¡Calabasó-só-só!

(from *Órbita de la poesía afrocubana: 1928–1937*. Ramón Guirao, ed. Havana: Ucar, García y Cía, 1938.)

Notes

Introduction

1. According to Nancy Pérez-Rodríguez, "carnival musicians [in Santiago] had to rehearse and move all around the city. And secretly they would remove the skins of their drums . . . and put guns and machetes inside them. In this way they were able to take weapons from the city to the countryside" (qtd. in Farr 214).

2. In my English-language translations I tend to use "Negro" when the original Spanish-language text hails from the nineteenth century or the early decades of the twentieth, given that the term was more commonly used than "black." When translating more recent texts I favor the latter term.

3. Moore refers to the events of 1912 as the "Guerrita del doce" [The Little War of 1912](69), but this is a misnomer that is commonly used in Cuba to describe what Helg more appropriately considers a "Racist Massacre." Helg also takes issue with another common moniker for the 1912 conflict—"The Race War of 1912"—which has been used by leading contemporary scholars such as Louis A. Pérez. According to Helg, those who see the conflict as a "Race War" fail to emphasize that white leaders took advantage of the circumstances to repress a racial group in order to terrify them and keep them out of power (*Rightful Share* 10, "Afro-Cuban Protest" 56). For more on the events of 1912 see Chapter 7—"The Racist Massacre of 1912"—in Helg's 1995 book *Our Rightful Share*.

4. For a complete account of the brawl that broke out between these two *comparsas*, see Helio Orovio's *El carnaval habanero* (31–33).

5. Figures for the number of blacks and mulattoes killed during the race war vary widely. Fermoselle (146) cites sources that put the number of dead Cubans of color at 3,000, but it is not clear if this figure includes the significant number of innocent civilians who lost their lives during the war. According to Helg, "official Cuban sources put the number of dead rebels at more than 2,000," while "U.S. citizens living in Oriente estimated it at 5,000 to 6,000." According to Helg, one of Estenoz's companions similarly guessed that around 5,000 Cuban blacks and mulattoes had perished (225). Pérez avoids citing figures in the main text of his study, but observes in a footnote that some estimates of the death toll "were as high as 35,000" ("Politics, Peasants, and People" 537, nt. 90).

6. "Gómez Sees End of Cuba Revolt." *New York Times*. May 23, 1912: 1. On May 25, for example, the *New York Times* reported that "The War Department received a dispatch from Jennings Cox, manager of mining properties at Juaragua [*sic*] . . . saying that the reports [of damage] had been much exaggerated and that everything was quiet around

his properties, which have not been burned or pillaged" ("Washington Wants Facts." *New York Times*. May 25, 1912: 2). The following day another article countered Cuban claims of widespread looting and extensive destruction by reporting that "depurations thus far have been confined to petty pillaging, and no large works have been burned or molested" ("Mobilize Fleet to go to Cuba." *New York Times*. May 26, 1912: 1)

7. As Robin Moore has noted, *tango* is a "generic term for African-derived dance in nineteenth-century Cuba. The term also applied to wandering groups of Afro-Cuban musicians" (286).

8. For a discussion of the history of Afro-Cuban carnival during the early decades of the Cuban Republic, see Robin Moore, (*Nationalizing Blackness* 62–86); Helio Orovio (*El carnaval habanero* 7–29); Judith Bettelheim ("Carnival in Santiago de Cuba" 94–127); Alejandra Bronfman (*Measures* 158–71); Virtudes Feliú Herrera (*Fiestas* 133–83, *Carnaval cubano* 7–31).

9. A *majá* is a large boa constrictor endemic in Cuba.

Chapter 1. Felipe Pichardo Moya's "La comparsa"

1. The first of Vasconcelos's editorials in *La Prensa* appeared on August 5, 1915 under the title "Confidencial" (Fernández Robaina, *El negro* 113). Like the majority of the articles that he published in the following years, it was signed with the pseudonym "Tristán."

2. A *bembé* is an "informal festival held for the enjoyment of the Yoruba *orishas*, to the accompaniment of the *bembé* drums. A Bantú term, the *bembé* has its origins in Nigeria, where it was originally performed for Ochún" (Orovio, *Cuban Music* 26). However, it should be pointed out here that the term was commonly misused in the early decades of the Republic to denote any rowdy Afro-Cuban dance or festivity. The term often carried sexual undertones, as can be seen in the following definition in the "Vocabulario" to Ramón Guirao's *Órbita de la poesía afrocubana*: "Baile africano ... traído por los mandingas o los lucumíes. El bembé es una danza sexual" (189) [African dance ... brought by the Mandinga or the Lucumí. The *bembé* is a sexual dance]. Like so many of the entries in Guirao's glossary, the first half of this one comes directly from Fernando Ortiz's *Glosario de afronegrismos* (52).

3. All citations from "La comparsa" are taken from its original publication in *Gráfico* 7.160 (March 25, 1916): 8.

4. Most subsequently published versions of "La comparsa" do not include the dedication to Ortiz, such as those in anthologies of *poesía negra* compiled by Hortensia Ruiz del Vizo (*Black Poetry* 18–21), Rosa E. Valdés-Cruz (89–91), and Aurora de Albornoz and Julio Rodríguez Luis (105–08). The dedication to Ortiz is also omitted from the 1992 reedition of Pichardo Moya's only published book of poems, *La ciudad de los espejos* [City of Mirrors] (1925).

5. Such opinions were not limited to Ortiz's first book. In several works from the 1920s—*La antigua fiesta afrocubana del Día de Reyes* [The Old Afro-Cuban Festival of Día de Reyes] (1920) and "Los cabildos afrocubanos" [The Afro-Cuban Cabildos] (1921) for example—Ortiz underscored the supposed atavistic nature of Afro-Cuban carnival celebrations. He also included many passages by other authors who describe traditional *comparsas* with demeaning terms. A citation from the 1920 essay, attributed to Aurelio

Pérez Zamora, is typical of those that Ortiz included—without further comment or contextualization—in his early writings on Afro-Cuban culture: "Innumerables grupos de comparsas de negros africanos recorren todas las calles de la capital; la turba es inmensa; su aspecto horroriza... El ruido que forman los tambores, los cuernos y los pitos aturde por doquiera los oídos del transeúnte.... cantan con monótono y desagradable sonido en lenguaje africano, las memorias del pueblo: y centenares de voces, chillonas unas, roncas las otras, y todas salvajes, responden en coro al rey etíope, formando un diabólico concierto difícil de describir" (14) [Innumerable groups of *comparsas* made up of African Negroes go through all the streets of the capital; the mob is immense; its appearance horrifies... Everywhere the noise made by the drums, the horns, and the whistles deafens the ears of the passerby... they sing the memories of the people with monotonous and disagreeable sounds in African languages; and hundreds of voices, some high-pitched, others hoarse, and all savage, respond in a chorus to the Ethiopian king, forming a diabolical concert that is difficult to describe].

6. The portion of this passage in quotes comes from a secondary source, but like so many such quotations in *Los negros brujos* it is incorporated into the main text as if it were Ortiz's own.

7. Ortiz further discusses the criminal nature of witchcraft in the final chapter of the study. See especially pages 185–90. For a complete and more reliable history of the case of Zoila Díaz see Ernesto Chávez Álvarez's book *El crimen de la niña Cecilia: la brujería en Cuba como fenómeno social*, 26–32 and Aline Helg, *Our Rightful Share*, 108–13.

8. See chapter VIII, "Noticias de prensa sobre la brujería" [News from the Press about Brujería](150–79).

Chapter 2. Carnival and Ñáñiguismo

1. *Revista de Avance.* 4.50 (Sept. 15, 1930): 260.

2. Page references here and throughout are to Alan West Durán's English-language translation.

3. Ortiz is using "potencia" here to refer to a specific Abakuá "group." The term technically refers to "the essential magical foundation, all powerful, of the group of drums, scepters, liturgical garments, and sacred personages owned by each Abakuá *juego*" (Brown, Glossary 70).

4. Fernando Ortiz also alluded to the alleged violence of the *ñáñigos* in some of his early writings (see, for example, "La antigua fiesta" 12), but he eventually called for a deeper understanding of their much-reviled traditions, even as he implicitly ignored his own role in reinforcing many of the prejudices against the Abakuá:

> El ñáñiguismo durante el siglo pasado fué envuelto en una tenebrosa atmósfera de criminalidad, más legendaria que verdadera... Parece que ya va siendo hora de ir alzando esos talones de tupida ignorancia y de necios prejuicios que impiden el conocimiento objetivo de las realidades étnicas de nuestros pueblos. ("La 'tragedia' de los ñáñigos" 79–80)

> [Ñáñiguismo in the past century was enveloped in a dark shroud of criminality, more legendary than true... It seems that it is now time to start retracting

those talons of rank ignorance and stupid prejudices that impede the objective knowledge of the ethnic realities of our peoples.]

5. For images of these clapperless bells, see Ortiz, *Los Instrumentos* Vol. 1, 271, 276–77.

6. The term "bongó" when used to refer to an Abakuá drum is often the cause of some confusion. While the *bonkó enchemiyá* is commonly called a bongó with a small "b," Brown explains that the sacred Abakuá drum known as *Ekue* to the Efó branch of Abakuá is called Bongó (with a capital "B") by those belonging to the Efí branch (*Light Inside* 47). However, it is clear from its mention along with the *ekón* in "Juego santo" that Carpentier is referring to the *bonkó enchemiyá*.

7. The spelling of the names of these drums, as well as other Abakuá terms, varies slightly. Sosa Rodríguez, for example, renders them as *biankomé*, *obi-apá*, and *kuchi-yeremá* (179). In his study of the Abakuá Brown lists the three *enkómos* as *Biapá*, *Kuchi Yeremá*, and *Aropabá*.

8. For a detailed discussion of Abakuá in Cuban music see Ivor Miller, "A Secret Society Goes Public" (170–74) and *Voice* (164–73).

9. Petit is perhaps best known as the founder of the syncretic religion known as La Regla de Kimbisa del Santo Cristo del Buen Viaje, or Regla Kimbisa for short. According to Brown, Regla Kimbisa "incorporated Lucumí (Yoruba), Palo Monte (Congo), spiritist (derived from the European-American spiritualism of Allen Kardec), and popular Catholic elements" (80). For more information on Petit's impact on Abakuá and his involvement in Regla Kimbisa see Brown, *Light Inside* (80–81, 90, 107–111, 237–39) and Ishemo (265–266).

Chapter 3. Carnival and Afro-Cuban Ritual in Nicolás Guillén's "Sensemayá: canto para matar una culebra"

1. Ortiz has expressed conflicting ideas about the relationship between Día de Reyes festivities and twentieth-century Afro-Cuban *comparsas*. In the epigraph to this chapter, for example, he clearly indicates that these traditions are intimately linked. Likewise, in his 1920 essay *La antigua fiesta afrocubana del Día de Reyes* (as well as in the 1960 reprint of the same essay) he states categorically that "las comparsas del carnaval habanero son supervivencias del Día de Reyes" (20 nt. 13) [the *comparsas* of Havana carnival are survivals of Día de Reyes]. However, in his essay "Los viejos carnavales habaneros" [Havana's Old Carnivals], which was originally published in the official program for Havana's 1954 carnival celebrations, Ortiz states that "Las comparsas en mascaradas no son . . . reminiscencias del Día de Reyes" (214) [Carnival masquerades are not . . . reminiscences of Día de Reyes], and then just a few paragraphs later he makes the following observation: "Muchas comparsas se desprendieron del pandemonium del Día de Reyes y sobre todo al cesar éste en 1884, trataron de perpetuarse transfiriendo sus mascaradas y ritos ambulatorios y danzarinos a las tardes y noches de carnestoladas, juntamente con los festejos análogos de los blancos" (214) [Many *comparsas* emerged from the pandemonium of Día de Reyes and above all when this tradition ended in 1884, they tried to stay alive by transferring their masquerades and ambulatory and dancing rites to the afternoons and evenings of Shrovetide, alongside the analogous festivities of the whites.]

2. A perusal of major Latin American poetry anthologies and popular college-level textbooks demonstrates that "Sensemayá" is rarely excluded from such books. In terms of its recital, "Sensemayá" was a standard piece among the repertoires of the most famous reciters of the poetry of Afrocubanismo, such as Eusebia Cosme and Luis Carbonell.

3. See, for example, Augier, *Nicolás Guillén* 141–42, "Inscripción geográfica" 270–71; González Pérez, *Acercamiento* 45–46; Mansour 195; Melon 210; Ruffinelli 47–48; Valdés-Cruz, *Poesía negroide* 75–76; Cintio Vitier "Hallazgo" 150; Lorna Williams 18; Jerome Branche 179.

4. Ortiz discusses "Mayombe" and related terms in *Los negros brujos* (115), *Glosario de afrocubanismos* (317), "Brujos y santeros" (88), and in many other later articles. "Mayombe" and "mayombero" are used frequently in Rafael Roche's study of *ñáñiguismo* and criminality in Cuba, *La policía y sus misterios en Cuba* (see 2nd ed. 153–55). Also see Rómulo Lachatañeré's article "La influencia bantú-yoruba en los cultos afrocubanos" [The Bantu-Yoruban Influence in Afro-Cuban Cults], which was originally published in *Estudios Afrocubanos* in 1940 and reprinted in *El sistema religioso de los afrocubanos* [The Religious System of the Afro-Cubans]. Havana: Ciencias Sociales, 2001. 205–216.

5. See Ramón Guirao, ed. *Órbita de la poesía afrocubana*; Emilio Ballagas, ed. *Mapa de la poeseía negra Americana*. These terms or variations of them are also defined in the following sources: Enrique Noble, ed. *Literatura afro-hispanoamericana* (46); Rosa E. Valdés-Cruz, ed. *La poesía negroide en América* (241); Luis Íñigo Madrigal, ed. Nicolás Guillén, *Summa poética* (95).

6. See for example: Migene González-Wippler 129–38; Brown, *Light Inside* 5, 62–63, *Santería Enthroned*, 28, 57; Ayorinde, 15–18; Mason 88, 133; Matibag 154–158.

7. I owe credit to Elliot Klein for suggesting to me in one of our many personal communications the notion that the name of the snake might also be hidden in the opening chant of "Sensemayá."

8. Though Cuellár's article seems to have gone largely unnoticed by modern critics of Guillén's poems, it is interesting nonetheless as it evokes the mystery that has long surrounded Guillén's apparently invented term. Cuellár was a close friend of Guillén, and was well known for his 1930s radio program (called "Sensemayá") that featured Afro-Cuban music. In the brief footnote to Cuellár's one-page article, the editor of *Adelante* suggests that the legend—which is condensed below—is authentic:

A boy named Didún is annoyed by his younger sister, Itana, who follows him everywhere. One day while Itana is secretly following Didún through the forest she sees him speaking to a beautiful woman, who tells him that she will help him become a strong man, and that if he ever finds himself in danger, he should call out to her for help. However, the beautiful woman explains to Didún that instead of calling out her name—which she must keep secret—he should call out the magical word, "Sensemayá," and she will appear.

The woman disappears, and Didún returns home. Several days later Itana again follows her brother into the forest where she finds him in the grips of a battle with an enormous, snake-like creature. When Didún realizes that he is losing the fight he tries to summon the beautiful woman, but he cannot remember the magical word. However, Itana remembers, and fearing her brother's death more than the punishment she might receive when he discovers that she has followed him, she shouts out "Sensemayá" two times. Though the beautiful woman does not appear, the chanting of "Sensemayá" has the following effect:

> empezó a llover muy fuerte . . . y el monstruo, que temía al agua más que todas las cosas, soltó a Didún. Y retrocediendo hacia lo profundo de la selva y hundiendo las patas en el fango creciente, se alejó para siempre, y sólo dejando un canto en el abismo:
> Mayombe-bombe mayombé . . .
> Mayombe-bombe mayombé . . . (15)
>
> [It began to rain very hard . . . and the monster, who feared water more than anything else, let Didún go. And retreating toward the depths of the jungle and hiding its legs in the deepening mud, it went away forever leaving a chant in the abyss:
> Mayombe-bombe mayombé . . .
> Mayombe-bombe mayombé . . .]

Given that in my readings of critical essays that have been published on "Sensemayá" since the poem first appeared in print in 1934, I had not encountered so much as a reference to this legend or to Cuéllar's article, I was dubious about its authenticity when I stumbled upon it by chance. After a bit of digging I found another article by Cuéllar (this one from 1962) titled "El Guillén que usted no conoce" [The Guillén that You Don't Know], in which the author effectively confirmed my doubts with the following admission: "Por cierto que el término 'sensemayá' es un fonema hijo de la inventiva de Nicolás Guillén. Yo escribí la leyenda con terminología Yoruba. Y con personajes Yorubas, claro está" (6) [In truth the term "sensemayá" is a phoneme of Guillén's own invention. I wrote the legend with Yoruba terminology. And with Yoruba characters, sure enough].

9. References to Sensemayá as a goddess in an Afro-Cuban religion can be found in Raquel Chang-Rodríguez and Malva E. Filer, ed. *Voces de Hispanoamérica: Antología literaria*. 3rd ed. Boston: Heinle and Heinle, 2003. 398; John F. Gargiano, et. al., eds. *Huellas de las literaturas hispanoamericanas*. 2nd ed. Upper Saddle River, NJ: Prentice Hall, 2002. 477; Gladys M. Varona-Lacey, ed. *Contemporary Latin American Literature: Original Selections from the Literary Giants for Intermediate and Advanced Studies*. Chicago: McGraw Hill, 2001. 88.

10. Antonio Olliz-Boyd suggests the possible relationship between Sensemayá and Yemayá (187–90), and Kubayanda (105), Zohn-Muldoon (137–38), and Octavio di Leo (93) support his idea with little or no elaboration. It should be noted, moreover, that none of these critics elaborates substantially on Yemayá's important connection with the image of the snake in Guillén's poem.

11. Kubayanda (105) and Zohn-Muldoon (137) both cite this reading, though they mistakenly render the term that Olliz-Boyd refers to as "sensa" instead of "Sansa."

12. It is worth noting that the term does not appear in Lydia Cabrera's *Vocabulario Congo*, and that several experts in Cuba that I have consulted are not familiar with it.

13. For example, in *Écue-Yamba-Ó* Carpentier refers to this sacred drum as *senseribó*

(173, 228), and in his poem "Bembé" Teófilo Radillo begins with the following chant: "Senseribó, / senseribó. / Sigue mi canto, / tamba tambó. / Senseribó, / apé mancó" (Guirao, *Órbita* 175). In the glossary to *Órbita*, this sacred drum is listed as "Senseribó," with "Cese-Eribó" offered as an alternate spelling. The name of this symbolic ritual drum is also prominent in some popular Cuban songs, such as Ernesto Lecuona's "Ecue senseribó." It is interesting to note, moreover, that in the Bríkamo language of the Abakuá, *Sése* signifies "el Gran Poder" (Cabrera, *La sociedad* 155). Likewise, Fernando Ortiz has observed that among various African peoples *sése* is an important term that denotes high-ranking deities, dignitaries, or more generally "the spirit of the Earth." Ortiz adds that in popular Cuban speech *sése* evolved into the more common *chéche*, and denotes "principal," "superior," "excellent," or "valiant" (*Instrumentos* Vol. 2, 103).

14. Adriana Tous (103, 106) and Antonio Olliz-Boyd (189) also establish this connection in their studies.

15. Guillén is referring here to the refrain from one of several widely disseminated, slave-era "cantos de comparsa," many of which appeared in print in contemporary publications such as *Los negros brujos*, which Guillén was reading at the time he wrote "Sensemayá." Ortiz transcribes one such chant in his description of how on Día de Reyes black slaves would parade through the streets carrying a giant artificial boa. The slaves would drop the snake effigy in front of the governor's palace, and then dance around it and pretend to chop it in half while chanting: "La culebra se murió, / Sángala muleque" (78). Ortiz cites the same chant in *La antigua fiesta afrocubana del Día de Reyes* (41).

In the years following the publication of "Sensemayá," various versions of snake chants appeared in anthologies of *poesía negrista* and *afrocubanista*. In his 1935 *Antología de la poesía negra hispanoamericana*, for example, Emilio Ballagas implicitly calls attention to the relationship between "Sensemayá" and such chants by including it in the same section as an anonymous slave-era composition that he titles "La Culebra: Canto de comparsa." In *Órbita de la poesía afrocubana* (1938), Ramón Guirao included his own renditions of several traditional chants under the general title "Cantos de comparsa" (see appendix).

16. In her English-language rendition of the poem, Kutzinski inaccurately translates "palo" as "pole" (*Against* 137), and later speaks of "the snake wrapped around the stick" (138, 139). Benítez-Rojo speaks of the snake who "comes and wraps himself around a staff" (297), revealing, perhaps, his debt to Kutzinski's interpretation of the key image of the snake wrapped around a "stick" as a metaphor for the Aesculapian staff. In his published English-language translation of "Sensemayá," Robert Márquez chooses "stick," while in their early translation of the poem Langston Hughes and Ben Frederic Carruthers render this key term as "stalk" (32).

17. Though Aesculapius's staff is widely recognized as a symbol for the medical professions, it is often confused with the caduceus, an ancient Greek or Roman wand with a pair of wings and two serpents wrapped around it, which was carried by the messenger god Hermes or Mercury.

18. Many of the explanations of the term "palo" as it relates to Palo Monte demonstrate the tendency to mistranslate the term. Mary Ann Clark explains that the mayombero's sacred cauldron—or *nganga*—"contains a variety of natural materials including

sticks from the forest. Hence the term 'palo' 'stick' in Spanish, in the name of many of these traditions" (93–94). Matibag provides a similar explanation stating that the name Palo Monte "denotes the 'sticks' and 'branches' of the 'mountain' used in the making of the nganga" (154). Matibag's explanation is doubly problematic, since, as any reader of Cabrera's *El Monte* will know, the term "monte" rarely denotes a "mountain" in Cuban Spanish, but rather "forest" or "jungle." On the first page of her seminal work Cabrera makes this very clear:

> En los montes y malezas de Cuba habitan, como en las selvas de África, las mismas divinidades ancestrales . . . El negro que se adentra en la manigua, que penetra de lleno en un 'corazón de monte,' no duda del contacto directo que establece con fuerzas sobrenaturales. (13)

> [In the forests and scrublands of Cuba live, as in the jungles of Africa, the same ancestral divinities . . . The black man who ventures into the thicket, who completely penetrates a 'heart of the forest,' does not doubt the direct contact with supernatural forces.]

In his seminal work *Santería Enthroned*, David H. Brown erroneously uses "stick" instead of "tree" in his translation of a well-known Afro-Cuban proverb: "Un solo palo no hace monte" ["One stick does not a forest make"] (xix). Ayorinde is more on track when she notes that "[palo] refers to the ritual use of *trees* and plants believed to have magical powers" (15 emphasis added).

19. See, for example, Roche y Monteagudo, *La policía* (3rd ed., n.p.), Sosa Rodríguez (n.p.), Brown, *Light Inside* (39), Miller, *Voice of the Leopard* (48, Plates 6,7,9).

20. Vasconcelos's letter and Guillén's response to it are reproduced in Alexander Pérez-Heredia, ed. *Epistolario de Nicolás Guillén*. Havana: Letras Cubanas, 2002. 33–34, 37–38.

Chapter 4. "Comparsa habanera," Emilio Ballagas's Emblematic Contribution to Afrocubanismo

1. For comments on "Comparsa habanera" as an emblematic poem of Afrocubanismo see Cartey (69), di Leo (91), Herrera (95), Rice (109).

2. Of the seventeen poets in the anthology twelve were from Cuba, and all but one—the Spanish poet Federico García Lorca—hailed from Latin America.

3. Ballagas did not include "comparsa" in the glossaries of *Cuaderno* (1934) or *Antología* (1935). The definition that Ballagas provides in the glossary to *Mapa de la poesía negra americana*, however, seems to imply that his poem was meant to be an evocation of the Afro-Cuban carnival celebrations that were popular during the nineteenth century: "Conjunto de negros esclavos y libertos que el Día de Reyes bailaban y cantaban al ritmo de tambores en calles y plazas. Las comparsas tal vez llevaran consigo sedimentos africanistas" [A group of Negro slaves and freemen that on Día de Reyes danced and sang to the rhythm of drums in the streets and plazas. The *comparsas* perhaps brought with them African sediments] (305). This last comment is, to be sure, highly ironic for two reasons. On the one hand, as we have noted, Ballagas included the poem in a section

that "evoked" Africa and, on the other hand, the poem contains an abundance of racial and ethnic markers.

4. The vitality of "Comparsa habanera" led José Antonio Fernández de Castro to opine that Ballagas's portrait of a traditional *comparsa* was less authentic than the somber spectacle presented in Pichardo Moya's 1916 composition (17).

5. All citations from "Comparsa habanera" come from *Cuaderno de la poesía negra*, the pages of which are unnumbered.

6. Throughout the early decades of the twentieth century the term *conga* was also used to refer to *comparsa* troupes hired by white Conservative Party members to promote their political campaigns and attract the votes of black men. Members of the black middle class found these to be especially offensive since they epitomized the exploitation of lower-class blacks and their culture by the white majority (see Acuña L'azcano, 7; Arredondo, *El negro en Cuba*, 143). *Congas* hired by the Liberal Party were usually referred to as *chambelonas*. For a complete discussion of the role of *congas* and *chambelonas* in early twentieth-century Cuban politics see Moore, 73–80. Conga is also a type of Cuban dance music that was popular in the United States and Europe in the 1930s.

7. For instance, Arturo Torres-Rioseco insists in his early evaluation of the poetry of Afrocubanismo that "Although Ballagas is a member of the white race, few poets have such an intimate knowledge of Negro psychology and folklore" (130).

8. Though Coulthard does not give specific examples, many poems serve to substantiate his claim. See, for example, José Zacarías Tallet's "La rumba" (1928), Alfonso Hernández Catá's "Rumba" (1931), and Teófilo Radillo's "Bembé" (ca. 1937).

9. In *El monte* Lydia Cabrera recounts the possession of a carnival queen by the *orisha* Oyá:

> Casimira . . . fué reina de una comparsa de chinos. Adornaba su cabeza una corona resplandeciente de inquietos pedacitos de espejos. Desfilando majestuosamente en su carroza, sentada en un trono no menos deslumbrante entre damas de honor y dragones de cartón . . . se desplomó de repente. Setenta y dos horas permaneció sin conocimiento, esta reina. Incapaz el médico de hacerla volver en sí, se hizo junta de babalawos. Determinaron kari Ocha: hacerle Santo. Recobró el sentido en la ceremonia, cuando la diosa Oyá tomó posesión de su cabeza. (269)

> [Casimira . . . was the queen of a *comparsa* of Chinese. She adorned her head with a resplendent crown of glistening little pieces of mirrors. Parading majestically on her float, seated on a no less dazzling throne among maids of honor and cardboard dragons . . . she suddenly collapsed. Seventy-two hours she remained unconscious, this queen. As the doctor was incapable of making her come to, he made an appointment with the *Babalawos* (literally, "fathers of secrets"). They determined to "make her a Saint." She regained consciousness during the ceremony, when the goddess Oyá took possession of her head.]

10. In the glossary to *Cuaderno de poesía negra* Ballagas gives the following definition for the phrase "Subirse el santo": "Sentirse poseído el brujo o el creyente de sus prácticas

por el espíritu que invoca" (n.p.)[When the sorcerer or believer in his practices feels possessed by the spirit that is invoked].

11. Roland E. Bush's claim that "the description of the dancer who reaches a state of total surrender suggests the ritualistic phenomenon which occurs in Santería when the dancer falls in a trance-like state because the orisha ("el santo") has overtaken him/her or has overtaken his/her body" makes a certain amount of sense (7). However, it seems more likely to me that Guillén was simply underscoring the widely held view that Afro-Cubans had a tendency to escape their harsh reality through heavy drinking. Indeed, "Canto negro" seems to express a notion that Guillén repeats in the fourth canto of "West Indies, Ltd.," that is "el problemático alcohol / que borra y ciega" (38)[problematic alcohol / that erases and blinds].

12. The introduction and the brief explanations that accompany the images are provided in both Spanish and English.

13. Images of lecherous black men appear in numerous *afrocubanista* poems. See for example, José Zacarías Tallet's "La rumba," Marcelino Arozarena's "La comparsa del majá," José Antonio Portuondo's "Rumba de la negra Pancha" [The Negress Pancha's Rumba], and Vicente Gómez Kemp's "Fuego con fuego" [Fire with Fire].

14. It is interesting to note that in the glossary to *Mapa de la poesía negra americana*, Ballagas downplays the term's supposed sexual undertones: "Es posible que metafóricamente haya pasado a significar sexualidad ardorosa" 304 [It's possible that metaphorically it has come to mean fiery sexuality].

15. See Ortiz's *Glosario* (156–57) and also the glossaries of the major collections of *poesía negra*, most of which provide "matón" (bully, lout, thug) as one of this term's meanings.

16. See my article "Carnival, Cultural Debate, and Cuban Identity in 'La comparsa' and 'Comparsa habanera'" *Revista de Estudios Hispánicos* 40 (2006): 64.

17. The relative obscurity of the original version of "Comparsa habanera" is illustrated by the fact that Robin Moore, despite specifically referring to *Cuaderno de poesía negra* in the main body of his study and correctly citing 1934 as the approximate date of the poem's composition, includes the truncated version of the poem in an appendix to *Nationalizing Blackness* (239–41).

Chapter 5. Drumming Up the Black Vote

1. For an example of a political handbill in the Bríkamo language see Sosa-Rodríguez (n.p.).

2. In his 1942 article "La poesía afrocubana," for example, José Juan Arrom makes a very brief reference to Tallet's recreation of the sound of the cornet in "Quintín Barahona" (394). In "*Afrocubanista* poetry and Afro-Cuban Performance," Miguel Arnedo likewise mentions Tallet's poem only in passing. Jorge María Ruscalleda Bercedóniz's analysis of the poem is the most extensive I have seen in print, but it still occupies just over a page (410–11) in his lengthy book *El negro en la poesía cubana (1608–1936)*.

3. For a discussion of the history of "La Chambelona" see Moore 74–77, Sublette 322, and Bianchi Ross's electronically published article "La Chambelona."

4. *Afro-Cuba: A Musical Anthology*. Rounder 1993. Track 27.

5. Even though "La Chambelona" was most typically associated with the Liberal Party, members of the Conservative Party sometimes adopted (and adapted) the tune as well. According to Francisco Martínez Chao "los partidarios de los Liberales o de los Conservadores salían en comparsas . . . cantando el pegajoso himno de La Chambelona" (n.p.) [The supporters of the Liberals as well as the Conservatives came out in *comparsas* . . . singing the catchy hymn of La Chambelona]. Bianchi Ross likewise notes that "aquel himno liberal, adoptando sus versos, lo cantaron también los afiliados al partido contrario" [Adopting its verses, those affiliated with the conservative party also sang that liberal hymn]. He then goes on to note that as early as 1916, the year that the tune gained widespread fame, Liberals and Conservatives in Las Villas bandied contrary versions of the song during the local elections.

6. Cuba's rural black population was not immune to such bribes from white politicians, as Facundo La Rosa, an Afro-Cuban peasant from Sabana de Robles, has pointed out. In the 1930s, when laborers like him earned just twenty cents for eight-hour days of cutting cane, well-dressed white politicians frequently traveled to rural villages offering money in exchange for the black vote: "Aquello era una desvergüenza . . . A mí uno de ellos me ofreció cinco pesos para que yo votara por un señor que no conocía" [That was a disgrace . . . One of them offered me five pesos to vote for a man that I didn't know] (Cited in Martínez Chao n.p.).

7. In *Écue-Yamba-Ó*, written in 1927 and published two years before Tallet's poem, Alejo Carpentier had similarly criticized Cuban politicians. As Menegildo describes the *chambelonas* he had witnessed in his youth, he also recalls how the politicians who courted the black vote never followed through with their empty campaign promises to Afro-Cubans: "Lo cierto es que la sabia administración de tales próceres había traído un buen rosario de quiebras, cataclismos, bancos podridos y negocios malolientes. Roída por el chancro del latifundio, hipotecada en plena adolescencia, la isla de corcho se había vuelto una larga azucarera incapaz de flotar" (114) [The truth of the matter is that the wise administration of such illustrious men had brought a long rosary of failures, cataclysms, rotten banks, and foul-smelling deals. Gnawed at by the chancre of the large estates, mortgaged in its very adolescence, the cork island had become a long sugar plantation incapable of floating].

8. For a discussion of Afro-Cuban militancy in the early decades of the twentieth century see Alejandro de la Fuente 94–95, 191–96.

Chapter 6. "La conga prohibida"

1. The Eusebia Cosme Papers, housed at the Manuscripts, Archives, and Rare Books Division of the Schomburg Center for Research in Black Culture (New York Public Library), include dozens of programs from Cosme's recitals of *poesía negrista* throughout Latin America and the United States from the early 1930s to the mid-1950s.

2. To the best of my knowledge, only one poem by Caignet, "Soy bongosero," has been anthologized, and only in two collections edited by Hortensia Ruiz del Vizo: *Poesía negra del Caribe y otras areas*. Maimi: Universal, 1971: 109; and *Black Poetry of the Americas: A Bilingual Anthology*. Miami: Universal, 1972: 59. Some of Caignet's poems, such as "Soy

bongosero" and "Coctel de son," were also part of the repertoire of the Cuban *declamador* Luis Carbonell.

3. Ortiz discusses the origins of the maraca at length in *Los instrumentos de la música afrocubana*. Vol. 1, 180–182.

4. Though Marcelino Arozarena poeticizes such traditions in his "Carnival de Santiago," this poem was not written until 1953, well over a decade after the poetry of Afrocubanismo had hit its height of popularity.

5. Pérez-Rodríguez reproduces several advertisements for the "artículos carnavalescos" [carnival items] that were sold during Santiago's winter and summer carnival seasons (see vol. 1, 212, 232). See Chapter 8 of this study for images of similar ads from Havana's newspapers.

6. This information is taken from an Edén advertisement, which was originally published in the Santiago newspaper *Adelante* on July 3, 1935 and is reproduced in Pérez-Rodríguez vol. 1, 14–15.

7. Bettelheim cites these same lines from Brea and Millet's articles, but translates the second-to-last line incorrectly: "Camacho doesn't want African congas; but I am coming with my trombone; *until they give me the prize* . . . bon! bon! bon!" (104, emphasis added). The line's true meaning more clearly conveys the group's defiance of the mayor's decree.

Chapter 7. Representations of Afro-Cuban Carnival in Three Poems by Marcelino Arozarena

1. "Liturgia etiópica" first appeared in *Adelante* 2.18 (Nov. 1936): 11.

2. In *Canción negra sin color* (1966), Arozarena provides specific dates for most of the poems. A note after "La conga," however, simply reads "Revista Miramar década de los 30." I have paged through most of the numbers of this short-lived publication of the Miramar Yacht Club, but have been unable to locate Arozarena's poem. An extensive search for information about the poem's original date of publication has been fruitless, but I believe that "La conga" was penned shortly after Afro-Cuban carnival celebrations were officially reinstated in Havana in 1937.

3. Emilio Ballagas's *Antologia de poesía negra hispanoamericana* (1935), Ramón Guirao's *Órbita de la poesía afrocubana* (1938), Rosa E. Valdés-Cruz's *La poesía negroide en América* (1970), and Jorge Luis Morales's *Poesía afroantillana y negrista* (1976, 1981, 200), just to name a few.

4. For a detailed discussion of these pantomimic dances see Fernando Ortiz's *La Antigua fiesta afrocubana del Día de Reyes* (41–42) and *Los bailes y el teatro de los negros en el folklore de Cuba* (118–120).

5. Given the breadth of the "Vocabulario" that follows Guirao's anthology, it is surprising that there is no entry for the term "murumba." This word is essential to the meaning of the poem since it represents the only obvious reference to Afro-Cuban witchcraft. In the glossary to *Canción negra sin color* Arozarena defines "murumba" as a "maleficio," which means a harmful curse or spell.

6. In their inaccurate English-language translation of "La comparsa del majá" Miriam Koshland and Sanders Russel evade the poem's obvious erotic subtext. For example, they

translate this stanza as if it were an innocent evocation of the unifying powers of song and dance: "Encarnasión! / I walk behind your body in the harmony of the dance,/ when the others look on / they see us as one / when they look from the side / they see us as two / and the song resounds anew." They translate one of the poem's most suggestive lines— "y cuando a mí te aproximas me vas haciendo bagazo"—as follows: "as I come closer you evade me / and it was only a joke I see" (145–46).

7. This was the first of many anthologies of Guillén's verse to be published in Cuba. The collection is introduced by a brief letter of appreciation by Miguel de Unamuno and includes forty-one poems. The book is divided into four sections that correspond to three previously published books—*Sóngoro cosongo* (1931), *West Indies Ltd.* (1934), *Cantos para soldadod y sones para turistas* (1937)—and one forthcoming title, *El son entero*, which was eventually published in Buenos Aires in 1946.

Chapter 8. An Outsider on the Inside

1. See, for example, Lázaro (231); Acosta (667); Baquero (220, 232, 240); Ruiz del Vizo (*Poesía negra*, 12–15, 21 and *Black Poetry* 13, 22); Fernández de la Vega and Pamies (104–06); González-Pérez (*Antología* 35); Albornoz and Rodríguez Luis (109); Albino Suárez (16–17). In *La poesía negrista*, Mónica Mansour studies several of Camín's poems, and without even mentioning the fact that he is Spanish or that he published his first *poemas negros* in 1925, she gives the following justification for including his work in her study: "Incluimos a Camín dentro del movimiento porque, aunque su estilo de poesía no refleja las innovaciones rítmicas y estructurales, características del *negrismo*, los temas que trata sí pertenecen a la ideología del movimiento y de la época . . ." (192–93 nt. 34) [We include Camín in this movement because, even though his poetic style does not reflect the rhythmic and structural innovations that are characteristics of *negrismo*, the themes that he treats do correspond to the ideology of the movement and the era . . .].

2. Unfortunately, I have been unable to locate the original version of this article, and have therefore had to rely on the information given by Camín in his bibliography.

3. For a discussion of the polemic that was unleashed by the article that Camín published in *El País*, see Camín's prologue to *Carey y nuevos poemas* (9–10), and *Entre palmeras* (562–66).

4. *Revista de Avance* 1.2 (March 15, 1927): 27.

5. World eBook Library PGCC Collection. http://WorldLibrary.net

Epilogue

1. These and many other verses from Hernández Santana's poem were inspired by his reading of Juan Luis Martin's decidedly unreliable study of Afro-Cuban religions, *Ecué, Changó y Yemayá* (1930). In a chapter titled "La medicina brujesca" [Witch Medicine], for example, Martin speaks of the sorceress Bulo, who by the grace of a deity named Likundu administers a magical potion known as the *libengue*.

2. In the same collection (63–67), Ayllón also includes a poem about the carnivalesque processions held on the feast day of the Virgen de Regla (September 7) in the working-class Havana neighborhood of Regla. The atmosphere of this unique poem shares much in common with the other poems discussed in this book. The Afro-Cuban participants

in the procession, for example, play drums, perform sacred rituals, sing chants, and, as the poetic voice puts it, "van tras la Regla *arrollando*" (64 emphasis in original).

3. Biabanga, established in December 1862, was the first Abakuá Lodge in Matanzas. It is worth pointing out that this *íreme*'s name recalls the *ñáñigo* ruffian in Marcelino Arozarena's 1936 poem "Cumbele Makumbele," which was first published in Guirao's *Órbita de la poesía afrocubana* (149–52).

4. According to Brea and Millet, the term *mamarrachos* historically refers to "a group of masked or costumed persons who danced rhythmically in the streets [of Santiago] following the *parrandas* or *comparsas* during the major festivals of July. These characters originally gained so much importance in the Santiago carnival that carnival itself became identified as the *Fiesta de mamarrachos*" and it was referred to as such until the twentieth century (Glossary 193).

5. Commenting on the carnival songs from Santiago de Cuba, Gladys María González stresses that, much like those from Havana, many *cantos de comparsa* and *congas* with deep political themes had double meanings, often hiding erotic themes just below the surface: "There's a carnival song lyric that goes: 'Con el cuero hinchao le dio un bocabajo,'" González observes. "Well, of course, there's a double meaning. The phrase could mean 'with a swollen penis he fucked her.' But this idiom comes from the days of slavery and also translates 'with a swollen whip he beat her.'" (qtd. in Farr 214).

6. My transcriptions of song lyrics are the products of careful listening to original recordings that are not always clear. There may be some errors, though none so grave as to detract significantly from the songs' meanings. Names in parentheses after song lyrics refer to the composers, under whose names the songs and appropriate information on the recordings are listed in the "Works Cited."

7. Robin Moore's translations of some lyrics actually serve to make certain songs appear to be more problematic than they actually are. For example, he translates the following two lines from Grenet's "Camina pa' 'lante"—"Ahí viene tumbando la sonora conga / ¿Por qué no te animas, negro, al golpe de la tambora"—as "There goes the sonorous conga felling everything in its path / Why don't you get excited, black man, at the sound of the drumbeat." Though "tumbar" does often mean "to fell" or "cut down" (a tree), in a musical sense it means "to beat a drum," and it is clearly used in that sense here. Moreover, "animarse" does not usually mean "excited" in a sexual sense, as suggested here, but rather "to get lively" or "to cheer up."

Works Cited

All entries marked with a "*" are signed either "Tristán" or "T."—pennames that Ramón Vasconcelos used in his column in *La Prensa*, "Palpitaciones de la Raza de Color: Crónica escrita para negros sin taparabos, mestizos no arrepentidos y blancos de sentido común."

Acha, Eduardo de. "La conga." Pérez-Rodríguez, Vol. 2, 8–11.
Acosta, Agustín. "Alfonso Camín, Miguel Ángel de la Torre y Yo." Camín, *Entre Palmeras* 667–69.
Acuña L'azcano, Tomás. "A la nación cubana: Exposición de la Asociación Adelante sobre las comparsas y las congas." *Adelante* 34 (March 1938): 7–8, 20.
Aguirre, Mirta. "Scottsboro." *Obra poética de Mirta Aguirre: Dinámica de una tradición lírica*. Ed. Susana A. Montero. Havana: Academia, 1987. 121.
Albornoz, Aurora de and Julio Rodríguez Luis, eds. *Sensemayá: La poesía negra en el mundo hispanohablante*. Madrid: Orígenes, 1980.
"El Alcalde de la Habana ha enviado al Consistorio un extenso mensaje extraordinario tratando del turismo." *Diario de la Marina*. Feb. 6, 1937: 3.
"El Alcalde reconoce que la labor de la policía en los carnavales es digna de loa." *Diario de la Marina*. Feb. 10, 1937: 9.
Anderson, Thomas F. "Carnival, Cultural Debate, and Cuban Identity in 'La comparsa' and 'Comparsa habanera.'" *Revista de Estudios Hispánicos* 40 (2006): 50–78.
———. "Inconsistent Depictions of Afro-Cubans and Their Cultural Manifestations in the Early Poetry of Marcelino Arozarena." *Afro-Hispanic Review* 27.2 (Fall 2008): 9–44.
Appelbaum, Nancy P., Ann S. Macpherson, and Karin Alejandra Rosemblatt, eds. *Race and Nation in Modern Latin America*. Chapel Hill: University of North Carolina Press, 2003.
Arias, Salvador, ed. *Recopilación de textos sobre Alejo Carpentier*. Havana: Casa de las Américas, 1977.
———. comp. "Habla Alejo Carpentier." Arias. 15–55.
Armas de Arenas, Bibi. "El carnaval habanero." *Luces y sombras de un destierro*. Hato Rey, PR: Ramallo, 1979. 94–96.
Arnaz y Alberni, Desiderio. "A mis convecinos." Pérez-Rodríguez, Vol. 1 337–38.
Arnedo, Miguel. "Afrocubanista Poetry and Afro-Cuban Performance." *Modern Language Review* 96.4 (Oct. 2001): 991–1005.

Arnedo-Gómez, Miguel. *Writing Rumba: The Afrocubanista Movement in Poetry*. Charlottesville: University of Virginia Press, 2006.

Arozarena, Marcelino. "El antillano domador de sones." *América: Revista de la Asociación de Escritores y Artistas Americanas* (Jan.-Feb. 1943): 37-42.

———."Canción del estudiante pobre" (1934). *Habrá que esperar: mínima poesía*. Havana: Letras Cubanas, 1983: 24-26.

———. "Canción negra sin color" (1935). Emilio Ballagas, ed. *Antología de la poesía negra hispanoamericana*. Madrid: Aguilar, 1935. 163-65.

———. *Canción negra sin color*. Havana: Unión, 1966.

———. *Canción negra sin color*. 2nd exp. ed. Havana: Unión, 1983.

———. "La canción del orate." *Canción negra sin color*. (1966). 132-34.

———. "Caridá" (1933). "La comparsa del majá" (1936). "Liturgia etiópica" (1936). Guirao 145-53.

———. "Carnaval de Santiago." *Canción negra sin color* (1966). 21-24.

———. "La conga" (c. 1935). *Canción negra sin color* (1966). 39-41.

———. "¡Evohé!" (1936). *Canción negra sin color* (1966). 18-19.

———. "Rebeldía paradojal." *Adelante* 1.5 (Oct. 1935): 15.

———. "We Rehearse the Snake Dance." Trans. Miriam Koshland and Sanders Russel. *Introduction to African Literature: An Anthology of Critical Writing from Black Orpheus*. Ed. Ulli Beir. Evanston: Northwestern University Press, 1967. 145-46.

Arozarena Himely, Georgina and Celia Pinto. "Marcelino Arozarena: abnegado trabajador de la cultura cubana." *Afro-Hispanic Review*. 17.2 (1998): 3-11.

Arredondo, Alberto. "Afrocubanismo poético." *Adelante* 3.33 (Feb. 1938): 7-8.

———. "El arte negro a contrapelo." *Adelante* 3.26 (July 1937): 5-6.

———. "Las comparsas." *Adelante* 2.22 (March 1937): 1.

———."Dos palabras más sobre el negro y la nación." *Adelante* 2.20 (Jan. 1937): 7-8.

———. "Eso que llaman afrocubanismo musical." *Adelante* 3.35 (Apr. 1938): 5-6.

———. "Un ¡Hurra! Para *Adelante*." *Adelante* 2.24 (May 1937): 7-8.

———. *El negro en Cuba*. Havana: Alfa, 1939.

Arróm, José Juan. "La poesía afrocubana." *Revista Iberoamericana* 4.8 (1942): 379-408.

Augier, Angel. "Una inscripción geográfica." Morejón, *Recopilación* 263-82.

———. *Nicolás Guillén: notas para un estudio biográfico-crítico*. 2 vols. 2nd rev. ed. Havana: Universidad Central de Las Villas, 1965.

———. *Nicolás Guillén*. Havana: UNEAC, 1971.

"Autorizado por el Alcalde el desfile de comparsas carnavalescas durante la noche de hoy si mantienen orden." *Diario de la Marina*. Feb. 20, 1937: 5.

Ayllón Morgan, Julio. *Romancero Cubano*. Havana: Rebeldía Estudiantil, 1946.

Ayorinde, Christine. *Afro-Cuban Religiosity, Revolution, and National Identity*. Gainesville: University Press of Florida, 2004.

Bachiller y Morales, Antonio and de Landaluze, Víctor Patricio. *Tipos y costumbres de la isla de Cuba*. Havana: Miguel de Villa, 1881.

Ballagas, Emilio, ed. *Antología de la poesía negra hispanoamericana*. Madrid: Aguilar, 1935.

———."Comparsa habanera." *Cuaderno de poesía negra*. Santa Clara: La Nueva, 1934, n.p.

―――, ed. *Mapa de la poesía negra americana*. Buenos Aires: Pleamar, 1946.
―――. "Poesía negra liberada." *Universidad* 4 (1937): 5-6.
―――. "Situación de la poesía afroamericana." *Revista Cubana* 21(1946): 5-65.
Baquero, Gastón. *Darío, Cernuda, y otros temas poéticos*. Madrid: Editora Nacional, 1969.
Barreal Fernández, Isaac et al. *Fiestas populares tradicionales cubanas*. Havana: Ciencias Sociales, 1998.
Benítez-Rojo, Antonio. "Música y literatura en el Caribe." *Horizontes: Revista de la La Pontífica Universidad Católica de Puerto Rico* (Sept. 6, 2004). http://www.pucpr/hz/007.html.
―――. "Música y nación: El rol de la música en la construcción de la nación cubana." *Encuentro* 8-9(1998): 43-54.
―――. *The Repeating Island: the Caribbean and the Postmodern Perspective*. 2nd ed. Trans. James E. Maraniss. Durham: Duke University Press, 1996.
Berreda-Tomás, Pedro M. "Alejo Carpentier: Dos visions del negro, dos conceptos de la novela." *Hispania* 55.1 (1972): 34-44.
Beruff Mendieta, Antonio et al. *Las comparsas populares del carnaval habanero, cuestión resuelta*. Havana: Molina y Cía, 1937.
―――. "Comunicación del Alcalde de La Habana al Presidente de la Sociedad de Estudios Afrocubanos solicitando la opinión y el consejo de dicha Sociedad sobre el resurgimiento de las comparsas populares habaneras." Beruff Mendieta et al. 7-8.
―――. Letter to Colonel José E. Pedraza (Chief of Cuba's National Police). Feb. 9, 1937. *Diario de la Marina*. Feb. 10, 1937: 9.
Betancourt, Juan René. *El negro: ciudadano del futuro*. Havana: Cárdenas y Cía, 1959.
Bettelheim, Judith. "Carnival in Santiago de Cuba." Betthelheim 94-126.
―――, ed. *Cuban Festivals: A Century of Afro-Cuban Culture*. Princeton: Markus-Wiener, 2001.
Bianchi Ross, Ciro. "La Chambelona." http://www.cirobianchi.blogia.com/2006/121902-la-chambelona.php.
Branche, Jerome. *Colonialism and Race in Luso-Hispanic Literature*. Columbia: University of Missouri Press, 2006.
Brandon, George. *Santería: from Africa to the New World*. Bloomington: Indiana University Press, 1993.
Brea, Rafael. "Un día en San Juan de Hoyos." *Del Caribe* [Santiago de Cuba] 2.5 (1985):62-65.
Brea, Rafael and José Millet. "Acerca de la presencia africana en los carnavales de Santiago de Cuba." *Revista de la Biblioteca Nacional José Martí* 3 (1987): 99-116.
―――. *Barrio, comparsa y carnaval santiaguero*. Santiago de Cuba: Casa del Caribe, 1997.
―――. "Glossary of Popular Festivals." Bettelheim. 173-205.
Bronfman, Alejandra. *Measures of Equality: Social Science, Citizenship, and Race in Cuba, 1902-1940*. Chapel Hill: University of North Carolina Press, 2004.
Brown, David H. "The Afro-Cuban Festival 'Day of the Kings': An Annotated Glossary." Bettelheim 41-93.

———. *The Light Inside: Abakuá Society, Arts, and Cuban Cultural History*. Washington, D.C.: Smithsonian, 2003.

———. *Santería Enthroned: Art, Ritual, and Innovation in an Afro-Cuban Religion*. Chicago: University of Chicago Press, 2003.

Bueno, Salvador. "Nicolás Guillén y el movimiento poético 'Afrocubano.'" *Revista de la Biblioteca Nacional José Martí* 24(1982): 53–66.

Bush, Roland E. "Cuba's Nicolás Guillén: A Poet of Negritude." *Afro-Hispanic Review* 4.2–3 (1985): 5–10.

Cabrera, Lydia. *Anaforuana: Ritual y símbolos de la iniciación en la sociedad secreta Abakuá*. Madrid: Ediciones R, 1975.

———. *Los animales en el folklore y la magia de Cuba*. Miami: Universal, 1988.

———. *El monte: notas sobre las religions, la magia, las supersticiones y el folklore de los negros criollos y el pueblo de Cuba*. (1954) 7th ed. Miami: Universal, 1992.

———. *Páginas sueltas*. Ed. Isabel Castellans. Miami: Universal, 1994.

———. *La sociedad secreta Abakuá, narrada por viejos adeptos*. (1959) Miami: Universal, 2005.

———. *Vocabulario Congo: el Bantú que se habla en Cuba*. Rev. ed. by Isabel Castellanos. Miami: Universal, 2000.

Caignet, Felix B. *A golpe de maracas: poemas negros en papel mulato*. Havana: Casin, 1950.

———. Letter to Eusebia Cosme. Feb. 12, 1936. *Eusebia Cosme Papers (1927–1973)*, Sc MG. Manuscripts, Archives and Rare Books Division, Schomburg Center for Research in Black Culture. New York Public Library.

Camacho Padro, José. "El bando del Alcalde prohibiendo las mascaradas de mal gusto. Cómo deberán proceder los grupos de máscaras que quieran pasear por la vía pública." Pérez-Ródríguez, Vol. 1. 244–46.

Camín, Alfonso. *Carey y nuevos poemas*. Mexico: Revista Norte, 1945.

———. "Carnaval en la Habana." *Maracas y otros poemas* 31–38.

———. "Demasajova." *Revista de Avance* 1.2 (March 15, 1927): 27.

———. *Entre palmeras: vidas emigrantes*. Mexico: Revista Norte, 1958.

———. *Maracas y otros poemas*. Mexico: Impresora Azteca, 1952.

Carbonell, Walterio. *Cómo surgió la cultura nacional*. Havana: Ediciones Yaka, 1961.

"Carnival Joys All Prohibited." *Havana Daily Post*. Feb. 18, 1917. 2.

Carpentier, Alejo. *Crónicas*. 2 vols. Havana: Arte y Literatura, 1976.

———. *Dos poemas afro-cubanos (Deux Poèmes afro-cubains)*. "Mari-Sabel" y "Juego santo." Música de Alejandro Carcía Caturla. Paris: Maurice Senart, 1930.

———. *Écue-Yamba-Ó*. (1933) *Obras completas de Alejo Carpentier*. Vol 1. Mexico: Siglo XXI, 1983. 21–193.

———. "Fiesta" (1929). *Poemas de las Antillas*. Trans. Carmen Suárez León. Havana: Instituto Cubano del libro, 1989.

———. "Juego santo" (1927). *Obras completas de Alejo Carpentier*. Vol 1. Mexico: Siglo XXI, 1983. 218–19.

———. "Liturgia." Guirao 77–80.

———. *Music in Cuba* (1946). Trans. Alan West-Durán. Minneapolis: University of Minnesota Press, 2001.

———. "Problemática de la actual novela latinoamericana." *Tientos y diferencias.* Mexico: UNAM, 1964. 5–46.

———. "El recuerdo de Amadeo Roldán." Carpentier, *Crónicas Vol. 2.* 130–38.

Carrión, Juan Manuel. Ed. *Ethnicity, Race and Nationality in the Caribbean.* Río Piedras: Institute of Caribbean Studies, University of Puerto Rico, 1997.

Cartey, Wilfred A. *Black Images.* New York: Teachers College Press, 1970.

Castellanos, Israel. "El diablito ñáñigo." *Archivos del Folklore Cubano* 3.4 (1928): 27–37.

———. "The Evolution of Criminology in Cuba." *Journal of Criminal Law and Criminology* 24.1 (1933): 218–29.

———. *Medicina legal y criminología afro-cubanas.* Havana: n.p., 1937.

———."El tipo brujo." *Revista Bimestre Cubana* 9.5 (Sep.–Oct. 1914): 328–49.

Castellanos, Orlando. "Felix B. Caignet, escritor radial." *Palabras grabadas.* Ed. Castellanos. Havana: Unión, 1996. 9–23.

Castillo Boloy, Estanislao. Letter. *La Prensa.* March 16, 1916: 4.

Chávez Álvarez, Ernesto. *El crimen de la niña Cecilia: La brujería en Cuba como fenómeno social (1902–1925).* Havana: Ciencias Sociales, 1991.

Clark, Mary Ann. *Santería: Correcting the Myths and Uncovering the Realities of a Growing Religion.* Eastport, CT: Praeger, 2007.

"Las comparsas." *Cuba y América* [Havana]. March 16, 1912: 8.

"Las comparsas." *Diario de la Marina.* Feb. 14, 1937: 1.

"Las comparsas carnavalescas constituirán una poderosa atracción turística." *Diario de la Marina.* Feb. 6, 1937: 3.

Cosme, Eusebia. *Eusebia Cosme Papers (1927–1973), Sc MG.* Manuscripts, Archives, and Rare Books Division, Schomburg Center for Research in Black Culture. New York Public Library.

Coulthard, G. R. *Race and Colour in Caribbean Literature.* Oxford: Oxford University Press, 1962.

Courlander, Harold. "Abakwa Meeting in Guanabacoa." *Journal of Negro History* 29.4 (1944): 461–70.

Cuéllar Vizcaino, Manuel. "El Guillén que usted no conoce." *La Gaceta de Cuba* 1.8–9 (1962): 6.

———."La leyenda de Sensemayá." *Adelante* 1.6 (Nov. 1935): 15.

Davis, Darién. "¿Criollo o mulato?: Cultural Identity in Cuba (1930–1960)." *Carrión.* 69–95.

DeCosta, Miriam, ed. *Blacks in Hispanic Literature.* Port Washington, NY: Kennikat, 1977.

DeCosta-Willis, Miriam. "Arozarena's Black Song." *Revista/Review Interamericana* 7 (Fall 1976): 348–55.

———. "Marcelino Arozarena's Journey to His Roots." *Afro-Hispanic Review.* 17.2 (1998): 12–18.

"El Departamento de Gobernación Municipal autoriza comparsas que saldrán hoy." *Diario de la Marina.* Feb.7, 1937.

Díaz-Ayala, Cristóbal. "De congas y comparsas." *Latin Beat Magazine* 15.1 (Feb. 2005): 30–31.

Di Leo, Octavio. *El descubrimiento de África en Cuba y Brasil*. Mexico City: Colibrí, 2001.

Duno-Gottberg, Luis. *Solventando las diferencias: la ideología del mestizaje en Cuba*. Madrid: Iberoamericana, 2003.

Ellis, Keith. *Cuba's Nicolás Guillén: Poetry and Ideology*. Toronto: University of Toronto Press, 1983.

Esquenazi Pérez, Martha E. "Fiestas de antecedente africano." Barreal Fernández et al. 74–87.

Estivil, Osvaldo. "Conga de la Habana." *Cuban Big Bands 1940–1942*. CD. Harlequin, 1996.

Farr, Jory. *Rites of Rhythm: The Music of Cuba*. New York: Harper Collins, 2003.

Feliú Herrera, Virtudes. *El carnaval cubano*. Havana: Ediciones Extramuros, 2002.

———. *Fiestas y tradiciones cubanas*. Havana: Centro de Investigación y Desarrollo de la Cultura Cubana Juan Marinello, 2003.

Fermoselle, Rafael. *Política y color en Cuba: La guerrita de 1912*. 2nd ed. Mexico City: Colibrí, 1998.

Fernández Carillo, Enrique. "El ñáñigo; carta cerrada y abierta." Bachiller y Morales 141–45.

Fernández de Castro, José Antonio. "La literatura negra actual de Cuba (1902–1934): Datos para un estudio." *Estudios Afrocubanos*. 4.1–4 (1940): 3–22.

Fernández de la Vega, Oscar and Alberto Herrera Pamies. *Iniciación a la poesía afroamericana*. Miami: Universal, 1973.

Fernández Retamar, Roberto. *Poesía contemporánea en Cuba*. Havana: Orígenes, 1954.

Fernández Robaina, Tomás. *Bibliografía sobre estudios afro-americanos*. Havana: Biblioteca Nacional José Martí, 1968.

———. *Bibliografía de temas afrocubanos*. Havana: Biblioteca Nacional José Martí, 1985.

———. *El negro en Cuba 1902–1958: Apuntes para la historia de la lucha contra la discriminación racial*. Havana: Ciencias Sociales, 1990.

"La Fiesta del Miramar." *Diario de la Marina*. Feb. 16, 1937. 7.

Font, Mauricio A. and Alfonso W. Quiroz, eds. *Cuban Counterpoint: The Legacy of Fernando Ortiz*. Lanham, MD: Lexington Books, 2005.

Freyre de Andrade, Fernando. "Los carnavales: Bando del alcalde." *Diario de la Marina*. Jan. 25, 1913, morning ed.: 5

Fuente, Alejandro de la. *A Nation for All: Race, Inequality, and Politics in Twentieth-Century Cuba*. Chapel Hill: University of North Carolina Press, 2001.

Fuentes, Carlos. *La nueva novela hispanoamericana*. Mexico City: Joaquín Mortiz, 1969.

García, Mariana and Ada Roda Le Riverend, eds. *Diccionario de la literatura cubana*. 2 vols. Havana: Letras Cubanas, 1980.

"Gómez Sees End of Cuba Revolt." *New York Times*. May 23, 1912: 1.

González, Ana. "Romance negro del negro" (1935). Ruiz del Vizo. *Black Poetry*. 81–82.

González, Hilario. "Alejo Carpentier: precursor del 'movimiento' afrocubano." Carpentier, *Obras completas*. 11–20.
González Echevarría, Roberto. *Alejo Carpentier: The Pilgrim at Home*. 2nd ed. Austin: University of Texas Press, 1990.
González-Pérez, Armando. *Acercamiento a la literature afrocubana*. Miami: Universal, 1994.
———. *Antología clave de la poesía afroamericana*. Madrid: Alcalá, 1976.
González-Wippler, Migene. *Santería: magia Africana en Latinoamérica*. Mexico City: Diana, 1976.
Graham, Richard, ed. *The Idea of Race in Latin America, 1870–1940*. Austin: University of Texas Press, 1990.
Grenet, Eliseo. "Cavalcada de las congas" [ca. 1933]. *Cubans in Europe 1929-1934*. Vol 2. CD. Harlequin, 1996.
Guerra, Pablo W. "Carnaval politico." Pérez-Rodríguez, Vol. 2, 324–26.
Guerra, Ramiro. *Calibán Danzante*. Havana: Letras Cubanas, 2008.
Guillén, Nicolás. "Cada año es carnaval." *Bohemia*. March 13, 1949. 44–45, 73–74, 80.
———. "La canción del bongó." *Summa Poética*. 77–78.
———. "Canto negro." *Summa poética*. 79–80.
———. *Cuba Libre. Poems by Nicolás Guillén*. Trans. Langston Hughes and Ben Frederic Carruthers. Los Angeles: Ward Richie, 1948.
———. "¡Negra, mueve la cintura!" (1941). *Prosa de Prisa*. Buenos Aires: Editorial Hernández, 1968. 20–23.
———. "Prólogo." *Sóngoro cosongo: poemas mulatos*. Havana: Ucar, García, y Cia, 1931. 9–10.
———. "Secuestro de la mujer de Antonio." *Summa Poética*. 85–86.
———. "Sensemayá." *West Indies, Ltd*. Havana: Ucar, García, y Cía, 1934. 27–29.
———. "Sones y soneros." *Diario de la Marina*. June 15, 1930. 3rd sec. 4.
———. *Summa poética*. Luis Íñigo Madrigal, ed. Madrid: Cátedra, 1990.
Guirao, Ramón. "Décimas." *Órbita de la poesía afrocubana* by Guiaro. 58-62.
———, ed. *Órbita de la poesía afrocubana: 1928–1937*. Havana: Ucar, García, y Cía, 1938.
Guzmán Moré, Jorgelina. "Notas para una historia de las comparsas en el centro Habana." http://www.lajiribilla.co.cu-/2005/n214_06/214_15.html.
Helg, Aline. "Afro-Cuban Protest: The Partido Independiente de Color, 1908–1912." *Cuban Studies* 21 (1991): 101–21.
———. "Black Men, Racial Stereotyping, and Violence in the U.S. South and Cuba at the Turn of the Century." *Comparative Studies in Society and History* 42.3 (July 2000): 576–604.
———. *Our Rightful Share: The Afro-Cuban Struggle for Equality, 1886–1912*. Chapel Hill: University of North Carolina Press, 1995.
———. "Race in Argentina and Cuba, 1880–1930: Theory, Politics, and Popular Reaction." Graham. 38–69.
Hernández Catá, Alfonso. "Rumba." Guirao 127.
Hernández Santana, Gilberto. *Semblanzas negras*. Havana: Alfa, 1939.
Herrera, Roberto. "La poesía mulata de Emilio Ballagas." *Círculo. Publicación de Cultura Panamericana* 10(1981): 93–103.

Ishemo, Shubi L. "From Africa to Cuba: an Historical Analysis of the Sociedad Secreta Abakuá (Ñáñiguismo)." *Review of African Political Economy* 92 (2002): 253–72.
Jackson, Richard L. "The *Afrocriollo* Movement Revisited." *Afro-Hispanic Review* 3.1 (1984): 5–9.
———. *The Afro-Spanish American Author: An Annotated Bibliography of Criticism.* New York: Garland, 1980.
———. *The Afro-Spanish American Author, II: The 1980s. An Annotated Bibliography of Criticism.* West Cornwall, CT: Locust Hill, 1989.
———. *The Black Image in Latin American Literature.* Albuquerque: University of New Mexico Press, 1976.
Jahn, Janheinz. *A History of Neo-African Literature.* Trans. Oliver Cobun. London: Faber and Faber, 1968.
———. *Muntu: An Outline of New African Culture.* Trans. Marjorie Grene. New York: Grove, 1961.
Janney, Frank. *Alejo Carpentier and his Early Works.* London: Tamesis, 1981.
Jiménez, Luis A. "Afro-Cuban Culture, Ecology, and Climate in 'La comparsa' by Felipe Pichardo Moya." *Climate and Literature: Reflections of Environment.* Janet Pérez and Wendell Aycock, eds. Lubbock: Texas Tech University Press, 1995. 123–30.
Klein, Elliot. "Re: Sensemayá and Juego santo." Message to the author. March 15, 2009. E-mail.
Kubayanda, Josaphat. *The Poet's Africa: Africanness in the Poetry of Nicolás Guillén and Aimé Césaire.* New York: Greenwood, 1990.
Kutzinski, Vera. *Against the American Grain: Myth and History in William Carlos Williams, Jay Wright, and Nicolás Guillén.* Baltimore: Johns Hopkins University Press, 1987.
———. "The Miraculous Weapons of Nicolás Guillén and Aimé Césaire." *Callaloo* 22 (1984): 140–50.
———. *Sugar's Secrets: Race and the Erotics of Cuban Nationalism.* Charlottesville: University of Virginia Press, 1993.
Lachatañeré, Rómulo. *Manual de Santería.* (1942) Havana: Ciencias Sociales, 1995.
———. *¡¡Oh, mío Yemayá!!* (1938). Havana: Ciencias Sociales, 1992.
———. *El sistema religioso de los afrocubanos.* Havana: Ciencias Socials, 2001.
Larrier, Renee. "Racism in the United States: an Issue in Caribbean Poetry." *Journal of Caribbean Poetry* 2.2 (1981): 51–71.
Lázaro, Ángel. "Alfonso Camín en México." Camín, *Maracas y otros poemas.* 229–34.
Leante, César. "Confesiones sencillas de un escritor barroco." *Arias* 57–70.
Leyva, Armando. "Sonsonete para un libro de sones." Caignet, *A golpe de maracas* 7–13.
Llarch, Enrique. "Las elecciones, los partidos políticos y los negros." *Adelante* 1.5 (Oct. 1935): 11.
Lohengrin. "Crisis de civismo." *La Prensa.* March 13, 1916: 4.
Madrigal, Luis Íñigo, ed. *Summa poética.* Nicolás Guillén. Madrid: Cátedra, 1990.
Mañach, Jorge. *Historia y estilo* (1944). *Edición facsimilar.* Miami: Editorial Cubana, 1994.
Mansour, Mónica. *La poesía negrista.* Mexico: Era, 1973.

Maribona, Armando. "La comparsa se va." *Diario de la Marina* (Sección Dominical). March 21, 1937: n.p.

Marinello, Juan. "Acción y omisión." *Adelante* 2.15 (Aug. 1936): 7, 10.

Márquez, Robert. "Introduction." *¡Patria o Muerte! The Great Zoo and Other Poems by Nicolás Guillén*. Ed. Márquez. 13–29.

Martín, Juan Luis. *Écue, Changó y Yemayá: Ensayos sobre la sub-religión de los afro-cubanos*. Havana: Cultural, 1930.

———. "Falsa interpretación afrocubana." *Adelante* 3.25 (June 1937): 7.

Martínez Chao, Francisco. "La Chambelona y las elecciones en Cuba." *Radio Cadena Habana*. Oct. 18, 2007. http://www.cadenahabana.cu/mirada/especiales/especialeselecciones01100807.htm.

Mason, Michael Atwood. *Living Santería: Rituals and Experiences in an Afro-Cuban Religion*. Washington: Smithsonian Institution, 2002.

Matibag, Eugenio. *Afro-Cuban Religious Experience: Cultural Reflections in Narrative*. Gainesville: University Press of Florida, 1996.

Melon, Alfred. "El poeta de la síntesis." Morejón, *Recopilación* 199–242.

Mendoza Marrero, Francisco. "El carnaval pasa . . ." *La Prensa*. March 12, 1916: 4.

Meruelo, Anisia. "Estampa habanera." Ruiz del Vizo, *Poesía negra*. 95–96.

Miahle, Pierre Toussaint Frédéric. *Albúm pintoresco de la Isla de Cuba*. Havana: B. May y Ca., c. 1855.

Miller, Ivor. "A Secret Society Goes Public: The Relationship Between Abakuá and Cuban Popular Culture." *African Studies Review* 43.1 (April 2000): 161–88.

———. *Voice of the Leopard: African Secret Societies and Cuba*. Jackson: University Press of Mississippi, 2009.

"Mobilize Fleet to Go to Cuba." *New York Times*. May 26, 1912: 1.

Moliner Castañeda, Israel. "Las comparsas." *Unión* (Jan.–Mar. 1986): 57–69.

Moore, Robin D. *Nationalizing Blackness: Afrocubanismo and Artistic Revolution in Havana, 1920–1940*. Pittsburgh: University of Pittsburgh Press, 1997.

Morales, Jorge Luis, ed. *Poesía afroantillana y negrista*. 2nd rev. ed. Río Piedras: University of Puerto Rico Press, 2000.

Morejón, Nancy. *Nación y mestizaje en Nicolás Guillén*. Havana: Unión, 1982.

———, ed. *Recopilación de textos sobre Nicolás Guillén*. Havana: Casa de las Américas, 1994.

Moreno Fajardo, Dennis. "Introducción." Barreal Fernández 5–19.

Mullen, Edward. *Afro-Cuban Literature: Critical Junctures*. Westport, CT: Greenwood, 1998.

Müller-Berg, Klaus. "Alejo Carpentier." *Latin American Writers*, Vol. 2. Eds. Carlos A. Solé and Maria Isabel Abreu. New York: Scribner's, 1989. 1019–1031.

Noble, Enrique, ed. *Literatura afro-hispanoamericana: poesía y prosa de ficción*. Lexington, MA: Xerox College Publishing, 1973.

Ojo-Ade, Femi. "De origen africano, soy cubano: African Elements in the Literature of Cuba." *African Literature Today. Number 9: Africa, America and the Caribbean*. Ed. Eldred Durosimi Jones. New York: Africana Publishing, 1978, 47–57.

Olliz-Boyd, Antonio. "The Concept of Black Esthetics as Seen in Selected Works of Three

Latin American Writers: Machado de Asis, Nicolás Guillén, and Adalberto Ortiz." Diss. Stanford University, 1974.

Orovio, Helio. *El carnaval habanero*. Havana: Extramuros, 2005.

———. *Cuban Music From A to Z*. Trans. Ricardo Bardo Portilla and Lucy Davies. Durham, NC: Duke University Press, 2004.

Orovio, Consuelo Naranjo and Miguel Ángel Puig-Samper Mulero. "Spanish Intellectuals and Fernando Ortiz (1900–1941)." Font and Quiroz 9–38.

Ortiz, Fernando. "The Afro-Cuban Festival Day of Kings." Trans. Jean Stubbs. Bettelheim 1–40.

———. *La antigua fiesta afrocubana del Día de Reyes*. (1920) Rev. ed. Havana: Ministerio de Cultura, 1960.

———. *Los bailes y el teatro de los negros en el folklore de Cuba*. (1951). Madrid: Música Mundana Maqueda, 1998.

———. "Brujos y santeros." *Estudios Afrocubanos*. 2.1–4 (1939): 88.

———. "Los cabildos afrocubanos." (1921). *Orbita de Fernándo Ortiz*. Ed. Julio Le Riverend. Havana: Unión, 1973. 121–34.

———. "Las carrozas americanas." *Cuba y América* [Havana] March 28, 1908: 3.

———. "Las comparsas de la Habana." *Social* 21.3 (March 1937): 1, 59–60.

———. *Estudios etnosociológicos*. Comp. Isaac Barreal Fernández. Havana: Ciencias Sociales, 1991.

———. "Los factores humanos de la cubanidad." (1939). *Fernando Ortiz y la cubanidad*. Ed. Norma Suárez. Havana: Unión, 1996. 1–35.

———. *Glosario de afronegrismos*. (1924). Havana: Ciencias Sociales, 1990.

———. *Hampa afro-cubana: Los negros brujos* (1906). Havana: Editorial de Ciencias Sociales, 1995.

———. *Hampa afro-cubana: Los negros esclavos*. Havana: Revista Bimestre Cubana, 1916.

———. "Informe del doctor Fernando Ortiz, presidente de la Sociedad de Estudios Afrocubanos, aprobado por la Junta Directiva de dicha Sociedad, pronunciándose en favor del resurgimiento de las comparsas populares habaneras." Beruff Mendieta 9–20. [Reprinted in *Estudios Afrocubanos* 5 (1945–1946): 129–41]

———. *Los instrumentos de la música afrocubana*. 2 Vols. (1952). Madrid: Música Mundana Maqueda, 1996.

———. Letter to Juilo Ayllón Morgan. Feb. 10, 1946. Ayllón Morgan 7–9.

———. "La religion en la poesía mulata" (1937). *Estudios etnosociológicos* 141–75.

———. "La tragedia de los ñáñigos." *Cuadernos Americanos* 9.4 (1950): 79–101.

———. "Los últimos versos mulatos." *Revista Bimestre Cubana* 5.35 (1935): 321–36.

———. "Los viejos carnavales habaneros." *Estudios etnosociológicos* 202–21.

Ortiz, Fernando, et al. "Las comparsas populares del carnaval habanero." *Estudios Afrocubanos* 5 (1945–1946): 129–148.

Palés Matos, Luis. "Majestad negra." *Tuntún de pasa y grifería*. San Juan: Biblioteca de autores puertorriqueños, 1937. 57–58.

Pancrazio, James J. *The Logic of Fetishism: Alejo Carpentier and the Cuban Tradition*. Lewisburgh, PA: Bucknell University Press, 2004.

Pedroso, Regino. "Hermano negro." *Antología de la poesía negra hispanoamericana*. Ed. Emilio Ballagas. Madrid: Aguilar, 1935. 155–57.

Pereda Valdés, Idelfonso. *Lo negro y lo mulato en la poesía cubana*. Montevideo: Ciudadela, 1970.

Pérez, Louis A. *Cuba: Between Reform and Revolution*. 2nd ed. New York: Oxford University Press, 1995.

———. *Cuba Under the Platt Amendment, 1902–1934*. Pittsburgh: University of Pittsburgh Press, 1986.

———. "Politics, Peasants, and People of Color: The 1912 'Race War' in Cuba Reconsidered." *Latin American Historical Review* 66.3 (1986): 509–39.

Pérez-Heredia, Alexander, ed. *Epistolario de Nicolás Guillén*. Havana: letras Cubanas, 2002.

Pérez-Rodríguez, Nancy. *El carnaval santiaguero*. 2 vols. Santiago de Cuba: Editorial Oriente, 1998.

Pichardo Moya, Felipe. *La ciudad de los espejos: antología poética*. Ed. Luis Suardíaz. Camagüey: Acana, 1992.

———. "La comparsa." *Gráfico* 7.160 (March 25, 1916): 8.

Piñeiro, Ignacio. "Noche de conga." *Septeto Nacional Ignacio Piñeiro*. CD. Egrem, 2006.

Pino y Águila, Ángel. "Decreto." Pérez Rodríguez, Vol. 2 15–16.

Pinto, Ángel C. "Una aclaración." *Adelante* 3.25 (June 1937): 10–11, 20.

Polit, Carlos E. "Imagen inocente del negro en cuatro poetas antillanos." *Sin Nombre* 5.2 (1974): 43–60.

Raigada, José. "Motivos de carnaval." Pérez Rodríguez, Vol. 2 48–49.

Rice, Argyll Pryor. *Emilio Ballagas: poeta o poesía*. Mexico: Ediciones de Andrea, 1966.

Roche y Monteagudo, Rafael. *La policía y sus misterios en Cuba*. 2nd ed. Havana: Rambla, Bouza, y Cía, 1914.

———. *La policía y sus misterios en Cuba*. 3rd exp. ed. Havana: La Moderna Poesía, 1925.

Rohmer, Sax. *The Insidious Dr. Fu Manchu* [1913]. World eBook Library PGCC Collection #173. http://WorldLibrary.net.

Roig de Leuchsenring, Emilio. "Las comparsas carnavalescas de La Habana en 1937." *Estudios Afrocubanos* 5 (1945–1946): 148–75.

———. "Dos actualidades cubanas: el interés por lo histórico; las comparsas habaneras." Beruff Mendieta 39–44.

Rojas, Jack. *Tambor Sin Cuero*. Madrid: Agora, 1968.

Rol Vinet, Raymundo. "Después de las comparsas." *Adelante* 2.23 (April 1937): 1.

Roy, Maya. *Cuban Music*. Trans. Denise Asfar and Gabriel Asfar. Princeton: Markus Wiener, 2002.

Ruffinelli, Jorge. *Poesía y descolonización: Viaje por la poesía de Nicolás Guillén*. Oaxaca: Oasis, 1985.

Ruiz del Vizo, Hortensia. *Black Poetry of the Americas*. Miami: Universal, 1972.

———. *Poesía negra del Caribe y otras áreas*. Miami: Universal, 1971.

Ruscalleda Bercedóniz, Jorge María. *El negro en la poesía cubana (1608–1936)*. Aguadilla, PR: Mester, 2001.

Saenz, José Manuel. "Las comparsas, su trayectoria histórica." *Actas del Folklore* 4 (April 1961): 21–25.
Salas Aranda, Mariano. Letter to Antonio Beruff Mendieta (Feb. 6, 1937). *Adelante* 2.22 (March 1937): 4.
Sánchez, María Luisa. "Zafra y comparsas." *Adelante* 2.23 (April 1937): 13.
"Se acerca la comparsa" [ca. 1940]. *Cuando salí de la Habana*. CD. Cubanacán, 1998.
Smart, Ian. "Arozarena's Poetic Language and the Issue of Ebonics." *Afro-Hispanic Review* 17.2 (1998): 19–27.
———. *Nicolás Guillén: Popular Poet of the Caribbean*. Columbia: University of Missouri Press, 1990.
Sosa Rodríguez, Enrique. *Los ñáñigos*. Havana: Casa de las Américas, 1982.
Staten, Clifford. *The History of Cuba*. New York: Palgrave, 2003.
Suárez, Adolfo. "Acusado de poeta: entrevista a Marcelino Arozarena." *La Gaceta de Cuba*. 96 (September 1971): 10–14.
Suárez, Albino. Introduction. *Alfonso Camín. Poemas*. Oviedo: Caja de Ahorros de Asturias, 1990. 7–29.
Sublette, Ned. *Cuba and Its Music: From the First Drums to the Mambo*. Chicago: Chicago Review, 2004.
Tallet, José Zacarías. "Quintín Barahona." Guirao 68–73.
———. "La rumba." Guirao 65–68.
Tarazona, Fernando. *Estampas afro-cubanas*. Havana: O. Echevarría y Cía, 1939.
Tejada, Valentín. "Las antologías de poesía cubana y Alfonso Camín." Camín, *Entre palmeras* 695–701.
Thomas, Hugh. *Cuba: The Pursuit of Freedom*. New York: Harper and Row, 1971.
"To Hold No Carnival In Havana This Year." *Havana Daily Post*. Feb. 17, 1917. 10.
Torre, Guillermo de. "Literatura de color." *Revista Bimestre Cubana* 38.1 (1937): 5–11.
Torres-Rioseco, Arturo. *The Epic of Latin American Literature*. New York: Oxford University Press, 1942.
Tous, Adriana. *La poesía de Nicolás Guillén*. Madrid: Cultura Hispánica, 1971.
Trujillo y Monegas, José. *Los criminales de Cuba y D. José Trujillo: Narración de los servicios prestados en el cuerpo de policía de la Habana por D. José Trujillo y Monegas*. Barcelona: Fidel Giró, 1882.
Urrutía, Gustavo E. "The Black Man's Contribution to Cuban Culture." *The Americas* 34.2 (1977): 244–51.
———. "Las comparsas." *Diario de la Marina*. May 9, 1931: 2.
———. "Una frase de Vasconcelos I." *Diario de la Marina*. Feb. 11, 1937: 2.
———. "Una frase de Vasconcelos II." *Diario de la Marina*. Feb. 12, 1937: 2.
Valdés-Cruz, Rosa E. *La poesía negroide en América*. New York: Las Américas, 1970.
———. "En torno al poema 'Liturgia' de Alejo Carpentier." *Explicación de Textos Literarios* 5.1 (1976): 29–33.
Vasconcelos, Ramón. "Alfilerazos" (Reply to letter from Estanislao Castillo Boloy). *La Prensa*. March 16, 1916: 4. *
———. "Al margen de los días. Complejos." Beruff Mendieta, 33–39.
———. "Al primer tapón, zurrapas." *La Prensa*. March 7, 1916: 4.*

———. "Comparsas." *La Prensa*. March 2, 1916: 4.*
———. "Dos letras." *La Prensa*. March 13, 1916: 4. *
———. "La fuga hacia la selva." *La Prensa*. March 24, 1916: 4. *
———. "Gracías, Lohengrin." *La Prensa*. March 10, 1916: 4, 7. *
———. "Motivos de son." *Diario de la Marina*. June 6, 1930: 4.
———. "Suma y sigue." *La Prensa*. March 8, 1916: 4.*
Vázquez, Eduardo "Jaruco." "La conga de Jaruco" [1937]. *Lecuona Cuban Boys Volume 5*. CD. Harlequin, 1993.
———. "Conga de la Habana" [1936]. *Lecuona Cuban Boys 1935-1938*. CD. Music Memoria, 1993.
Venture Young, Ann. "The Black Woman in Afro-Caribbean Poetry." DeCosta 137–42.
Villa, Álvaro de. "La comparsa." *Mi Habana . . . poemas desde el destierro*. Miami: Universal, 1971, 83–84.
Villoch, Federico. "Las comparsas de 1939." *Carteles*. March 1939. 18-19.
Vitier, Cintio. "Hallazgo del son." Morejón 147–58.
———. "Introducción." *Obra poética de Emilio Ballagas*. Miami: Mnemosyne, 1969.
"Washington Wants Facts." *New York Times*. May 25, 1912: 2.
Williams, Claudette. *Charcoal and Cinnamon: The Politics of Color in Spanish Caribbean Literature*. Gainesville: University Press of Florida, 2000.
Williams, Lorna V. *Self and Society in the Poetry of Nicolás Guillén*. Baltimore: Johns Hopkins University Press, 1982.
Zamcois, Eduardo. "Loa al progreso del negro." *La Prensa*. Nov. 14, 1915: 6.
Zohn-Muldoon, Ricardo. "The Song of the Snake: Silvestre Revueltas' *Sensemayá*." *Latin American Music Review* 19.2 (Fall/Winter 1998): 133–59.

Index

Page references in italics refer to illustrations

Abakuá brotherhoods, 20, 29; Carpentier's knowledge of, 56–57; conflicts among, 62–65; government actions against, 80; of Havana, 221–22; healing system of, 98; ideograms of, 98, *98*; in "Juego santo," 54, 57–65; lodges of, 58, 62–65, *63*, *75*, 301n3, 312n3; multiethnic members of, 74; musical instruments of, 58–60, 66–67; music of, 65–69; processions of, *55*; silk scarves of, 68–69; snake protectors of, 103; as symbol for Afrocubanismo, 61; terminology of, 58, 65; violence associated with, 62–64, 222; voting influence of, 141. *See also Ñáñiguismo*

Abakuá rites: and carnival ensembles, 60–61; *comparsas* and, 70, 77, 96; Divine Voice in, 225; government propaganda on, 61–62; *íremes* in, 61; in "Juego santo," 54, 57–65; percussion in, 66–67; religious syncretism in, 76; unofficial festivals during, 59, 60; use of Catholic objects, 224–25

Abasí (Abakuá supreme being), 225

Acuña L'azcano, Tomás: on *comparsas* debate, 196; *La conga*, 17

Adelante (journal), 15, *16*, 17; *comparsas* debate in, 14, 15, *15*, 196, 201; Sensemaya legend in, 303n8

Aesculapian staff, imagery of, 96–97, 305nn16–17

Afrocubanismo: Abakuá brotherhoods and, 61; African elements in, 12–13; Camín's role in, 214–17, 248–52; caricatures in, 181; Carpentier's role in, 20; distancing from colonialism, 241; in eastern Cuba, 164; exoticism in, 185, 187–88; founders of, 50; goals of, 108–13; in "Juego santo," 65–66; non-Cuban contributors to, 251; political agendas of, 46–47, 179; precursors of, 20, 26; *senseribo* in, 87; superficiality in, 181; waning years of, 185, 218

Afrocubanista poetry: African-derived culture in, 110; carnival and, 17–19; demonic possession in, 121; depiction of Afro-Cubans, 22, 127, 128; feminist critics on, 188; intoxication in, 125; negative Afro-Cuban imagery in, 122; *orishas* in, 182; outsider perspective of, 112–13; Papá Montero in, 131; precursors of, 20; racial hierarchy in, 112; sociopolitical concerns of, 113; stereotypes in, 22, 143, 185, 198; terminology of, 19–20; verbal orchestration in, 116

Afro-Cubans: in Afrocubanista poetry, 22, 127, 128; in Batista regime, 209; in Castro revolution, 208; characterization as instinctual, 116; defiance of *comparsas* bans, 26, 92; depictions as drunken, 4, 22, 124–25, 139, 308n11; disparagement of traditions, 165–68; divisions among, 27; equality for, 4, 5–6, 197–201, 209; fusion with whites, 111; governmental violence against, 152; hedonism of, 23; importance to nation, 157–58; involvement in political process, 157; job discrimination against, 151; in labor market, 51; lascivious stereotypes of, 34–35, 44–45, 194, 308n13; mainstream attitudes toward, 5; marginalization of, 5, 151; militancy among, 309n8; middle-class, 3, 4, 167, 168, 200; opposition to imperialism, 200; political apathy among, 156–59, 210; political influence of, 140–41; politicians' exploitation of, 144, 146, 149–50, 153; pseudo-scientific

Afro-Cubans—*continued*
discussions of, 203; repression of, 7; resistance to slavery, 90; rural, 309n6; slaughter under Gómez, 152; stereotypes of, 15, 22, 31, 34–35, 42, 43–45, 109; superficial depictions of, 115; support for Castro, 208; support for Gómez, 152; as symbols of oppression, 23; tourist interest in, 110, 111; visual depictions of, 127–28; in Wars of Independence, 150–51, 270; in white carnivals, 91, 92. *See also* Voters, Afro-Cuban; Women, Afro-Cuban

Aguinaldos (tips), slaves' petitions for, 1

Aguirre, Mirta: "Scottsboro," 200

El Alacrán (carnival ensemble), 36, 56; brawling by, 4; *cantos* of, 271; dances of, 256; founding of, 222; multiracial membership of, 222; traditionalism of, 227

Animal sacrifice, in "Juego santo," 70–71

Ánima sola, 136

Arará drums, 240

Armas de Arenas, Bibi: "El carnaval habanero," 267–68

Arnaz, Desi, 171

Arnaz, Desiderio: *conga* edict against, 171–72

Arnedo-Gómez, Miguel, 188, 308n1; *Writing Rumba*, 182

Arozarena, Marcelino, 87, 159; on Afrocubanismo, 181; in Asociación Adelante, 197; commitment to Afro-Cubans, 184; Cosme's recitations of, 189; depiction of Afro-Cubans, 184, 211; on Guillén, 210–12; knowledge of Afro-Cuban culture, 182, 184, 185; literary studies on, 184; Marxism of, 199, 209; sociopolitical messages of, 184–85, 186, 198, 212; support for *comparsas*, 190, 197; use of Lucumí lore, 182; West African roots of, 190

—"El antillano dormador de sones," 210–11

—*Canción negra sin color*, 199, 310n2; glossary of, 310n5

—"Canción negra sin color," 23, 198–99, 208; Afro-Cuban music in, 199; sociopolitical aspects of, 212

—"Caridad," 182; female eroticism in, 186–88; hedonism of, 211; Oshún in, 188

—"Carnaval de Santiago," 18, 23, 206–10, 310n4; music in, 208; negative images in, 186, 206, 207; poetic voice of, 207–8; political message of, 208–10; sociopolitical aspects of, 212; summer carnival in, 206

—"La comparsa del majá," 23, 95, 182; black poetic voice of, 192–93, 194, 195; eroticism of, 185, 194–95, 310n6; exoticism in, 190; folkloric antecedents of, 254; hedonism of, 211; original title of, 191; rehearsal in, 191, 192, 193; snake dances in, 190–91; stereotypes in, 189–96, 206; witchcraft in, 193

—"La conga," 23, 185, 201–6; Afro-Cuban culture in, 201, 212; composition of, 310n2; dance in, 203; exoticism in, 201; historical context of, 205; political subtext of, 204, 212; resistance in, 205; stereotypes in, 206

—"Cumbele Makumbele," 312n3

—"¡Evohé!," 198, 201, 208; Afro-Cuban music in, 199; sociopolitical aspects of, 212

—"Liturgia etiópica": dance in, 188–89; dedication to Tallet, 182, 189; first appearance of, 183

Arredondo, Alberto: on *comparsas*, 14, 15–17, 47, 197–98; on *congas*, 196–97; on political *comparsas*, 148. Works: *El negro en Cuba*, 154; "Rebeldía paradojal," 197–98

Arrollaos (dances): in "La comparsa," 34, 35, 36; criticism of, 17; in Cuban popular song, 275–76; perception as destructive, 35; snake imagery of, 34

Arróm, José Juan: on Afro-Cuban sexuality, 131–32; on Cuban unity, 111, 112; "La poesía Afro-Cubana," 110, 111, 120, 308n2

Asociación Adelante: Arozarena in, 197; on *comparsas*, 14–15, 17; on *congas*, 196, 203–4

Aspiazu, Leopoldo, 156

Assemblies, Afro-Cuban: white fear of, 136, 260

Atavism, African: attacks on, 4, 9; in *comparsas*, 26, 39, 94; in *congas*, 201; of *íremes*, 125; *ñáñiguismo* and, 30; Ortiz on, 300n2

Augier, Angel, 89, 94

Ayllón Morgan, Julio: "Romance de la comparsa," 258–59

Ayorinde, Christine, 151

Aznar, Manuel, 214

Bacardí, Emilio, 77

Bacardí Rum, sponsorship of carnival, 177, 247

Bacchanalia, Roman, 199
Bachiller y Morales, Antonio: *Tipos y costumbres de la isla de Cuba*, 71
Baile de la chancleta, in "Juego santo," 54, 68
Balbuena de Moro, Elvira: "Canto africano," 261
Ballagas, Emilio, 38; on Camín, 250; conception of Afro-Cubans, 127; knowledge of Afro-Cuban ritual, 120; poetic agenda of, 112; social concerns of, 134; in Sociedad de Estudios Afrocubanos, 137; use of nonsense words, 116–17; use of snake imagery, 95; view of *ñáñigos*, 125, 127
—*Antología de la poesía negra hispanoamericana*, 108–9, 114–15, 213, 250, 306n2
—"Comparsa habanera," 21–22, 253, 254; "Africanness" of, 115; African terms in, 256; as Afrocubanista poem, 306n1; Afro-Cuban religion in, 120; Afro-Cuban sexuality in, 128–30, 139; Afro-Cuban women in, 130, 131; in anthologies, 108, 114, 134; black performers in, 117–18, 120; *bozal* speech in, 121–22, 139; *brujería* in, 135, 139; Christianity in, 128; and "La comparsa," 117; *comparseros* in, 139; composition of, 115, 308n17; demonic possession in, 120–22, 128; *diablitos* in, 125; intoxication in, 124–25; *jitanjáforas* of, 116, 121; *marugas* in, 136–37; Papá Montero in, 130, 131; political message of, 132–34; prejudice in, 120; racial markers in, 307n3; sinister aspects of, 134–37; slavery images in, 135, 138; snake imagery in, 133; stereotypes in, 115, 122; superstition in, 135–37, 139; truncated version of, 22, 134–39; witchcraft in, 138, 193
—*Cuaderno de la poesía negra*, 121, 130; "Subirse el santo" in, 307n10; cover of, *126*, *127*; glossaries of, 306n3
—*Mapa de la poesía negra americana*, 110, 134, 250, 306n3, 308n14
Banda Rará (carnival ensemble), 257
Bantu Africans, 74, 87
Bantu language, Cuban speakers of, 87
Baquero, Gastón, 216
Batista, Fulgencio: popularity among Afro-Cubans, 209; populism under, 10
Beltrán, Daniel: "¡Bomba!," 261–62; "Carnaval," 263

Bembés (Yoruba rituals), 192, 193, 300n2; snakes in, 84
Benítez-Rojo, Antonio, 82, 86, 89; on "Sensemayá," 91, 107; on snake imagery, 305n16
Beruff Mendieta, Antonio, 10, 148, 203
Betancourt, Juan René, 122
Bettelheim, Judith, 17, 170, 176, 300n8, 310n7
Biabanga (Abakuá lodge), 312n3
Biapá (drum), 58, 302n7
Bocú (drum), 166–67, 173
Las Bolleras (carnival ensemble), 226, 264; chants of, 230; costumes of, 229–30; distribution of fritters, 230
Bombas (drums), 83
Bombe, 81; meanings of, 83–84
Bombos (bass drums), 83
Bonkó drums, 59, 66, 302n6; bans on, 164
Botellas (government sinecures), 156
Bozal speech: Caignet's use of, 165; in "Comparsa habanera," 121–22, 139; in "La conga prohibida," 169; in Cuban popular music, 274
Brandy Fundador, sponsorship of carnival, 242, *243*
Brea, Rafael, 34, 174, 310n7; on *congas* ban, 178; on *mamarrachos*, 312n4; on police violence, 205
Brikamo language, 128, 305n13; political messages in, 141, 308n1
Bronfman, Alejandra, 11, 14, 17
Brown, David H.: on Abakuá ceremonies, 59, 61; on Afro-Cuban syncretism, 224; on animal sacrifice, 70; on Arará drum, 240; on "juego," 58; on *mayomberos*, 81; on *ñáñiguismo*, 29–30; on Nasakó, 98. Works: *The Light Inside*, 8; *Santería Enthroned*, 306n18
Brujería, 34–35, 44–45; arrival of saint in, 121, 124, 127–28, 307n10; in "La comparsa," 31; in "Comparsa habanera," 139; criminalization of, 40; curses in, 136, 193; newspaper depictions of, 44; Vasconcelos on, 29; white targeting of, 9, 113
La brujería y los brujos en Cuba (1900), 122, *123*
Brujos: fear of, 8, 26; perception of criminality among, 42, 45; reports of epilepsy among, 42; stereotypes of, 43–44; use of crabs, 71–73
Bueno, Salvador, 38–39

330 · Index

Bulo (sorceress), 311n1
Bush, Roland E., 308n11

Cabildos (carnival troupes), 240; banning of, 170–71
Cabildos de nación, 1, 240
Cabrera, Lydia: Abakuá informants of, 63–64; on animal sacrifice, 70–71; on animal superstitions, 135; on birth of Abakuá, 98; on curses, 136; on *juegos*, 30; on *majás*, 84; on *mayombé*, 81; on *orishas*, 307n9; on snake imagery, 104–5, 193. Works: *El monte*, 81, 307n9; *Vocabulario Congo*, 84, 87
Caignet, Felix B.: Cosme and, 160, 161, 163; disinterest in politics, 179; radio soap operas of, 163; as social poet, 164–68; *sones* of, 165–66; as songwriter, 163; support for congas, 175; use of *bozal* speech, 165, 169
—"El bongosero," 164
—"La conga prohibida," 254, 259; Afro-Cuban tradition in, 177–78; black speaker of, 169–70, 173, 174, 177, 178; *bozal* speech in, 169; political aspects of, 178, 179–80; racial divide in, 176; Santiago *congas* in, 170; sources for, 177
—*A golpe de maracas*, 161, 162
—"Lamento veterano," 180
—"¡Que muera er son!," 165, *166*, 168
—"Soy bongosero," 309n2
—"¡Soy maraquero!," 164–65
Calunga (erotic desire), 130, 308n14
Camacho Padro, José, 171, 178, 261
Camín, Alfonso, 19; autobiography of, 213, 214, 219, 224, 234; Ballagas on, 250; Cosme's performance of, 217; defense of *sones*, 217; on European carnival, 219; journalism career of, 214; marginalization of, 248–52; observation of *comparsas*, 224, 234, 237; polemic with Mañach, 214–15, 248–49; residence in Cuba, 213–14; role in Afrocubanismo, 214–17, 248–52
—*Carey y nuevos poemas*, 215–16, 250
—"Carnaval en la Habana," 23–24, 213, 218–19; African-derived carnival in, 221; class divisions in, 24; commercialization in, 241–42; *comparsas* in, 239, 251; diablitos in, 222, 223, 239–40; *ñáñigos* in, 221; negative stereotypes in, 223–24; poetic voice of, 224, 227; publication of, 218; syncretism in, 224–25, 240; white carnival in, 232–37, 248; white women in, 233, 234
—*Carteles*, 216
—"Demasajova," 215, 216, 251
—"Elogio a la negra," 215, 217, 250
—*Entre palmeras*, 213–14
—"La negra Panchita," 215, 216
—"Negro," 217
Cantos de comparsa, 24, 254; of carnival ensembles, 268–72; double meanings in, 312n5; female sensuality in, 269; Guillén on, 305n15; sources for, 271–72; themes of, 268–71; twentieth-century, 268–72
Cantos de Eribó, 75
Carabalí people, 74; in Cuban popular song, 273
Caravia, Enrique: carnival posters of, 229, *231*, *237*, *238*
Carbonell, Luis, 310n2
Caribbean, musical instruments of, 165
Carnival: in Casa Cuba de Puerto Rico, 267–68; commercialization of, 241–42; European, 219, 232; idealization of, 264; mixed-race, 265–66; multicultural, 225–26; newspaper poems on, 259–63; as outlet for frustrations, 257, 258, 259, 261, 266; posters for, 229, *231*, *236*, *237*, *238*, *239*, *239*; role in national identity, 24, 266–68; socioeconomic divisions in, 233. *See also* Chambelonas; Comparsas; Congas
Carnival, Afro-Cuban: and Abakuá processions, 60–61; Afro-Cuban intellectuals on, 197; Afrocubanista poetry and, 17–19; banning of, 2, 20; colonial, 1–2; commercialization of, 13, 177; in "La comparsa," 20; demise of, 133; on Día de Reyes, 1–2; during early Republic, 3–5, 300n8; in *Écue-Yamba-Ó*, 56; mass appeal of, 276; *ñáñiguismo* in, 95; negative images of, 185–86; political activism during, 3, 299n1; in popular music, 272–76; pre-Lenten, 27; rehearsals for, 191–92; as remnant of past, 139–40, 207; role in national identity, 24, 266–68; of Santiago, 2, 170,

259–61; scholarship on, 17–18; "Sensemayá" and, 88–95; snake killing in, 80, 190–91
Carnival, white, 24, 173, 235; advertisements for, 245–46; Afro-Cubans in, 91, 92; blackface groups in, 248; in "Carnaval en la Habana," 232–37; *comparsas* and, 234, 248; corporate sponsorship of, 177, 241–42; of early Republic, 118, *119*; European aspects of, 232; floats in, 233, 235, 237, 242, *242*, *243*; of Havana, 218, 242, 244, 247–48; hypocrisy in, 179; materialism in, 241–42; private festivities in, 233; queens of, 220, 233, *235*, 307n9; of Santiago, 259, 262–63; traditional carnival in, 218
Carnival ensembles, 254; brawls between, 4, 299n4; chants of, 256; costumes of, 229–30; in Gómez campaign, 141; Haitian, 257; of Havana, 226, 242, 264; Liberal Party's use of, 142; rivalries among, 12, 28; romanticized, 267; of Santiago, 176. *See also Juegos*
Carpentier, Alejo: in anthologies, 49; on Cuban national identity, 61; interest in African-derived culture, 49; knowledge of Abakuá brotherhoods, 56–57; literary fame of, 49; musical settings of, 49, 50; at *ñáñigo* rituals, 57–58; reading of Ortiz, 50, 54; role in Afrocubanismo, 20, 53–54; use of Afro-Cuban ritual, 54
—"Canción," 131
—*Dos poemas Afro-Cubanos*, 50, *51*
—*Écue-Yamba-Ó*: carnival in, 56; *chambelonas* in, 142–43; *ñáñigo* criminality in, 64–65; politicians in, 309n7; senseribó in, 304n13; snake killing in, 56; sources for, 57
—"Fete," 255
—"Juego santo," 20–21, 56–78, 254; Abakuá music in, 65–69; Abakuá rites in, 54, 57–65; Afrocubanismo of, 65–66; animal sacrifice in, 70–71; dance in, 59–60, 74; *farolas* in, 68; inaccuracies in, 58–59, 78; *íremes* in, 74; manuscript of, *73*, 73–74; *ñáñiguismo* in, 20, 54; percussion in, 66–68, 74, 76; score of, *52*; syncretism in, 54, 58; title of, 58
—"Liturgia," 50, 74; carnival in, 56; *ñáñigos* in, 54, 255; Papá Montero in, 131
—"Marí-Sabel," 50
—*La música en Cuba*, 56–57, 91

—"Problemática de la actual novela latinoamericana," 57
—*La rebambaramba*, 56
—"El recuerdo de Amadeo Roldán," 53, 56
—*Reino de este mundo*, 106
Carreño, Mario: carnival poster of, *236*, 237, 240
Cartey, Wilfred: *Black Images*, 211
Casa Cuba de Puerto Rico, carnival in, 267–68
Castellanos, Israel, 62, 203; *La brujería y el ñáñiguismo*, 37; on *ñáñigo* violence, 64; "El tipo brujo," 28, 42
Castellanos, Orlando, 179
Castro, Fidel: Afro-Cuban support for, 208; attack on Santiago, 206, 209
Castro Revolution, exile poetry following, 24, 263–68, 276
Cencerros (bells), 66, 224; in Cuban popular music, 274
Cervecería Polar, sponsorship of carnival, 242, *243*
"La Chambelona" (song), 146–47, 308n3; political use of, 155–56, 309n5; in "Quintín Barahona," 158; sociopolitical implications of, 147; version of 1916, 155–56
Chambelonas (political *comparsas*), 22; black voters in, 149–50; in *Écue-Yamba-Ó*, 142–43; Liberal Party's, 146; in "Quintín Barahona," 144, 149; twentieth-century, 307n6; violence in, 153; white intellectuals on, 147; white politicians' use of, 148–49
Changó (*orisha*), 122
Chéveres (ruffians), 131, 308n15
Christianity: in "Comparsa habanera," 128; snakes in, 103, 104
Clark, Mary Ann, 305n18
Club Atenas, 141
Cocuyos (fireflies), superstitions concerning, 135–36
Comisión Asesora de Turismo Municipal (Havana), 228, 237
Commerce, Cuban: Spanish dominance in, 242, 244, 247
Communism, Cuban, 200
Comparsa del majá (carnival ensemble), 190–91

Comparsas: Abakuá processions and, 70, 77, 96; acceptance in Cuban culture, 13; Arozarena's support for, 190, 197; association with snakes, 94, 95, 133; association with witchcraft, 9; atavism in, 26, 39, 94; in "Carnaval en la Habana," 221, 239, 251; colonial associations of, 47; condemnation of, 3–4, 11–12; in Cuban national identity, 10–11, 139, 264, 267, 276; in Cuban popular music, 274; cultural heterogeneity in, 137; de-Africanization of, 139, 227–28; desert wind imagery of, 35, 43; and Día de Reyes festivals, 302n1; of early Republic, 4; economic impact of, 258; effect on Cuban society, 30; evolving vision for, 138; in exile poetry, 24, 263–68, 276; following Racist Massacre, 9; government opposition to, 93–94; held in darkness, 36–37; lascivious behavior in, 34; middle-class Afro-Cubans on, 168; multicultural aspects of, 118, 226; *ñáñiguismo* in, 54, 60, 95–96, 255; national pride in, 10–11, 113–14; negative stereotypes of, 223; neighborhood, 26; of 1916, 3, 9, 26, 27, 28, 31, 48; nostalgia for, 227; pathological metaphors for, 28–29; perception as destructive, 35; political, 142, 148, 149–50, 307n6; prejudice against, 276; print debates over, 14, 137, 196, 201; proximity to Christian sites, 128; racist attitudes toward, 32; reauthorization of, 9–17, 113, 137, 148, 203, 222; reconciliation of injustice through, 264; reemergence of, 9–17, 226–32; regulation of, 12, 139; rehearsals for, 191–92; respectability of, 138–39; role in Cuban nationalism, 10, 137; of Santiago de Cuba, 3; in "Sensemayá," 21, 91; sinister descriptions of, 134–37, 203, 258; as slave-era throwbacks, 134–39; symbolic eradication of, 100–101; syncretism in, 224–25; themes of, 228; in tourism, 11, 12, 13; twentieth-century, 79; violence in, 28, 30–31; and white carnival, 234, 248; white intellectuals on, 14–15, 17; white participation in, 237. See also *Cantos de comparsa*; Carnival; Chambelonas; Congas; Music, *comparsa*
Comparsas bans, 3, 4, 26–27; Afro-Cuban defiance of, 92; Freyre de Andrade's, 9, 27; Guillén's opposition to, 92–93; in Havana, 30, 115; under Machado, 91–92, 94, 142, 205; in Santiago, 167; "Sensemayá" and, 79, 94; sociocultural debates concerning, 132
Las comparsas populares del carnaval habanero (1937), 228
Comparsas troupes. See Carnival ensembles
Comparseros: African origins of, 46; of "Comparsa habanera," 139; demonic possession of, 122; economic sacrifices by, 258–59; lanterns of, 68; stereotypes of, 21–22
Congas, 18; in Afrocubanista poetry, 19, 120; Arozarena's support for, 190; association with snakes, 95; atavism in, 201; Bantu roots of, 120; chants of, 230; in Cuban national identity, 276; in Cuban popular music, 273, 274, 275; dance in, 17, 74, 203; debate over, 196–97; enforcement of prejudices, 186; governmental objections to, 171–73; Guillén on, 92; images of criminality in, 203–4; menacing aspects of, 201; middle-class Afro-Cubans on, 168, 206; moral objections to, 172–74, 179; music of, 24; national pride in, 266; negative impacts of, 186; as obstacles to progress, 35, 196–97, 206; political, 145, 148–49; political apathy in, 210; prejudice against, 205, 276; print debates over, 14, 196; romanticization of, 267; salon, 272, 275; of Santiago de Cuba, 3, 67–68, 167, 168–79; in "Sensemayá," 91; social protest in, 178; in white carnival balls, 175; white hypocrisy concerning, 170, 173–76, 178, 262; white politicians' use of, 148–49. See also Carnival; Chambelonas; *Comparsas*
Congas ban, 3, 22, 29; defiance of, 178, 262, 310n7; protests against, 261–62; in Santiago, 168, 169, 170–74, 178, 261–62
Congo people, in Cuban popular song, 273. See also Kongo fundamento
Congo priests, snake protectors of, 34
Consumer goods, American, 244
Corpus Christi festivals: *comparsas* and, 77; purification in, 105; serpent monsters in, 89
Cosme, Eusebia, 160–61, *161*, 163; performance of Camín, 217; recitation of Arozarena, 189
Costumbristas, depiction of Afro-Cubans, 109
Coulthard, G. R., 121, 307n8
Courlander, Harold, 59; on percussion instruments, 67

Cox, Jennings, 299n6
Crabs, *brujos*' use of, 71–73
Crusellas y Compañía, Spanish ownership of, 244
Cruz, Celia, 242, 276
Cuba, colonial: carnival processions of, 1–2; persecution of *ñáñigos*, 61; racial tension in, 8, 27
Cuba, eastern: Afro-Cuban culture of, 23; Afrocubanismo in, 164; Afro-Cubans of, 7; Afro-Cuban voters of, 178–79; carnival celebrations of, 186, 206. *See also* Santiago de Cuba
El Cubano Libre (newspaper), 171
Cuban Republic: Afro-Cuban culture in, 5; Afro-Cuban marginalization under, 151; carnival processions of, 3–5, 300n8; civility of, 4; demographics of, 5; election of 1916, 146–47, 155–56, 158; fear of witchcraft in, 43; Fifty Percent Law, 154–55; fragmentation of, 11; Ku Klux Klan in, 141; Morúa's Law, 6; religious syncretism in, 76–77, 128; universal male suffrage in, 140–41
Cuba y América (daily), 34
Cuéllar Vizcaino, Manuel: "El Guillén que usted no conoce," 304n8; "La leyenda de Sensemayá," 85, 303n8
La Culebra (*comparsa* ensemble), 56, 94, 101, 133; dances of, 255; founding of, 222; traditionalism of, 227
Culture, African-derived, 1, 28, 108–9, 133; in Afrocubanista poetry, 49, 110; Camín's use of, 251; commercialization of, 201; in "La Comparsa," 35; in *comparsas*, 138; control of, 8; Ortiz on, 20; problematic aspects of, 197; in "Sensemayá," 91; in twentieth century, 21; Vasconcelos on, 27; white intellectuals on, 101
Culture, Afro-Cuban: assimilation into mainstream, 114; in early Republic, 5; in eastern Cuba, 23; governmental suppression of, 140; middle-class rejection of, 167; and Racist Massacre, 5–9; and struggle for equality, 197–201, 209; suppression of, 8
Culture, white Cuban: foreign domination of, 241; Spanish influence on, 252
Curses, in *brujería*, 136, 193

Dahomey, snake cult of, 190
Dance, Afro-Cuban: Afro-Cuban denigration of, 167; in "Carida," 186, 187; celebrating *majás*, 191; collective, 17, 34, 35, 274; in *congas*, 17, 74, 203; demonic possession in, 308n11; of *íremes*, 67, 71; in "Juego santo," 59–60; lascivious, 34–35, 194; in "Liturgia etiópica," 188–89; as obstacle to equality, 197–201; Ortiz on, 39; pantomimic, 67, 190, 310n4; in poster art, 237, 238; ritual, 41, 42; of Santiago, 164; sensuality in, 68, 131, 186, 195, 223–24, 234, 254, 255, 258, 268–69, 272; snake imagery in, 34; snake killing in, 190–91; stereotypes in, 186–87
Los Dandys (carnival ensemble), 226, 228–29, 264; costumes of, 229; and Ku Klux Klan, 229
Darío, Rubén: influence on Guillén, 216; "La negra Dominga," 217
De la Fuente, Alejandro, 6; on Afro-Cuban voters, 140, 141; on Cuban Communism, 200
Demonic possession, 124, 308n11; in Afro-Cuban music, 41, 42; of carnival queens, 307n9; in "Comparsa habanera," 120–22, 128; of *comparseros*, 122
El Derecho de nacer (soap opera), 163
De Villa, Álvaro: "La comparsa," 264
Diablitos: in "Carnaval en la Habana," 222, 223, 239–40; dance of, 67; in Día de Reyes, 77; epileptic appearance of, 258; in "Juego santo," 54; persecution of, 125; violence associated with, 222, 223. *See also Íremes*
Día de Reyes festivals, 222; Abakuá violence during, 62–63; association with snakes, 94, 95; banning of, 2, 3; in "Carnaval en la Habana," 221; colonial, 1–2; *comparsas* and, 302n1; as *diablitos* festival, 77; in Havana, 125; *ñáñigos* in, 20, 56; "Sensemayá" and, 21, 79, 89–91, 107; snake killing chants in, 133, 305n15; symbolic emancipation in, 89, 90, 221
Díaz, Zoila: murder of, 45, 301n7
Díaz-Ayala, Cristóbal, 36
Drums, banning of, 164, 240, 275. *See also specific names of drums*

Duno-Gottberg, Luis, 11, 12; on Afro-Cuban sexuality, 130; on Ballagas, 115; on Ortiz, 39
Economy, Cuban: foreign domination of, 241, 242, 244
Edén Tobacco, sponsorship of carnival, 177
Ekón (bell), 59–60, 66, 67
Ekue (drum), 302n6
Ékue (Abakuá father figure), 76
Elections, Cuban: Afro-Cuban nonparticipation in, 156–59; of 1916, 146–47, 155–56, 158
Eleguá (*orisha*), 136
Empegó (drum), 74–75
El Encanto (department store): carnival advertisements of, 246; Spanish ownership of, 244
Enkanikás (ritual bells), 67
Enkómos (drums), 67
Eribó (divinity), 76; cantos de, 75
Estenoz, Evaristo, 5, 6, 152; press attacks on, 8
Estivil, Osvaldo: "Conga de la Habana," 275
Europe: carnival traditions of, 219; *negrismo* in, 110–11
Exiles, Cuban: carnival poems of, 24, 263–68, 276

Farolas (paper lanterns), 28, 36, 36, 69, 240, 267; in "Juego santo," 54, 68
Faroleros, 37
Farr, Jory, 2–3
Feast of the Epiphany. *See* Día de Reyes
Feliú Herrera, Virtudes, 153, 219
Fermoselle, Rafael, 299n4
Fernández de Castro, José Antonio, 137, 307n4
Fernández de la Vega, Oscar, 213
Fernández Retamar, Roberto: *Poesía contemporánea en Cuba*, 251
Fifty Percent Law (Cuba), 154–55
Floats, carnival, 233, 235, 237, 242; commercial sponsors of, 242, 243
Forests, Cuban: terms for, 306n18
Freyre de Andrade, Fernando, 5; *comparsas* decree of, 9, 27
Fuentes, Carlos, 163

García Caturla, Alejandro, 50
García Lorca, Federico, 217, 306n2; "Son," 250
García Menocal, Mario: in election of 1916, 146–47; government sinecures under, 156

El Gavilán (carnival ensemble), 4
Gener (cigar brand), 247
Goats, sacrifice of, 70–71
Gómez, José Miguel, 6, 61, 64; antiblack propaganda of, 152; black support for, 152; government sinecures under, 156; on Racist Massacre, 8; soliciting of black vote, 141, 151; suppression of Afro-Cuban uprising, 152
González, Ana: "Romance negro del negro," 200
González, Gladys María, 312n5
González, Hilario, 50
González-Pérez, Armando, 85
Grafico (magazine), "La comparsa" in, 25, 30, 31
Grau San Martín, Ramón: black support for, 153, 154; populism under, 10; pro-labor reforms of, 154; in "Quintín Barahona," 155
Grenet, Eliseo: "Camina pa' 'lante," 312n7; "Cavalcada de las congas," 273
Los Guajiros (carnival ensemble), 271
Guarachas (songs), 68
Guerra, Pablo W., 149–50
Güijes (river spirits), 136
Guillén, Nicolás: anthologies of, 311n7; Arozarena on, 210–12; on *cantos de comparsa*, 305n15; on carnival rehearsals, 191–92; childhood of, 90; Cosme's recitations of, 161; Darío's influence on, 216; depiction of Afro-Cubans, 210–11; on national identity, 92; opposition to *comparsas* ban, 92–93; reading of Ortiz, 90, 93, 94, 103, 305n15; sociopolitical themes of, 184–85; *son* poems of, 101–2; use of African words, 116; on white hypocrisy, 175
—"El abuelo," 211
—"Balada del güije," 88
—"Balada de los dos abuelos," 211
—"Cada año es carnaval," 93
—"La canción del bongó," 66, 167–68, 211
—"Cantaliso en un bar," 211
—"Canto negro," 255–56; intoxication in, 125
—"Elegía a un soldado vivo," 211
—"Maracas," 164
—"¡Negra, mueve la cintura!," 92
—"No se por qué piensas tú," 211
—"Rumba," 210
—"Secuestro de la mujer de Antonio," 195, 210
—"Sensemayá," 19, 78, 254; African-derived

traditions in, 91; in anthologies, 303n2; carnival and, 88–95; chant in, 80, 81; and *comparsas* bans, 79; *comparsas* in, 91, 94; composition of, 89–90, 91; critical appraisals of, 80; criticism of government, 94; defense of *comparsas*, 94; Día de Reyes and, 21, 79, 89–91, 107; extermination metaphors in, 101; formal qualities of, 19; *jitanjáforas* of, 82; key terms of, 79; Mayombe/*mayombé* in, 81, 83, 97; meaning of title, 85–87; misunderstanding of terms, 79, 80–88; and *ñáñiguismo*, 95–102; Ortiz's influence on, 85, 87; ritual violence in, 90; snake imagery in, 80, 94, 96; snake killing in, 21, 81, 83, 87–89, 90, 94–95, 100–101, 103–5; sociopolitical resistance in, 107; twentieth-century *comparsas* and, 79
—"Sones y soneros," 101–2
—*Sóngoro socongo*, 12, 92, 210
—"El velorio de Papá Montero," 131, 210
—*West Indies, Ltd.*, 94
—"West Indies, Ltd.," 308n11
Guirao, Ramón, 19, 54; anthologies of, 53; "Bailadora de rumba," 50; *Órbita de la poesía afrocubana, 1928–1937*, 50, 109–10, 143, 190, 195, 213; role in Afrocubanismo, 251
Gutiérrez, Agustín, 70

Haitians, carnival ensembles of, 257
Havana: Abakuá brotherhoods of, 221–22; Afro-Cuban neighborhoods of, 3, 35; carnival ensembles of, 226, 242, 264; carnival regulations in, 4; carnival season in, 24, 195, 218, 252; carnival violence in, 31; Catholic Cathedral, 128, 240; Comisión Asesora de Turismo Municipal, 228, 237; commercialization of carnival in, 241–42; *comparsas* bans in, 30, 115; criminological studies of, 37; Día de Reyes festivals in, 125; election of 1916, 155–56, 158; hurricane of 1926, 230; Jesús María neighborhood, 3, 26, 63–64, 222; reauthorization of *comparsas* in, 113, 203, 226; Los Sitios neighborhood, 26, 60, 61, 229; underworld of, 20, 37, 38; white carnival in, 218, 242, 244, 247–48
Helg, Aline, 6–7; on Afro-Cuban stereotypes, 43; on Cuban society, 111–12; on Racist Massacre, 299nn3,5

Hernández Catá, Alfonso: "Rumba," 255
Hernández-Santana, Gilberto, 311n1; "Comparsa de semana santa," 256–57
Hughes, Langston: role in Afrocubanismo, 251

Immigration, Spanish: during early Republic, 5
Imperialism, U.S., 10, 11, 21; Afro-Cuban opposition to, 200; and Cuban national pride, 271; Cuban resistance to, 90; and *poesía negra*, 113
La Independencia (newspaper), carnival poems in, 261, 262–63
Institución Hispano-Cubana de Cultura, 244
Intellectuals, Afro-Cuban: on carnival processions, 197
Intellectuals, white: on carnival, 14–15, 17; on *chambelonas*, 147; criticism of black art, 214; defense of *comparsas*, 225; view of Afro-Cuban sexuality, 132
Íremes (Abakuá masquerader), 59; in Abakuá processions, 61; as atavistic figures, 125; crab movements of, 72; dance of, 67, 71; implements of, 127; in "Juego santo," 74. *See also* Diablitos
Isué (Abakuá bishop), 75
Ivonet, Pedro, 6, 152

Jackson, Richard L., 112; on Arozarena's criticism, 211; *The Black Image in Latin American Literature*, 184
Jahn, Janheinz, 58, 188
La Jardinera (carnival ensemble), 226; *cantos* of, 269; costumes of, 230
Juego (set of drums), 58
"*Juego*," meanings of, 58
Juegos (Abakuá lodges), 58; conflicts among, 62–65, 63; officers of, 75; *potencia* of, 301n3, rival, 30
Juegos (rituals), 58, 69; white, 70. *See also* Abakuá rites

Kikongo language, "Sensemayá" in, 86
Kongo fundamento: healing system of, 98; snake protectors of, 103. *See also* Congo people
Kubayanda, Josaphat, 83, 104, 304n11; on snake imagery, 106

Ku Klux Klan: in Cuba, 141; Los Dandys and, 229
Kutzinski, Vera: on Afrocubanismo, 112; on Arozarena, 189; on Ballagas, 133–34; on "La comparsa," 26, 32, 38, 41, 46; on Mayombe, 82; on "Sensemayá," 82, 86, 89, 90, 91, 96, 97, 106; on snake imagery, 305n16; *Sugar's Secrets*, 26, 27

Lachantañeré, Rómulo, 82, 303n4
Landaluze, Víctor Patricio de: *Día de Reyes*, 2; *El ñáñigo*, 71, 72
La Rosa, Facundo, 309n6
Lasciviousness, stereotypes of, 34–35, 44–45, 194, 308n13
Lent: carnival during, 176, 220–21; sugar harvest during, 221
Liberal Party, Cuban, 22; *chambelonas* of, 146; *congas* hired by, 307n6; in election of 1916, 146; use of carnival ensembles, 142
Lisaza, Blanca: "Himno del Carnaval," 262–63
Literature, Cuban: dependence on Spanish literature, 214
Little War (1879–1880), 2
Llorana (river spirit), 136
Lombroso, Cesare, 42
Lucumí lore, Arozarena's use of, 182
Lucumí people: in Cuban popular song, 273; fritter vendors, 229–30
Lucumí priests, snake protectors of, 34

Maceo, Antonio, 141
Machado, Gerardo: Afro-Cuban policies of, 141; banning of *comparsas*, 91–92, 94, 142, 205; ouster of, 10, 153
Madrigal, Luis Íñigo, 85
Majá (Cuban boa), 84; dance celebrating, 191; erotic symbolism of, 193, 194
Majá de Santa María (snake), 86
Mamarrachos (masqueraders), 260, 312n4
Mambises (freedom fighters), 3
Los Mambises (carnival ensemble), 269–70
Mañach, Jorge: hispanophilia of, 249; "Historia y estilo," 249; polemic with Camín, 214–15, 248–49
Mansour, Mónica: *La poesía negrista*, 31–32, 311n1

Maracas: banning of, 165; origins of, 310n3
Maribona, Armando, 13
Los Marqueses (carnival ensemble), 264
Márquez, Robert, 305n16
Martin, Juan Luis: *Ecué, Changó y Yemayá*, 311n1
Martínez Chao, Francisco, 309n5
Marugas (maracas), 136–37
Massaguer, Cornado, 31
Matibag, Eugenio, 65; *Afro-Cuban Religious Experience*, 86; on *bombe*, 83–84; on *nganga*, 306n18
Mayombé, 81; in Bantu culture, 82; Ortiz on, 303n4; snake imagery of, 97
Mayomberos (priests), 81; cauldrons of, 305n18; *nganga judía* of, 135; Ortiz on, 94; police targeting of, 81; snake protectors of, 103
Mayombe sect, 81; snake rite of, 81, 97
Mbóri (sacrificial goat), 70
Mendoza Marrero, Francisco, 4; on violence in *comparsas*, 30
Mercury, staff of, 305n17
Meruelo, Anisia: "Estampa habanera," 267
Meza, Jaramillo: "Himno del Carnaval," 262–63
Meza y Suárez, Ramón, 125
Mialhe, Pierre Toussaint Frédéric: *Día de Reyes*, 2, 2, 56
Middle class, Afro-Cuban: rejection of Afro-Cuban culture, 167; view of carnivals, 3, 4; view of *congas*, 168, 206
Middle class, white Cuban, 92; ambivalence toward Afro-Cubans, 21; hypocrisy concerning *congas*, 178; perception of Afro-Cubans, 198
Miller, Ivor, 271; *The Voice of the Leopard*, 95–96, 98
Millet, José, 310n7; on *mamarrachos*, 312n4; on police violence, 205
Miramar Yacht Club, carnival ball of, 248; publication of, 310n2
Moliner Castañeda, Israel, 227–28
Montero, Papá (underworld figure), 130–31
Moore, Robin: on *cantos de comparsa*, 268, 270; on "La Chambelona," 147, 156; on "Comparsa habanera," 308n17; on Cuban popular song, 272; on *diablitos*, 125; on Platt Amendment, 10; on Racist Massacre, 299n3;

on *sones*, 168; on *tangos*, 300n7; translations by, 312n7; on white carnival, 248
Morejón, Nancy, 134
Moreno Fajardo, Dennis, 233
Moreno Frangial, Manuel, 194
Morúa's Law, 6
Mpegó (scribe), 75
Mulattoes: in Abakuá lodges, 74, 222; in Cuban culture, 108; followers of Castro, 209; intellectuals, 138, 214; in Machado administration, 141; massacre of, 7, 299n5; middle-class, 167; opposition to *comparsas*, 14, 17; view of carnivals, 3, 4; women, 130, 186, 189, 193, 194, 203, 223, 268, 272
Müller-Berg, Klaus, 50
El Mundo (newspaper), on *congas*, 173–74
Murumbas (curses), 193, 310n5
Music, Afro-Cuban: Abakuá, 65–69; Afro-Cuban denigration of, 167; commercial, 272; of *congas*, 24; demonic possession in, 41, 42; embodiment of oppression, 209; literary possibilities of, 31; as obstacle to equality, 197–201; official attitudes toward, 164; in Santiago, 164. *See also* Popular music, Cuban
Music, *comparsa*, 13, 24, 41, 42; Abakuá influence on, 96; instruments of, 66. *See also Cantos de comparsa*
Musical instruments, Afro-Cuban: banning of, 113, 164–65, 170, 204–5; *ñáñigo*, 58–60, 66–67; percussion, 66–68, 74, 76, 302n6; police destruction of, 205
Musical instruments, Caribbean, 165

Ñangabión (snake): Divine Voice of, 102; sign of, 98
Ñáñigos: in "Carnaval en la Habana," 221; Carpentier's knowledge of, 56–57; during colonial era, 61; in *comparsas*, 54, 95 96, 255; depiction as criminals, 62–63, 131, 301n4; in Día de Reyes celebrations, 56; fear of, 8, 26; initiation ceremonies of, 20, 54, 56–57, 255; musical instruments of, 58–60, 66–67; newspaper depictions of, 64; outlawing of, 61; perception of violence among, 62–65, 301n4; public appearances of, 60–61; recordings of, 57; white, 70, 237

Ñañiguismo: association with irrationality, 29–30; association with violence, 30, 222; birth of, 97, 97; in carnival processions, 95; in *comparsas*, 54, 60, 95–96, 255; in Día de Reyes festivals, 20; dissimulation of, 57–58; governmental suppression of, 95; in "Juego santo," 20, 54; perception of violence in, 62–65; and "Sensemayá," 95–102; Vasconcelos on, 29; white targeting of, 9, 113. *See also* Abakuá brotherhoods
Nasakó (Abakuá officer), 98; snake companion of, 102
National identity, Cuban: African elements of, 250; Afro-Cuban contributions to, 114; blending of culture in, 61; *comparsas* in, 10–11, 139, 264, 267, 276; *congas* in, 276; Guillén on, 92; mixed-race, 225; PIC and, 6; popular songs in, 276; pride in, 113–14, 137; role of carnival in, 24, 266–68; white majority in, 22
Negrismo, in Europe, 110–11
Nganga (sacred cauldron), 305n18
Nkíko (sacrificial rooster), 71
Noble, Enrique, 50; *Literatura afro-hispano-americana*, 85

Obatalá (Yoruba deity), 145
Ojo-Ade, Femi, 87, 184
Olliz-Boyd, Antonio, 83, 305n14; on "Sensemayá," 87, 304nn10–11
El Oriental (newspaper), on *chambelonas*, 149–50
Orishas: in Afrocubanista poetry, 182; in Arozarena's poetry, 182, 184; avatars of, 86; festivals of, 300n2
Orovio, Helio, 13, 24; on "Canto negro," 256; *El carnaval habanero*, 218, 256, 272; on carnival sponsorship, 242; on Cuban national identity, 276; on white carnival, 247–48; on white hypocrisy, 175
Ortiz, Fernando: on Abakuá musical instruments, 68; on African-derived culture, 20, 48, 94; on Afrocubanismo exoticism, 187–88; on Afro-Cuban sexuality, 44–45; on Ayllón Morgan, 258; on *ánima sola*, 136; on Arará drum, 240; on atavism, 300n2; on brujería, 39, 40, 41, 101, 124;

Ortiz, Fernando—*continued*
on "Caridad," 187; on *comparsas*, 10, 12, 14, 118, 301n6; criminal anthropology of, 38; on de-Africanized carnival, 228; dedication of "La comparsa" to, 20, 38, 41, 48, 300n5; on demonic possession, 41, 124; on Día de Reyes, 125, 302n1; on European carnival, 219; on Guillén's poetry, 88; Guillén's reading of, 90, 93, 94, 103, 305n15; on Havana underworld, 20; influence on Carpentier, 54, 60; influence on Pichardo Moya, 38–48; influence on "Sensemayá," 85, 86, 87, 103; and Institución Hispano-Cubana de Cultura, 244; on maracas, 310n3; on "Mayombe," 303n4; on *mayomberos*, 82, 94; on name taboos, 85; on *ñáñigos*, 58, 301n4; on national pride, 113–14, 137; on Old Woman figures, 220; racist themes of, 38–40; on Rey Momo, 220; on "Sensemayá," 86; on snake killing, 88–89, 106; Tarazona's use of, 128; on witchcraft, 301n7. Works: *La antigua fiesta afrocubana del Dia de Reyes*, 85, 302n1; *Glosario de afronegrismos*, 82, 83, 300n2, 303n4, 308n15; *Hampa afrocubana*, 20; *Los negros brujos*, 28, 37, 38, 82, 94, 124, 128, 305n15; *Los negros esclavos*, 28; "La religion en la poesía mulata," 86; "Los viejos carnavales habaneros," 302n1
Oshún (*orisha*), 188, 300n2
Oyá (*orisha*), 307n9

Palés Matos, Luis: "Canción festiva para ser llorada," 9; "Pueblo negro," 215; role in Afrocubanismo, 251
Palo Mayombe, 82; rites of, 21, 95, 96
Palo Monte, 305n18; *ramas* of, 81; rites of, 98
Pamies, Alberto Herrera, 213
Partagás (cigar brand), 247
Partido Independiente de Color (PIC), 5–6; banning of, 141; press attacks on, 8; in Racist Massacre, 6–7, 152
Paseos, white, 173
Pedroso, Regino, 112, 159, 185; "Hermano negro," 199–200
Pereda Valdés, Idelfonso: *Lo negro y lo mulato en la poesía cubana*, 134, 190; role in Afrocubanismo, 251

Pérez, Louis A., 6–7, 151, 152; on Racist Massacre fatalities, 299n5
Pérez-Rodríguez, Nancy, 170, 263; on carnival items, 310n5; on carnival musicians, 299n1
Pérez Zamora, Aurelio, 300n5
Petit, Andrés, 76, 302n9
Pichardo Moya, Felipe: Ballagas's biography of, 38; view of Afro-Cuban religion, 43
—"La comparsa," 5, 18, 30–48, 253; *arrollaos* in, 34, 35, 36; *brujería* in, 31; "Comparsa habanera" and, 117; dedication to Ortiz, 20, 38, 41, 48, 300n4; demonic possession in, 41, 42; illustrations of, 31, 32; original version of, 30–31; Ortiz's influence on, 38–48; pathological themes of, 41, 42; point of view of, 32; as precursor of Afrocubanismo, 26, 31, 38, 46–47; publication of, 20, 25, 30, 31; racial markers in, 46; sexuality in, 44; simún imagery in, 35; sinister descriptions in, 122, 134, 203, 260; snake imagery in, 33, 95; stereotypes in, 42; suspicion in, 47–48; underworld in, 38–48; white prejudice in, 31; witchcraft in, 42–43, 46
Piñeiro, Ignacio, 70; "Noche de conga," 274
Pino y Águila, Angel, 170
Pla, José Armando, 157, 159
Plantes, Abakuá, 60; public phases of, 76; snakes in, 84
Platt Amendment, 10, 113, 154
Plaza de Armas (Havana), celebrations at, 1
Plazas (Abakuá dignitaries), 59, 98
Poesía negra, 19; artificiality of, 110; audience of, 112; *chéveres* in, 131; Cuban contributions to, 109; female sexuality in, 187, 195; racial markers in, 46; U.S. imperialism and, 113; women's sexuality in, 131
Polit, Carlos E., 131
Politicians, white: buying of votes, 156; exploitation of Afro-Cubans, 144, 146, 149–50, 153; hypocrisy concerning *congas*, 178; use of bribery, 309n6
Popular music, Cuban, 24; Afro-Cuban carnival in, 272–76; Afro-Cuban exoticism in, 272; *arrollaos* in, 275–76; *bozal* speech in, 274; collective dancing in, 274; *comparsas* in, 274; *congas* in, 273, 274, 275; in Cuban national identity, 276; female sensuality in,

272; stereotypes in, 274; themes of, 273. *See also* Music, Afro-Cuban
Portel Vilá, Heriberto: *Comparsa*, 68, 69
Posters, carnival, 229, *231*, *236*, *237*, *238*, *239*, *239*
Pozo, Chano, 229
Los Precios Fijos, carnival advertisement of, *245*
La Prensa (daily), Vasconcelos in, 3, 27
Puente, M.: *Fiesta ñáñiga*, 54, 55

Queens, carnival, 220, 233, 235; demonic possession of, 307n9

Racial equality, 5–6; carnivals and, 4
Racial tension, Cuban, 48; in colonial era, 8, 27; in early Republic, 152
Racist Massacre (1912), 4–5, 150, 299nn3,5; Afro-Cuban culture and, 5–9; causes of, 6–7; *comparsas* following, 9; consequences of, 7, 9, 32; fatalities in, 141, 299n5; fear of crowds following, 260; looting in, 300n6; PIC in, 6–7; suspicion following, 47–48
Radillo, Teófilo: "Bembé," 305n13
Rebellions, Afro-Cuban: fear of, 4–5, 8, 25–26
Rebellions, slave: punishment for, 2, 3
Regla Kimbisa (religion), 302n9
Religions, Afro-Cuban: Bantu, 120; in "Comparsa habanera," 120; fear of, 33–34; governmental denigration of, 77–78; snakes in, 34, 103–4; syncretism in, 224–25; terminology of, 82; trees in, 96; white fear of, 43–44, 45, 46; white involvement in, 46; white understanding of, 122, 124
"Rey Momo" (king of carnival), 220
Rice, Argyll Pryor, 133
Roche y Monteagudo, Rafael, 62, 203; on Abakuá, 98; on Afro-Cuban religion, 124; on *mayomberos*, 82, 94; on *ñáñigo* violence, 64; *La policía y sus misterios en Cuba*, 37, 63, 70, 82, 87, 124, 303n4; on "Sensemayá," 87–88
Rodrigueroa (pseudonym), "Versificación sobre los carnavales cultos," 259–61
Rohmer, Sax: Fu Manchu novels of, 222, 223
Roig de Leuchsenring, Emilio, 137, 138; on Las Bolleras, 229–30; "Las comparsas carnavalescas de la Habana en 1937," 271–72; on de-Africanized carnival, 228;

on multicultural carnival, 225–26; on political *comparsas*, 148
Rojas, Jack: "La reina del carnaval," 264, 265–67; "Llora el bongó," 264, 265
Roldán, Amadeo, 53
Roosters, sacrifice of, 70, 71, 74
Ross, Bianchi, 309n5
Roy, Maya, 92
Ruiz, Rosendo, 167
Ruiz del Viso, Hortensia, 213, 216, 248–49; on "Llora el bongó," 265
Rumba columbia (Abakuá dance), 60, 67
Rumbas, 54, 67–68, 93, 164, 176
Ruscalleda Bercedóniz, Jorge María, 150, 308n2

Saints, arrival of (*brujería*), 121, 124, 127–28, 307n10
Santa Clara, Día de Reyes festivities of, 256
Santería, 61, 145; rituals of, 21; syncretism in, 225
Santiago de Cuba: Afro-Cuban music of, 164; carnival celebrations of, 2, 170, 259–61; carnival ensembles of, 176; carnival poems from, 24, 259–63; carnival season in, 310n5; Castro's attack on, 206, 209; *comparsas* ban in, 167; *conga* ban in, 22, 168, 169, 170–74, 178, 261–62; *congas* in, 29, 67–68, 167, 168–79; police violence in, 205; slave-era carnivals of, 177; sociopolitical hypocrisy in, 169, 170; summer carnival in, 176, 177; white carnival of, 259, 262–63; winter carnival in, 176–77
Sardines, Spanish symbolism of, 220–21
Scottsboro Boys, in Afro-Cuban poetry, 200
"Se acerca la comparsa" (song), 275
Secret societies, Afro-Cuban, 29
Sensemayá: definition of, 85–87; legends of, 303n8; as serpent goddess, 85–86, 304n9; and Yemaya, 304n9. *See also* Guillén, Nicolás: "Sensemayá"
Sese eribó (drum), 74, *75*, 75–76, 87; in *Écue-Yamba-Ó*, 304n13; and Holy Sacrament, 76; types of, 76
Sexuality, Afro-Cuban: in "Caridad," 187; in "Comparsa habanera," 128–30; Ortiz on, 44–45; white fear of, 44, 130. *See also* Women, Afro-Cuban: sensual images of

Sikán (Abakuá initiate), 71
Simún (desert wind), 35
Slave ancestors, evocation of, 136
Slavery, Afro-Cuban resistance to, 90
Slaves, African: celebrations of, 1, 135, 138, 176
Snake imagery, 305nn16–17; in "La comparsa," 33, 95; in "Comparsa habanera," 133; eroticism in, 193, 194–96; rebirth in, 80; in "Sensemayá," 80, 96–97; trees in, 80, 96–97, 97, 98
Snake killing: in carnivals, 80, 190–91; chants for, 133, 195, 305n15; as cultural renewal, 102–7; dances celebrating, 190–91; deception in, 105–6; in *Écue-Yamba-Ó*, 56; Ortiz on, 88–89; as purification ritual, 89, 105; in "Sensemayá," 21, 81, 83, 87–89, 90, 94–95, 100–101, 103–5; as symbolic exorcism, 105; symbolic rebirth in, 105–6
Snakes: in Afro-Cuban religion, 34, 84, 96–97; association with Divine Voice, 102; in *bembé* rituals, 84; in carnival celebrations, 190; in Christianity, 103, 104; in *comparsas*, 94, 95, 133; as protectors, 98, 102–3; regenerative powers of, 103, 104–5, 106–7; Western depictions of, 84
Sociedad de Estudios Afrocubanos, 10, 14; Ballagas in, 137; on national pride, 11
Society, Cuban: Afro-Cubans in, 3, 13, 15; divisions in, 24, 111–12; effect of *comparsas* on, 30; foreign domination of, 241
Soldiers, Afro-Cuban: exploitation of, 150–51
Sones: in Caignet's poetry, 165–66; Camín's defense of, 217; Guillén's, 101–2; origins of, 167; Papá Montero in, 131; popularity of, 168
Sonora Matancera (musical ensemble), 242
Suárez, Adolfo, 181, 182
Suárez, Albino, 216–17
Suárez León, Carmen, 255
Sublette, Ned, 1; on Cuban popular music, 272; on percussion instruments, 67; on political *comparsas*, 142
Sugar production: forced labor in, 271; Haitian workers in, 257; sexual imagery of, 194–95
Sundays: "de la piñata," 220; "de la sardina," 220–21; "de la vieja," 220; "del figurín," 220

"Ta Julia" (eighteenth-century chant), 195–96
Tallet, José Zacarías: dedication of "Liturgia etiópica" to, 182, 189; influence on Arozarena, 182; role in Afrocubanismo, 251; use of rumba, 54
—"Quintín Barahona," 19, 143–59, 175, 254; black political consciousness in, 157–58; "La Chambelona" in, 158; *chambelonas* in, 22, 144, 149; electoral corruption in, 156–57; Grau regime in, 155; political message of, 145; protagonist of, 144–46, 149, 150, 153, 155, 156–57, 158, 169; racial stereotypes in, 143; sociopolitical issues in, 143
—"La rumba," 22, 50, 143; composition of, 113; dancers in, 176; exoticism of, 182
Tambor de cajón (percussion instrument), 67
Tangos, 9, 300n7
Tarazona, Fernando: *La Conga*, 18, 254–55; *Estampas afro-cubanas*, 127; "The Saint's Protégé," 127, 128, *129*; use of Ortiz, 128
Tata Nkisi (Palo Monte practitioners), 98
Tejada, Valentín, 213, 250
Ten Years' War (1868–1878), 2
Thomas, Hugh, 209
Toques (celebrations), snakes in, 84
Torre, Guillermo de: "Literatura de color," 110–11
Torres-Rioseco, Arturo, 307n7
Tourism: *comparsas* in, 11, 12, 13; view of Afro-Cubans in, 198
Tous, Adriana, 305n14
Trees: in Afro-Cuban religions, 96; magical powers of, 306n18; snakes entwined in, 80, 96–97, *97*, 98
Trujillo y Monegas, José: *Los criminales de Cuba*, 62
Tumbas (drums), 67–68

Unamuno, Miguel de, 311n7
Underworld, Afro-Cuban, 37; in "La comparsa," 38–48
Urrutía, Gustavo E., 159

Valdés-Cruz, Rosa E., 122
Varona Suárez, Manuel, 156
Vasconcelos, Ramón: on *arrollaos*, 35; on *brujería*, 44; on *comparsas*, 11–12, 27–28, 101, 139; on Guillén's *sones*, 101–2; pathological metaphors of, 28. Works: "Al primer tapón, zurrapas," 28, 35; "Comparsas," 27–28, 29;

"Confidencial," 300n1; "Palpitaciones de la Raza de Color," 27; "Suma y sigue," 29

Vázquez, Eduardo "Jaruco": "La conga de Jaruco," 274–75; "Conga de la Habana," 273–74

Virgen de Regla, feast of, 311n2

Voters, Afro-Cuban: of Oriente, 178–79; in political *comparsas*, 149–50; white politicians' courting of, 140–41, 151; women, 154

War of Independence, Cuban (1895), 3; Afro-Cubans in, 150–51, 270

White children, ritual murder of, 81

Whites, Cuban: on Afro-Cuban culture, 101; carnival balls of, 175, 247, 248; fear of Afro-Cuban gatherings, 45; fear of rebellion, 4–5, 8, 25–26; fear of witchcraft, 8, 26; fusion with Afro-Cubans, 111; hypocrisy concerning *congas*, 170, 173–76, 178, 262; middle-class, 21, 92, 178, 198; *ñáñigos*, 70; participation in *comparsas*, 237; popularity of *sones* with, 168; popular songs of, 272; propagation of black stereotypes, 43. *See also* Carnival, white

Williams, Claudette, 187

Witchcraft: animals in, 135–36; in "La comparsa," 42–43, 46; in "La comparsa del majá," 193; in "Comparsa habanera," 138, 193; Ortiz on, 301n7; secret societies and, 29; white fear of, 8, 26

Women, Afro-Cuban: in *cantos de comparsa*, 269; in "Comparsa habanera," 130, 131; poetry by, 261; sensual images of, 68, 131, 186, 187–89, 194–95, 223–24, 234, 254, 255, 258, 268–69, 272; stereotypes of, 130–31; voting rights for, 154

Women, white: in "Carnaval en la Habana," 233, 234; observers of carnival, 240

Yellow peril, 223

Yemayá (*orisha*): association with snakes, 86–87, 304n10; avatars of, 86; and Sensemayá, 304n10

Yoruba deities, 34, 256; pairing with Catholic saints, 225

Zohn-Muldoon, Ricardo, 304n11

Thomas F. Anderson is associate professor of Latin American literature at the University of Notre Dame. He is the author of *Everything in Its Place: The Life and Works of Virgilio Piñera*.